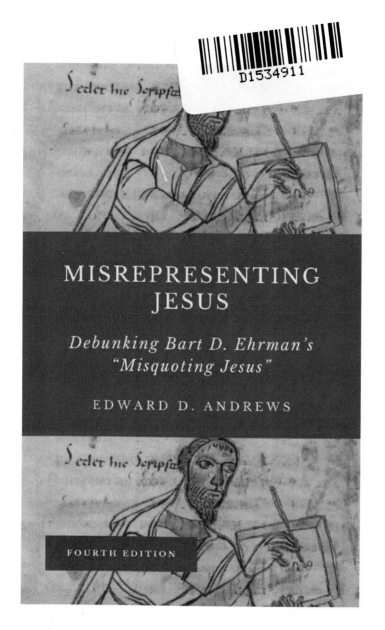

MISREPRESENTING JESUS

Debunking Bart D. Ehrman's "Misquoting Jesus"

EDWARD D. ANDREWS

FOURTH EDITION

i

MISREPRESENTING JESUS

Debunking Bart D. Ehrman's "Misquoting Jesus"

FOURTH EDITION

Edward D. Andrews

Christian Publishing House

Cambridge, Ohio

Christian Publishing House
Professional Conservative Christian
Publishing of the Good News!

CPH Since 2005

Unless otherwise stated, Scripture quotations are from Updated American Standard Version (UASV) Copyright © **2019** by Christian Publishing House

MISREPRESENTING JESUS: Debunking Bart D. Ehrman's "Misquoting Jesus" by Edward D. Andrews

ISBN-13: **978-1-949586-95-4**

ISBN-10: **1-949586-95-2**

Significant English Bible Translations

Unless otherwise indicated, Scripture quotations are from the *New American Standard Bible* (NASB) Copyright © 1960, 1962, 1963, 1968, 1971, 1972, 1973, 1975, 1977, 1995 by The Lockman Foundation

Below are some of the most significant English Bible translation of the twentieth and now twenty-first centuries. The word significant is used broadly and does not necessarily suggest a preferred or accurate translation.

ASV American Standard Version, 1901 Public Domain

CEV Contemporary English Version, 1995 by American Bible Society

CSB Christian Standard Bible, 2017 by Holman Bible Publishers

ESV English Standard Version, 2001 by Crossway Bibles, a publishing ministry of Good News Publishers

GNT Good News Translation, 1992 by American Bible Society

KJV King James Version, 1611 Public Domain

REB Revised English Bible, 1989 by Oxford University Press and Cambridge University Press

RSV Revised Standard Version, 1946, 1952, and 1971 the Division of Christian Education of the National Council of the Churches of Christ in the United States of America

NASB New American Standard Bible, 1960, 1962, 1963, 1968, 1971, 1972, 1973, 1975, 1977, 1995 by the Lockman Foundation

NEB New English Bible, 1961 by Oxford University Press and Cambridge University Press

NIV New International Version, 2011 973, 1978, 1984, 2011 by Biblica, Inc.®

NKJV New King James Version, 1982 by Thomas Nelson

NLT New Living Translation (second edition), 2004 by Tyndale House Foundation

NRSV New Revised Standard Version, 1990 by the Division of Christian Education of the National Council of the Churches of Christ in the United States of America

TNIV Today's New International Version, 2005 by Biblica (Formerly International Bible Society)

UASV Updated American Standard Version, NT 2019 OT, 2020 by Christian Publishing House – https://www.uasvbible.org/

Publication Abbreviations

AA Aland-Aland = *The Text of the New Testament, An Introduction to the Critical Editions and to the Theory and Practice of Modern Textual Criticism*, by Kurt Aland and Barbara Aland (Grand Rapids, 1987; 2nd ed., 1989).

BAA *Griechisch-Deutsches Wörterbuch zu den Schriften des Neuen Testaments und der frühchristlichen Literatur*, by W. Bauer, K. Aland, and B. Aland (6th ed.; Berlin: de Gruyter, 1988)

BAGD *A Greek-English Lexicon of the New Testament and Other Early Christian Literature*, by W. Bauer, W. F. Arndt, F. W. Gingrich, and F. W. Danker (2d ed.; Chicago: University of Chicago Press, 1979)

BDB *A Hebrew and English Lexicon of the Old Testament*, by F. Brown, S. R. Driver, and C. A. Briggs (Oxford: Clarendon, 1907)

BDF *A Greek Grammar of the New Testament and Other Early Christian Literature*, by F. Blass, A. Debrunner, and R. W. Funk (Chicago: University of Chicago Press, 1961)

BDR *Grammatik des neutestamentlichen Griechisch*, by F. Blass, A. Debrunner, and F. Rehkopf (Göttingen: Vandenhoeck & Ruprecht, 1984)

FJAH F. J. A. Hort's "Notes on Select Readings," in *The New Testament in the Original Greek*, the Text Revised by Brooke Foss Westcott and Fenton John Anthony Hort; [vol. ii] *Introduction [and] Appendix* (Cambridge and London, 1881; 2nd ed., 1896).

GMAW *Greek Manuscripts of the Ancient World* (2nd ed., E. G. Turner)

GELNTBSD Johannes P. Louw and Eugene Albert Nida, *Greek-English Lexicon of the New Testament: Based on Semantic Domains* (New York: United Bible Societies, 1996).

HIBD Brand, Chad, Charles Draper, and England Archie. *Holman Illustrated Bible Dictionary: Revised, Updated and Expanded*. Nashville, TN: Holman, 2003.

ISBE *International Standard Bible Encyclopedia* (4 vols., Bromiley) [1979–1988]

LSJ *A Greek-English Lexicon*, by H. G. Liddell, R. Scott, and H. S. Jones (Oxford: Clarendon, 1968)

LXX *Septuaginta: With Morphology*, electronic ed. (Stuttgart: Deutsche Bibelgesellschaft, 1979)

LXX Swete Henry Barclay Swete, The Old Testament in Greek: According to the Septuagint (Cambridge, UK: Cambridge University Press, 1909)

MCEDONTW Mounce, William D. *Mounce's Complete Expository Dictionary of Old & New Testament Words*. Grand Rapids, MI: Zondervan, 2006.

MM *The Vocabulary of the Greek Testament: Illustrated from the Papyri and Other Non-literary Sources*, by J. H. Moulton and G. Milligan (repr. Grand Rapids: Eerdmans, 1980)

(MT) Masoretic Text

NA[26] *Novum Testamentum Graece* (26th ed., Nestle-Aland) [1979]

NA[27] *Novum Testamentum Graece* (27th ed., Nestle-Aland) [1993]

NA[28] *Novum Testamentum Graece* (27th ed., Nestle-Aland) [2012]

NBD Wood, D R W. *New Bible Dictionary* (Third Edition). Downers Grove: InterVarsity Press, 1996.

NIDNTT *The New International Dictionary of New Testament Theology*, edited by L. Coenen, E. Beyreuther, and H. Bietenhard; English translation edited by C. Brown (4 vols.; Grand Rapids: Zondervan, 1975–86)

NU text of Nestle-Aland 26th/27th/28th [N] and the United Bible Societies 3rd/4th/5th [U]

TCGNT A TEXTUAL COMMENTARY ON THE GREEK NEW TESTAMENT by Bruce M. Metzger (German Bible Society, 1970; 2nd ed., 1994)

TDNT *Theological Dictionary of the New Testament*, edited by G. Kittel and G. Friedrich; translated and edited by G. W. Bromiley (10 vols.; Grand Rapids: Eerdmans, 1964–76)

TENTGM THE TEXT OF THE EARLIEST NEW TESTAMENT MANUSCRIPTS A Corrected, Enlarged Edition of The Complete Text of the Earliest New Testament Manuscripts by Philip W. Comfort and David P. Barrett (Tyndale House Publishers, 1999, 2nd ed., 2001)

TTNT-A *The Text of the New Testament, An Introduction to the Critical Editions and to the Theory and Practice of Modern Textual Criticism*, by Kurt Aland and Barbara Aland (Grand Rapids, 1987; 2nd ed., 1989).

TTNT-M *The Text of the New Testament, Its Transmission, Corruption, and Restoration*, by Bruce M. Metzger (Oxford, 1964; 3rd ed., 1992).

TNTCR The Text of the New Testament in Contemporary Research: Essays on the Status Quaestionis (New Testament Tools, Studies, and Documents, by Bart D. Ehrman and Michael W. Holmes (Brill, 1995; 2nd ed., 2012)

UBS³ United Bible Societies' *Greek New Testament* (3rd ed., Metzger et al) [1975]

UBS⁴ United Bible Societies' *Greek New Testament* (4th corrected ed., Metzger et al) [1993]

UBS⁵ United Bible Societies' *Greek New Testament* (4th corrected ed., Metzger et al) [2014]

VCEDONTW Vine, W E. *Vine's Expository Dictionary of Old and New Testament Words*. Nashville: Thomas Nelson, 1996.

WHI Westcott and Hort, *Introduction* = *The New Testament in the Original Greek*, the Text Revised by Brooke Foss Westcott and Fenton John Anthony Hort; [vol. ii] *Introduction [and] Appendix* (Cambridge and London, 1881; 2nd ed., 1896).

WPNT Robertson, A.T. *Word Pictures in the New Testament*. Oak Harbor, MI: Logos Research Systems, 1933, 1997.

WSNT Vincent, Marvin. Word Studies in the New Testament. Bellingham: Logos Research Systems, 2002.

WWSGNT Wuest, Kenneth S. *Wuest's Word Studies from the Greek New Testament*: For the English Reader. Grand Rapids: Eerdmans, 1997, c1984.

ABBREVIATIONS: Manuscripts and Ancient Versions

Textual scholars employ a symbol (called sigla; singular siglum), which indicate a manuscript and to identify the copyist or corrector of a text. Below are the sigla used in THE READING CULTURE OF EARLY CHRISTIANITY, as well as the content to the nearest book (sometimes chapter) and its date. We are only providing a few examples each. For the complete list, please see the introduction and appendixes to UBS5 and NA[28].

- Dates are given to the nearest 25-50-year increment.

- A small cross (†) shows the content the nearest chapter, while other times the verses are sometimes listed. For example, P11 would read 1 Corinthians 1-7 † because it has many verses throughout chapters 1-7: 1:17-22, 25-27; 2:6-8, 9-12, 14; 3:1-3, 5-6, 8-10, 20, 4:3-5; 5:7-8; 6:5-9, 11-18; 7:3-6, 10-14.

- Symbol c. for "circa," or "about."

- Exact dates, like 316 C.E. for P^{10} are the result of being found with, being tied to a document with an exact date, or having an exact date on the manuscript.

- Abbreviation for text families is as follows: Alexandrian Alex.; Western West.; Caesarean Caes.; Byzantine Byz.

- Independent text is abbreviated as Ind.

PAPYRI

Papyrus, Papyri: named for the Egyptian plant from which it is made. In the proper climate this is a very durable writing material that was made by bonding vertical strips of the papyrus' pith to horizontal strips. Writing could easily be done on the side with the horizontal strips, and with some difficulty on the other side (called an "opisthograph" when written on both sides). The oldest manuscripts of the NT were written on papyrus; some of them are as early as the second century.

P^4+ Luke 1–6; same as P^{64}+P^{67} Matt 3; 5; 26; c. 160-180 C.E. (Alex. esp. P^{75})

P^{45} Gospels and Acts †; c. 200 C.E. (Mark Caes.; Matt, Luke and John Alex. and West.; Acts Alex. esp. ℵ A B and C)

P^{46} Rom 5-6; 8-16; 1 Cor.; 2 Cor.; Gal.; Eph.; Php; Col.; 1 Thess.; Heb.; c. 200 C.E. (Proto-Alex. esp. B in Eph., Col., and Heb.) P46 and P13 are nearly the same text. There are only seventeen disagreements out of eighty-eight variation units.

P[52] John 18:31-34, 37-38; c. 110-125 C.E. (Seems to be Alex.)

P[66] John 1:1-6:11; 6:35-14:26, 29-30; 15:2-26; 16:2-4, 6-7; 16:10-20:20, 22-23; 20:25-21:9, 12, 17; c. 150 C.E. (Alex. esp. close to P[75], B, 016) Because P[66] is an early Papyrus near complete codex of the Gospel of John, we are adding more here. Fee studied the corrections (i.e., P[66c]) of P[66] in John 1-9 with P[75]. He found that the corrections are in more of an agreement with P[75] than the original scribe of P[66], which means that P[66] was corrected with a manuscript akin to P[75], as far as John 1-9 goes. The agreement is increased significantly when the corrections (P[66c]) of John 10:1-15:8 are compared to P[75] and 15:9-21:22 with B (this section is missing from P[75]).

P[66c1] this corrector is designated as the original scribe by Comfort and Barrett.

P[66c2] this corrector is designated as a second scribe in the scriptorium by Comfort and Barrett.

P[66c3] this corrector is designated as a third scribe who was also the paginator by Comfort and Barrett.[1]

P[75] Luke 3:18-24:53 and John †; c. 175-200 C.E. (Alex.) The Christian scribe of P[75] was a professional. This was the kind of text that was used to make Codex Vaticanus. Porter shows that there is an 87% agreement between P[75] and B.

UNCIALS

Uncial: a term commonly used to refer to majuscule (q.v.) letters (4th to 8th centuries C.E.). It is agreed, however, that the term, taken from Latin and meaning "one-twelfth," should be applied only to a particular type of Latin script or document.

ℵ (Sinaiticus) most of NT; c. 330–360 C.E.

ℵ[a] designates corrections that were done by several scribes before the manuscript left the scriptorium.

---

[1] James Royse states that other than John 13:19, the corrections are all by the hand of the original scribe. (Royse 2008, pp. 409-21)

א^{ca} designates a group of correctors working at Caesarea in about the sixth or seventh century C.E., who corrected the manuscript in both the Old and New Testament.

A (Alexandrinus) most of NT; c. fifth century C.E.

B (Vaticanus) most of NT; c. 300–325

B¹ designates a corrector who was contemporary with the original scribe.

B² designates a tenth or eleventh century corrector, who also retraced the original writing, as well as adding accents and punctuation marks.[2]

C (Ephraemi Rescriptus) most of NT with many lacunae; fifth century C.E.

D (Bezae) Gospels, Acts; fifth century C.E.

D (Claromontanus) Paul's Epistles; sixth century C.E. (different MS than Bezae)

E (Laudianus 35) Acts; sixth century C.E.

MINUSCULES

Minuscule: from a Latin word meaning "somewhat smaller," a set of small, cursive Greek letters as opposed to majuscules (q.v.). In a loose sense, minuscules are often thought of as lowercase Greek letters. They seem to have been invented in the ninth century to speed and lower the cost of book production, usually on vellum or parchment

1 Gospels, Acts, Paul's Epistles; twelfth century C.E.

20 Gospels; eleventh century C.E.

22 Gospels; twelfth century C.E.

28 Gospels; eleventh century C.E.

33 All NT except Rev; ninth century C.E.

2344 Rev; eleventh century C.E.

f¹ (a family of manuscripts including 1, 118, 131, 209) Gospels; twelfth-fourteenth century C.E.

---

[2] Bruce M. Metzger, *Manuscripts of the Greek Bible: An Introduction to Greek Palaeography*, New York, Oxford: Oxford University Press, 1991, p. 74.

f¹³ (a family of manuscripts that include 13, 69, 124, 174, 230, 346, 543, 788, 826, 828, 983, 1689, 1709, known as the Ferrar group) Gospels; eleventh-fifteenth c.

Maj The **Majority Text**: a text of the NT in which variant readings are chosen that are found in the majority of all Greek NT manuscripts (cf. "Byzantine Family" above). One could consider this external (objective) evidence and maintain that it is the leading criterion for establishing the text. Credit for this text is due primarily to Zane Hodges and Arthur Farstad, though the latter once humbly told me (Wilkins) that the text was mainly Hodges' work. Hodges maintained that mathematical probabilities pointed to the text with the greatest number of surviving manuscripts as the one closest to the original. Thus, the name is an accurate description, though Hodges' theory about the text's relation to the original is arguable at best. Of greater value and importance, the Majority Text has essentially purged the Byzantine text of its negative association with the Textus Receptus. Nevertheless, most textual critics maintain that those favoring the MT rely heavily on theological arguments and thin objective evidence in their defense of the text. In particular, easier readings tend to prevail over harder in the MT and BT.

Maj^a This siglum only occurs in Revelation and indicates a large group of manuscripts which contain a commentary on Revelation by Andreas of Caesarea.

Maj^k This siglum also occurs only in Revelation and indicates the large group of manuscripts which do not contain Andreas's commentary.

LECTIONARIES

Lectionaries: books of NT passages chosen by the Christian church for reading at services. For the most part, they represent the Byzantine text and are of use in reconstructing the history of that text. Below are some of the lectionaries cited in the critical editions. At present, there are 2,412 lectionaries extant.

𝑙 1 Evangelistarion (uncial); tenth century C.E.
𝑙 2 Evangelistarion (uncial); tenth century C.E.
𝑙 3 Evangelistarion (uncial); eleventh century C.E.
ANCIENT VERSIONS
Syriac (syr)
syr^c (Syriac Curetonianus) Gospels; fifth century C.E.
syr^h (Syriac Harclean) All NT; 616 C.E.
syr^h** This siglum denotes a reading in syr^h that is set off by asterisks, which questions its originality.

syr[hmg] This siglum denotes a reading from the margin of syr[h].

syr[p] (Peshitta) All NT except Revelation and shorter General Epistles; fourth-fifth century C.E.

syr[pal] (Palestinian Syriac) Gospels; fifth-sixth century C.E.

syr[s] (Syriac Sinaiticus) Gospels; fourth century C.E.

Old Latin (it)

it[a] (Vercellensis) Gospels; fourth century C.E.

it[aur] (Aureus) Gospels; seventh century C.E.

it[b] (Veronensis) Gospels; fifth century C.E.

it[c] (Colbertinus) Gospels; twelfth century C.E.

it[d] (Cantabrigiensis, the Latin text of Bezae) Gospels, Acts, 3 John; fifth century C.E.

it[e] (Palatinus) Gospels; fifth century C.E.

it[f] (Brixianus) Gospels; sixth century C.E.

it[ff2] (Corbeiensis II) Gospels; fifth century C.E.

it[g1] (Sangermanensis) Matthew; eighth-ninth century C.E.

it[gig] (Gigas) Gospels; Acts; thirteenth century C.E.

it[h] (Fleury palimpsest) Matt 3–14; 18–28; Acts; Revelation; Peter's Epistles; 1 John; fifth century C.E.

it[i] (Vindobonensis) Mark 2–15; Luke 10–23; fifth century C.E.

it[k] (Bobbiensis) Matthew, Mark; c. 400 C.E.

it[l] (Rehdigeranus) Gospels; Acts 8-11; 15; James; 1 Peter; John's Epistles; eighth century C.E.

it[q] (Monacensis) Gospels; sixth-seventh century C.E.

it[r] (Usserianus) Gospels, Paul's Epistles, Peter's Epistles, 1 John; seventh century C.E.

it[w] (Wernigerodensis) Acts; 14th–15th c.; Peter's Epistles; 1 John; sixth century C.E.

Vulgate

The following sigla represent the major editions of the Vulgate.

vg[cl] (Clementine) *Biblia Sacra Vulgatae Editionis Sixti Quinti Pont. Max. iussu recognita atque edita*; 1592

vg[st] (Stuttgart) *Biblia sacra iuxta Vulgatam versionem*; 1969

vg[ww] (Wordsworth and White) *Novum Testamentum Domini nostri Iesu Christi latine secundum editionem Sancti Hieronymi*; 1889–1954

lat Indicates a reading supported by the Vulgate and some of the Old Latin MSS.

Coptic

The Coptic translations of the New Testament date from the 3rd century onward.

cop^{ach} (Akhmimic) John; James; fourth century C.E.

cop^{ach2} (Subakhmimic) John; fourth century C.E.

cop^{bo} (Bohairic = north Egypt) All NT; ninth century C.E.

cop^{fay} (Fayyumic = central Egypt) John; fourth-fifth century C.E.

cop^{G67} (a Middle Egyptian ms) Acts; fifth century C.E.

cop^{mae} (Middle Egyptian) Matthew; fourth-fifth century C.E.

cop^{sa} (Sahidic = southern Egypt) All NT; fourth-fifth century C.E.

Armenian

arm All NT; twelfth century C.E.

Ethiopic

eth All NT; fourteenth century C.E.

Georgian

geo All NT; eleventh century C.E.

Slavonic

slav All NT; tenth- twelfth century C.E.

Ancient Authors

The following abbreviations are used for ancient works.

1 Apol. Justin Martyr, *First Apology*

1 Clem. 1 Clement

Ann. Tacitus, *Annals*

Ant. Josephus, *Jewish Antiquities*

b. Ber. Babylonian tractate *Berakot*

Bacch. Euripides, *Bacchanals*

Cels. Origen, *Against Celsus*

Claud. Suetonius, *Claudius*

Comm. Jo. Origen, *Commentary on John*

Comm. Matt. Origen, *Commentary on Matthew*

Comm. Rom. Origen, *Commentary on Romans*

Cons. Augustine, *De consensus evangelistarum*(Harmony of the Gospels)

Dial. Justin Martyr, *Dialogue with Trypho*

Dial. Pseudo-Athanasius, *Dialogue with Zaccheus*

Did. Didache

Epist. Jerome, *Epistulae*

Fel. Augustine, *Against Felix*

Geogr. Ptolemy, *Geography*

Gos. Pet. Gospel of Peter
Haer. Irenaeus, *Against Heresies*
Hist. eccl. Eusebius, *Ecclesiastical History*
J.W. Josephus, *Jewish War*
Life Josephus, *The Life*
LXX Septuagint
Marc. Tertullian, *Against Marcion*
Onom. Eusebius, *Onomasticon*
Or.Bas. Gregory of Nazianzus, *Oratio in laudem Basilii*
Pan. Epiphanius, *Panarion (Refutation of all Heresies)*
Phaen. Aratus, *Phaenomena*
Prom. Aeschylus, *Prometheus Bound*
Pyth. Pindar, *Pythian Odes*
Quaest. Mar. Eusebius, *Quaestiones ad Marinum*
Tg. Ps.-J. Targum Pseudo-Jonathan

INTRODUCTION Bart D. Ehrman and Misquoting Jesus

Dr. Bart D. Ehrman has written or edited thirty books, including five New York Times bestsellers: How Jesus Became God, Misquoting Jesus, God's Problem, Jesus Interrupted and Forged. Ehrman is the James A. Gray Distinguished Professor of Religious Studies at the University of North Carolina, Chapel Hill, and is a leading authority on the New Testament and the history of early Christianity.

His work has been featured in Time, the New Yorker, the Washington Post and other print media, and he has appeared on NBC's Dateline, The Daily Show with Jon Stewart, CNN, The History Channel, National Geographic, the Discovery Channel, the BBC, major NPR shows, and other top media outlets.

The last 40 plus years have seen a rise in interest in what are known as pseudo-gospels, epistles, and apocalypses discovered in the 1950s in Nag Hammadi[3] and other places in Egypt. Generally, these documents and

---

[3] NAG HAMMADI (Nàg Hăm ma' dē) Modern Egyptian village 300 miles south of Cairo and about 60 miles north of Luxor or ancient Thebes. Because of the close proximity of Nag Hammadi to the site of an important discovery of ancient documents relating to Gnosticism, the collection of documents is usually referred to as the Nag Hammadi Documents or Library. — Chad Brand, Charles Draper, Archie England et al., Holman Illustrated Bible Dictionary (Nashville, TN: Holman Bible Publishers, 2003), 1167-68.

others have been referred to as Gnostic or Apocryphal writings. The term "Gnostic" is a reference to knowledge; especially knowledge of secret spiritual truths, while apocryphal refers to what is hidden or concealed. Both of these terms are used to refer to books that are considered by conservative Christians, as not being part of the inspired, authorized canon of Scripture. The writers of these uncanonical works were attempting to emulate the Gospels, Acts, and letters.

The Conspiracy Theory

Because of the liberal scholarship of such persons as Dr. Bart D. Ehrman, Elaine Pagels, Karen L. King, and Marvin W. Meyer; many have become suspicious and skeptical that the Bible is the Word of God. They also reject that there was one true Christianity that Jesus Christ started and the apostle grew from 120 disciples on Pentecost 33 C.E.[4] to more than one million disciples by 130 C.E. and that heresies grew out of this one pure form of Christianity centuries later.

The Gnostic or Apocryphal writings as presented by the agnostic, atheist, and liberal-to-moderate Bible scholar, to the churchgoers, have created an acceptance never considered by the orthodox community. Both the teachings of Jesus and first-century Christianity have been dealt a new hand in the history books by these writings.

The modern-day scholarship has used these documents to propagate the theory that there was a variety of Christian movements in the first-century, along with what we know as orthodox Christianity, and these varieties just continued to grow until the fourth century. The fourth-century saw the orthodox variety take the prominent position until it was considered the Church. After that, it conspired to erase any evidence that other types of Christianity existed in the first-century.

According to these Bible scholars, this conspiratorial church developed the new history that there was only one true Christianity in the first and second century and by the end of the second and beginning of the third-century division was causing breakaway groups. The new Orthodox Church changed the story around to say that these fragment groups developed in the late second to early third centuries, but never took hold because the orthodox was always the real source of Christianity. This Orthodox Church supposedly suppressed the gnostic and apocryphal writings, while at the

---

[4] B.C.E. means "before the Common Era," which is more accurate than B.C. ("before Christ"). C.E. denotes "Common Era," often called A.D., for *anno Domini*, meaning "in the year of our Lord."

same time; they altered what we know to be the canonical Gospels: Matthew, Mark, Luke, and John.

Elaine Pagels, a professor of religion, put it this way,

> Yet even the fifty-two writings discovered at Nag Hammadi offer only a glimpse of the complexity of the early Christian movement. We now begin to see that what we call Christianity, and what we identify as Christian tradition, actually represents only a small selection of specific sources, chosen from among dozens of others. Who made that selection, and for what reasons? Why were these other writings excluded and banned as 'heresy'? What made them so dangerous? Now, for the first time, we have the opportunity to find out about the earliest Christian heresy; for the first time, the heretics can speak for themselves. (Pagels 1989, xxxv)

For scholars like Elaine Pagels and Bart D. Ehrman, Marvin W. Meyer, and others, the Bible is just one source that Christians should look to for their understanding of God. These scholars and others believe that these apocryphal books are just as canonical, authorized and authoritative as the ones we have always accepted, giving more weight to their credibility than the 27 books that have been accepted for almost 2,000 years as the only canonical New Testament. This popular message is resonating with this generation of Christians that are so busy trying to eke out a living; they do not have the time to investigate the truth of the matter. I believe that our investigation into Bart Ehrman, will add to what other authors have exposed, it is all theory, smoke, and mirrors (deception), nothing more.

The Importance of Being Informed

Almost all Christians today are uninformed about the very book they carry. Sure, many love the Bible, and some see it as the inspired and fully inerrant Word of God. However, let me draw you an analogy. Every Christian also likely believes that the Bible says we are allowed to defend ourselves against physical harm. Nevertheless, most do not take classes in unarmed self-defense. But then again, some do because they live in rough neighborhoods. Christians that live in high crime areas, where mugging, carjacking, robbery, assault, sexual assault, rape, and murder, are everyday experiences, are more prone to take such classes. Surviving in such a climate may very well depend on their training in unarmed self-defense. It may be the difference between life and death for themselves, family, friends, or of a spiritual brother or sister.

Today we Christians live in a world that assaults the Word of God and Christianity using every possible method. The Bible critic uses such tools as

19

the radio, television, movies, books, schools, billboards, lawsuits, and so on. They are figuratively robbing us, as well as our loved ones with their misleading words, their trickery, their cunning deception, and blatant lies. No place is safe. Do you prepare your Christian children for the onslaught that they face in today's school system? Do you prepare yourself? One may believe that they do not need to defend what they know to be true, but that does not always end with the best results, as many are walking away from the faith. This is precisely what we saw with Bart D. Ehrman, who went from an evangelical, conservative Christian to an agnostic Bible scholar.

Suppose you are online on a Christian Facebook group, and someone begins raising doubts about the Bible. The issues they raise cannot just be set aside because Christians new in their faith may be on the group with you. If none of the Christians on the group defends the Bible against the critic, the new Christians may assume we have no answers and start reading books, which leads them into a spiritual shipwreck. This too is a matter of life and death. Moreover, listen to Peter's words, as he spells out our obligation as Christians, "in your hearts honor Christ the Lord as holy, **always being prepared to make a defense** to anyone who asks you for a reason for the hope that is in you."–1 Peter 3:15.

William Lane Craig writes, "I think the church is really failing these kids. Rather than provide them training in the defense of Christianity's truth, we focus on emotional worship experiences, felt needs, and entertainment. It's no wonder they become sitting ducks for that teacher or professor who rationally takes aim at their faith. In high school and college, students are intellectually assaulted with every manner of non-Christian philosophy conjoined with an overwhelming relativism and skepticism. We've got to train our kids for war. How dare we send them unarmed into an intellectual war zone? Parents must do more than take their children to church and read them Bible stories. Moms and dads need to be trained in apologetics themselves and so be able to explain to their children simply from an early age and then with increasing depth why we believe as we do. Honestly, I find it hard to understand how Christian couples in our day and age can risk bringing children into the world without being trained in apologetics as part of the art of parenting."[5]

Craig also writes, "If the gospel is to be heard as an intellectually viable option for thinking men and women today, then it's vital that we as Christians try to shape American culture in such a way that Christian belief cannot be dismissed as mere superstition. This is where Christian apologetics

[5] Craig, William Lane. On Guard: Defending Your Faith with Reason and Precision (Kindle Locations 267-274). David C. Cook. Kindle Edition.

comes in. If Christians could be trained to provide solid evidence for what they believe and good answers to unbelievers' questions and objections, then the perception of Christians would slowly change. Christians would be seen as thoughtful people to be taken seriously rather than as emotional fanatics or buffoons. The gospel would be a real alternative for people to embrace. I'm not saying that people will become Christians because of the arguments and evidence. Rather I'm saying that the arguments and evidence will help to create a culture in which Christian belief is a reasonable thing. They create an environment in which people will be open to the gospel. So becoming trained in apologetics is one way, a vital way, of being salt and light in American culture today."[6]

A Look Into Ehrman's Misquoting Jesus

This fourth edition will be dealing with the Greek text of our New Testament, through the Eyes of Dr. Bart D. Ehrman, in his New York Times bestseller: *Misquoting Jesus: The Story Behind Who Changed the Bible and Why* (2005). First, in this introduction, we will look into Bart D. Ehrman's early life and spiritual decline as he moved from being an evangelical conservative Christian to becoming an agnostic skeptic. Second, we will open with chapter one covering the book writing process of the New Testament authors and early Christian scribes. Then, we will spend three lengthy chapters covering the reading culture of early Christianity because of Ehrman's claim of just how low the literacy rates were in early Christianity. After that, we will take one chapter to investigate the early Christian copyists because of Ehrman's claim that most of the scribal errors come from the first three centuries. Following this will be one of the most critical chapters examining Ehrman's claim of 400,000 textual variants [errors] and what impact they have on the integrity of the Greek New Testament. We will then investigate Bible Difficulties and what they mean for the trustworthiness of God's Word. Thereafter, we will give the reader the fundamentals of some of Ehrman's complaints, debunking them as we investigate each one throughout seven chapters.

Discovering the Ehrman Mindset

"My questions were complicated even more as I began to think increasingly about the manuscripts that conveyed the words. The more I studied Greek, the more I became interested in the manuscripts that preserve the New Testament for us, and in the science of textual

---

[6] IBID.

criticism, which can **supposedly** help us reconstruct what the **original** words of the New Testament were. I kept reverting to my basic question: how does it help us to say that the Bible is the inerrant word of God if in fact we don't have the words copied by the scribes—sometimes correctly but sometimes **(many times!***)* **incorrectly?** What good is it to say that the autographs (i.e., the **originals**) were inspired? *We* **don't have the original!** We have **only error ridden copies**, and the **vast majority of these are centuries removed from the originals and different from them, evidently, in thousands of ways.**" Bold mine. (Ehrman, 2005, p. 7)

Please notice the mental disposition, "supposedly," "many times!" "don't have the originals!" "error-ridden copies," "vast majority of," "centuries removed," "different from," and "thousands of." Well, this sounds quite ominous does it not? We might all just as well throw up our hands and go home, and give up Christianity because we could never possess the Word of God in the New Testament. Do not my latter words sound a bit sarcastic toward Ehrman? Yes, they are meant to come across that way, because I had the agenda to be sarcastic. The point being, one can tell the intent of what is being expressed by the wording. Now, what would we think Ehrman's objective is, by the way, he is writing in the above? We will get back to that soon enough.

The above quote comes from Bart D Ehrman's bestseller *Misquoting Jesus: the Story behind Who Changed the Bible and Why*. Bart D. Ehrman is a New Testament scholar extraordinaire. He chairs the department of religious studies at the University of North Carolina, Chapel Hill. He is one of the world's leading authorities on early Christianity and the life of Jesus Christ. In fact, he has authored over twenty books in this field of study.

Moreover, his books are New York Times bestsellers. Ehrman was raised in a conservative Christian family of five in the heartland of America—Lawrence, Kansas. It was the 1950s and 1960s, a time when the American citizens took religion very seriously.

His early life was filled with a conservative Christian influence. Christian youth camp and a camp leader that he calls "Bruce" influenced his middle teens. It was here that Ehrman was moved by his 'born-again' experience to take the Bible more serious. Therefore, the next stage was all too natural; he signed on at Moody Bible Institute in 1973, a conservative religious institution that takes Bible education serious in the extreme. The school name itself carries a reputation of knowing that it educates nothing but the most skilled Christians, who accept the Bible as nothing short of fully inerrant, with every word being inspired of God. In his telling of his early life, Ehrman reveals that he was not such a student, as Bart was very concerned as he got to know that there were no autograph manuscripts still extant (available today).[7]

Even more disturbing to him was that textual scholars do not also have the first published copies of the autographs or the second and third generation of copies. This issue alone seemed to push Ehrman into the field of textual studies. This weighed heavy on his young mind as he entered yet another evangelical university of extraordinary reputation in producing some of the best scholars the world has to offer: Wheaton College. Wheaton, being conservative, seemed though to pale in comparison to his former days at Moody. It was now time to peak outside of the box of just accepting things and not raising any issues about discrepancies that had been plaguing his mind. It was here that he met scholars, who were not afraid of asking the tough questions concerning their faith. While this is certainly reasonable, it was one more step toward the slippery slope that was going to consume young Ehrman. It was here that we see the mindset of Ehrman starting to develop, as our initial quote at the outset of this piece, in the above.

As he settled into the field of textual criticism, Ehrman would head on to yet another big named school, but one that was now moving away from his founding conservative principles, to a more liberal progressive stance: Princeton Theological Seminary. It is here that Bart D. Ehrman would study under the renowned textual scholar, Bruce M. Metzger. When writing an initial paper, for a Princeton professor by the name of Cullen Story at the beginning of his stay, Bart tried to give a long, complicated answer to overturn a discrepancy found in the Gospel of Mark. (Mark 2:26; 1 Sam 21:1-6) It was the response of this professor, on Bart's paper, which sent Ehrman onto the road of Agnosticism: "Maybe Mark just made a mistake." Here is Bart's established mindset from *Misquoting Jesus* before he even enters his first chapter,

> **p. 7**: How does it help us to say that the Bible is the inerrant word of God if in fact we don't have the words of God inerrantly inspired, but only the words copied by the scribes - sometimes correctly, but sometimes (many times!) incorrectly?

---

[7] The manuscript penned by one of the New Testament writers: Matthew, Mark, Luke John, Paul, Peter, James, or Jude. However, it may not have been personally penned, as the writer may have dictated to a scribe, as he took things down in shorthand, to later create a rough draft, which would be corrected by the Bible writer ad scribe, before being signed and published.

p. 10: It is one thing to say that the originals were inspired, but the reality is that we don't have the originals - so saying they were inspired doesn't help me much.

p. 10: Not only do we not have the originals, we don't have the originals of the first copies. We don't even have copies of the copies of the originals, or copies of the copies of the copies of the originals.[8]

p. 11: If one wants to insist that God inspired the very words of scripture, what would be the point if we don't have the very words of scripture? In some places, as we will see, we simply cannot be sure that we have constructed the original text accurately. It's a bit hard to know what the words of the Bible mean if we don't even know what the words are!

p. 11: The fact that we don't have the words surely must show, I reasoned, that he did not preserve them for us. And if he didn't perform that miracle, there seemed to be no reason to think that he performed the earlier miracle of inspiring those words.

It seems that Ehrman has a mindset that is perpetuated by a blind spot, the fact that we do not have the originals. We will start with Ehrman's obstacle of Mark 2:26. At Mark 2:26, many translations have Jesus saying that David went into the house of God and ate the showbread "when Abiathar was high priest." Since Abiathar's father, Ahimelech was the high priest when that event took place; such a translation would seem to result in a historical error.

Ehrman explains his assignment of having to write a paper dealing with the discrepancy of Mark 2:26: 'he was overly concerned with the idea of turning in anything that did not keep the validity of inerrancy alive.' He claimed that he had to do "fancy exegetical foot-work" for that to happen. The context of his recounting of the story was that he had to bend heaven and earth to get something resembling an explanation that avoided a historical error, which was not only a daunting task but time-consuming as well. Ehrman writes,

At the end of my paper, [Professor Story] wrote a simple one-line comment that for some reason went straight through me. He wrote: "Maybe Mark just made a mistake." I started thinking about it, considering all the work I had put into the paper, realizing that I had to do

---

[8] This may very well be an exaggeration because we do have some very early papyri.

some pretty fancy exegetical foot-work to get around the problem, and that my solution was in fact a bit of a stretch. I finally concluded, "Hmm . . . maybe Mark *did* make a mistake."

Once I made the admission, the floodgates opened. For if there could be one little, picayune mistake in Mark 2, maybe there could be mistakes in other places as well.... This kind of realization coincided with the problems I was encountering the more closely I studied the surviving Greek manuscripts of the New Testament. It is one thing to say that the original were inspired, but the reality is that we do not have the originals—so saying they were inspired doesn't help much, **unless I can reconstruct the originals.**[9]

Before looking at Ehrman's "fancy exegetical footwork" that he says, 'took much work,' let us say that this Bible difficulty is solved with simple reasoning. Is it not true that if we referred to the Roman Emperor Tiberius, before the time of his becoming emperor, we would say Roman Emperor Tiberius? Why? Because it is a title and position that he is known for throughout history. This would hold true with Abiathar as well. Therefore, Mark's reference to Abiathar as high priest is simply a reference to the position he had in history.

Mark 2:26 (NET): "he [being David] entered the house of God when Abiathar was high priest."

This rendering is certainly a historical error if taken outside of the way we usually talk about people in history. Let us start by looking at an interlinear, to get an understanding of the Greek words involved.

ΚΑΤΑ ΜΑΡΚΟΝ 2:26 (WHNU) *

How he entered into the house of the God upon Abiathar
26 πῶς εἰσῆλθεν εἰς τὸν οἶκον τοῦ θεοῦ ἐπὶ Ἀβιάθαρ
chief priest and the loaves of the presentation he ate which not it is lawful
ἀρχιερέως καὶ τοὺς ἄρτους τῆς προθέσεως , οὓς οὐκ ἔξεστιν
to eat if not the priests and he gave also to the (ones together with him
φαγεῖν εἰ μὴ τοὺς , καὶ ἔδωκεν καὶ τοῖς σὺν αὐτῷ
being?
οὖσιν;

* WHNU stands for the master critical Westcott and Hort Greek text of 1881, the 28th edition of the Nestle-Aland Greek text of 2013 and the fourth edition of the United Bible Societies Greek text of 2014. Of course,

---

[9] Ehrman, Bart D.: Misquoting Jesus: The Story Behind Who Changed the Bible and Why. New York: HarperCollins, 2005, pp. 9-10.

WH alone would refer to Westcott and Hort, while NA28 alone would stand for the Nestle-Aland text and UBS5 alone would stand for the United Bible Societies Greek text.

The Greek structure of Mark 2:26 is similar to that of Mark 12:26 and has been used by the translations below in their rendering of 2:26. This is perfectly acceptable, and there was no need for any "fancy exegetical footwork." The only exegetical footwork that I see is Ehrman's attempt at exaggerating a small Bible difficulty and not giving the complete picture. One has to keep in mind that original readers did not need to go to the length that we do today. It was written to them, in their language and their historic setting. We are 2,000 years removed and in a modern era that can hardly relate to them. Therefore, in translation and explanation, there is work to be done. Yet, any beginning Bible student with the reference works could have resolved this Bible difficulty in a matter of minutes. In fact, any churchgoer with the *Big Book of Bible Difficulties* by Norman Geisler or the *Encyclopedia of Bible Difficulties* by Gleason L. Archer could have found a reasonable answer the moment they opened the book. Why Ehrman struggled so when he had three years at Moody Bible Institute and two years at Wheaton College is beyond this writer.

Mark 12:26 (USB4): epi tou batou pos

upon the thorn bush how

Mark 12:26: epi tou batou ["*in the time of* the burning bush"]

Mark 2:26 (NASB): "in the time of Abiathar"

Mark 2:26 (ESV): "in the time of Abiathar"

Mark 2:26 (HCSB): "in the time of Abiathar"

Mark 2:26:   epi abiathar ["*in the time of* Abiathar"]

Mark 12:26: epi tou batou ["*in the time of* the burning bush"]

Luke 20:37: epi tes batou ["*in the time of* the burning bush"]

Acts 11:28:   epi klaudiou ["*in the time of* Claudius"]

Hebrews 1:2: epoiesen tous aionas ["*in the time of* the last days."]

Actually, if we look at Jesus' words: "He [David] entered the house of God, **in the time** of Abiathar, the high priest, and ate the bread of the Presence;" Jesus did not state that Abiathar was high priest at the time of this incident, only "**in the time of** . . ."[10] Contextually, Abiathar is actually present when the event took place. And in the story just after the murder of his father and would be high priest, a position, and title of which one would refer to him as thereafter, even in discussing events before his receiving that position. This is just a loose citation of Scripture. Today, we do it all the time. Therefore, it was in the time of Abiathar, but not during the time, he occupied the chief priest position. 1 Sam 22:9-12, 18; 23:6; 1 Sam 21:1-6; 22:18-19.

This is actually the argument that Ehrman had given to his professor, Cullen Story, which is a reasonable argument. Here are Ehrman's own words,

> In my paper for Professor Story, I developed a **long and complicated** argument to the effect that even though Mark indicates this happened "when Abiathar was the high priest," it doesn't really mean that Abiathar was the high priest, **but that the event took place in the part of the scriptural text** that has Abiathar as one of the main characters. My argument was based on the meaning of the Greek words involved and was a bit **convoluted.** *Misquoting Jesus* (p. 9)

Ehrman believes that his argument to Professor Story was "long and complicated argument." Ehrman says that his argument was also "convoluted," which means that it was extremely intricate: too complex or difficult to understand easily. This does not seem to be the case at all. I made the same argument on one page of typed text and wrote on a level that could be easily understood. I do not personally see mine as "long and complicated," nor "convoluted." Sadly, it gets even worse for Ehrman and his case, because he actually expresses himself in the same way that Jesus did, which is a common way of expressing things. If we look at page 9, the very page of his complaint, we will find Ehrman saying:

> Jesus wants to show the Pharisees that "Sabbath was made for humans, not humans for the Sabbath" and so reminds them of what the great **King David** had done when he and his men were hungry, how they went into **the Temple** "when Abiathar was the high priest" and ate the show bread, which was only for the priests to eat. *Misquoting Jesus* (p. 9)

First, David was **not a king at the time** of Ehrman's reference. Second, there was **no Temple at the time**; it was the Tabernacle. This is just a loose reference to Scripture by Ehrman as he refers to the person and place

---

[10] Ἀβιαθὰρ ἀρχιερέως *under, in the time of, Abiathar the high priest* **Mk** 2:26. ἐ. ἀρχιερέως Ἄννα καὶ Καιάφα **Lk** 3:2. ἐ. Κλαυδίου **Ac** 11:28

involved. We know David as King David, so we are not bewildered by his loose reference and recognize this is a way of referencing things. He also knows we think of it as a Temple, not the Tabernacle; we generally think of the Tabernacle being associated with Moses. Moreover, it was David's son, Solomon, who would eventually build the Temple. Here we have a world-renowned Bible scholar, who uses a loose reference in his book, and expects that his audience will understand what he means by his way of wording things. Was Ehrman technically chronologically wrong? Yes, in the strictest sense of things, if one wishes to be unreasonable. However, if we recognize this is an acceptable way of human expression; then, no really, he is not wrong because he knows his audience will understand his loose reference, and so it goes with Jesus as well. If only, Ehrman was as reasonable with Mark, who was recording Jesus' words.

Misleading by Failing to Qualify

If a textual scholar writes a book and says that the NT Greek manuscripts contain 400,000 errors or variants without qualifying that statement, this alone can be quite staggering to think about and will certainly dishearten the reader. A fuller explanation of how we count variants will be given in a future chapter, 'How to Count Textual Variants.' Below is the gist of what will be found in Chapter 10.

The critical text is as close as we get to what the original would have been like (99.95% restored).[11] Therefore, we use the reading in the critical text as the original reading, and anything outside of that in the manuscript history is a variant: 'spelling, word order, omission, addition, substitution, or a total rewrite of the text.' If we have the words of the original document, we do not need the documents themselves. What we have is not a miraculously preserved text but a painstakingly restored text involving hundreds of years, dozens of world-renowned textual scholars, and 5,836+ Greek New Testament manuscripts, not to mention thousands of versions and patristic quotations.

Misleading by Exaggeration

For example sake alone: if we find numerous overdone statements and exaggerated explanations, with missing information and many exclamation points to emphasize the negative, but seldom mentioning the

---

[11] While it is true that some scholars, like Philip Comfort, argue that, the NU could be improved upon, because in many cases it is too dependent on internal evidence when the documentary evidence should be more of a consideration as to the weightiness of the matter. Again though, this is a handful of places, when one considers 138,020 words in the Greek New Testament.

positive; we can eventually see **a pattern.** If this proves to be the case, the writer is certainly doing a disservice to the reader. If we find 200 texts that are supposed to be full of historical, geographical, or scientific errors, and they are highlighted; yet this person fails to explain to the reader that each of the 200 errors have reasonable and logical explanations; then, this is a pattern of misleading the reader by failing to disclose all of the facts. Many who have read Ehrman's *Misquoting Jesus* are simply churchgoers that occasionally study the Bible, who are not aware of the apologetic answers to the claims. Scholars are hardly moved by them, as they are well aware of the alternative explanations.

If we find repeated behavior that reflects an agenda of highlighting minute issues, while ignoring a massive amount of positives, one can hardly avoid the conclusion that we have an agnostic scholar, who wishes others to join his ranks. Why dramatically point to Mark 2:26 as the obstacle with the exclamation points and act as though the historical error is a fact, and only "fancy exegetical footwork" can possibly undo it? This we will look at repeatedly because each of his textual issues has explanations that he largely fails to share with his reader. Let us look at one more text before moving on.

Mark 4:31: "It is like a grain of mustard seed, which, when sown on the ground, is the smallest of all the seeds on earth"—ESV.

Critic: Today we know that the mustard seed is not the smallest seed on earth. If Jesus were the Son of God, he would have known that.

Bart D. Ehrman: "Jesus says later in Mark 4 that the mustard seed is 'the smallest of all seeds on the earth,' maybe I don't need to come up with a fancy explanation for how the mustard seed is the smallest of all seeds when I know full well it isn't"—p. 9-10.

Some commentators argue that Jesus was referring to the seed for the black mustard plant. However, while this could be the case, it need not be that complicated. Jesus was talking to Jewish farmers, to which the mustard seed was the smallest. Jesus was not giving a lesson in botany but was attempting to make a point by using what the people knew. In fact, the mustard seed is one of the tiniest seeds, and to those, to whom Jesus was speaking to, it was. The Bible is not a science textbook, nor is to be treated as such in our interpretation.

Is there a Need for Concern?

Is there a pattern forming here? Is the problem anything more than a Bible difficulty for the regular churchgoer, who has the potential to find a reasonable answer within minutes? Does Ehrman's expression "fancy explanation" imply more than one needing some Bible background knowledge that takes less than five minutes to acquire? To this writer, it does, when considered with his other phrase that we have already seen. In addition, remember, we have not even made it out of the introduction of Ehrman's book yet. Ehrman said that he had to do "some pretty fancy exegetical footwork to get around the problem," [of Mark 2:26's 'when Abiathar was high priest'] and in fact, my solution was a bit of a stretch." I found the answer that is accepted by some of the best translations and commentators, as well as apologetics within a few minutes.[12] There was no need for some "fancy exegetical footwork." It seems that Bart D Ehrman, the "happy agnostic" as he calls himself is attempting to make his points in an exaggerated fashion in *Misquoting Jesus*. A person that intends to exaggerate his claims allows '**some** manuscripts' to become '**the majority** of manuscripts,' and **the 'majority** of manuscripts' becoming '**all manuscripts,**' and '**some cases** of intentional errors by scribes' becomes '**all cases.**' One certainly has to question the credibility of any scholar that would tend to exaggerate numbers, overstate the extent, embellish reports and leave out other information that would derail his point.

I want us to keep the phrase "**accuracy of the statement**" in mind, as I am going to be using it all through our investigation of *Misquoting Jesus*. We will look at several of his comments throughout his publication, evaluating them as we go. Before we begin this journey, let it be said here that no Bible student is responsible for restoring the original text. However, *every*, and I do mean *every* Bible student is responsible for having a basic knowledge of the issues at hand, the art and science of textual criticism (TC). Textual criticism is not to be confused with higher criticism. TC 'is the study of any written work of which the autograph is unknown, with the purpose of ascertaining the original text.' (Greenlee, 1995) Literally, hundreds of textual scholars over the last 400-years have given their lives to this work. One can feel most confident that our NA^{28} and our UBS^5 master Greek texts are predominately the same as the originals that were penned so long ago. Bible scholars Norman L. Geisler and William Nix conclude: "The New Testament, then, has not only survived in more

---

[12] Gleason L. Archer Jr.: *Encyclopedia of Bible Difficulties*. Grand Rapids, MI: Zondervan, 1984, p. 329;

[12] Norman L. Geisler; Thomas Howe: *The Big Book of Bible Difficulties*. Grand Rapids, MI: Baker Books, 1992, p. 345; Kaiser, Walter C.; Davids, Peter H.; Bruce F. F.; Brauch, Manfred T.: Hard Sayings of the Bible. Downer Groves, Illinois: InterVarsity Press, 1996, pp 411-412; Comfort, Philip W.: New Testament Text and Translation Commentary. Carol Stream, Illinois: Tyndale House Publishers, 2008, p. 102

manuscripts than any other book from antiquity, but it has survived in a purer form than any other great book – a form that is 99.5 percent pure."[13]

On this, Stanley E. Porter writes,

The most important observation is that the number of variants being investigated by Ehrman and others with respect to their theological influences, when compared to the entirety of the New Testament, is fairly small, despite sometimes sensationalist claims to the contrary. We now have somewhere over 5,800 New Testament Greek manuscripts in part (mostly) and in whole, ranging from the second century to the fifteenth or sixteenth centuries. Within those manuscripts, if one counts every possible type of variant, there are well over one hundred thousand variants (a number I will return to below). Nevertheless, despite all of this purported textual evidence of variance, calculations have indicated that, on the basis of the editions of the Greek New Testament produced by Tischendorf, Westcott and Hort, Hermann von Soden, Heinrich Joseph Vogels, Augustin Merk, and José Maria Bover, 62.9 percent of the verses of the Greek New Testament show no variants. The individual books range from a low of 45.1 percent of verses with no variants (in Mark) to a high of 81.4 percent of verses with no variants (in 1 Timothy). According to the estimates of Aland and Aland, when one compares the two major text-types for the Greek New Testament— the Byzantine and the Alexandrian— they "actually exhibit a remarkable degree of agreement, perhaps as much as 80 percent!" Other scholars have estimated this degree of agreement to be as high as 90 percent. Even this is perhaps not high enough, however. Most recently, Martin Heide has compared and calculated the stability of the New Testament manuscripts. Manuscripts vary in their textual stability from about 89 to 98 percent. As he states, "The stability of the New Testament text under consideration, from the early papyri to the Byzantine text, achieves an average of 92.6 percent." This means that the textual evidence confirms the existence of a stable text, with the lack of variation indicating that we probably have 80– 90 percent, if not more, of the Greek text of the New Testament unquestionably established, so far as that can be determined from our existing manuscripts; and that is really all we have on which to base such a decision. The impression sometimes given in discussions of the text of the New Testament is that the text itself is entirely fluid and unstable, and that it was subject to so much variation and change

---

[13] Geisler, Norman L.; Nix, William E.: *A General Introduction to the Bible.* Chicago, Illinois, Moody Press, 1980 Reprint, p. 361.

through especially the first two centuries that its very stability is threatened. This simply is not true.[14]

---

[14] Stanley E. Porter. How We Got the New Testament (Acadia Studies in Bible and Theology) (p. 23-24). Baker Publishing Group.

CHAPTER 1 The Book Writing Process of the New Testament: Authors and Early Christian Scribes

Ehrman wrote: This is obviously a crucial task, since we can't interpret the words of the New Testament if we don't know what the words were. Moreover, as I hope should be clear by now, knowing the words is important not just for those who consider the words divinely inspired. It is important for anyone who thinks of the New Testament as a significant book. Misquoting Jesus (p. 70).

Ehrman wrote: In particular, as I said at the outset, I began seeing the New Testament as a very human book. The New Testament as we actually have it, I knew, was the product of human hands, the hands of the scribes who transmitted it. Then I began to see that not just the scribal text but the original text itself was a very human book. This stood very much at odds with how I had regarded the text in my late teens as a newly minted "born-again" Christian, convinced that the Bible was the **inerrant Word** of God and that the biblical words themselves had come to us by the **inspiration** of the Holy Spirit. As I realized already in graduate school, even if God had **inspired** the original words, we don't have the original words. So the **doctrine of inspiration was** in a sense **irrelevant** to the Bible as we have it, since the words **God reputedly inspired** had been changed and, in some cases, lost. Moreover, I came to think that **my earlier views of inspiration** were **not only irrelevant**, they were **probably wrong**. For the only reason (I came to think) for God to inspire the Bible would be so that his people would have his actual words; but if he really wanted people to have his actual words, surely he would have miraculously preserved those words, just as he had miraculously inspired them in the first place. Given the circumstance that he didn't preserve the words, the conclusion seemed inescapable to me that he hadn't gone to the trouble of inspiring them. Misquoting Jesus (p. 211).

The Place of Writing

When we think of the apostle Paul penning his books that would make up most of the New Testament, some have had the anachronistic tendency to impose their modern way of thinking about him, such as presupposing where he would have written. As I am writing this page, I am tucked away in my home office, seeking privacy from the hustle and bustle of our modern world. This was not the case in the ancient world where Paul lived and traveled. People of that time favored a group setting, not isolation. The apostle Paul probably would have been of this mindset. Paul would not have necessarily sought a quiet place to pen his letters, to escape the noise of those around him. As for myself, I struggle to get back on track if I am interrupted for more than a couple of minutes.

Most during Paul's day would have been surprised by this way of thinking, i.e., seeking quiet and solitude to focus all of one's energy on the task of writing. Those of Paul's day, including himself, would not have even noticed people talking around them, nor would they have been troubled by what we perceive as interruptions, such as the discussions of others, which were neither relevant nor applicable to the subject of their letter writing.

The Scribe of the New Testament Writer

Ancient Greco-Roman society employed secretaries or scribes for various reasons. Of course, the government employed some scribes, working for chief administrators. Then, there were the scribes who were employed in the private sector. These latter scribes (often slaves) usually were employed by the wealthy. However, even high-ranking slaves and freed slaves employed scribes. Many times, one would find scribes who would pen letters for their friends. According to E. Randolph Richards, the skills of these unofficial secretaries "could range from a minimal competency with the language and/or the mechanics of writing to the highest proficiency at rapidly producing an accurate, proper, and charming letter."[15] Scribes carried out a wide range of administrative, secretarial, and literary tasks, including administrative bookkeeping, shorthand and taking dictation, letter-writing, and copying literary texts.

The most prominent ways that a scribe would have been used in the first century C.E. would have been as (1) a recorder, (2) an editor, and (3) as a secretary for an author. At the very bottom of the writing tasks, he would be used to record information, i.e. as a record keeper. The New Testament scribes, when they were needed or desired, were being used as secretaries, writing down letters by dictation. Tertius, in taking down the book of Romans with its 7,000+ words, would have simply written out the very words that the apostle Paul spoke. Some have argued that longhand in dictation was not feasible in ancient times because the author would have to slow down to the point of speaking syllable-by-syllable. They usually cite Cicero as evidence for this argument because of the numerous references to dictation in his writings. Cicero stated in a letter to his friend Varro that he had to slow down his dictation to the point of "syllable by syllable" for the sake of the scribe. However, the scribe he was

---

[15] (Richards, The Secretary in the Letters of Paul 1990, 11)

using at that time was inexperienced, not his regular scribe. Of course, it would be very difficult to retain one's line of thought in such a dictation process. It should be noted that Cicero had experienced scribes who could take down dictation at a normal pace of speaking, even rapid speech.[16] Therefore, since there is evidence that there were scribes in those days who were skilled enough to take down dictation at the normal rate of speech, we should not assume that the apostles would not have had access to such scribes in the persons of Tertius, Silvanus, or even Timothy.

In fact, Marcus Fabius Quintilianus (b. 35 C.E. d. 100 C.E.) complained that a scribe who could write at the speed of normal speech can lead to the speaker feeling rushed, to the point of not having time to ponder his thoughts.

> On the other hand, there is a fault which is precisely the opposite of this, into which those fall who insist on first making a rapid draft of their subject with the utmost speed of which their pen is capable, and write in the heat and impulse of the moment. They call this their rough copy. They then revise what they have written, and arrange their hasty outpourings. But while the words and the rhythm may be corrected, the matter is still marked by the superficiality resulting from the speed with which it was thrown together. The more correct method is, therefore, to exercise care from the very beginning, and to form the work from the outset in such a manner that it merely requires being chiseled into shape, not fashioned anew. Sometimes, however, we must follow the stream of our emotions since their warmth will give us more than any diligence can secure. The condemnation which I have passed on such carelessness in writing will make it pretty clear what my views are on the luxury of dictation which is now so fashionable. For, when we write, however great our speed, the fact that the hand cannot follow the rapidity of our thoughts gives us time to think, whereas the presence of our amanuensis hurries us on, and at times we feel ashamed to hesitate or pause, or make some alteration, as though we were afraid to display such weakness before a witness. As a result, our language tends not merely to be haphazard and formless, but in our desire to produce a continuous flow we let slip positive improprieties of diction, which show neither the precision of the writer nor the impetuosity of the speaker. Again, if the amanuensis is a slow writer or lacking in intelligence, he becomes a stumbling-block, our speed is checked, and the thread of our ideas is

---

[16] (Richards, *Paul And First-Century Letter Writing: Secretaries, Composition and Collection* 2004, 29-30); Murphy-O'Connor, *Paul the Letter-Writer*, 9–11; Shorthand references Plutarch, *Cato Minor*, 23.3–5; Caesar, 7.4–5; Seneca, *Epistles*, 14.208.

interrupted by the delay or even perhaps by the loss of temper to which it gives rise.[17]

Therefore, again, we do have evidence that some scribes were capable, skilled to the point of writing at the normal speed of speech. While Richards says that this is by way of shorthand, saying it was more widespread than originally thought, where the secretary uses symbols in place of words, forming a rough draft that would be written out fully,[18] this need not be the case. True, there is some evidence that shorthand existed a hundred years before Christ. However, it was still rare, with few scribes having the ability. Whether this was true of the scribes that assisted our New Testament authors is an unknown. It is highly unlikely but not necessarily impossible.

Who in the days of the New Testament authors would use the services of scribes? Foremost would be those who did not know how to read and write. Within ancient contracts and business letters, one can find a note by the scribe (illiteracy statement), who penned it, stating he had done so because his employer could not read or write. For example, an ancient letter concludes with, "Eumelus, son of Herma, has written for him because he does not know letters."[19] It may be that they were able to read, but struggled with writing. Then again, it may simply be that they wrote slowly, and were not willing to spend the time on improving their skills. An ancient letter from Thebes, Egypt, penned for a certain Asklepiades, concludes, "Written for him hath Eumelus the son of Herma ..., being desired so to do for that he writeth somewhat slowly." (Deissmann 1910, 166-7)

On the other hand, whether one knew how to read and write was not always the decisive issue in the use of a secretary. John L. McKenzie writes, "Even people who could read and write did not think of submitting their readers to unprofessional penmanship. It was probably not even a concern for legibility, but rather a concern for beauty, or at least for neatness," (McKenzie 1975, 14) which moved the ancients to turn to the services of a secretary. Although the educated could read and write, some likely very well, writing was tedious, trying, and frustrating, particularly where lengthy and elaborate texts were concerned. It seems that if one could avoid the tremendous task of penning a lengthy letter, entrusting it to a scribe, so much the better.

The apostle Paul had over 100 traveling companions; like Aristarchus, Luke and Timothy served by the apostle's side for many years. Then, there

---

[17] Institutio Oratoria, 10.3.17–21

[18] (Richards, Paul And First-Century Letter Writing: Secretaries, Composition and Collection 2004, 72)

[19] See examples in Francis Exler, *The Form of the Ancient Greek Letter: A Study In Greek Epistolography* (Washington D.C.: Catholic University of America, 1922), pp. 126-7

are others such as Asyncritus, Hermas, Julia, or Philologus, of whom we barely know more than their names. Many of Paul's friends traveled for the sake of the gospel, such as Achaicus, Fortunatus, Stephanas, Artemas, and Tychicus. We know that Tychicus was used by Paul to carry at least three letters now included in the Bible canon: the epistles to the Ephesians, the Colossians, and to Philemon. Tychicus was not simply some mail carrier. He was a well-trusted carrier for the apostle, Paul. The final greeting from Paul to the Colossians reads,

Colossians 4:7-8 New American Standard Bible (NASB)

7 As to all my affairs, Tychicus, *our* beloved brother and faithful servant and fellow bond-servant in the Lord, will bring you information. 8 *For* I have sent him to you for this very purpose, that you may know about our circumstances and that he may encourage your hearts;

Richards offers the following about a letter carrier, saying he "was often a personal link between the author and the recipients in addition to the written link. . . . [One purpose] for needing a trustworthy carrier was, he often carried additional information. A letter may describe a situation briefly, frequently with the author's assessment, but the carrier is expected to elaborate for the recipient all the details." (Richards, The Secretary in the Letters of Paul 1990, 7) Many of Paul's letters deal with teachings, as well as one crisis after another; the carrier was expected to be aware of these on a much deeper level so that he could orally explain, and answer any questions. Therefore, he needed to be a highly trusted messenger who was literate.

Tertius was the scribe Paul used to pen his letter to the Romans. We cannot assume that all of Paul's companions were proficient readers and writers, but we can infer that Paul would task coworkers, who were able to carry and read letters, as well as understand the condition of the people or congregation where they were being sent or stationed. In addition, the scribes whom Paul used, such as Tertius, would very likely have been semi-professional or professional. It would have been simply senseless to entrust the secretarial work of taking down the monumental words of the book of Romans, for example, to an inexperienced scribe. What skills would Tertius need to carry out the task of penning the book of Romans?

The ordinary coworker of Paul would likely have been able to read proficiently, but barely be able to write. Paul would have chosen workers whose skills would have equipped them to carry out their assignments. Tertius would have been the exception to the rule, most likely having been a professional scribe. He would have to have been able to glue the sheets together if it was to be a roll or stitch the pages together if a codex. He would need to know the appropriate mixture of soot and gum to make ink and to be able to use his knife to make his own reed pen. Richards writes that a professional scribe would also "draw lines on the paper. Small holes were often pricked down each side, and then a straight edge and a lead disk were used to lightly draw evenly spaced lines across the sheet."[20] If Tertius had not been trained as a copyist of documents, he would have made many minor errors because his attention would have been on the sense of what he was penning, as opposed to the exact words, as is typical of the unconscious mind.

Did Tertius take Paul's exact dictation, word for word? Robert H. Mounce writes,

> The only legitimate question about authorship relates to the role of Tertius, who in 16:22 writes, 'I Tertius, who wrote down this letter, greet you in the Lord.' We know that at that time in history an amanuensis [scribe] that is, one hired to write from dictation, could serve at several levels. In some cases, he would receive dictation and write it down immediately in longhand. At other times, he might use a form of shorthand (*tachygraphy* [ancient shorthand]) to take down a letter and then later write it out in longhand. In some cases, an amanuensis would simply get the gist of what a person wanted to say and then be left on his own to formulate the ideas into a letter. (R. H. Mounce 2001, 22)

It might seem quite the task for Tertius to take down Paul's words in longhand. However, this is not to say that it was impossible, just difficult. Paul might have had to speak in a slow to a normal rate of speech, **but not** syllable-by-syllable. It is true that Tertius would have been writing on a papyrus sheet with a reed pen, with the intention of being legible; however, he would have been very skilled in his trade. Then again, there is the slight possibility of Tertius taking it down in shorthand and thereafter making out a full draft, which would have been reviewed by both Paul and Tertius. The last option by Mounce in the above is contrary to the attitudes that both the scribes and the New Testament authors would have had toward what was being penned. God chose to convey a message through Matthew, Mark, Luke, John, Peter, Jude, James, and Paul, not Tertius and Silvanus, or others. We cannot say with any certainty whether Tertius or Silvanus took their authors' words down in shorthand or longhand. We can say, however, that the Word of God was being dictated by the human author to the scribe, and in no way composed by the scribe.

---

[20] (Richards, Paul And First-Century Letter Writing: Secretaries, Composition and Collection 2004, 29)

Inspiration and Inerrancy in the Writing Proce

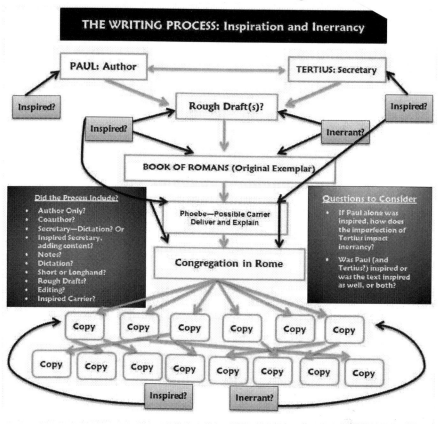

THE WRITING PROCESS: Inspiration and Inerrancy

PAUL: Author

TERTIUS: Secretary

Inspired?

Inspired?

Rough Draft(s)?

Inspired?

Inerrant?

BOOK OF ROMANS (Original Exemplar)

Did the Process Include?
- Author Only?
- Coauthor?
- Secretary—Dictation? Or
- Inspired Secretary, adding content?
- Notes?
- Dictation?
- Short or Longhand?
- Rough Drafts?
- Editing?
- Inspired Carrier?

Phoebe—Possible Carrier Deliver and Explain

Questions to Consider
- If Paul alone was inspired, how does the imperfection of Tertius impact inerrancy?
- Was Paul (and Tertius?) inspired or was the text inspired as well, or both?

Congregation in Rome

Copy Copy Copy Copy Copy Copy

Copy Copy Copy Copy Copy Copy Copy Copy

Inspired?

Inerrant?

All Scripture is Inspired by God

In this context, inspiration is **the state** of a human being moved by the Holy Spirit, which results in an inspired, fully inerrant written Word of God.

Chicago Statement on Biblical Inerrancy ICBI

Article VII

We affirm that **inspiration** was the work in which God by His Spirit, through human writers, gave us His Word. The origin of Scripture is divine. The mode of divine **inspiration** remains largely a mystery to us. We deny that **inspiration** can be reduced to human insight, or to heightened states of consciousness of any kind.

Article VIII

We affirm that God in His Work of **inspiration** utilized the distinctive personalities and literary styles of the writers whom He had chosen and prepared. We deny that God, in causing these writers to use the very words that He chose, overrode their personalities.

Article IX

We affirm that **inspiration**, though not conferring omniscience, guaranteed true and trustworthy utterance on all matters of which the Biblical authors were moved to speak and write. We deny that the finitude or fallenness of these writers, by necessity or otherwise, introduced distortion or falsehood into God's Word.

Article X

We affirm that **inspiration**, strictly speaking, applies only to the autographic text of Scripture, which in the providence of God can be ascertained from available manuscripts with great accuracy. We further affirm that copies and translations of Scripture are the Word of God to the extent that they faithfully represent the original. We deny that any essential element of the Christian faith is affected by the absence of the autographs. We further deny that this absence renders the assertion of Biblical **inerrancy** invalid or irrelevant.

Article XI

We affirm that Scripture, having been given by divine inspiration, is infallible, so that, far from misleading us, it is true and reliable in all the matters it addresses. We deny that it is possible for the Bible to be at the same time infallible and errant in its assertions. Infallibility and inerrancy may be distinguished, but not separated.

Inerrancy of Scripture

Inerrancy of Scripture is **the result** of the state of a human being moved by the Holy Spirit from God, which results in an inspired, fully inerrant written Word of God.

Article XII

We affirm that Scripture in its entirety is **inerrant**, being free from all falsehood, fraud, or deceit. We deny that Biblical infallibility and **inerrancy** are limited to spiritual, religious, or redemptive themes, exclusive of assertions in the fields of history and science. We further deny that scientific hypotheses about earth history may properly be used to overturn the teaching of Scripture on creation and the flood.

Article XIII

We affirm the propriety of using **inerrancy** as a theological term with reference to the complete truthfulness of Scripture. We deny that it is proper to evaluate Scripture according to standards of truth and error that are alien to its usage or purpose. We further deny that **inerrancy** is negated by Biblical phenomena such as a lack of modern technical precision, irregularities of grammar or spelling, observational descriptions of nature, the reporting of falsehoods, the use of hyperbole and round numbers, the topical arrangement of material, variant selections of material in parallel accounts, or the use of free citations.

Article XV

We affirm that the doctrine of **inerrancy** is grounded in the teaching of the Bible about **inspiration**. We deny that Jesus' teaching about Scripture may be dismissed by appeals to accommodation or to any natural limitation of His humanity.

Article XVI

We affirm that the doctrine of **inerrancy** has been integral to the Church's faith throughout its history. We deny that inerrancy is a doctrine invented by Scholastic Protestantism, or is a reactionary position postulated in response to negative higher criticism.

Authoritative Word of God

The **authoritative** aspect of Scripture is that God by way of inspiration gives the words the authors chose to use power and authority, so that the outcome (i.e., originals) is the very Word of God, as though God were speaking to us himself.

Article I

We affirm that the Holy Scriptures are to be received as the **authoritative** Word of God. We deny that the Scriptures receive their authority from the Church, tradition, or any other human source.

2 Timothy 3:16-17 Updated American Standard Version (UASV)

[16] All Scripture is inspired by God and profitable for teaching, for reproof, for correction, for training in righteousness; [17] so that the man of God may be fully competent, equipped for every good work.

What does this mean? The phrase "inspired by God" (Gr., *theopneustos*) literally means, "Breathed out by God." A related Greek word, *pneuma*, means "wind," "breath," life, "Spirit." Since *pneuma* can also mean "breath," the process of "breathing out" can rightly be said to be the work of the Holy Spirit inspiring the Scriptures. The result is that the originals were accurate, fully inerrant and authoritative. Thus the Holy Spirit moved human writers so that the result can truthfully be called the Word of *God*, not the word of man.

2 Peter 1:21 Updated American Standard Version (UASV)

[21] for no prophecy was ever produced by the will of man, but men carried along by the Holy Spirit spoke from God.

The Greek word here translated "men moved by (NASB)," *phero*, is used in another form at Acts 27:15, 17, which describes a ship that was driven along by the wind. So the Holy Spirit, by analogy, 'navigated the course' of the Bible writers. While the Spirit did not give them each word by dictation,[21] it certainly kept the writers from inserting any information that did not convey the will and purpose of God.

The heart of what the International Council on Biblical Inerrancy (ICBI) stood for is apparent in "A Short Statement," produced at the Chicago conference in 1978:

A SHORT STATEMENT

1. God, who is Himself Truth and speaks truth only, has inspired Holy Scripture in order thereby to reveal Himself to lost mankind through Jesus Christ as Creator and Lord, Redeemer and Judge. Holy Scripture is God's witness to Himself.

2. Holy Scripture, being God's own Word, written by men prepared and superintended by His Spirit, is of infallible divine authority in all matters upon which it touches: it is to be believed, as God's instruction, in all that it affirms, obeyed, as God's command, in all that it requires; embraced, as God's pledge, in all that it promises.

3. The Holy Spirit, Scripture's divine Author, both authenticates it to us by His inward witness and opens our minds to understand its meaning.

4. Being wholly and verbally God-given, Scripture is without error or fault in all its teaching, no less in what it states about God's acts in creation, about the events of world history, and about its own literary origins under God, than in its witness to God's saving grace in individual lives.

5. The **authority of Scripture** is inescapably impaired if this total divine **inerrancy** is in any way limited or disregarded or made relative to a view

---

[21] (Wilkins) Exactly how the Spirit guided the writers is a mystery, and the words "thus says the Lord" in prophecy most likely do introduce a dictated message. However, those familiar with Greek can easily see stylistic differences between the NT writers which seem to reflect different personalities and rule out verbatim dictation from a single source.

of truth contrary to the Bible's own; and such lapses bring serious loss to both the individual and the Church.

Questions to Consider

We have been using the book of Romans as our example, so we will continue with it. We know that Paul was the author who gave us the inspired content of Romans, Tertius was the secretary who recorded Romans, and Phoebe was likely the one who carried the letter to Rome or else accompanied the one who did. Thus, we have at least three persons: the author, the secretary (scribe), and the carrier.

What is inspiration?

Inspiration is a "theological concept encompassing phenomena in which human action, skill, or utterance is immediately and extraordinarily supplied by the Spirit of God. Although various terms are employed in the Bible, the basic meaning is best served by Gk. *theopneustos* "God-breathed" (2 Tim. 3:16), meaning "breathed forth by God" rather than "breathed into by God" (Warfield)." (Myers 1987, 524) **Verbal plenary inspiration** holds that "every word of Scripture was God-breathed." A significant role was played by the human writers. Their individual backgrounds, personal traits, and literary styles were authentically theirs but had been providentially prepared by God for use as his instrument in producing Scripture. "The Scriptures had not been dictated, but the result was as if they had been (A. A. Hodge, B. B. Warfield)." (Myers 1987, 525)

Benjamin B. Warfield: "Inspiration is, therefore, usually defined as a supernatural influence exerted on the sacred writers by the Spirit of God, by virtue of which their writings are given Divine trustworthiness."[22]

Edward J. Young: "Inspiration is a superintendence of God the Holy Spirit over the writers of the Scriptures, as a result of which these Scriptures possess Divine authority and trustworthiness and, possessing such Divine authority and trustworthiness, are free from error."[23]

Charles C. Ryrie: "Inspiration is ... God's superintendence of the human authors so that, using their own individual personalities, they composed and recorded without error His revelation to man in the words of the original autographs."[24]

---

[22] B. B. Warfield, *The Inspiration and Authority of the Bible* (Philadelphia: Presbyterian and Reformed, 1948), p. 131.

[23] Edward J. Young, *Thy Word Is Truth* (Grand Rapids: Eerdmans, 1957), p. 27.

[24] Charles C. Ryrie, *A Survey of Bible Doctrine* (Chicago: Moody, 1972), p. 38.

Paul P. Enns: "There are several important elements that belong in a proper definition of inspiration: (1) the divine element—God the Holy Spirit superintended the writers, ensuring the accuracy of the writing; (2) the human element—human authors wrote according to their individual styles and personalities; (3) the result of the divine-human authorship is the recording of God's truth without error; (4) inspiration extends to the selection of words by the writers; (5) inspiration relates to the original manuscripts."[25]

Were both Paul and Tertius inspired, or just Paul?

Only Paul and other Old and New Testament authors were inspired. First, as was stated above, **Verbal plenary inspiration** holds that "every word of Scripture was God-breathed." God **did not**, generally speaking, dictate the books of the Bible word by word to the Bible authors as if they were dictating machines.

2 Thessalonians 3:17 New American Standard Bible (NASB)

[17] I, Paul, write this greeting with my own hand, and this is a distinguishing mark in every letter; this is the way I write.

An appended note to every letter with his signature "distinguishing mark" is like a boss signing a letter that he dictated to a secretary. It is unthinkable that Paul would sign or make a distinguishing mark on anything without reading through it and make any necessary corrections. This supposes that Paul looked over all of his letters, which would also suppose that the scribe could not have been inspired because if he were, then there would have been no mistakes in the document, which means it would not have been needed to be looked over let alone corrected. So again, there would have been no need for Paul to check the work of an inspired secretary. If Tertius had been inspired, the moment he set the pen down, Paul would have had no need to look the text over. There is no need to read into silence and suggest that the secretary was inspired. While the secretary was certainly engaged in his work being that they were coworkers and traveling companions,

However, in some cases, information was transmitted by verbal dictation, word for word. For example, when God delivered the large body of laws and statutes of his covenant with Israel, Jehovah instructed Moses: "Write for yourself these words." (Ex 34:27, LEB) In another example, the prophets were often given specific messages to deliver. (1 Ki 22:14; Jer. 1:7; 2:1; 11:1-5; Eze. 3:4; 11:5) More importantly, the Bible authors did dictate

---

[25] Paul P. Enns, *The Moody Handbook of Theology* (Chicago: Moody Press, 1989), p. 161.

what they received under inspiration to their secretaries, i.e., amanuenses/scribes.

Jeremiah 36:4 New American Standard Bible (NASB)

[4] Then Jeremiah called Baruch the son of Neriah, and Baruch wrote on a scroll at **the dictation of Jeremiah** all the words of the Lord which He had spoken to him. (Bold mine)

If Paul alone was inspired, how does the imperfection of Tertius affect inerrancy?

First, we should state that just because Paul used Tertius, Peter used Silvanus, or Jeremiah used Baruch, to pen the Word of God, they did not thereby detract from or weaken the authority of God's Word or the inerrancy of Scripture. The dictation that Paul gave Tertius was the result of divine inspiration as he, Paul, was moved along by Holy Spirit. Tertius merely recorded Paul's dictation, word by word. Whether Tertius was a professional scribe[26] or had the skills of a semi-professional scribe, he must have made at least a few slips of the pen. Afterward, however, Paul would have reviewed the document with Tertius, correcting any errors before publishing the official, authoritative text.

What about Phoebe, what role did the carrier have in the process?

Those used by New Testament authors to deliver the Word of God to people or congregations would have been some of Paul's most trusted, competent coworkers. Certainly, in the case of congregations contacting Paul with questions and concerns, to which Paul responded with an inspired letter, the carrier would be made aware of those questions and concerns. Paul would have spoken to the carrier at length about these matters, going over what he meant by what he wrote. This would have provided the carrier sufficient knowledge; in case the person or congregation had any question that the carrier could address. This process is not indicated within the Scriptures; but are we to believe God and Paul for that matter would send a simple carrier who was left in the dark as to what he was carrying, and that no congregational leader would have follow-up questions, which God would have foreseen? Hardly.

The Publishing, Copying and Distributing Process

In the above, we spoke of the initial aspect of the publishing process, i.e., the moment Paul decided to pen a letter to a congregation like the Romans, the Ephesians, the Colossians, or to a person such as Philemon.

---

[26] In the strictest sense, a professional scribe is one who was specifically trained in that vocation and was paid for his services.

We discussed the process that Paul went through with his secretary (e.g., Tertius), to the carrier (e.g., Phoebe, Tychicus) and the recipients. Now we turn to the circulation aspect, i.e., getting the book out to more and more readers. Harry Y. Gamble says the following in *The Publication and Early Dissemination of Early Christian Books*:

> The letters of Paul to his communities, the earliest extant Christian texts, were dictated to scribal associates (presumably Christian), carried to their destinations by a traveling Christian, and read aloud to the congregations.[27] But Paul also envisioned the circulation of some of his letters beyond a single Christian group (cf. Gal. 1: 2, 'to the churches of Galatia', Rom. 1:7 'to all God's beloved in Rome'—dispersed among numerous discrete house churches, Rom. 16: 5, 10, 11, 14, 15), and the author of Colossians, if not Paul, gives instruction for the exchange of Paul's letters between different communities (Col. 4: 16), which must indeed have taken place also soon after Paul's time.[28] The gospel literature of early Christianity offers only meager hints of intentions or means of its publication and circulation. The prologue to Luke/Acts (Luke 1: 1–4) provides a dedication to 'Theophilus', who (whether or not a fictive figure) by that convention is implicitly made responsible for the dissemination of the work by encouraging and permitting copies to be made. The last chapter of the Gospel of John, an epilogue added by others after the original conclusion of the Gospel (20: 30–1), aims at least in part (21: 24–5) to insure appreciation of the book and to promote its use beyond its community of origin. To take another case, the Apocalypse, addressed to seven churches in western Asia Minor, was almost surely sent in separate copy to each. Even so, the author anticipated its wider copying and dissemination beyond those original recipients, and so warned subsequent copyists to preserve the integrity of the book, neither adding nor subtracting, for fear of religious penalty (Rev. 22: 18–19). The private Christian copying and circulation that is presumed in these early writings continued to be the means for

---

[27] On the dictation of Paul's letters to a scribe, see E. R. Richards, The Secretary in the Letters of Paul (WUNT 42; Tubingen: Mohr, 1991), 169–98; for couriers see Rom. 16: 1, 1 Cor. 16: 10, Eph. 6: 21, Col. 4: 7, cf. 2 Cor. 8: 16–17. Reference to their carriers is common in other early Christian letters (e.g. 1 Pet. 5: 12, 1 Clem. 65: 1, Ignatius, Phil. 11.2, Smyr. 12.1, Polycarp, Phil. 14.1). For the general practice see E. Epp, 'New Testament Papyrus Manuscripts and Letter Carrying in Greco-Roman Times', in B. A. Pearson (ed.), The Future of Early Christianity (Minneapolis: Fortress, 1991), 35–56. Reading a letter aloud to the community, which seems to be presupposed by all the letters, is stipulated only in 1 Thess. 5: 27.

[28] This is shown for an early time by the generalization of the original particular addresses of some of Paul's letters (Rom. 1: 7, 15; 1 Cor. 1: 2; cf. Eph. 1: 1).

46

the publication and dissemination of Christian literature in the second and third centuries. It can be seen, for example, in the explicit notice in The Shepherd of Hermas (Vis. 2.4.3) that the book was to be published or released in two final copies, one for local use in Rome, the other for the transcription of further copies to be sent to Christian communities in 'cities abroad'. It can also be seen when Polycarp, bishop of Smyrna, had the letters of Ignatius copied and sent to the Christian community in Philippi, and had copies of letters from them and other churches in Asia Minor sent to Syrian Antioch (Phil. 13). It is evident too in the scribal colophons of the Martyrdom of Polycarp (22.2–4), and must be assumed also in connection with the letters of Dionysius, bishop of Corinth (fl. 170 ce; Eusebius, H.E. 4.23.1–12).

From another angle, the physical remains of early Christian books show that they were produced and disseminated privately within and between Christian communities. Early Christian texts, especially those of a scriptural sort, were almost always written in codices or leaf books—an informal, economical, and handy format—rather than on rolls, which were the traditional and standard vehicle of all other books. This was a sharp departure from convention, and particularly characteristic of Christians. Also distinctive to Christian books was the pervasive use of nomina sacra, divine names written in abbreviated forms, which was clearly an in-house practice of Christian scribes. Further, the preponderance in early Christian papyrus manuscripts of an informal quasi-documentary script rather than a professional bookhand also suggests that Christian writings were privately transcribed with a view to intramural circulation and use.[29]

If Christian books were disseminated in roughly the same way as other books, that is, by private seriatim copying, we might surmise that they spread slowly and gradually in ever-widening circles, first in proximity to their places of origin, then regionally, and then transregionally, and for some books this was doubtless the case. But it deserves notice that some early Christian texts appear to have enjoyed surprisingly rapid and wide circulation. Already by the early decades of the second century Papias of Hierapolis in western Asia Minor was acquainted at least with the Gospels of Mark and Matthew (Eusebius, H.E. 3.39.15–16); Clement of Rome, Ignatius of Antioch, and Polycarp of Smyrna

---

[29] On these features see H. Gamble, Books and Readers in the Early Church (New Haven: Yale University Press, 1995), 66–81, and L. Hurtado, The Earliest Christian Artifacts (Grand Rapids: Eerdmans, 2006).

were all acquainted with collections of Paul's letters; and papyrus copies of various early Christian texts were current in Egypt.[30] The Shepherd of Hermas, written in Rome near the mid-second century, was current and popular in Egypt not long after.[31] Equally interesting, Irenaeus' Adversus haereses, written about 180 in Gaul, is shown by papyrus fragments to have found its way to Egypt by the end of the second century, and indeed also to Carthage, where it was used by Tertullian.[32]

The brisk and broad dissemination of Christian books presumes not only a lively interest in texts among Christian communities but also efficient means for their reproduction and distribution. Such interest and means may be unexpected, given that the rate of literacy within Christianity was low, on average no greater than in the empire at large, namely in the range of 10–15 percent.[33] Yet there were some literate members in almost all Christian communities, and as long as texts could be read aloud by some, they were accessible and useful to the illiterate majority. Christian congregations were not reading communities in the same sense as elite literary or scholarly circles, but books were nevertheless important to them virtually from the beginning, for even before Christians began to compose their own texts, books of Jewish scripture played an indispensable role in their worship, teaching, and missionary preaching. Indeed, Judaism and Christianity were the only religious communities in Greco-Roman antiquity in which texts had any considerable importance, and in this, as in some other respects, Christian groups bore a greater

---

[30] For Clement, Ignatius, and Polycarp, see A. F. Gregory and C. M. Tuckett, eds., The Reception of the New Testament in the Apostolic Fathers (Oxford: OUP, 2005), 142–53, 162–72, 201–18, 226–7. For early Christian papyri in Egypt see Hurtado, Earliest Christian Artifacts, appendix 1 (209–29). The most notable case is P52 (a fragment of the Gospel of John, customarily dated to the early 2nd cent.).

[31] Some papyrus fragments of Hermas are 2nd cent. (P.Oxy. 4706 and 3528, P.Mich. 130, P.Iand. 1.4).

[32] For the A.H. in Egypt: P.Oxy. 405; for Tertullian's use of A.H. in Carthage, see T. D. Barnes, Tertullian (Oxford: Clarendon, 1971), 127–8, 220–1.

[33] The fundamental study of literacy in antiquity is still W. V. Harris, Ancient Literacy (Cambridge, Mass.: Harvard University Press, 1989); see now also the essays in J. H. Humphrey, ed., Literacy in the Roman World (Journal of Roman Archaeology, suppl. ser. 3; Ann Arbor: University of Michigan, 1991), and in W. A. Johnson and H. N. Parker, eds., Ancient Literacies (Oxford: OUP, 2009).

resemblance to philosophical circles than to other religious traditions.[34]

If smaller, provincial Christian congregations were not well-equipped or well-situated for the tasks of copying and disseminating texts, larger Christian centers must have had some scriptorial capacity: already in the second century: Polycarp's handling of Ignatius' letters and letters from other churches shows its presence in Smyrna; the instruction about the publication of Hermas' The Shepherd suggests it for Rome; and it can hardly be doubted for Alexandria, since even in a provincial city like Oxyrhynchus many manuscripts of Christian texts were available.[35] The early third-century Alexandrian scriptorium devised for the production and distribution of the works of Origen (Eusebius, H.E. 6.23.2), though unique in its sponsorship by a private patron and its service to an individual writer, surely had precursors, more modest and yet efficient, in other Christian communities. It also had important successors, not the least of which was the library and scriptorium that flourished in Caesarea in the second half of the third century under the auspices of Pamphilus.[36] Absent such reliable intra-Christian means for the production of books, the range of texts known and used by Christian communities across the Mediterranean basin by the end of the second century would be without explanation.[37] (Hill and Kruger 2012, 32-35)

---

[34] M. Beard, 'Writing and Religion: Ancient Religion and the Function of the Written Word in Roman Religion', in Humphrey, Literacy in the Roman World, 353–8, argues that texts played a relatively large role in Greco-Roman religions, yet characterizes that role as 'symbolic rather than utilitarian', which was clearly not the case in early Christianity. The kind of careful reading, interpretation, and exposition of texts that we see in early Christianity and in early Judaism (whether in worship or school settings) provides, mutatis mutandis, an interesting analogy to the activity of elite literary circles.

[35] On the question of early Christian scriptoria (the term may be variously construed), see Gamble, Books and Readers, 121–6. Hurtado, Earliest Christian Artifacts, 185–9, rightly calls attention to corrections by contemporary hands in early Christian papyri as pointing to at least limited activity of a scriptorial kind.

[36] The role of Pamphilus and the Caesarean library/scriptorium in the private production and dissemination of early Christian literature, esp. of scriptural materials, was highlighted by Eusebius in his Life of Pamphilus, as quoted by Jerome in his Apology against Rufinus (1.9).

[37] Beyond the uses of Christian texts in congregational settings, there were already in the 2nd cent. some Christian circles that pursued specialized and technical engagements with texts, usually in the service of theological arguments and exegetical agendas. The 'school-settings' of teachers such as Valentinus and Justin, and a little later of Theodotus, Clement, and Origen, were Christian approximations to the kinds of literary activity associated with 'elite' reading communities in the early empire.

When we think of publishing a book today, there are some similarities to the ancient process, but of course, it was not the same for Christian communities in the ancient world of the Roman Empire. Paul dispatched Tychicus as a carrier with a letter to the Ephesians, to the Colossians, and Philemon, as well as a potential fourth letter to the Laodiceans. Tychicus was a competent, trusted, skilled coworker, who delivered these letters hundreds of miles from an imprisoned Paul, with enough information to bring God's Word to the first-century Christian congregations. However, in the letter to the Colossians, Paul said, "When this letter has been read among you, have it also read in the church of the Laodiceans; and see that you also read the letter from Laodicea." (Col. 4:16) In other words, it was to be a circuit letter. Paul had also stated to the Thessalonians in a letter to them, "I put you under oath before the Lord to have this letter read to all the brothers." (1 Thess. 5:27) Paul encouraged the distribution of his books.

Remember the process from the above; the book would be shared with friends of similar interests, and then the circles grew wider and wider to friends of friends and others. First, Paul's primary level of friends would be his more than one hundred traveling companions and fellow workers, some being the carriers who delivered the books. Second, the friends in the Christian congregation would have the letter read to them, who would then share it with other fellow congregations. In the secular circle of friends, interested readers who wished to have a copy would have their slaves (i.e., scribes) make a copy or copies of a book. The same would have been true within the Christian congregation. When the Laodiceans read the letter that had been sent by Paul to the Colossians, they would have had one of their wealthy members use his literate and trained scribe to make a copy for their congregation and maybe even a few copies for other members. Now the same would hold true when the Colossians received the letter that had been written to the Laodiceans. Eventually, Paul's letters would be gathered together so that they circulated as a group, such as P^{46}.

The scriptorium was a room for copying manuscripts, where a lector would read aloud from his exemplar with a room full of copyists taking down his dictation. Recent scholarship has suggested that we remove the concept of the scriptorium in the time of Jesus and the apostles of the first century C.E., on the grounds that this was not a practice until the fourth century C.E. Harry Y. Gamble addresses this effectively when he writes,

> It is difficult to determine just when Christian scriptoria came into existence. The problem is partly of definition, partly of evidence. If we think of the scriptorium as simply a writing center where texts were copied by more than a single scribe, then any of the larger Christian communities, such as Antioch or Rome, may have already had scriptoria in the early second century, and

in view of Polycarp's activity something of the kind can be imagined for Smyrna. If we think instead of a scriptorium as being more structured, operating, for example, in a specially designed and designated location; employing particular methods of transcription; producing certain types of manuscripts; or multiplying copies on a significant scale, then it becomes more difficult to imagine that such institutions developed at an early date. (Gamble 1995, 121)

Gamble goes on to inform us that Origen's scriptorium of about 230 C.E. was an exception. The scriptorium of Cyprian just a few short years later was a more official version of what we think of when picturing scriptoria. Then, there is the scriptorium that was attached to the Christian library in Caesarea, which we know was commissioned to produce fifty New Testament manuscripts in short order. It may even have been added in the third century when Pamphilus (latter half of the 3rd century–309 C.E.) built the library. It is likely that a more official type of scriptorium could be found in this period at other Christian epicenters, such as Rome, Jerusalem, and Alexandria. Gamble adds, "It was only during the fourth and fifth centuries that the scriptoria on monastic communities came into their own, also in association with monastic libraries." (Gamble 1995, 121-2)

While it is extremely difficult, if not impossible to identify a specific Alexandrian scriptorium for our early manuscripts of the second century, or even if they were produced in a scriptorium at all, we do know that professional scribes produced them. There are many possibilities: (1) the professional scribe could have produced them in a Christian scriptorium. On the other hand, (2) the professional scribe could have been a Christian who worked for a scriptorium, who then used his skills to produce copies. Then again, (3) it could have been that the scribe formerly worked in a scriptorium, but now was the private scribe of a wealthy Christian, who used his skills to make copies. What we do know is that there were about a million Christians spread throughout the Roman Empire at the beginning of the second century. Therefore, the copying of manuscripts could very well have been within the Christian community, i.e., from Christian congregation to Christian congregation, as well as wealthy Christians acquiring personal copies for themselves.

We have a number of early manuscripts that evidence that they were very likely produced in a scriptorium, even if it was simply a room attached to a Christian library, which had a handful of copyists. For example, P[46] (150 C.E.) was certainly done by a professional scribe because it contained stichoi marks, which are notes at the end of sections, stating how many lines were copied. This was a means of calculating how much a scribe should be paid. It is likely that an employee of the scriptorium numbered the pages, indicating the stichoi marks. Moreover, this same scribe made corrections as he went. Another example would be P[66], according to Comfort:

It is also fairly certain that P[66] was the product of a scriptorium or writing center. The first copyist of this manuscript had his work thoroughly checked by a diorthotes [corrector], according to a different exemplar—just the way it would happen in a scriptorium. Of course, it can be argued that an individual who purchased the manuscript made all the corrections, which was a common practice in ancient times. But the extent of corrections in P[66] and the fact that the paginator (a different scribe) made many of the corrections speaks against this (see description of P[66] in chap. 2). It was more the exception than the rule in ancient times that a manuscript would be fully checked by a diorthotes. P[66] has other markings of being professionally produced. The extant manuscript still shows the pinpricks in the corners of each leaf of the papyri; these served as a guide for left hand justification and right hand. The manuscript also exhibits a consistent set of marginal and interlinear correction signs. Another sign of professionally produced manuscript is the use of the diple (>) in the margin, which was used to signal a correction in the text and/or the need for a correction in the text. There are very few of these in the extant New Testament manuscripts. (P. W. Comfort 2008, 26)

The production and distribution of New Testament manuscripts were carried out at the congregation and individual Christian level in the early days of Christianity.

Moreover, this process did not negate the use of professional scribes. Just as Paul would not have used an inexperienced scribe to produce the book of Romans, congregations and wealthy Christians would have likely used professional scribes to make copies. Of course, there are exceptions to the rule and some congregations may not have had access to a professional scribe, so they would have to have chosen to use the best person available to them. Nevertheless, if a congregation had access to a semi-professional or professional scribe, it would have been a lack of good sense or practicality not to take advantage of such a person. Think of anything we want to have done in our Christian congregation today: would we not seek out a professional, if we had access to one as a member, be it plumbing, wiring, teaching, or computer technology? We naturally look to the most skilled person that we can find even if we have a clogged up a commode. Would we do any less if we were in the first century and had just received a letter from the apostle Paul, who was imprisoned hundreds of miles away in Rome?

CHAPTER 2 Books, Reading, and Writing; Literacy In Early Christianity

Ehrman wrote: Rome during the early Christian centuries, or even Greece during the classical period. The best and most influential study of literacy in ancient times, by Columbia University professor William Harris, indicates that at the very best of times and places—for example, Athens at the height of the classical period in the fifth century B.C.E.—literacy rates were rarely higher than 10–15 percent of the population. To reverse the numbers, this means that under the best of conditions, 85–90 percent of the population could not read or write. In the first Christian century, throughout the Roman Empire, the literacy rates may well have been lower. Misquoting Jesus (pp. 37-38).

Before delving into the discussion, we should mention that Ehrman has one aspect right in that there is a severe difficulty of defining what literacy was in the ancient Roman Empire of the first three centuries of Christianity and just how literate was the populace. However, he is far off into the weeds of exaggeration again when he claims a 10-15 percent literacy rate. The next two chapters will show a gar higher literacy rate for the Roman Empire in the first three centuries of Christianity and an even higher rate among the Jews and Christians. However, first, let's take a moment to offer some way to measure literacy.

Full Illiteracy: This one has *no* reading or writing *skills*, no math skills, and is incapable of signing his name for daily living and employment beyond fundamental manual labor. He would work at fruit and vegetable picking, handling materials or low-level tools, manual digging or building, farming, or working in large workshops that produced items such as dishes or pots, as well as household slaves.

Fragmentary Literacy: (inconsistent or incomplete in some areas) The *very basic ability* to understand spoken words, a *very basic grasp* of written words, *very basic math skills* (buying in the market place), and the ability to sign one's name for daily living and employment. He would work as a manual laborer in the market place not requiring math, a shop assistant that performs manual labor, or a soldier.

Fundamental Literacy: The *basic ability* to understand spoken words, an *elementary grasp* of written words, *basic* math skills and the ability to sign one's name and the *ability* to read and write simple words for daily living and employment, such as work as a craftsman, works in the marketplace, or soldier.

Functional Literacy: This one has the *competent ability* to understand spoken words, a *beginner-intermediate level grasp* of written words, and the ability to prepare *basic documents* for daily living and employment tasks that require reading skills beyond a basic level. He is a semiliterate writer who is untrained in writing but has the ability to read or write simple sentences and can take on some basic jobs, such as a copyist or scribe.

Proficient Literacy: This one is a *highly skilled* person, who can understand spoken words, and has an *intermediate-advanced level grasp* of written words. He has the *proficient ability* to prepare short texts for daily living and employment tasks that require reading skills at the *intermediate* level. He is a literate writer who is trained in writing and can take on jobs, such as a copyist or scribe, a tax collector or clerk.

Full Literacy: This one is a *highly skilled expert*, who can understand spoken words, an *advanced level grasp* of written words. He has the *professional ability* to prepare long texts for daily living and employment tasks that require reading skills at the *advanced* level. He is a fully literate writer who is professionally trained in writing and can take on jobs, such as a copyist or scribe, a tax collector, teacher, lawyer, or a clerk to high-ranking positions like Senators.

Rome was a complex society. Levels of literacy were fluid because of the conditions of the day being as culturally and ethnically diverse as it was. The Roman Empire from the first century to the fourth century was as culturally and ethnically diverse as New York City and its five boroughs: the Bronx, Brooklyn, Manhattan, Queens, and Staten Island. A person's literacy level to carry out different job functions and skills for daily living and employment would not be the same in Nazareth as would have been the case in Rome. The need or desire for literacy would not be as important in Nazareth as it would have been in Rome. As we will see, the need or desire for literacy was likely not as important to the pagan as it would have been to the Jew or the Christian.

Therefore, when we look at all of the evidence over the next two chapters, we will discover that literacy on all levels was more prominent than has long been held by historians, who have felt literacy in ancient Rome was no greater than 10-20 percent. It is clear that a *far greater proportion* of the population of the Roman Empire from the days of Jesus Christ to the time of Constantine the Great could make use of their skills in understanding the spoken word, grasping the written word, math skills, and writing. The Roman world was in this time that we speak of overflowing with documents, a range of literacies as we can see from above, as well as different literary genres: historical, religious, military, commercial, poetry, and so on. These were distinguished by the social location of those who possessed them, by the method in which they were produced, the material used to receive the writing, the publication, and circulation, as well as the languages, the kinds of text, and those who used them.

The city of Rome is founded in 753 B.C.E., some 750 years before Jesus was born. The Roman citizens had long believed that reading and writing strengthened them. It gave them confidence that their rulers were not going to take advantage of them. It is a given that as an empire grows, what is expected out of their subjects grows exponentially as well. When a state bureaucracy develops, the use of documents grows right alongside it and the people have no choice but to become *functionally literate*.[38]

Based on what you will learn over the next two chapters consider the accuracy of the following quote from Dr. Bart D. Ehrman, who is a prominent scholar of early Christianity and the history of the Greek manuscripts of the New Testament.

> The best and most influential study of literacy in ancient times, by Columbia University professor William Harris, indicates that at the very best of times and places—for example, Athens at the height of the classical period in the fifth century B.C.E.— literacy rates were rarely higher than 10–15 percent of the population. To reverse the numbers, this means that under the best of conditions, 85–90 percent of the population could not read or write. In the first Christian century, throughout the Roman Empire, the literacy rates may well have been lower. (B. D. Ehrman, *Misquoting Jesus: The Story Behind Who Changed the Bible and Why* 2005, 37-38)

On this Larry Hurtado writes, "A few decades ago, it became fashionable in some scholarly circles, including NT/Christian Origins, to hold the view that in the Roman period there was an extremely low level of literacy, and that only elite levels of society had that skill. One still sees this view touted today (typically by those echoing what they believe to be authoritative pronouncements on the matter by others). But a number of studies show that such generalizations are simplistic, and that "literacy" was both more diverse and much more widely distributed than some earlier estimates. The earlier claims of an extremely low level of literacy resurfaced in some comments, so I take the time to draw attention to some previous postings on the subject. Likewise, the older (early 20th century) notion that early Christian circles were composed of slaves and unlearned nobodies has rightly been corrected by various studies. The pioneering study by Edwin Judge, *The Social Pattern of Christian Groups in the First Century* (1960),

---

[38] Hopkins, K. (1991) 'Conquest by book', in Humphrey (1991) 11.

was followed by a number of works focused on the social description of early Christian groups." – *Larry Hurtado's Blog*[39]

Literacy in the First Century

Craig A. Evans writes, "In recent years, a number of scholars have suggested that Jesus could not read, and that in all likelihood none of his disciples could read either. They maintain this because of studies that have concluded that rates of literacy in the Roman Empire were quite low, and that Jesus and his earliest followers were probably not exceptions."[40] We will see this is not the case below but for now, let it be said that we cannot take aggregate data and apply it to individuals. In other words, we cannot say that the literacy level in the Roman Empire of the first four centuries of our Common Era is less than ten percent; therefore, Jesus, the apostles, and the New Testament authors were illiterate. This is especially true when we can extrapolate from the data that we have, that this is not the case. This would be like saying the average income for Columbus, Ohio is 52,000 dollars a year, so John Smith who lives in Columbus makes 52,000 dollars a year. You cannot apply that aggregate data to individuals unless you have direct information, such as tax records.

How can we, modern readers, know so much about letters from the ancient Roman Empire? We have two different sources that provide us some insight into the writer and his letters. Lucius or Marcus Annaeus Seneca, known as **Seneca the Elder** (54 B.C.E.-39 C.E.), was a Roman rhetorician[41] and writer, born of a wealthy equestrian family of Cordoba, Hispania. Seneca lived through the reigns of three significant emperors: Augustus, Tiberius, and Caligula. For our purpose here we are particularly interested in his letters, which were published; i.e., someone paid to have a scribe produce a copy of them. As was the case with many works of antiquity, the process was repeated over and over again throughout the centuries. Today, we have critical editions of them.

Our other source for insight into the development of the letter-writing process is found in the letters of ordinary people, uncovered by archaeologists. These were never published, as they were simply discarded after they served their purpose. In many cases, in order to save costs, these

---

[39] Retrieved Tuesday, March 26, 2019 (Larry Hurtado's Blog Comments on the New Testament and Early Christianity (and related matters)

https://larryhurtado.wordpress.com/2018/11/01/literacies-in-the-roman-world/

[40] Craig A. Evans (2012-03-16). Jesus and His World: The Archaeological Evidence (Kindle Locations 1403-1406). Westminster John Knox Press. Kindle Edition.

[41] A rhetorician is a speaker whose words are primarily intended to impress or persuade.

writers would simply flip a letter over and use the other side for something else. Many such letters ended up in garbage dumps. However, some recipients of these letters valued them, so they stored them as though they were a treasure. Therefore, when archaeologists uncovered homes, these letters would be found within the ruins of the home.

In some cases, they were even buried with the deceased because they were so valued. Hundreds of thousands of letters have been discovered over the past century by archaeologists. These were the work of common folk, writing about everyday things. On the subjects of an empire learning a language so as not to be exploited by a powerful kingdom, Gregory Wolf writes,

> This is wonderfully illustrated by the Roman Empire by the personal archive of the Jewish woman named Babatha, found in the Cave of Letters on the shore of the Dead Sea and dating to the early second century C.E.[42] Babatha's papers comprised thirty-five documents written in Greek, Nabatean, and Aramaic or a mixture of these languages, with occasional transliterated Latin terms for Roman institutions. The archive included documents relating to the sale of land, dates and probably also wine, various marriage contracts and probably details of a dowry, a bequest, a court summons, various notices of deposits and loans, a court summons and a deposition, petitions, and an extract from the minutes of the council of Petra relating to the guardianship of her son. Much of this was generated by private transactions-both commercial and disputes arising from her complicated family life. But it was the recourse to law, and to civic and provincial administration, that generated this mass of material, which she kept with her until her death in the disturbances arising from the Bar Kokhba war.[43]

Most of us have heard of Marcus Tullius Cicero, or simply Cicero (106 B.C.E. – 43 B.C.E.), who was a Roman philosopher, politician, lawyer, orator, political theorist, consul, and constitutionalist. He came from a wealthy municipal family in Rome. In his everyday affairs, he penned letters in order to correspond with others. However, while Cicero was writing letters to one person, he knew that others would be reading them as well. Therefore, he took advantage of these opportunities to use writing to communicate points persuasively, using logic and reason, philosophical

---

[42] N. Lewis 1989.

[43] William A Johnson; Holt N Parker. Ancient Literacies: The Culture of Reading in Greece and Rome (Kindle Locations 655-659). Kindle Edition.

arguments, and the like. His letters grew from concise letters to far longer, intricate rhetorical letters.

We find yet another famous Roman named Seneca in the days of the apostle Paul. He was the second son of Seneca the Elder. Lucius Annaeus Seneca, or simply **Seneca the Younger** (c. 4 B.C.E.–65 C.E.), was a Roman Stoic philosopher, statesman, and dramatist, i.e., a very famous, skilled, and effective speaker. As for written works, Seneca is known for twelve philosophical essays, 124 letters to Lucilius Junior, nine tragedies, and an uncertain satire. Seneca was a representative of the Silver Age of Latin literature. In his letters to his friend Lucilius, dealing with moral issues, he delved into philosophical ideas, setting aside the simple and bare letters of the day for something far more complex.

The apostle Paul, as we have seen, used personal letters and letter carriers as a substitute until he could visit churches and key people. He produced through his scribe Tertius 433 verses, 7,111 words in the book of Romans, which would have taken two days to copy. Like the skilled rhetoricians before him, Paul knew that many others would be reading his letters. In fact, he exhorted them to do so. – Colossians 4:16.

We should note that the level of literacy in the first century is a somewhat subjective measurement, because of the limited available evidence, as well as one's interpretation of that evidence. Consider as an analogy the historian today, as compared to the historian during the first few centuries of Christianity. Today, we are capable of covering almost anything that goes on in life, from the most insignificant to the most noteworthy. We in the United States may watch live on television or a laptop as some firefighters in New Zealand rescue a puppy that had been trapped in a storm drain. Then again, we can observe a 9.0 earthquake as it hits Japan, causing the deaths of over 15,000 people.

What about the first few centuries of Jesus, the apostles, and the earliest Christians? The coverage of people, places, and events are not even remotely comparable. The coverage at that time was of the most prominent people, like Seneca the Elder, Cicero, Seneca the Younger, Mark Antony, and Augustus, i.e., the emperor of Rome, senators, generals, the wealthy, with very little press being given to the lower officials, let alone the lower class. We do not have much information on Pontius Pilate at all, but what we do have is an exception to the rule.

History from antiquity, then, is recoverable but incomplete due to the limited extent and frequently tendentious nature of the sources. Ancient historiography, more than its modern counterpart, is to a greater degree approximate or provisional. A new discovery may alter previous perceptions. Until the discovery of Claudius's Letter to the Alexandrians, written on his accession in 41 but lost until modern times, that emperor's steely resolve could not have been guessed. In short, evidence from Greco-Roman antiquity is fragmentary, generally devoted to "important" people and events and its texts overtly "interpreted." (Barnett 2005, 13)

According to E. Randolf Richards, literacy in the first century was determined by being able to read, not write.[44] The need for writing today is far greater than antiquity. Richards offers an excellent analogy when he says, "I am right handed, so to pen a long paper with my left hand would be quite difficult, and not very legible. The man of antiquity would write with the same difficulty because the need to write was so seldom."[45] This author finds this to be true of himself, now that we have entered an era of texting and typing. I have not written a paper by hand in many years. When I fill out a form or even sign my name, I struggle to write, because it is so seldom required. Many have argued that the lower class of antiquity was almost entirely illiterate. However, recent research shows that this was not the case,[46] as literacy was more of an everyday need than they had thought.[47]

Richard's definition of literacy is too simplistic because defining literacy among historians has been plagued by many different definitions. It is also relative to the person determining how the word should be defined. For some historians of the first three centuries of Christianity under the Roman Empire, literacy could refer to any ancient person who merely had the ability to write one's name. For another, it might be as Richard's suggested, one who can read but cannot write. Then, again, it could be a semiliterate writer who is untrained in writing but could prepare short documents, to a literate writer who has had experience in making lengthy documents and has an understanding of what he is writing, to the professional who is paid

---

[44] (Richards, Paul And First-Century Letter Writing: Secretaries, Composition and Collection 2004, 28)

[45] (Richards, Paul And First-Century Letter Writing: Secretaries, Composition and Collection 2004, 28)

[46] "Throughout the Hellenistic and Roman world the distinction prevailed in that there were educated people who were proficient readers and writers, less educated ones who could read but hardly write, some who were readers alone, some of them only able to read slowly or with difficulty and some who were illiterate."--Millard, Alan Reading and Writing in the Time of Jesus (Sheffield, Sheffield Academic Press, 2000), p. 154

[47] Exler, Form. P. 126 warns, "The papyri discovered in Egypt have shown that the art of writing was more widely, and more popularly, known in the past, than some scholars have been inclined to think." For example, see PZen. 6, 66, POxy. 113,294, 394, 528, 530, 531 and especially 3057.

to write for others. The levels of literacy that was laid out at the beginning of this chapter cover the different levels of literacy in early Christianity.

In passing, I will mention something that few historians or textual scholars will address, the gift of languages. An extraordinary gift conveyed through the Holy Spirit to a number of disciples starting at Pentecost 33 C.E. that made it possible for them to speak or otherwise glorify God in a tongue in addition to their own. Therefore, the ability to be miraculously able to speak a foreign language in the Roman Empire would have been greatly appreciated. In conjunction with this, we must also remember that Christianity grew out of a melting pot of languages: Hebrew, Aramaic, Greek, Latin, Coptic, and Syriac (an Aramaic dialect). Thus, when we think about it, the first and second century Jewish Christian **in Palestine** may be quite familiar with Hebrew, Greek, and even Aramaic but be illiterate when it comes to Latin. On the other hand, the Gentile Christian may be very familiar with Greek, somewhat familiar with Hebrew and a little familiar with Aramaic but possess the very basic ability to understand spoken words and have an elementary grasp of written words when it comes to Latin. Then, **in Rome**, the Gentile and Jewish Christian might be literate when it comes to Latin and also be quite familiar with Greek, and yet be wholly illiterate when it comes to Hebrew and Aramaic.

Even though Greek was very much used **in Egypt**, in time, the need to have a translation in the native language of the growing Egyptian Christian population would come. Coptic was a later form of the ancient Egyptian language. In the late first or early second century C.E., a Coptic alphabet was developed using somewhat modified Greek letters (majuscules and seven characters from the demotic,[48] representing Egyptian sounds the Greek language did not have). At least by the end of the second or the beginning of the third century (c. 200 C.E.), the first translation of parts of the New Testament had been produced for the Coptic natives of Egypt. Various Coptic dialects were used in Egypt, and in time, different Coptic versions were made. Therefore, In the Egyptian part of the Roman Empire, the Christian may be literate when it comes to Coptic but struggles with Greek. And whether the Egyptian Christian is Gentile or Jew, he may or may not have any working knowledge when it comes to Hebrew or Aramaic.

Syria was a region with the Mesopotamia to its East, with the Lebanon Mountains on the West, the Taurus Mountains to it's North, and Palestine and the Arabian Desert to its south. Syria played a very prominent role in the early growth of Christianity. The city of Antioch in Syria was the third-

---

[48] Demotic is a simplified form of Egyptian hieroglyphics. Hieroglyphics is a writing system that uses symbols or pictures to denote objects, concepts, or sounds.

largest city in the Roman Empire. Luke tells us of "those who were scattered because of the persecution that occurred in connection with Stephen [shortly after Pentecost, yet just before the conversion of Paul in 34 or 35 C.E.] made their way to Phoenicia and Cyprus and **Antioch**, speaking the word to no one except to Jews alone. But there were some of them, men of Cyprus and Cyrene, **who came to Antioch** [of Syria] and began speaking to the Greeks also, preaching the Lord Jesus." (Ac 11:19-20, bold mine) Because of the thriving interest of the Gospel manifested in Antioch, where many Greek-speaking people were becoming believers, the apostles in Jerusalem sent Barnabas, who then called Paul in from Tarsus to help. (Ac 11:21-26) Both Barnabas and Paul remained there for a year, teaching the people. Antioch became the center for the apostle Paul's missionary journeys.

Moreover, "the disciples were first called Christians in Antioch." (Ac 11:26) While the New Testament letters were written in Koine Greek, the common language of the Roman Empire, Latin being the official language, it was thought best to **translate the New Testament books into Syriac in mid-second century C.E.** as Christianity spread throughout the rest of Syria.

However, let us assume for the sake of discussion that literacy was very low among the lower class, and even relatively low among the upper class, who had the ability to pay for the service. What does this say about individual Christians throughout the Roman Empire? It is believed that more than 30–40 million people lived in the combined eastern and western Roman Empire (50–200 C.E.). Now, assume that statistically, the literacy rate is low in a specific area, or a particular city, like Rome (slave population). Does this mean that everyone is illiterate in that region or city? Do we equate the two? If we accept the belief that the lower class were likely to be illiterate, meaning they could not write, or struggled to write; what does this really mean for individuals or Christianity? Very little, because if there are 40-100 million people living throughout the Roman Empire and one million of them were Christian by 125-150 C.E., we are only referring to one or two percent of the population. There is no way to arrive at a specific statistical level of literacy for this small selection, in a time when history focused on the prominent. If a person from that period said anything about the lower class, this was only based on the sphere of whom he knew or what he had seen in his life, which would be very limited when compared to the whole. The last 20 years or so has seen many new directions in the field of literacy in the ancient world. Johnson and Parker offer the following.

> The moment seems right, therefore, to try to formulate more interesting, productive ways of talking about the conception and construction of 'literacies' in the ancient

world—literacy not in the sense of whether 10 percent or 30 percent of people in the ancient world could read or write, but in the sense of text-oriented events embedded in particular sociocultural contexts. The volume in your hands [*ANCIENT LITERACIES*] was constructed as a forum in which selected leading scholars were challenged to rethink from the ground up how students of classical antiquity might best approach the question of literacy, and how that investigation might materially intersect with changes in the way that literacy is now viewed in other disciplines. The result is intentionally pluralistic: theoretical reflections, practical demonstrations, and combinations of the two share equal space in the effort to chart a new course. Readers will come away, with food for thought of many types: new ways of thinking about specific elements of literacy in antiquity, such as the nature of personal libraries, or the place and function of bookshops in antiquity; new constructivist questions, such as what constitutes reading communities and how they fashion themselves; new takes on the public sphere, such how literacy intersects with commercialism, or with the use of public spaces, or with the construction of civic identity; new essentialist questions, such as what "book" and "reading" signify in antiquity, why literate cultures develop, or why literate cultures matter. (Johnson and Parker 2011, 3-4)

Books, Reading, and Writing; Literacy and Early Jewish Education

The priests of Israel (Num. 5:23) and leading persons, such as Moses (Ex. 24:4), Joshua (Josh. 24:26), Samuel (1 Sam 10:25), David (2 Sam. 11:14-15), and Jehu (2 Ki 10:1, 6), were capable of reading and writing. The Israelite people themselves generally could read and write, with few exceptions. (Judges 8:14; Isa. 10:19; 29:12) Even though Deuteronomy 6:8-9 is used figuratively, the command to write the words of the Law on the doorposts of their house and their gates implied that they were literate. Yes, it is true that even though Hebrew written material was fairly common, few Israelite inscriptions have been discovered. One reason for this is that the Israelites did not set up many monuments to admire their accomplishments. Thus, most of the writing, which would include the thirty-nine books of the Bible were primarily done with ink on papyrus or parchment. Most did not survive the damp soil of Palestine. Nevertheless, the Hebrew Old Testament Scriptures were preserved throughout the centuries by careful, meticulous copying and recopying.

During the first seven years of Christianity (29-36 C.E.), three and a half with Jesus' ministry and three and a half after his ascension, only Jewish people became disciples of Christ and formed the newly founded Christian congregation. In 36 C.E. the first gentile was baptized: Cornelius.[49] From that time forward Gentiles came into the Christian congregations. However, the church still consisted mostly of Jewish converts. What do we know of the Jewish family, as far as education? Within the nation of Israel, everyone was strongly encouraged to be literate. The texts of Deuteronomy 6:8-9 and 11:20 were figurative (not to be taken literally). However, we are to ascertain what was meant by the figurative language, and that meaning is what we take literally.

Deuteronomy 6:8-9 Updated American Standard Version (UASV)

8 You shall bind them [God's Word] as a sign on your hand and they shall be as frontlets bands between your eyes.[50] 9 You shall write them on the doorposts of your house and on your gates.

Deuteronomy 11:20 Updated American Standard Version (UASV)

20 You shall write them on the doorposts of your house and on your gates,

The command to bind God's Word "as a sign on your hand," denoted constant remembrance and attention. The command that the Word of God was "to be as frontlet bands between your eyes," denoted that the Law should be kept before their eyes always, so that wherever they looked, whatever was before them, they would see the law before them. Therefore, while figurative, these texts implied that Jewish children grew up being taught how to read and to write. The Gezer Calendar (ancient Hebrew writing), dated to the 10th-century B.C.E., is believed by some scholars to be a schoolboy's memory exercise.

The Jewish author Philo of Alexandria (20 B.C.E.–50 C. E.) a Hellenistic Jewish philosopher, whose first language was Greek, had this to say about Jewish parents and how they taught their Children the Law and how to read it. Philo stated, "All men guard their own customs, but this is especially true of the Jewish nation. Holding that the laws are oracles vouchsafed by God and having been trained [*paideuthentes*] in this doctrine from their earliest years, they carry the likenesses of the commandments enshrined in their souls." (Borgen 1997, 187) This certainly involved the ability to read and write at a competent level. Philo also wrote, "for parents, thinking but little of their own advantage, think the

---

[49] Cornelius was a centurion, an army officer in charge of a unit of foot soldiers, i.e., in command of 100 soldiers of the Italian band.

[50] I.e. on your forehead

virtue and excellence of their children the perfection of their own happiness, for which reason it is that they are anxious that they should obey the injunctions which are laid upon them, and that they should be obedient to all just and beneficial commands; for a father will never teach his child anything which is inconsistent with virtue or with truth."[51] In the nation of Israel some 1,550 years before Philo, everyone was strongly encouraged to be literate. (Deut. 4:9; 6:7, 20, 21; 11:19-21; Ps 78:1-4) Not only the father to the children but also prophets, Levites, especially the priests, and other wise men served as teachers. Fathers taught their sons a trade, while mothers taught their daughters the domestic skills. Fathers also taught their children the geography of their land, as well as the rich history. As Philo informs us of the Jewish people of his day, saying that it is the father, who is responsible for educating the children academically, philosophically, physically, as well as moral instruction and discipline.

Josephus (37-100 C.E.), the first-century Jewish historian, writes, "Our principle care of all is this, to educate our children [*paidotrophian*] well; and we think it to be the most necessary business of our whole life to observe the laws that have been given us, and to keep those rules of piety that have been delivered down to us." (Whiston 1987, Against Apion 1.60) Even allowing for an overemphasis for apologetic purposes; clearly, Jesus was carefully grounded in the Word of God (Hebrew Old Testament), as was true of other Jews of the time. Josephus also says, "but for our people, if anybody do but ask any one of them about our laws, he will more readily tell them all than he will tell his own name, and this in consequence of our having learned them immediately as soon as ever we became sensible of anything, and of our having them, as it were engraven on our souls. Our transgressors of them are but few; and it is impossible when any do offend, to escape punishment." (Whiston 1987, Against Apion 2.178) He also says: "[the Law] also commands us to bring those children up in learning [*grammata* paideuein] and to exercise them in the laws, and make them acquainted with the acts of their predecessors, in order to their imitation of them, and that they may be nourished up in the laws from their infancy, and might neither transgress them, nor yet have any pretense for their ignorance of them." (Whiston 1987, Against Apion 2.204) Again, this clearly involves at a minimum the ability to read and write at a competent level.

From the above, we find that the Jewish family education revolved around the study of the Mosaic Law. If their children were going to live by the Law, they needed to know what it says, as well as understand it. If they were going to know and understand the Law, this would require the ability

---

[51] Charles Duke Yonge with Philo of Alexandria, *The Works of Philo: Complete and Unabridged* (Peabody, MA: Hendrickson, 1995), 590–591.

to read it, and hopefully apply it. Emil Schurer writes: "All zeal for education in the family, the school and the synagogue aimed at making *the whole people a people of the law*. The common man too was to know what the law commanded, and not only to know but to do it. His whole life was to be ruled according to the norm of the law; obedience thereto was to become a fixed custom, and departure therefrom an inward impossibility. On the whole, this object was to a great degree attained." (Schurer 1890, Vol. 4, p. 89) Scott writes that "from at least the time of Ezra's reading of the law (Neh. 8), education was a public process; study of the law was the focus of Jewish society as a whole. It was a lifelong commitment to all men. It began with the very young. The Mishnah[52] requires that children be taught 'therein one year or two years before [they are of age], that they may become versed in the commandments.' Other sources set different ages for beginning formal studies, some as early as five years."[53] (Scott 1995, 257)

It may be that both Philo and Josephus are presenting their readers with an idyllic picture, and what they have to say could possibly refer primarily to wealthy Jewish families who could afford formal education. However, this would be shortsighted, for the Israelites had long been a people who valued the ability to read and write competently. In the apocryphal account of 4 Maccabees 18:10-19, a mother addresses her seven sons, who would be martyred, reminding them of their father's teaching. There is nothing in the account to suggest that they were from a wealthy family. Herein the mother referred to numerous historical characters throughout the Old Testament and quoted from numerous books – Isaiah 43.2; Psalm 34:19; Proverbs 3:18; Ezekiel 37:3; Deuteronomy 32:39.

Jesus would have received his education from three sources. As was made clear from the above, Joseph, Jesus' stepfather would have played a major role in his education. Paul said that young Timothy was trained in "the sacred writings" by his mother, Eunice, and his grandmother Lois. (2 Tim. 1:5; 3:15) Certainly, if Timothy received education in the law from his mother because his Father was a Greek (Acts 16:1), no doubt Jesus did as well after Joseph died.

Jesus would have also received education in the Scriptures from the attendant at the synagogue. In the first-century C.E., the synagogue was a place of instruction, not a place of sacrifices. The people carried out their sacrifices to God at the temple. The exercises within the synagogue covered such areas as praise, prayer, and recitation and reading of the Scriptures, in addition to expository preaching. – Mark 12:40; Luke 20:47

---

[52] The Mishnah was the primary body of Jewish civil and religious law, forming the first part of the Talmud.

[53] Mishnah *Yoma* 8:4

Before any instruction in the holy laws and unwritten customs are taught... from their swaddling clothes by parents and teachers and educators to believe in God, the one Father, and Creator of the world. (Philo *Legatio ad Gaium* 115.)

The Mishnah tells us the age that this formal instruction would have begun, "At five years old one is fit for the scripture... at thirteen for the commandments." (Mishnah *Abot* 5.21.) Luke 4:20 tells of the time Jesus stood to read from the scroll of Isaiah in the synagogue in Nazareth, and once finished, "he rolled up the scroll and gave it back to the attendant." An attendant such as this one would have educated Jesus, starting at the age of five. As Jesus grew up in Nazareth, he "increased in wisdom and in stature and in favor with God and man." (Lu 2:52) Jesus and his half-brothers and sisters would have been known to the people of the city of Nazareth, which was nothing more than a village in Jesus' day. "As was his custom, [Jesus] went to the synagogue on the Sabbath day," each week. (Matt. 13:55, 56; Lu. 4:16) While Jesus would have been an exceptional student, unlike anything that the Nazareth synagogue would have ever seen, we must keep in mind that the disciples would have been going through similar experiences as they grew up in Galilee. Great emphasis was laid on the need for every Jew to have an accurate knowledge of the Law. Josephus wrote,

> for he [God] did not suffer the guilt of ignorance to go on without punishment, but demonstrated the law to be the best and the most necessary instruction of all others, permitting the people to leave off their other employments, and to assemble together for the hearing of the law, and learning it exactly, and this not once or twice, or oftener, but every week; which thing all the other legislators seem to have neglected. (Whiston 1987, Against Apion 2.175)

The high priest questioned Jesus about his disciples and his teaching. Jesus answered him, "I have spoken openly to the world. I have always taught in synagogues and in the temple, where all Jews come together. I have said nothing in secret." (John 18:19-20) We know that another source of knowledge and wisdom of Jesus came from the Father. Jesus said, "My teaching is not mine, but his who sent me," i.e., the Father. – John 7:16.

Mark 1:22 Updated American Standard Version (UASV)	Mark 1:27 Updated American Standard Version (UASV)
22 And they were astounded[54] at his teaching, for he taught them as	

---

[54] **Astounded:** (Gr. *ekplēssō*) This is one who is extremely astounded or amazed, so much so that they lose their mental self-control, as they are overwhelmed emotionally.–Matt. 7:28; Mark 1:22; 7:37; Lu 2:48; 4:32; 9:43; Ac 13:12.

one who had authority, and not as the scribes.	27 And they were all **astonished**,[55] so that they questioned among themselves, saying, "What is this? A new teaching **with authority!** ..."

At first, in the days of Ezra and Nehemiah, the priests served as scribes. (Ezra 7:1-6) The scribes referred to here in the Gospel of Mark are more than copyists of Scripture. They were professionally trained scholars, who were experts in the Mosaic Law. As was said above, a great emphasis was laid on the need for every Jew to have an accurate knowledge of the Law. Therefore, those who gave a great deal of their life and time to acquire an immense amount of knowledge were admired, becoming scholars, forming a group separate from the priests, creating a systematic study of the law, as well as its exposition, which became a professional occupation. By the time of Jesus, these scribes were experts in more than the Mosaic Law (entire Old Testament actually) as they became experts on the previous experts from centuries past, quoting them in addition to quoting Scripture. In other words, if there was any Scriptural decision to be made, these scribes quoted previous experts in the law, i.e., their comments on the law, as opposed to quoting applicable Scripture itself. The scribes were among the "teachers of the law," also referred to as "lawyers." (Lu 5:17; 11:45) The people were **astonished** and **amazed** at Jesus' **teaching** and **authority** because he did not quote previous teachers of the law but rather referred to Scripture alone as his authority, along with his exposition.

Jesus' Childhood Visits to Jerusalem

Only one event from Jesus' childhood is given to us, and it is found in the Gospel of Luke. It certainly adds weighty circumstantial evidence to the fact that Jesus could read and, therefore, was literate.

Luke 2:41-47 Updated American Standard Version (UASV)

41 Now His parents went to Jerusalem every year at the Feast of the Passover. 42 And when he [Jesus] was twelve years old, they went up according to the custom of the feast. 43 And after the days were completed, while they were returning, the boy Jesus stayed behind in Jerusalem. And his parents did not know it, 44 but supposing him to be in the company, they went a day's journey; and they began looking for him among their relatives and acquaintances. 45 and when they did not find him, they returned to Jerusalem, looking for him. 46 Then, it occurred, after three days they found him in the temple, sitting in the midst of the teachers and

---

55 **Astonished:** (Gr. *thambeō*; derivative of *thambos*) This is one who is experiencing astonishment, to be astounded, or amazed as a result of some sudden and unusual event, which can be in a positive or negative sense.–Mark 1:27; 10:32; Lu 4:36; 5:9; Acts 3:10.

listening to them and **questioning them.** [47] And all those listening to him were **amazed at his understanding** and his answers.

As we pointed out earlier in chapter 2, this was no 12-year-old boy's questions of curiosity. The Greek indicates that Jesus, at the age of twelve did not ask childlike questions, looking for answers, but was likely challenging the thinking of these Jewish religious leaders.

This incident is far more magnificent than one might first realize. Kittel's *Theological Dictionary of the New Testament* helps the reader to appreciate that the Greek word *eperotao* (to ask, to question, to demand of), for "questioning" was far more than the Greek word erotao (to ask, to request, to entreat), for a boy's inquisitiveness. *Eperotao* can refer to questioning, which one might hear in a judicial hearing, such as a scrutiny, inquiry, counter questioning, even the "probing and cunning questions of the Pharisees and Sadducees," for instance those we find at Mark 10:2 and 12:18-23.

The same dictionary continues: "In [the] face of this usage it may be asked whether . . . [Luke] 2:46 denotes, not so much the questioning curiosity of the boy, but rather His successful disputing. [Verse] 47 would fit in well with the latter view." Rotherham's translation of verse 47 presents it as a dramatic confrontation: "Now all who heard him were beside themselves, because of his understanding and his answers." Robertson's Word Pictures in the New Testament says that their constant amazement means, "they stood out of themselves as if their eyes were bulging out."

After returning to Jerusalem, and three days of searching, Joseph and Mary found young Jesus in the temple, questioning the Jewish religious leaders, at which "they were astounded." (Luke 2:48) Robertson said of this, "second aorist passive indicative of an old Greek word [*ekplesso*]), to strike out, drive out by a blow. Joseph and Mary 'were struck out' by what they saw and heard. Even they had not fully realized the power in this wonderful boy."[56] Thus, at twelve years old, Jesus, only a boy, is already evidencing that he is a great teacher and defender of truth. BDAG says, "to cause to be filled with amazement to the point of being overwhelmed, amaze, astound, overwhelm (literally, Strike out of one's senses).[57]

Some 18 years later Jesus again confronted the Pharisees with these types of interrogative questions, so much so that not "anyone [of them]

---

[56] A.T. Robertson, Word Pictures in the New Testament (Nashville, TN: Broadman Press, 1933), Lk 2:48.

[57] William Arndt, Frederick W. Danker and Walter Bauer, A Greek-English Lexicon of the New Testament and Other Early Christian Literature, 3rd ed. (Chicago: University of Chicago Press, 2000), 308.

dare from that day on to ask him any more questions." (Matthew 22:41-46) The Sadducees fared no better when Jesus responded to them on the subject of the resurrection: "And no one dared to ask him any more questions." (Luke 20:27-40) The scribes were silenced just the same after they got into an exchange with Jesus: "And from then on no one dared ask him any more questions." (Mark 12:28-34) Clearly, this insight into Jesus' life and ministry provide us with evidence that he had the ability to read very well and likely write. There is the fact that Jesus was also divine. However, he was also fully human, and he grew, progressing in wisdom, because of his studies in the Scriptures.

Luke 2:40, 51-52 Updated American standard Version (UASV)

[40] And the child continued growing and became strong, **being filled with wisdom**. And the favor of God was upon him. [51] And he went down with them and came to Nazareth, and he continued in subjection to them; and his mother treasured all these things in her heart. [52] And Jesus kept **increasing in wisdom** and stature, and in favor with God and men.

Jesus was often called "Rabbi," which was used in a real or genuine sense as "teacher." (Mark 9:5; 11:21; 14:45; John 1:38, 49 etc.) We find "*Rabbo(u)ni*" (Mark 10:51; John 20:16) as well as its Greek equivalents, "schoolmaster" or "instructor" (*epistata*; Luke 5:5; 8:24, 45; 9:33, 49; 17:13) or "teacher" (*didaskalos*; Matt. 8:19; 9:11; 12:38; Mark 4:38; 5:35; 9:17; 10:17, 20; 12:14, 19, 32; Luke 19:39; John 1:38; 3:2). Jesus used these same terms for himself, as did his disciples, even his adversaries, and those with no affiliation.

Another inference that Jesus was literate comes from his constant reference to reading Scripture, when confronted by the Jewish religious leaders: law students, Pharisees, Scribes and the Sadducees. Jesus said, "**Have you not read** what David did when he was hungry, and those who were with him ... Or **have you not read in the Law** how on the Sabbath the priests in the temple profane the Sabbath and are guiltless? (Matt. 12:3, 5; reference to 1 Sam 21:6 and Num 28:9) Again, Jesus responded, "**Have you not read** that he who created them from the beginning made them male and female." (Matt. 19:3; a paraphrase of Gen 1:27) Jesus said to them, "Yes; **have you never read**, "'Out of the mouth of infants and nursing babies you have prepared praise'?" (Matt. 21:16; quoting Psa. 8:2) Jesus said to them, "**Have you never read in the Scriptures**: "'The stone that the builders rejected has become the cornerstone; this was the Lord's doing, and it is marvelous in our eyes'? (Matt. 21:42; Reference to Isaiah 28:16) Jesus said to him, "**What is written in the Law? How do you read it?**" (Lu. 10:26) Many of these references or Scripture quotations were asked in such a way to his opponents; there is little doubt Jesus himself had read them. When Jesus asked in an interrogative way, "have you not read," it was taken for granted that he had read them. Jesus referred to or quoted over 120 Scriptures in the dialogue that we have in the Gospels.

The data that have been surveyed are more easily explained in reference to a literate Jesus, a Jesus who could read the Hebrew Scriptures, could paraphrase and interpret them in Aramaic and could do so in a manner that indicated his familiarity with current interpretive tendencies in both popular circles (as in the synagogues) and in professional, even elite circles (as seen in debates with scribes, ruling priests and elders). Of course, to conclude that Jesus was literate is not necessarily to conclude that Jesus had received formal scribal training. The data do not suggest this. Jesus' innovative, experiential approach to Scripture and to Jewish faith seems to suggest the contrary.[58]

How did Jesus gain such wisdom? Jesus, although divine, was not born with this exceptional wisdom that he demonstrated at the age of twelve and kept increasing. It was acquired. (Deut. 17:18-19) This extraordinary wisdom was no exception to the norm, not even for the Son of God himself. (Luke 2:52) Jesus' knowledge was acquired by his studying the Hebrew Old Testament, enabling him to challenge the thinking of the Jewish religious leaders with his questions at the age of twelve. Therefore, Jesus had to be very familiar with the Hebrew Old Testament, as well as the skill of reasoning from the Scriptures.

Books, Reading, and Writing; the Literacy Level of the Apostle Peter and John

Acts 4:13 Updated American Standard Version (UASV)	Acts 4:13 New American Standard Bible (NASB)
[13] Now when they saw the boldness of Peter and John, and perceived that **they were uneducated**[59] and untrained men, they were astonished, and they recognized that they had been with Jesus.	[13] Now as they observed the confidence of Peter and John and understood that **they were uneducated** and untrained men, they were amazed, and *began* to recognize them as having been with Jesus.

---

[58] (Evans, Jesus and His World: The Archaeological Evidence 2012)

[59] Or *unlettered* (YLT) that is, not educated in the rabbinic schools; not meaning illiterate.

How are we to understand the statement that Peter and John **were uneducated**? (ESV, NASB, HCSB, LEB, UASV, and others) [*unlettered* (YLT) or *unlearned* (ASV)] This did not necessarily mean that they could not read and write, as the letters that were penned by these apostles (or their secretaries) testify that they could. What this means is that they were not educated in higher learning of the Hebrew schools, such as studying under someone like Gamaliel, as was the case with Paul (Ac 5:34-39; 22:3).[60] The Greek words literally read καταλαβομενοι [having perceived] οτι [that] ανθρωποι [men] αγραμματοι [unlettered] εισιν [they are] και [and] ιδιωται [untrained]. This means that the disciples were not educated in rabbinic schools. It did not mean that they were illiterate. In other words, they lacked scribal training. In addition, ιδιωται [untrained], simply means that in comparison to professionally trained scribes of their day, they were not specialists, i.e., were not trained or expert in the scribal duties. This hardly constitutes the idea that they were illiterate.

It was the same reason that the Jewish religious leaders were surprised by the extensive knowledge that Jesus had. They said of him, "How is it that this man has learning when he has never studied?" (John 7:15) This is our best Scriptural evidence that Jesus could read. Let us break it down to what the religious leaders were really saying of Jesus. They asked πως [how] ουτος [this one] γραμματα [letters/writings] οιδεν [has known] μη [not] μεμαθηκως [have learned]. First, this is a reference to the fact that Jesus did not study at the Hebrew schools, i.e., scribal training. In other words, 'how does this one [Jesus] have knowledge of letters/writings, when he has not studied at the Hebrew schools. This question means more than Jesus' ability to read because as we saw in the above, Jewish children were taught to read.

Another example: Luke 4:16-30 says that Jesus "came to Nazareth, where he had been brought up. And as was his custom, he went to the synagogue on the Sabbath day, and he stood up to read. And the scroll of the prophet Isaiah was given to him. He unrolled the scroll and found" (Lu 4:16-17) Jesus was able to take the scroll of Isaiah and read what is now known as Isaiah 61:1-2. While the parallel account in Mark 6:1-6 does not refer to Jesus reading this text, scholars have long known that the gospel writers shared the events through their separate viewpoints, i.e., they drew attention to what stood out to them, and what served their purpose for writing their Gospel accounts.

Within the Roman Empire from the first to the fourth century, we find public writings in and throughout all of the cities. It encompasses

---

[60] Gamaliel was a Pharisee and a leading authority in the Sanhedrin, as well as a teacher of the law, of which Acts says, Paul was "educated at the feet of Gamaliel according to the strict manner of the law of our fathers." (Ac 22:3)

inscriptions, which are "dedications, lists of names, imperial decrees, statements or reminders of law, quotations of famous men and even rather pedestrian things, such as directions. Many gravestones and tombs are inscribed with more than the name of the deceased; some have lengthy, even poetic obituaries; others have threats and curses against grave robbers (literate ones, evidently!). The impression one gains is that everybody was expected to be able to read; otherwise, what was the point of all of these expensive inscriptions, incised on stone?"[61] This impression does not end with inscriptions, because archaeology can extrapolate that between the fourth and sixth centuries C.E., millions upon millions of documents came out of Oxyrhynchus, just one city, based on the more than 1.5 million documents found in their garbage dumps. Of these, five hundred thousand have been recovered.

The **Library of Celsus** (45-ca. 120 C.E.) is an ancient Roman building in Ephesus (completed in 135 C.E.) which contained some 12,000 scrolls. The library was also built as a monumental tomb for Celsus. He is buried in a stone coffin beneath the library. The **Ancient Library of Alexandria**, Egypt (third-century to 30 B.C.E.), was one of the largest and most important libraries of the ancient world. Most of the books were kept as papyrus scrolls. King Ptolemy II Philadelphus (309–246 B.C.E.) is believed to have set 500,000 scrolls as a goal for the library. Apparently, by the first century C.E., the library contained one million scrolls. The **Library of Pergamum** (Asia Minor) was one of the most significant libraries in the ancient world. It is said to have housed roughly 200,000 volumes. Historical records say that the library had a large central reading room. We have not even mentioned Rome, Athens, Corinth, Antioch (Syria), and the rest. The Mediterranean world from Alexander the Great (356-323 B.C.E.) to Constantine the Great (272-337 C.E.), some 700 years, saw hundreds of major libraries, as well as thousands of moderate to minor ones, with hundreds of millions of documents being written and read. Certainly, this does not suggest illiteracy, but literacy.

Some point out that "Celsus,[62] the first writer against Christianity, makes it a matter of mockery, that labourers, shoemakers, farmers, the most uninformed and clownish of men, should be zealous preachers of the Gospel."[63] Paul explained it this way: "For consider your calling, brothers: not many of you were wise according to worldly standards, not many were

---

[61] (Evans, Jesus and His World: The Archaeological Evidence 2012)

[62] This Celsus was a second-century Greek philosopher and opponent of early Christianity, who should not be confused with the previously mentioned Celsus, Roman Senator Tiberius Julius Celsus Polemaeanus.

[63] The History of the Christian Religion and Church, During the Three First Centuries, by Augustus Neander; translated from the German by Henry John Rose, 1848, p. 41

powerful, not many were of noble birth. But God chose what is foolish in the world to shame the wise; God chose what is weak in the world to shame the strong." (1 Cor. 1:26-27) It seems that these so-called illiterate Christians were able to grow from 120 in Jerusalem about 33 C.E., to some one million by 125 C.E., a mere 92 years later. This growth in the Christian population all came about because they effectively evangelized, using the Septuagint (Greek Old Testament). They were so effective with the Septuagint that the Jews abandoned it and went back to the Hebrew Old Testament.

In any case, Celsus was an enemy of Christianity. Also, as was stated above, what Celsus observed was only within the sphere of his personal experiences. How many Christians could he have known out of almost a million at the time of his writing? Moreover, although not highly educated in schools, it **need not** be assumed that most or all of the early Christians were entirely illiterate, but rather a good number of them could read and write (with difficulty). Many had a *very basic* ability to understand spoken words, a *very basic* grasp of written words, *very basic* math skills (buying in the market place), and the ability to sign one's name for daily living and employment.

Let us return to Peter and John. We will assume for the sake of argument that literacy was between five and ten percent, with most readers being men. We will accept that Peter and John were entirely illiterate in the sense the modern historian believes it to be true (even though they likely were not). The time of the statement in Acts about the two apostles' being "**uneducated**" (i.e., unlettered) was about 33 C.E.[64] Peter would not pen his first letter for about 30 more years. Throughout those 30 years, Peter progressed spiritually, maturing into the position of being one of the leaders of the entire first-century Christian congregation. A few years later, Peter and John were viewed as developing and growing into their new position, as leaders in the Jerusalem congregation; as Paul said of them, "James and Cephas and John, who seemed to be pillars" of the Christian community. John, on the other hand, did not pen his books until about 60 years after Acts 4:13. Are we to assume that he too had not grown in 60 years? Could education in the first century have become more accessible?

The Birth of Koine Greek

After the conquests of Alexander the Great and the extension of Macedonian rule in the fourth-century B.C.E., a transferal of people from

---

[64] B.C.E. means "before the Common Era," which is more accurate than B.C. ("before Christ"). C.E. denotes "Common Era," often called A.D., for *anno Domini*, meaning "in the year of our Lord."

Greece proper to the small Greek communities in the Middle East took place. Throughout what became known as the Hellenistic period, the Attic dialect, spoken by the educated classes as well as by the traders and many settlers, became the language common to all the Middle East. From about 300 B.C.E. to about 500 C.E. was the age of Koine, or common Greek, a combination of different Greek dialects of which Attic was the most significant. Koine soon became the universal language. It had a tremendous advantage over the other languages of this period, in that it was almost universally used. "Koine" means the "common" language, or dialect common to all. The Greek vocabulary of the Old Testament translation, the Septuagint, was the Koine of Alexandria, Egypt, from 280 to 150 B.C.E. Everett Ferguson writes,

> Literacy became more general, and education spread. Both abstract thought and practical intelligence were enhanced in a greater proportion of the population. This change coincided with the spread of Greek language and ideas, so that the level and extent of communication and intelligibility became significant. (Ferguson 2003, 14)

> Education was voluntary, but elementary schools at least were widespread. The indications, especially on the evidence of the papyri, are that the literacy rate of Hellenistic and early Roman times was rather high, probably higher than at any period prior to modern times. Girls as well as boys were often included in the elementary schools, and although education for girls was rarer than for boys, it could be obtained. The key for everyone was to get what you could on your own. (Ferguson 2003, 111)

By the time we enter the first-century C.E., the era of Jesus and the apostles, Koine Greek had become the international language of the Roman Empire. The Bible itself bears witness to this; e.g. when Jesus was executed by the Roman Pontius Pilate, the inscription above his head was in Aramaic, the language of the Jews, in Latin, the official language of Rome. It was also in Greek, which was the language spoken on the streets of Alexandria to Jerusalem, to Athens, to Rome and the rest of the Empire. (John 19:19, 20; Acts 6:1) Acts 9:29 informs us that Paul was preaching in Jerusalem to Greek-speaking Jews. As we know, Koine, a well-developed tongue by the first-century C.E., would be the tool that would facilitate the publishing of the 27 New Testament books.

Books, Reading, and Writing; Archaeological Evidence for Literacy In Early Christianity

Archaeologists have discovered hundreds of thousands of examples of graffiti on the outsides of buildings throughout the ancient Roman world, over 11,000 in Pompeii alone.

Graffiti and Literacy in Early Christianity

Pompeii was a prosperous, populace (15,000), economically diverse ancient Roman city near modern Naples in the Campania region of Italy. Over 11,000 graffiti samples, etched into the plaster or painted on the walls, in both public and private places, have been uncovered in the excavations of Pompeii. Archaeologists have been studying and recording graffiti in Pompeii since the 1800s.

Mount Vesuvius blew a column of gas, magma, and debris for thirty-six hours that literally darkened the sky as though it were night, which caused a dreadful rain of ash and lapilli (small lava rock fragments ejected from a volcano). It only took two days until Pompeii and an enormous area of rural area were covered with a thick layer, with the average depth of about eight feet [2.5 m]. The earth continued to be shaken by violent tremors that released into the air a huge cloud of poisonous gases. These gases were invisible but deadly, which covered the city, bringing death. As Pompeii was being buried, the small Roman town Herculaneum vanished instantly, being preserved more or less intact. "Lava flowed down on Herculaneum, submerging that town under a mass of mud and volcanic debris to a depth that reached twenty-two meters [72 feet] near the shore." (Dell'Orto 1990, 131)

CIL IV, 03494 National Archaeological Museum of Naples (inv. N. 111482), Scenes of osteria, Pompeian fresco (50 x 205 cm) from the Caupona of Salvius (VI, 14, 35-36) with "comics."

It is these buried cities that have helped us to understand the ancient Roman world better and specifically it's Graffiti that has enabled us to understand its literary level better. The Graffiti of the ancient Roman world was **writing** in charcoal, scratched with a stylus or stick, painted with a brush, **or drawings** scribbled, scratched, or painted with a brush on a wall or other surface in a public place. In the ancient world of the first-century Roman Empire, graffiti was a valued form expression, which was even interactive, and should not be confused with the modern-day criminal defacement we now see in most of our modern cities.

CIL IV, 10237 A graffito from Pompeii that shows musicians, the emperor, and a fight between a murmillō and a secūtor.

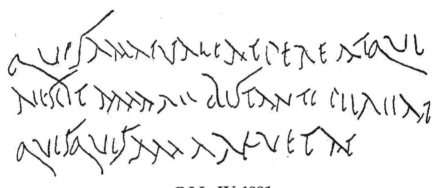

C.I.L. IV 4091
QVIS AMAT VALEAT PEREAT QVI
NESCIT AMARE BIS TANTI PEREAT
QVISQVIS AMARE VETAT

CIL IV, 4091 "Whoever loves, let him flourish, let him perish who knows not love, let him perish twice over whoever forbids love"

Some scholars as we have already seen from above and others not mentioned herein have attempted to downplay the importance of the texts of the Greek New Testament within early Christianity. Instead, they argue that the oral gospel played a far more important, dominant role. This is largely supported by the long-held belief that the vast majority of those in the ancient Roman world was unable to read and write. Many scholars throughout the twentieth century have argued that the low literacy level is evidence that the early Christians did not place a significant value of the texts of the New Testament. On this Alan Millard, professor of Hebrew and ancient Semitic languages, writes, "Another authority stated, 'there was a gap of several decades between the public ministry of Jesus and the writing down of his words by the authors of the Gospels. During this time what was known about Jesus was handed on orally.'" The Jesus Seminar, fifty critical Biblical scholars and one-hundred laymen founded in 1985 by Robert Funk, even argue that Jesus' early disciples "were technically illiterate." (Millard 2000, 185)

From the last forty to fifty years, the evidence supports that people of all sorts knew how to read and write in the first century. The Hebrew, Aramaic, and Greek languages were common at all levels of society during Jesus' life and ministry and the apostle's lifetime. The argument that the Gospels came out of an utterly illiterate society is a false narrative because the evidence tells another story entirely, as reading and writing would be quite common throughout the Roman Empire. In almost every circumstance there would be people who could write something that someone tells them, be it for their personal use, or the benefit of another.

C.I.L. IV 5092
AMORIS IGNES SI SENTIRES MVLIO
MAGI PROPERARES VT VIDERIS VENEREM
DILIGO IVVENEM (PVERVM) VENVSTVM ROGO PVNGE IAMVS
BIBISTI IAMVS PRENDE LORA ET EXCVTE
POMPEIOS DEFER VBI DVLCIS EST AMOR
MEVS ES

CIL IV, 5092 Graffiti from Pompeii, in verse. The writer, burned by the flames of love, incites the mule driver to stop drinking and goad the mules to get to Pompeii first, where a handsome boy, whose writer is in love, awaits him, and where love is sweet.

For example, consider the commonness of the graffiti in Pompeii and throughout the Roman Empire. The elites that argue for orality do not include this kind of evidence into the discussion, which they should because it would detract from their theme of literacy impacting the production, publication, and distribution of a written text. Think about graffiti by its very nature cannot be derived from the wealthy, prominent members of Roman society. Who would argue that such memorable writers as Vergil (or Virgil), Horace, Catullus, Propertius, Tibullus, and Ovid were found scribbling on the side of some public building? On this, Kristina Milnor writes, "The corpus of Pompeian wall writings, moreover, has been seen as

79

a window onto the language of everyday life in the ancient Roman world, one of our few opportunities to read words written by ordinary people performing an activity (writing graffiti) that we in the modern day do not associate with the cultural elite."[65]

As Milnor rightly points out, the graffiti is not by the hands of elite writers but rather common everyday people. She makes the acute observation that the prominent Latin poets of the day had mixed feelings and concerns about the production of their book that they knew would be read and reread, which meant being copied and copied. They knew this also meant that human error would creep into the work and copyist may even take liberties. Moreover, these published authors knew that they also faced public criticism, while the authors of the graffiti knew their work was an autograph and never had to face any production, publication, and distribution issues. The author of a graffito simply concerned himself with the **technical** aspects of his written work: its properties and techniques as seen from a literary and language perspective. In many cases, the Latin poet's work may become known throughout the entire empire, while the graffito author is simply a local phenomenon.

We need to view graffiti in the light of all written works that had an impact on the ancient Roman culture of the day. Some might mistakenly believe that graffiti was at the bottom of the written record spectrum. However, we might place the graffiti above the daily writings of advertisements for rental properties, shopping lists, or signs throughout the city offering public information to the passerby. We might even place the graffiti on the same level as the local newspaper or rather something like the tabloid magazine of the first century C.E., with writers showing much interest in the classics, who dabbled in poetry and mythology, as well as local gossip, with a mixture of advertisements. While it is true that the messages were likely more impactful on the urban level, let's not think the elites were any less impacted by the graffiti than the elites of today and TMZ. The readers were incidental in nature, happening upon the graffiti, not seeking it out like a published book. However, the workers of the elites likely communicated these things to their employers or masters if the subject or context was relevant, and there is nothing to say that when a wealthy person walked the streets through the shops, they never paused to read the graffiti. The general conclusion being "It seems clear that a significant percentage of wall writers and readers were literate in Greek, although the

---

[65] William A. Johnson; Holt N. Parker, *Ancient Literacies: The Culture of Reading in Greece and Rome* (Oxford: Oxford University Press, 2011), 291.

common practice of transliteration suggests that there may have been more speakers than writers/readers."[66]

While we have focused on the public places of Pompeii and the Roman empire as a whole, graffiti can also be found in the catacombs and on various early Christian monuments. Throughout the Roman Empire of the first three centuries of Christianity, graffiti could have been in the millions engraved into or painted on walls, floors and engraved on tombstones. Craig A. Evans informs us that Israel was not exempt from graffiti, stating, "There are many examples in Israel too, though not nearly as 'colourful' as those preserved on the scorched walls of Pompeii and Herculaneum. At the very least these graffiti and inscriptions attest to a crude literacy that reached all levels of society." Evans sites Rock Inscriptions and Graffiti Project (3 vols, SBLRBS 28, 29, 31; Atlanta: Scholars Press, 1992-4), "Stone and his colleagues catalogued some 8,500 inscriptions and graffiti found in southern Israel: the Judean desert, the desert of the Negev and Sinai. The inscriptions are in several languages, including Hebrew, Aramaic, Greek, Latin, Nabatean, Armenian, Georgian, Egyptian hieroglyphs and others. Not many date to late antiquity, because, unlike the graffiti and inscriptions of Pompeii and Herculaneum, the graffiti and inscriptions in the deserts of Israel were exposed to the eroding elements."[67] The graffiti help us to illustrate literacy and the literary sources of the life of the early Christians.

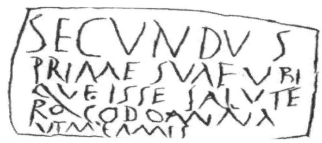

Figure 1 CIL IV, 8364 Pompeyan inscription Translation: "I subscribe to your dear Prima in every place a cordial greeting, I beg of you, my mistress, to love me."

---

[66] William A. Johnson; Holt N. Parker, *Ancient Literacies: The Culture of Reading in Greece and Rome* (Oxford: Oxford University Press, 2011), 295.

[67] Craig A. Evans, *Jesus and His World: The Archaeological Evidence* (Westminster: John Knox Press, 2012), Section 3317, KDP.

Public Writing

Theodotus Inscription to Greek-Speaking Jews: The inscription reads: "Theodotus son of Vettenus, priest and synagogue-president, son of a synagogue-president and grandson of a synagogue-president, has built the synagogue for the reading of the Law and the teaching of the Commandments, and (he has built) the hostelry and the chambers and the cisterns of water in order to provide lodgings for those from abroad who need them—(the synagogue) which his fathers and the elders and Simonides had founded." (*Biblical Archaeology,* by G. Ernest Wright, 1962, p. 240)

The text was carved on a limestone slab measuring 72 cm (28 in.) in length and 42 cm (17 in.) in width. It was discovered early in the 20th century on the hill of Ophel in Jerusalem. The inscription, written in Greek, refers to a priest, Theodotus. It has been dated to shortly before the destruction of Jerusalem in 70 C.E. It is evidence that there were Greek-speaking Jews in Jerusalem in the first century C.E. (Ac 6:1) Some believe that the writing is referring to "the synagogue of the Freedmen (as it was called)." The inscription also references that Theodotus, as well as his father Vettenus and his grandfather, had the title *archisynagogos* (**leader of a synagogue**, local ruler of the community),[68] a title that used a number of times in the Greek New Testament. (Mark 5:22, 35-36, 38; Lu 8:49; 13:14; Ac 13:15; 18:8, 17, etc.).

---

[68] James Swanson, *Dictionary of Biblical Languages with Semantic Domains: Greek (New Testament)* (Oak Harbor: Logos Research Systems, Inc., 1997).

There has been a countless number of archaeological finds that seem to suggest that many within the Roman Empire could read. Literally, throughout the Roman Empire, we find literally hundreds if not thousands of public inscriptions like the Theodotus Inscription shown above. These inscriptions range from a list of names, general public information, imperial decrees, laws and regulations, quotations from famous people, as well as directions, or distances from one place to another. In addition, even in the graveyards and the tombs, we find far more inscribed on the gravestones then merely the names of the deceased. On these tombstones, we find graffiti as mentioned above but also an inscription on the stone itself, such as threats and curses against any suspecting grave robbers who might happen upon their burial site. Indeed, it seems that they believed that the lowest criminal elements of the day could read. The impression from all of this public writing is that the public as a whole could read; otherwise, what is the point of spending all of the time and money so that a mere 5-10 percent of 100 million people could read it.

Literacy and the Literature from Egyptian Garbage Heaps

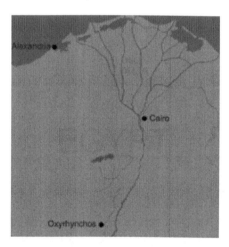

Beginning in 1778 and continuing to the end of the 19th century, many papyrus texts were accidentally discovered in Egypt that date from 300 B.C.E. to 600 C.E., almost 500 thousand documents in all. About 130 years ago, there began a systematic search. At that time, a continuous flow of ancient texts was being found by the native fellahin, and the Egypt Exploration Society, a British non-profit organization, founded in 1882, realized that they needed to send out an expedition team before it was too late. They sent two Oxford scholars, Bernard P. Grenfell and Arthur S. Hunt, who received permission to search the area south of the farming region in the Faiyūm district. Grenfell chose a site called Behnesa because of its ancient Greek name, Oxyrhynchus. A search of the graveyards and the ruined houses produced nothing. The only place left to search was the town's garbage dumps, which were some 30 feet [9 m] high. It seems to Grenfell and Hunt that all was lost but they decided to try.

Grenfell (left) and Hunt (right) in about 1896

In January of 1897, a trial trench (excavation or depression in the ground) was dug, and it only took a few hours before ancient papyrus materials were found. These included letters, contracts, and official documents. The sand had blown over them, covering them, and for nearly 2,000 years, the dry climate had served as a protection for them.

Illustrates excavations at Oxyrhynchus

It took only a mere three months to pull out and recover almost two tons of papyri from Oxyrhynchus. They shipped twenty-five large cases back to England. Over the next ten years, these two courageous scholars returned each and every winter, to grow their collection. They discovered ancient classical writing, along with royal ordinances and contracts mixed

84

in with business accounts private letters, shipping lists, as well as fragments of many New Testament manuscripts.

Of what benefit were all these documents? Foremost, the bulk of these documents were written by ordinary people in Koine (common) Greek of the day. Many of the words that would be used in the marketplace, not by the elites appeared in the Greek New Testament Scriptures, which woke scholars up to the fact that Biblical Greek was not some special Greek, but instead, it was the ordinary language of the common people, the man on the street. Thus, by comparing how the words had been used in these papyri, a clearer understanding of Biblical Greek emerged. As of the time of this writing, less than ten percent of these papyri have been published and studied. Most of the papyri were found in the top 10 feet 93 m] of the garbage heap because the other 20 feet [6 m] had been ruined by water from a nearby canal. If we look at it simply, this would mean that the 500 thousand documents found could have been two million in total. Then, we must ponder just how many documents must have come through Oxyrhynchus that were never discarded in the dumps.

We have almost a half million papyrus documents (likely there were millions more that did not survive) in garbage dumps in the dry sands of Oxyrhynchus, Egypt. This is but one city in the entirety of the Roman Empire. Are we to believe that Oxyrhynchus is the exception, and some of the biggest cities, such as Rome, Corinth, Athens, Pergamum, Ephesus, Smyrna, Antioch, Jerusalem, Alexandria, and Carthage, which numbered anywhere from one hundred thousand to over a million in their population, did not have equal or greater writings discarded in their dumps? Then we should consider the temples and the libraries that boasted of tens of thousands of books. Reportedly, by the first century C.E., the Alexandrian library housed one million scrolls. In fact, Mark Antony took 200,000 scrolls from the library at Pergamum to replenish the Alexandrian library for Cleopatra. Because of moisture damage and they're being written on perishable material, we cannot discover the documents of these centers of education as we have in the dry sands of Egypt. Yet, should we for a moment believe that their garbage dumps saw any fewer books that were discovered at Oxyrhynchus, Egypt?

Clearly, the tremendous amount of document discoveries begs for widespread literacy not low levels. We are not trying to overturn the apple cart here. The common consensus of the historians is that in the Roman Empire of the first three centuries of Christianity were 5-10 percent literate and they were male. We **are not** trying to suggest that widespread means the 80-90 percent literacy but instead at least 40-50 percent, if not more. We think of the immense production of the twenty-seven New Testament books of the first century and the Apostolic Fathers in the late first and early second centuries, as well as the Apologists from near the middle of the second century through its end. Then, we consider the publication of these books, the copying of these books, as well as their circulation, and we conclude that the use of these books in the early Christian Church are apparent. They, along with all else that has been discussed in this chapter give us clear visible proof of some level literacy within Christianity, but it cannot offer us the exact extent. We would argue the percentage be broken down instead of trying to suggest a one size fits all.

Full Illiteracy (20%): This one has no reading or writing skills, no math skills, and is incapable of signing his name for daily living and employment beyond fundamental manual labor. He would work as fruit and vegetable picking, handling materials or low-level tools, manual digging or building, farming, or working in large workshops that produced items such as dishes or pots, as well as household slaves.

Fragmentary Literacy (40%): (inconsistent or incomplete in some areas) The very basic ability to understand spoken words, a very basic grasp of written words, very basic math skills (buying in the market place), and the ability to sign one's name for daily living and employment. He would work as a manual laborer in the market place not requiring math, a shop assistant that performs manual labor, or a soldier.

Fundamental Literacy (20%): The basic ability to understand spoken words, an elementary grasp of written words, basic math skills and the ability to sign one's name and the ability to read and write simple words for daily living and employment, such as work as a craftsman, works in the marketplace, or soldier.

Functional Literacy (15%): This one has the competent ability to understand spoken words, a beginner-intermediate level grasp of written words, and the ability to prepare basic documents for daily living and employment tasks that require reading skills beyond a basic level. He is a semiliterate writer who is untrained in writing but has the ability to read or write simple sentences and can take on some basic jobs, such as a copyist or scribe.

Proficient Literacy (3%): This one is a highly skilled person, who can understand spoken words, and has an intermediate-advanced level grasp of written words. He has the proficient ability to prepare short texts for daily living and employment tasks that require reading skills at the intermediate level. He is a literate writer who is trained in writing and can take on jobs, such as a copyist or scribe, a tax collector or clerk.

Full Literacy (2%): This one is a highly skilled expert, who can understand spoken words, an advanced level grasp of written words. He has the professional ability to prepare long texts for daily living and employment tasks that require reading skills at the advanced level. He is a fully literate writer who is professionally trained in writing and can take on jobs, such as a copyist or scribe, a tax collector, teacher, lawyer, or a clerk to high-ranking positions like Senators.

CHAPTER 3 The Reading Culture of Early Christianity

Ehrman wrote: There were always exceptions, of course, like the apostle Paul and the other authors whose works made it into the New Testament and who were obviously skilled writers; but for the most part, Christians came from the ranks of the illiterate. This is certainly true of the very earliest Christians, who would have been the apostles of Jesus. In the Gospel accounts, we find that most of Jesus's disciples are simple peasants from Galilee—**uneducated fishermen, for example. Two of them, Peter and John, are explicitly said to be "illiterate"** in the book of Acts (4:13). The apostle Paul indicates to his Corinthian congregation that "not many of you were wise by human standards" (1 Cor. 1:27)—which might mean that some few were well educated, but not most. As we move into the second Christian century, things do not seem to change much. As I have indicated, some intellectuals converted to the faith, but **most Christians were from the lower classes and uneducated. Misquoting Jesus (pp. 39-40).**

Acts 4:13 Updated American Standard Version (UASV)

[13] Now when they saw the boldness of Peter and John, and perceived that they were uneducated[69] and untrained men, they were astonished, and they recognized that they had been with Jesus.

Unlettered (YLT) that is, not educated in the rabbinic schools. This does not mean illiterate.

There is evidence of universality in the early orthodox Christian manuscripts. While the elite of the Roman society preferred the roll or scroll for their pagan literature, the Christian preferred the codex book form. This is even the case with the roll or scroll being preferred for apocryphal apostate Christian literature as opposed to the codex. Except for P[22] (John 15:25–16:2, 21–32), all of the third/fourth-century canonical gospel manuscripts were papyrus codices. Going back to the second/third centuries, we also find that the Gospel codices were given some special status, as they were all produced in standard sizes that were smaller than the other canonical NT books. The gospels were 11.5–14 cm in width and height at least 3 cm higher than width, while other NT books were 12–14 cm in width and height not quite twice that. Even so, while the other NT books might have been a little taller, they all were easily carried. (Hill and

---

[69] Or *unlettered* (YLT) that is, not educated in the rabbinic schools; not meaning illiterate.

Kruger 2012, 38) The codex came to be used toward the end of the first century, and the Christians were commonly using it after the first century.[70] The evidence for such a conclusion comes from our earliest Christian manuscripts that are still in existence, which were produced in codex form. The manuscripts include the Old Testament that was used by the Christians and the New Testament texts, as well as the Apostolic Fathers, the Apologists, and other early Church Fathers.

Another piece of evidence of universality in the early orthodox Christian manuscripts was the *nomina sacra* (Lat. "sacred names"), which were contractions and abbreviations of several frequently occurring divine names or titles in the early texts, the Greek counterparts of God, Lord, Jesus, Christ, Son, Spirit, David, Cross, Mother, Father, Israel, Savior, Man, Jerusalem, and Heaven. (Metzger 1981, 36-37) Early on there was universality with the four divine names or titles God, Jesus, Christ, and Lord, to which were later added the other sacred names above. Even how the sacred names were to be contracted in the manuscripts was standardized and universal. It was decided early that regardless of whether sacred names were used in a sacred or mundane way, they were to be contracted. For example, whether the Greek *kurios* (Lord) was used in reference to the Son Jesus (sacred) as opposed to the master of a household (mundane/non-sacred), it was to be contracted. Another example of whether the Greek *pater* (Father/father) was used in reference to the Father (sacred) or a father in some narrative or parable (mundane/non-sacred), it was to be contracted. For example, in P[66] (c. 200 C.E.),[71] *kurios* ("Lord") is contracted through the entire manuscript whether it was sacred or mundane in its use. We have the same situation with *pneuma* (spirit) in P[75] (c. 175-225 C.E.),[72] even when it is a reference to an unclean spirit. This is evidence of a universal, systematic approach to the Christian canonical books, which shows a concern for the accuracy of the content and the handiness, convenience, and portability of the New Testament books in the latter half of the second-century C.E.[73]

---

[70] T. C. Skeat, *Zeitschrift für Papyrus und Epigraphic* 102 (1994): 263–68.

[71] CONTENTS: John 1:1–6:11; 6:35–14:26, 29–30; 15:2–26; 16:2–4, 6–7; 16:10–20:20, 22–23; 20:25–21:9, 12, 17.

[72] CONTENTS: Luke 3:18–22; 3:33–4:2; 4:34–5:10; 5:37–6:4; 6:10–7:32, 35–39, 41–43; 7:46–9:2; 9:4–17:15; 17:19–18:18; 22:4–24:53; John 1:1–11:45, 48–57; 12:3–13:1, 8–10; 14:8–29; 15:7–8.

[73] What we have learned here and in the whole of THE TEXT OF THE NEW TESTAMENT undermine what secular scholars such as Walter Bauer, Robert A. Kraft, and agnostic Bart D. Ehrman maintain. These argue that **Gnosticism** (a false philosophy, speculation, and pagan mysticism of apostate Christianity), **Montanism** (a heresy based on the teachings of the charismatic prophet Montanus), and **Marcionism** (condemned as a Christian heresy that rejected the Old Testament) were just alternative forms of Christianity, just as

The Reading Culture of Early Christianity

Textual scholar Larry Hurtado (Hill and Kruger 2012, 49) borrows an approach from William A. Johnson in his book *Readers and Reading Culture in the High Roman Empire: A Study of Elite Communities*, and I would like to take the liberty of borrowing this concept as well. Johnson, under the heading, CONTEXTUALIZING READING COMMUNITIES, writes, "The more proper goal, as I [Johnson] have argued, is to understand the particular reading cultures that obtained in antiquity, rather than to try to answer decontextualized questions that assume in 'reading' a clarity and simplicity it manifestly does not have." (Johnson 2012 (Reprint), 14) Johnson focuses his reading culture on "'the reading of Greek literary prose texts by the educated elite during the early empire (first and second centuries AD)'" (Hill and Kruger 2012, 49), just one of many surrounding reading cultures of the time. We are going to focus our attention on the reading culture of early Christianity, namely, the first three centuries. Just as the manuscript evidence above gave us proof of a universal approach of early Christianity to the publication of their canonical books, showing concern for the accuracy of the content, this will be an extension of that.

What made Johnson's work so appetizing for Hurtado is the Roman elite reading culture and how he demonstrated that their approach was actually designed to keep out anyone who could not handle the difficulty with which their reading community functioned. The Roman literary world had long had word separation within their texts, but the elite reading culture of the Roman world in the second and third centuries returned to *scriptio continua* (Lat. for "continuous script"), a style of writing without spaces or other marks between the words and sentences. This choice of writing style over others that were current and common, with spaces between words and sentences as well as punctuation, diacritical marks that indicate how words are to be pronounced, and distinguished letter case, is

---

organized and fast-growing if not faster. They have maintained, moreover, that the form of Christianity in Rome prevailed in the fourth century and became the standard, causing these groups and others to be seen as apostate forms of Christianity. This is not the case. First, the early evidence is that these groups were only tiny apostate offshoots of true Christianity, who broke away, abandoning the truth. Second, they were busy arguing amongst themselves over doctrine, as opposed to making disciples. Third, the apocryphal non-canonical Gospel of Thomas, the Gospel of Mary, the Gospel of Peter, the so-called Egerton Gospel, and the Gospel of Judas were composed in the second century C.E. by no apostle or anyone associating directly with Jesus, not to mention that they all indicate that they were private manuscripts, having no earmarks that they were meant to be universal. Finally, if these heresies and their apocryphal writings were just as far-reaching as Orthodox Christianity, why are there no citations of them in the second/third century apostolic fathers? Only the Gospel of Thomas has two early third-century citations. If they were as impactful as the canonical gospels, they should have been cited as much. The early papyri do not support Walter Bauer, Robert A. Kraft, and Bart D. Ehrman's in their views of early Christianity.

evidence that they were putting up roadblocks to keep the uneducated out of their elite reading culture.

This is even further evidenced when we consider that they ignored the codex and stayed with the rolls or scrolls that were held horizontally, with the text being read vertically. The text was in "columns ranging from 4.5 to 7.0 centimetres in width, about 15–25 letters per line, left and right justification, and about 15–25 centimetres in height, with about 1.5–2.5 centimetres spacing between columns. The letters were carefully written, calligraphic in better quality manuscripts, but with no spacing between words, little or no punctuation, and no demarcation of larger sense-units. The strict right-hand justification was achieved by 'wrapping' lines (to use a computer term), ending each line either with a given word or a syllable, and continuing with the next word or syllable on the next line, the column 'organized as a tight phalanx of clear, distinct letters, each marching one after the other to form an impression of continuous flow, the letters forming a solid, narrow rectangle of written text, alternating with narrower bands of white space'." (Hill and Kruger 2012, 50)

Another feature of this elite reading culture was the fact that they cared deeply about the elegant and beautiful or artistic handwriting that was pleasing to the eyes, but not as reader-friendly as the rounded, unadorned writing in the Christian texts. Indeed, the elite reading culture cared about the accuracy of the content in their documents as well, but it took a backseat to visually stimulating handwriting. The reader had the task of bringing to life this text with no sense breaks or punctuation.

The early codex manuscripts present us a picture of early Christianity that was a book-buying, book-reading, and book-publishing culture unlike no other, as they turned to the book form, i.e., the codex, finding it handy, convenient, and portable. Matthew, Mark, Luke, John, Paul, Peter, James, and Jude were moved along by the Holy Spirit, penning their books. The writings were then delivered and distributed by a trusted traveling companion, who then read it aloud to the Christian congregation(s).

Paul in his final greeting to the Ephesians writes, "So that you also may know how I am and what I am doing, Tychicus the beloved brother and faithful minister in the Lord will tell you everything. I have sent him to you for this very purpose, that you may know how we are, and that he may encourage your hearts." (Eph. 6:21-22, ESV) Paul tells the Christians in Colossae, "Tychicus will tell you all about my activities. He is a beloved brother and faithful minister and fellow servant in the Lord. I have sent him to you for this very purpose, that you may know how we are and that he may encourage your hearts." (Col. 4:7-8, ESV) The first Christians were encouraged to read the Scriptures during their religious services and to discuss them. (1 Cor. 14:26; Eph. 5:18-19; Col. 3:16; 1 Tim. 4:13; See Matt. 24:15; Mark 13:14; Rev. 1:3)

The members of these early Christian congregations were from a wide-ranging spectrum; the poor, slaves, freedman (emancipated from slavery), male and female, old and young, children, workers, business owners, landowners, and even some from the wealthy segment of society. Generally, the powerful political leaders of the day and the very wealthy were missing from these Christian meetings. The apostle Paul exhorted Timothy, "devote yourself to the **public reading** of Scripture, to exhortation, to teaching." (1 Tim 4:13, UASV) Writing about 155 C.E., Justin Martyr says of the weekly Christian meetings, "And on the day called Sunday, all who live in cities or in the country gather together to one place, and the memoirs of the apostles or the writings of the prophets are read, as long as time permits; then, when the reader has ceased, the president verbally instructs, and exhorts to the imitation of these good things.[74]

Gamble says that Justin Martyr's words suggest what was typical in mid-second century weekly Christian meetings in Asia Minor and Rome. Scholars agree that the reading of Scripture at Christian meetings, offering an exposition of what had been read, was common and likely universal in Justin's day, the practice originating with the first-century Christians. (Gamble 1995, 151-152) By the end of the first century, it is likely that every Christian community in the then-known world had as many of the New Testament books as were available (excluding the Gospel of John, his three epistles, and the book of Revelation, since they were written between 95-98 C.E.). Also, they would have had Old Testament books as well. These congregations would have had several readers who were responsible for the congregation's library. Further, it is highly likely that many Christians themselves could read. In addition, it is likely that these assigned readers were also serving as scribes. In some cases, these readers/scribes would likely have had the same training as the Jewish Sopherim (scribes), meaning that they possessed excellent reading, copying, translating, and interpreting skills. It might even have been that these were Jewish converts to Christianity, very familiar with the synagogue practice of copying manuscripts, studying the texts, and reading and interpreting the texts. As Comfort points out, 'the relationship between scribes and readers is found in the subscription to 1 Peter and to 2 Peter in P[72], wherein both places, it says, "Peace to the one having written [i.e., the scribe] and to the one having read [i.e., the lector].' As such, the scribe of P[72] was asking for a blessing of God's peace on the scribe [presumably himself] and on the lector. As such, the scribe knew that the publication of 1 Peter and 2 Peter

---

[74] Justin Martyr, "The First Apology of Justin," in *The Apostolic Fathers with Justin Martyr and Irenaeus*, ed. Alexander Roberts, James Donaldson, and A. Cleveland Coxe, vol. 1, The Ante-Nicene Fathers (Buffalo, NY: Christian Literature Company, 1885), 186.

was dependent on the twofold process—the copying of the text and the oral reading of it."[75]

When we look at the evidence for the first three centuries of Christianity, we find that most early Christians were from a lower social stratum, a minority from the middle level, and a minute few from the upper levels of society. (Hill and Kruger 2012, 55) It would seem that the early Christian manuscripts were prepared for the early Christian reading culture. We have already spoken at length about the book form of the codex, as opposed to the roll or scroll with its continuous text. Unlike the elite reading culture that Johnson surveyed, the Christian reading culture was not aiming for what was pleasing to the eyes, i.e., elegant handwriting. The highest priority was creating a text that was accurate in content and reader-friendly. While the elite reading culture during this same period was creating texts designed to keep the uneducated out (too overwhelming for the average reader), the Christian texts were prepared in such a way that they placed fewer demands on the reader (more Christians could reach out to be readers), so as to bring this to a more diverse audience. If we are to understand fully early Christianity, the early reading culture, and their view of their text, we need to look to the early papyri and scribal activity, the patristic quotations, and any early attitudes that have been expressed about textual transmission.

Literacy in the Roman Empire and the Early Church

The question of reading, writing, and literacy levels in the Roman Empire and the early Church is not as settled or decided as secular scholarship might like us to believe. We can start by noting that there is a difference between what we deem literate today, and what the situation was in the Roman Empire and the first three centuries of the Church. Being literate today means having the ability to read and write, while literacy in the Roman Empire mainly applied to those who could read. The ability to write was not necessarily assumed.[76] Secular sources suggest that the literacy level in the Greco-Roman world was rarely if ever more than twenty percent. Scholars argue that the average was possibly not much more than ten percent in the Roman Empire. They point out that it varied within different regions, which however would be true for any period. They further argue that in the western province's literacy never rose above five percent.[77] Some Bible scholars are unfamiliar with the reading culture of early Christianity.

---

[75] Philip Comfort, *Encountering the Manuscripts: An Introduction to New Testament Paleography & Textual Criticism* (Nashville, TN: Broadman & Holman, 2005), 52.

[76] See Eric A. Havelock, The Literate Revolution in Greece and its Cultural Consequences (Princeton, N.J.: Princeton University Press, 1982), 38-59.

[77] William V. Harris, *Ancient literacy* (Harvard University Press, 1989) 328.

In many cases, the scholars fail to mention the overabundance of evidence for a literate culture between 50 B.C.E. and 325 C.E. What is more; there is considerable evidence that the early Christians' literacy rates were higher than those of the Roman Empire in general. Bible scholar Christopher D. Stanley offers us the commonly accepted misconception about the literacy level among the early Christians:

> Literacy levels were low in antiquity, access to books was limited, and most non-Jews had little or no prior knowledge of the Jewish Scriptures. Of course, Gentile Christians who had been Jewish sympathizers (Luke's "God-fearers") would have been exposed to the Jewish Scriptures, but we have no reason to think that their literacy levels differed appreciably from their contemporaries.[78]

In the Greco-Roman world, education was voluntary. Nevertheless, we do know that elementary schools were widespread. The archaeological evidence, especially the papyri, actually point to a literacy rate in the Hellenistic-Roman world that was higher than at any other time outside modern history. We have already spoken at length on the literacy level of early Christianity in the previous chapter and will briefly look at more evidence here in this chapter.

THE DAILY NEWSPAPER OF ROME

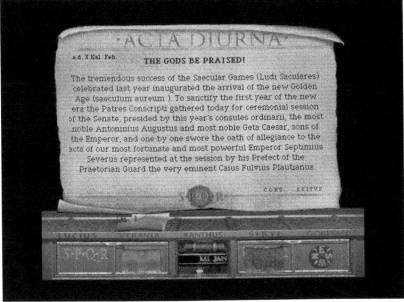

---

[78] Christopher D. Stanley, *Arguing with Scripture: The Rhetoric of Quotations in the Letters of Paul* (London; New York: T&T Clark, 2004), 3.

From the days of Gaius Octavius, who became the first emperor of Rome (thereafter known as Caesar Augustus), to almost two centuries after the execution of Christ (59 B.C.E. to 222 C.E.), the Roman Empire published and distributed a regular news publication for the city of Rome. The Latin phrase *Acta Diurna* (Daily Acts/Events or Daily Public Records) were the official notices from Rome, a sort of Daily Roman Times. Much of the news out of the city of Rome was also published broadly across the Empire as well.[79] Acta Diurna introduced the expression "publicare et propagare," meaning, "Make public and propagate." The expression was placed at the end of the news release, which was to both Roman citizens and non-citizens. There was a daily *papyrus* newspaper, which informed all who could read of the daily events. It was distributed throughout Rome, in such places as the public bathhouses,[80] as well as message boards.

Pliny the Elder (23 C.E. – 79 C.E.) was a Roman author, naturalist, and natural philosopher, as well as a naval and army commander. Pliny informs us that there were different grades of papyrus, such as the low-grade Saitic paper, so called from the city of that name in Lower Egypt, as well as the taeniotic paper, possibly from Alexandria.[81] These low-grade papyruses were likely used for the public notices, which would also explain why we have never discovered a single piece of the Acta Diurna (Daily Events). This Daily Newspaper of Rome covered such important information as royal or senatorial decrees and events, military and political news, deaths, crimes, trials, as well as economic insights. It also offered social information like wedding and divorces, births, festivals, astrology, human-interest stories, and even gossip. On this, Brian J. Wright writes,

> The Latin term *Acta* in its broadest sense means 'the things that have been done,'[82] or more simply, 'events'. Without any additional qualifiers, these events could – and did – include public and private activities; secular and sacred matters; government and civilian affairs. With additional qualifiers, these events had a narrower and even more specialized meaning. The *Acta Militaria* refers to published military events,[83] the *Acta Senatus* indicates

---

[79] Propertius 2.7.17–18; Pliny the Elder, *Naturalis historia* 35.2.11; *Epigrams* 7.17; *Epigrams* 5.5; *Tristia* 4.9.20-25; *Tristia* 4.10.130.

[80] The largest of these was the Baths of Diocletian, which could hold up to 3,000 bathers.

[81] Pliny, *Natural History*, book 13, ch. 23

[82] John Percy Vyvian Dacre and Andrew William Lintott, 'Acta', in *The Oxford Classical Dictionary*, 4th ed., ed. Simon Hornblower and Antony Spawforth (Oxford: UP, 2012), 10.

[83] The first-century papyrus PSI 13.1307 is one example. For further details, see J. F. Gilliam, 'Notes on PSI 1307 and 1308', Classical Philology 47.1 (1952), 29-31. Cf. Sergio Daris, 'Osservazioni AD alcuni papyri di carattere militare', *Aegyptus* 38 (1958), 151-58, esp. 157-58;

published senatorial events,[84] and the *Acta Triumphorum* denotes the published triumphs of emperors.[85] The main qualifier for the purposes of this study is diurna, which simply means 'daily'. Thus, the Acta Diurna represents published 'daily events'.[86] Though there are no authentic fragments of these specific kinds of acta,[87] and thus no physical features to discuss, there are ample references to them in ancient authors (again, by various nomenclature). Both Tacitus and Suetonius used these Acta as sources for information about the Empire's earlier emperors when they were writing their histories of Rome.[88] (Wright 2016)[89]

Sergio Daris, 'Note di lessico e di onomastica militare', *Aegyptus* 44 (1964), 47-51. For other examples from inscriptions and ancient authors see M. Léon Renier, *Inscriptions Romaines de l'Algérie* (Paris: Imprimerie Impériale, 1855); J. F. Gilliam, 'Some Military Papyri from Dura', in *Yale Classical Studies: Volume 11*, ed. Harry M. Hubbell (New Haven, CT: Yale University Press, 1950), 171-252, esp. 209–252.

[84] The bulletin of daily news was almost exclusively a private affair before Julius Caesar made it regular and official in 59 BC. Although private publications continued, he ordered that these occasionally published *Acta* were to be published daily for mass consumption under the authority of the government from the court reporters' notes (e.g. Seneca the Younger *Apocolocyntosis* 9). After Julius Caesar's death, a custom arose that future emperors (and their magistrates every January) were to swear to keep and respect all previous *Acta Senatus* from their predecessors (e.g. Dio Cassius 47.48; cf. 37.20); with a few exceptions (e.g. Dio Cassius 56.33). For inscriptional evidence of how emperors dealt with the *acta* of their predecessors, see Benjamin Wesley Kicks, 'The Process of Imperial Decision-Making from Augustus to Trajan' (Ph.D. dissertation, Rutgers, 2011), 86-91, the case study regarding the *Epistula Domitiani ad Falerienses*. For additional details and texts, see, among others, William Smith, William Wayte, and G. E. Marindin, eds., *A Dictionary of Greek and Roman Antiquities* (London: John Murray, 1890); Harry Thurston Peck, ed., *Harper's Dictionary of Classical Literature and Antiquities* (New York: Cooper Square, 1965), 14-15.

[85] *Pliny,* Naturalis historia. *37.6.*

[86] Too much emphasis should not be placed on the word 'daily' since it is possible that it could mean 'everyday' events, as in 'current events.'

[87] I say 'authentic' here because some forgeries have been published. For example, eleven fragments of the *Acta Diurna* were published in 1615 by Pighius, and defended by Dodwell. Though the fragments were exposed as a fifteenth century forgery (by Wesseling, Ernesti et al.), some scholars still attempted to defend their authenticity at least as far as 1844; with Lieberkühn. For more details and background to this story, see Wilhelm Sigismund Teuffel, *A History of Roman Literature: Volume One, The Republican Period*, trans. Wilhelm Wagner (London: George Bell and Sons, 1873), 381. Cf. Hermann L. G. Heinze, ' *De Spuriis Actorum Diurnorum Fragmentis Undecim: Fasciculus Prior'* (Ph.D. dissertation, University of Greifswald, 1860), 11-24; Andrew Lintott, 'Acta Antiquissima: A Week in the History of the Roman *Republic,'* Papers of the British School at Rome *54 (1986), 213-28.*

[88] A. W. Mosley, 'Historical Reporting in the Ancient World', *NTS* 12.1 (1965), 10-26.

[89] COMING FALL 2017

Brian J. Wright, *Communal Reading in the Time of Jesus: A Window into Early Christian Reading Practices* (Minneapolis: Fortress Press, 2017).

Moreover, it should be noted that the Roman *Acta Diurna* (Daily Acts/Events or Daily Public Records) was not the only newspaper of its kind during this period of 59 B.C.E. to about 222 C.E. Around 225 C.E., we find a Roman official ordering several mayors in the Hermopolite region of Egypt to post copies of his letter 'in well-known places so that all may be aware of his pronouncements' (P. Oxy. 2705). When we consider these things on face value, they indicate that notices were being written so that the populace could be updated about current affairs by reading them, not having them read to them.

We can conclude from these facts that reading, writing, and the dissemination of information was far more extensive than has long been held, with a much higher basic literacy level, which then adds to our understanding of the writing, publication, and distribution of the Greek New Testament letters that were read in the Christian congregations throughout the Roman Empire (Col. 4:46; 1 Thess. 5:27; 1 Tim. 4:13; Jam. 1:1; Rev. 1:3). Evidence indicates a far higher level of basic literacy throughout the Roman Empire than thought, as well as Christians who originated primarily as Jewish converts who prided themselves on their ability to read and write, coupled with a message that they were commanded to evangelize to the whole inhabited earth (Matt. 24:14; 28:19-20; Ac 1:8). As a result, it is no exaggeration to say that Christians were able to take over the Roman power that had a military unlike any other up to that time, by growing the faith in a pagan world. They went from 120 disciples at Pentecost in 33 C.E. to over one million disciples about a century later.

Jewish education under this same period was significantly different as to the content, though in some respects they had stages similar to Greco-Roman education. The primary objective of Jewish education was knowledge of the Hebrew Scriptures. The parents were the first and primary educators of their Jewish children, especially their earlier elementary education in reading, writing, and understanding the Torah (2 Tim 1:5; 3:14-15). We read briefly of young Jesus as he grew up in Nazareth. He would have received his education from three sources: Joseph, Jesus' stepfather, would have played a major role in his education. Paul said that young Timothy was trained in "the sacred writings" by his mother, Eunice, and his grandmother Lois (2 Tim. 1:5; 3:15). Certainly, if Timothy received education in the Scriptures from his mother though his Father was a Greek (Acts 16:1), no doubt Jesus did as well from Joseph during his childhood. Jesus would have also received education in the Scriptures from the attendant at the synagogue, which was a place of instruction.

We know that another source of knowledge and wisdom for Jesus was the divine Father. Jesus said, "My teaching is not mine, but his who sent me," i.e., the Father (John 7:16, UASV). Mark 1:22 reads, "And they were **astounded at his teaching,** for he taught them as **one who had authority,** and not as the scribes" (UASV).

The third century Rabbi Judah b. Tema outlines the stages of Jewish education. "At five years old *one is fit* for the Scripture, at ten years for Mishnah, at thirteen for the commandments, at fifteen for Talmud, at eighteen for marriage, at twenty for retribution (a vocation)."[90] Again, the home was the primary place of Jewish education in reading, writing, and the memorization of the Hebrew Scriptures. In the first century, there were a number of primary schools in Jerusalem, but it was not until the second century C.E. that they grew more numerous outside of Jerusalem. Children began their studies as early as age 4-5 in primary school **Beth Sefer** ("house of reading"). Both boys and girls could attend the class in the synagogue, or in an adjoining room. (Ferguson 2003, 112)

First-century Jewish historian Josephus (30-100 C.E.) said of the Jewish life, "Our principle care of all is this, to educate our children well."[91] In speaking of what the Mosaic Law commands, he wrote, "It also commands us **to bring those children up in learning** and to exercise them in the laws, and make them acquainted with the acts of their predecessors, in order to their imitation of them, and that they may be nourished up in the laws from their infancy, and might neither transgress them, nor yet have any pretense for their ignorance of them."[92] We have even more texts, especially from the later Rabbis, which make similar statements. If we take these comments at face value, it is evidence of a reading culture among the Jews that is surely higher than that of the Roman Empire, which was certainly higher than the secular sources claim.

Five hundred years from now, what if we were to ask the historian, "how well could the Amish in America read and write?" It would be difficult to be accurate because they teach themselves. It is 2017, and they have one-room county schoolhouses with chalkboards, which remind us of the pioneer days in America, or some Laura Ingalls Wilder novels. The historian might find slate chalkboards and tablets that are blank, so they could only guess at the level of the reading and writing. Would it surprise anyone that this highly religious community, who value the ability to read their religious books, very similar to the first-century Jewish community,

---

[90] Robert Henry Charles, ed., *Pseudepigrapha of the Old Testament*, vol. 2 (Oxford: Clarendon Press, 1913), 710.

[91] Flavius Josephus and William Whiston, *The Works of Josephus: Complete and Unabridged* (Peabody: Hendrickson, 1987).

[92] Flavius Josephus and William Whiston, *The Works of Josephus: Complete and Unabridged* (Peabody: Hendrickson, 1987).

can speak two to three languages (Dutch or German and English), as well as read and write well?

When we see signs of a reading environment, it suggests a populace with at least a basic reading level. In the first-century Roman Empire, there were hundreds of public inscriptions of dedications, imperial decrees, lists of names, laws, and regulation, and even directions. Even the gravestones of the time were meant to do more than mark the name of the person. Some had lines of poetry; others had threats and curses for any who even thought of robbing the graves. The painstaking time taken to publish these things indicates the expectation that the public is able to read them, even lowly grave robbers.

We have almost a half million papyrus documents (likely there were millions more that did not survive) in garbage dumps in the dry sands of Oxyrhynchus, Egypt. This is but one city in the entirety of the Roman Empire. Are we to believe that Oxyrhynchus is the exception, and some of the biggest cities, such as Rome, Corinth, Athens, Pergamum, Ephesus, Smyrna, Antioch, Jerusalem, Alexandria, and Carthage, which numbered anywhere from one hundred thousand to over a million in their population, did not have equal or greater writings discarded in their dumps? Then we should consider the temples and the libraries that boasted of tens of thousands of books. Reportedly, by the first century C.E., the Alexandrian library housed one million scrolls. In fact, Mark Antony took 200,000 scrolls from the library at Pergamum to replenish the Alexandrian library for Cleopatra. Because of moisture damage and they're being written on perishable material, we cannot discover the documents of these centers of education as we have in the dry sands of Egypt. Yet, should we for a moment believe that their garbage dumps saw any fewer books than were discovered at Oxyrhynchus, Egypt?

We have such great quantities of written material as to suggest a much higher literacy level than most are willing to accept. Only ten percent of the Oxyrhynchus papyri have been investigated, but they offer insight that indicates a more literate society, not less. Many men and women who wrote had scribes pen their words, indicating that they were literate by what they said, while their signatures at the end of letters show only that some of them had poor penmanship. We should not judge their literacy level by the limitations of their penmanship. We must remember, in that period, that it was reading that dictated one's level of literacy.

We also have the Vindolanda Writing Tablets. "The writing tablets are perhaps Vindolanda's greatest discovery and have been previously voted by experts and the public alike as 'Britain's Top Treasure.' Delicate, wafer-thin slivers of wood covered in spidery ink writing, the tablets were found in the oxygen-free deposits on and around the floors of the deeply buried early wooden forts at Vindolanda and are the oldest surviving handwritten documents in Britain. Like postcards from the past, the tablets allow a rare insight into the real lives of people living and working at Vindolanda near Hadrian's Wall nearly 2000 years ago. They provide a fascinating and compelling insight into private and military lives from a very different time but are hauntingly familiar, covering matters from birthdays through to underpants! Have we changed that much in two millennia?"[93]

The Vindolanda Writing Tablets, like the papyri in the dry sands of Oxyrhynchus, offer us insights into the literacy of the Roman officers who we would expect to be literate but also indicate the literacy of the low-ranking soldiers, wives, friends, and servants. The handwriting of these tablets ranges from writing that is barely legible, to the professional hand. We have to ask ourselves the same question: if these common soldiers had some basic writing skills, some even to the document hand level, and even a few at the professional hand, what are we to think of the literacy level of the Roman Empire?[94] Must we keep disputing the obvious? If the evidence suggests, as it does, a far higher literacy level than a mere 5-10 percent throughout the Roman Empire, what are we to expect from the Christian community that grew out of the Jewish populace that so valued reading, writing, and memorization, that was commissioned with evangelizing the entire inhabited earth?

---

[93] Vindolanda Writing Tablets - Roman Vindolanda and Roman ..., https://www.vindolanda.com/roman-vindolanda/writing-tablets (accessed March 23, 2017).

[94] (Bowman 1998, 82-99)

CHAPTER 4 The Early Christian's View of the Integrity of the Greek New Testament Books

Ehrman wrote: We appear, then, to have a paradoxical situation in early Christianity. This was a bookish religion, with writings of all kinds proving to be of uppermost importance to almost every aspect of the faith. Yet most people could not read these writings. How do we account for this paradox? In fact, the matter is not all that strange if we recall what was hinted at earlier, that communities of all kinds throughout antiquity generally **used the services of the literate for the sake of the illiterate.** For in the ancient world "reading" a book did not mean, usually, reading it to oneself; it meant reading it aloud, to others. One could be said to have read a book when in fact one had heard it read by others. There seems to be no way around the conclusion that books—as important as they were to the early Christian movement—were almost always read aloud in social settings, such as in settings of worship. **Misquoting Jesus (pp. 41-42).**

Paul was the author of fourteen letters within the Greek New Testament.[95] Paul's earliest letters were 1 Thessalonians (50 C.E.), 2 Thessalonians (51 C.E.), Galatians (50-52 C.E.), 1&2 Corinthians (55 C.E.), Romans (56 C.E.), Ephesians, Philippians, Colossians, Philemon (60-61 C.E.), Hebrews (61 C.E.), 1 Timothy, and Titus (61-64 C.E.). 2 Timothy was penned last, about 65 C.E. This means that the apostle Peter could have been aware of at least thirteen out of fourteen Pauline letters at the time of his penning 2 Peter in 64 C.E., in which he writes,

2 Peter 3:15-16 Updated American Standard Version (UASV)

[15] and regard the patience of our Lord as salvation; just as also **our beloved brother Paul,** according to the wisdom given him, wrote to you, [16] as also **in all his letters,** speaking in them of these things, in which are some things hard to understand, which the untaught and unstable distort, as they do also **the rest of the** Scriptures, to their own destruction. [bold is mine]

---

[95] This author accepts that Paul is the author of the book of Hebrews. For further information see the CPH Blog article, Who Authored the Book of Hebrews: A Defense for Pauline Authorship

https://christianpublishinghouse.co/2016/11/02/who-authored-the-book-of-hebrews-a-defense-for-pauline-authorship/

Notice that Peter speaks of Paul's letters, referring to them as a collection. Thus, Peter is our earliest reference to Paul's letters that were gathered together as a collection. Peter also states that the letters were viewed as being on equal footing with the Hebrew Scriptures when he says that "the untaught and unstable distort" Paul's letters as they do "the rest of the Scriptures." Günther Zuntz was certain that there was a full collection of Pauline letters by 100 C.E. (Zuntz 1953, 271-272) In 65 C.E.[96] Peter could say of Paul, "in all his letters," and his readers would know who Paul was and of Paul's many letters. Also, his readers would have accepted the idea that Paul's letters were equal to the Hebrew Scriptures, which indicates that they were being collected among the churches.

1 Timothy 5:18 Updated American Standard Version (UASV)

[18] For **the Scripture says,** "You shall not muzzle the ox while he is threshing," and "The laborer is worthy of his wages." [bold is mine]

Notice that Paul says, "the Scripture says" (λέγει γὰρ ἡ γραφή), just before he quotes from two different Scriptures. The first half of the quote, "You shall not muzzle the ox while he is threshing," is from Deuteronomy 25:4. The Second half, "The laborer is worthy of his wages," seems to be from Luke 10:7. Here Paul is doing exactly what Peter did in the above at 2 Peter 3:16, placing the Gospel of Luke on par with the Hebrew Scriptures.

---

[96] 2 Peter generally is wrongly dated to about 100-125 C.E. (e.g. J. N. D. Kelly, A *Commentary on the Epistles of Peter and of Jude: Introduction and Commentary*; J. D. Mayor, the *Epistle of St. Jude and the Epistle of Second Peter*; D. J. Harrington, Jude and 2 Peter). Other Bible scholars date 2 Peter to 80-90 C.E. (e.g., R. Bauckham *Jude, 2 Peter*; B. Reicke, *The Epistle of James, Peter and Jude*). We should begin with a date of about 64 C.E. for 2 Peter. Then, the Greek makes it apparent that the author is a contemporary of the apostle Paul because it suggests that Paul is speaking to the churches at the time of this writing. The Greek ἐν πάσαις ἐπιστολαῖς λαλῶν ("*in all letters [he] speaking*") strongly implies such. The author of the document says that he is "Simon Peter, a bond-servant and apostle of Jesus Christ" (2 Pet. 1:1, NASB). He refers to this as "the second letter I am writing to you" (2 Pet. 3:1, NASB). The author clearly states that he was an eyewitness to the transfiguration of Jesus Christ, at which only Peter, James, and John were present (Matt. 17:1-13; Mark 9:1-13; Lu 9:28–36; See 2 Pet. 1:16-21). The author mentions that Jesus foretold his death, "knowing that the laying aside of my *earthly* dwelling is imminent, as also our Lord Jesus Christ has made clear to me" (2 Pet. 1:14; John 21:18, 19.). The argument that the style is different from 1 Peter is moot because the subject and the purpose in writing were different. The implication of the phrases "in all *his* letters" and "the rest of the Scriptures" is that many of Paul's letters (thirteen of them) were viewed as "Scripture" by the first-century Christian congregation and should not be "twisted" or "distorted." In addition, Second Peter was regarded as canonical by a number of authorities prior to the Third Council of Carthage (i.e., Irenaeus of Asia Minor c. 180 C.E., Origen of Alexandria c. 230 C.E., Eusebius of Palestine c. 320 C.E., Cyril of Jerusalem c. 348 C.E., Athanasius of Alexandria c. 367 C.E., Epiphanius of Palestine c. 368 C.E., Gregory Nazianzus of Asia Minor c. 370 C.E., Philaster of Italy c. 383 C.E., Jerome of Italy c. 394 C.E., and Augustine of N. Africa c. 397 C.E.).

Some have tried to dismiss 1 Timothy 5:18 by saying that Paul was just quoting oral tradition, but that can hardly be the case when he says, "**the Scripture says,**" which requires a written source and it happens that we have such a source: The Gospel of Luke. Luke was written about 56-58 C.E. in Caesarea, and First Timothy was written about 61-64 C.E. in Macedonia. Then, there is the fact that Luke was a faithful traveling companion and co-worker of the apostle Paul. Luke was one of Paul's closest traveling companions from about 49 C.E. until the time of Paul's martyrdom. The Gospel of Luke was written just after the two of them returned from Paul's third missionary journey, while Paul was imprisoned for two years at Caesarea, after which Paul was transferred to Rome in about 58 C.E. Other "scholars believe Luke wrote his Gospel and the book of Acts while in Rome with Paul during the apostle's first Roman imprisonment. Apparently, Luke remained nearby or with Paul also during the apostle's second Roman imprisonment. Shortly before his martyrdom, Paul wrote that 'only Luke is with me' (2 Tim. 4:11)."[97] Either way, Luke was a very close co-worker with Paul for almost twenty years. In fact, Luke's writing shows evidence of Paul's influence (Lu 22:19-20; 1 Cor. 11:23-25). We must remember that Luke was a first-rate historian, as well as being inspired. He says that he "investigated everything carefully from the beginning, to write it out" (Lu 1:3). Regardless, the apostle Paul had access to Luke's Gospel for many years before penning 1 Timothy, where it appears that he made a direct quote from what we know now as Luke 10:7, referring to it as Scripture.

The use of the well-known phrase, "**it is written,**" further confirms the authority of the New Testament books. We understand that when this phrase is used, it is a reference to the Scriptures of God, the inspired Word of God. It should be noted that the gospel writers themselves use the phrase "**it is written**" some forty times when referring to the inspired Hebrew Scriptures.

The *Epistle of Barnabas* dates after the destruction of the Second Temple in 70 C.E., but it dates before the Bar Kochba Revolt of 132 C.E. At Barn 4:14, we read, "let us be on guard lest we should be found to be, as **it is written,** 'many called, but few chosen.'"[98] Immediately after using the phrase "it is written," Barnabas quotes Jesus' words found in Matthew 22:14, "For many are called, but few are chosen."

The *Letter of Polycarp to the Philippians* dates to about 110 C.E. Poly 12:1 reads, "For I am convinced that you are all well trained in the sacred

---

[97] T. R. McNeal, "Luke," ed. Chad Brand et al., *Holman Illustrated Bible Dictionary* (Nashville, TN: Holman Bible Publishers, 2003), 1056–1057.

[98] Michael William Holmes, *The Apostolic Fathers: Greek Texts and English Translations*, Third ed. (Grand Rapids, MI: Baker Books, 2007), 373.

Scriptures and that nothing is hidden from you (something not granted to me). Only, as it is said in these Scriptures, 'be angry but do not sin,' and 'do not let the sun set on your anger.' Blessed is the one who remembers this, which I believe to be the case with you."[99] The first phrase "be angry but do not sin" is a quotation from Ephesians 4:26, where Paul is quoting Psalm 4:5. However, the latter part of the quote, "do not let the sun set on your anger" is Paul's words alone. It is clear here that Polycarp is referring to both the Psalm and the book of Ephesians when he writes, "it is said in these Scriptures."

Clement of Rome (c. 30-100 C.E.) penned two books: we focus on the second, *An Ancient Christian Sermon* (2 Clement), which dates to about 98-100 C.E. II Clement 2:4 reads, "And another Scripture says, 'I have not come to call the righteous, but sinners.'"[100] Here Clement is quoting Mark 2:17 or Matt. 9:13, which is likely the earliest quotation of a New Testament passage as Scripture. In the Gospel of Mark and Matthew, Jesus is quoted as saying, "I came not to call the righteous, but sinners" (ESV). II Clement 14:2 reads, "But if we do not do the will of the Lord, we will belong to those of whom the Scripture says, 'My house has become a robbers' den'" which is a quote from Matthew 21:13, Mark 11:17, and Luke 19:46, where Jesus himself is quoting Jeremiah 7:11 after cleansing the temple of greedy merchants.

Indeed, we can garner from this brief look at early Christianity's view of Scriptures that the New Testament books were placed on the same footing as the Hebrew Scriptures quite early, starting with the words of Peter about the apostle Paul's letters. Again, Justin Martyr tells us that at the early Christian meetings "the memoirs of the apostles or the writings of the prophets are read, as long as time permits; then, when the reader has ceased, the president verbally instructs and exhorts to the imitation of these good things" (1 Apology 67).[101] Ignatius of Antioch (c. 35-108 C.E.), Theophilus of Antioch (d. 182 C.E.), and Tertullian (c. 155-240 C.E.) also spoke of the Prophets, the Law, and the Gospels as equally authoritative.

---

[99] Ibid., 294.

[100] Ibid., 141.

[101] Justin Martyr, "The First Apology of Justin," in *The Apostolic Fathers with Justin Martyr and Irenaeus*, ed. Alexander Roberts, James Donaldson, and A. Cleveland Coxe, vol. 1, The Ante-Nicene Fathers (Buffalo, NY: Christian Literature Company, 1885), 186.

The Early Christian View of the Integrity of the Greek New Testament Originals

If the early Christians' view of the New Testament books were on the same footing as the Hebrew Scriptures, then we would see them guarding the integrity of the New Testament in the same way the Old Testament authors and the scribes in ancient Israel guarded the Hebrew Old Testament.

Deuteronomy 4:2 Updated American Standard Version (UASV)	Deuteronomy 12:32 Updated American Standard Version (UASV)
[2] You shall **not add to** the word which I am commanding you, **nor take away** from it, that you may keep the commandments of Jehovah your God which I command you.	[32] "Everything that I command you, you shall be careful to do; you shall **not add to** nor **take away from** it.

There certainly were severe consequences, even death to some, if scribes or copyists were to add to or take away from God's Word, disregarding these warnings. Eugene H. Merrill observes, "There is a principle of canonization here as well in that nothing is to be added to or subtracted from the word. This testifies to the fact that God himself is the originator of the covenant text and only he is capable of determining its content and extent."[102]

Proverbs 30:6 Updated American Standard Version (UASV)

[6] **Do not add to** his words,
lest he reprove you and you be found a liar.

This is an ongoing command about God's words given to the Israelites in Deuteronomy 4:2 and 12:32. There is no need to add to or take away from God's Word, for it is sufficient. Duane A. Garrett tells us that "Verse 6 is an injunction against adding to God's words similar to the injunctions found in Deut. 12:32 and Rev 22:18. It is noteworthy that this text does not warn the reader not to reject or take away from divine revelation; it is more concerned that no one supplements it. This is therefore not a warning to the unbelieving interpreter but rather to the believer. The temptation is to improve on the text if not by actually adding new material then by interpreting it in ways that make more of a passage's teaching than is really there. It is what Paul called "going beyond what is written" (1 Cor. 4:6).[103]

---

[102] Eugene H. Merrill, *Deuteronomy*, vol. 4, The New American Commentary (Nashville: Broadman & Holman Publishers, 1994), 229.

[103] Duane A. Garrett, *Proverbs, Ecclesiastes, Song of Songs*, vol. 14, The New American Commentary (Nashville: Broadman & Holman Publishers, 1993), 237.

The attitude of the Jewish people and their Hebrew Scriptures can be summed up in the words of Josephus, the first-century (37 – c.100 C.E.) Jewish historian, who wrote, "We have given practical proof of our reverence for our own Scriptures. For, although such long ages have now passed, no one has ventured either to add, or to remove, or to alter a syllable; and it is an instinct with every Jew, from the day of his birth, to regard them as the decrees of God, to abide by them, and, if need be, cheerfully to die for them."[104] The longstanding view of the Jews toward the Hebrew Scriptures is very important, especially in view of what the apostle Paul wrote to the Roman Christian congregation. The apostle says, the Jews "were entrusted with the sayings[105] of God" (Rom. 3:1-2).

Galatians 3:15 Updated American Standard Version (UASV)

[15] Brothers, I speak according to man:[106] even though it is only a man's covenant, yet when it has been ratified, **no one sets it aside or adds conditions to it.**

The letter from Paul to Galatians was penned about **50-52 C.E.** Here Paul's words in dealing with the covenant to Abraham and his descendants echo the words from the Law of Moses at Deuteronomy 4:2, when he says, "no one sets it aside or adds conditions to it," i.e., "not add to... nor take away." The covenant word of God was not to be altered.

Revelation 22:18-19 Updated American Standard Version (UASV)

[18] I testify to everyone who hears the words of the prophecy of this book: if anyone **adds to them,** God will add to him the plagues which are written in this book; [19] and if anyone **takes away from** the words of the book of this prophecy, God will take away his part from the tree of life and out of the holy city, which are written in this book.

The letter from John to the seven congregations was penned about 95 C.E. Kistemaker and Hendriksen write, "The solemn warning not to add to or detract from the words of this book is common in ancient literature. For instance, Moses warns the Israelites not to add to or subtract from the decrees and laws God gave them (Deut. 4:2; 12:32). This formula was attached to documents much the same as copyright laws protect modern manuscripts. In addition, curses were added in the form of a conditional sentence, 'If anyone adds or takes away anything from this book, a curse

---

[104] Josephus, *The Life/Against Apion*, vol. 1, LCL, ed. by H. St. J. Thackeray (Cambridge, MA: Harvard University Press, 1976), pp. 177–181.

[105] **Sayings:** (Gr. *logia, on* [only in the plural]) A saying or message, usually short, especially divine, gathered into a collection–Acts 7:38; Romans 3:2; Hebrews 5:12; 1 Peter 4:11.

[106] Or *in terms of human relations*; or *according to a human perspective*; or *using a human illustration*

will rest upon him.' Paul wrote a similar condemnation when he told the Galatians that if anyone preached a gospel which was not the gospel of Christ, 'let him be eternally condemned' (Gal. 1:6–8). Now Jesus pronounces a curse on anyone who distorts his message."[107]

The Didache (The Teaching of the Twelve Apostles) dates to about 100 C.E. At 4:13, it reads, "You must not forsake the Lord's commandments, but must guard what you have received, neither adding nor subtracting anything."[108] This author is drawing on the command in Deuteronomy 4:2 and 12:32.[109] The point here is that while the author makes use of "the Lord" (i.e., Jehovah, that is, the Father) in Deut. 4:2, 12:32, he is actually referring to Jesus' teaching found in the Gospels. Therefore, the Gospels and more specifically Jesus' teaching are equal to the Hebrew Scriptures.

Papias of Hierapolis about 135 C.E. records what he had to tell about the details surrounding the personal life and ministry of each of the apostles. Papias 3:3-4 says, "I will not hesitate to set down ... everything I carefully learned then from the elders and carefully remembered, guaranteeing their truth. For unlike most people I did not enjoy those who have a great deal to say, but those who teach the truth. Nor did I enjoy those who recall someone else's commandments, but those who remember the commandments given by the Lord to the faith and proceeding from the truth itself. And if by chance someone who had been a follower of the elders should come my way, I inquired about the words of the elders— what Andrew or Peter said, or Philip, or Thomas or James, or John or Matthew or any other of the Lord's disciples."[110]

Papias says of Mark's Gospel: "Mark, having become Peter's interpreter, wrote down accurately everything he remembered." Further confirming the Gospel's accuracy, Papias continues: "Consequently Mark did nothing wrong in writing down some things as he remembered them, for he **made it his one concern not to omit anything** which he heard **or to make any false statement in** them."[111] This is a clear reference to Deuteronomy 4:2 while referencing Mark's Gospel, again showing that Christians viewed the New Testament books as being equal to the Hebrew

---

[107] Simon J. Kistemaker and William Hendriksen, *Exposition of the Book of Revelation*, vol. 20, New Testament Commentary (Grand Rapids: Baker Book House, 1953–2001), 594.

[108] Michael William Holmes, *The Apostolic Fathers: Greek Texts and English Translations*, Third ed. (Grand Rapids, MI: Baker Books, 2007), 351.

[109] (LXX 13:1.)

[110] Michael William Holmes, *The Apostolic Fathers: Greek Texts and English Translations*, Third ed. (Grand Rapids, MI: Baker Books, 2007), 735.

[111] Ibid, 739-40.

Scriptures. Papias offers testimony that Matthew initially penned his Gospel in the Hebrew language. Papias says, "So Matthew composed the oracles in the Hebrew language, and each person interpreted them as best he could."[112] As the overseer of Hierapolis in Asia Minor, Papias was in a position to enquire and carefully learn from the elders throughout the church at the time, establishing the authenticity and divine inspiration of the New Testament. Sadly, though, only scanty fragments of the writings of Papias survived.

The *Epistle of Barnabas*, dated about 130 C.E., declares, "You shall guard what you have received, **neither adding nor subtracting** anything" (Barn 19:11).[113] Here again, Barnabas is drawing on Deuteronomy 4:2 as he expresses his concern about the Word of God, as he speaks about "the way of light" in chapter 19 of his letter, making multiple references to New Testament teachings and principles.

Dionysius of Corinth wrote in about 170 C.E. about those who had dared to alter his own writings. He writes, "For I wrote letters when the brethren requested me to write. And these letters the apostles of the devil have filled with tares [false information], **taking away some things and adding others**, for whom a woe is in store. It is not wonderful, then, if some have attempted to adulterate the Lord's writings when they have formed designs against those which are not such."[114] Here Dionysius is referring to Deuteronomy 4:2 and 12:32, noting the curse or a woe that is in store for altering his own writings, and all the more so for daring to alter the Scriptures themselves. The reference to adulterating "the Lord's writings" is a reference to the New Testament writings – "A probable, though not exclusive, reference to Marcion, for he was by no means the only one of that age that interpolated and mutilated the works of the apostles to fit his theories. Apostolic works—true and false—circulated in great numbers, and were made the basis for the speculations and moral requirements of many of the heretical schools of the second century."[115]

---

[112] Ibid, 741.

[113] Ibid, 437.

[114] Dionysius of Corinth, "Fragments from a Letter to the Roman Church," in *Fathers of the Third and Fourth Centuries: The Twelve Patriarchs, Excerpts and Epistles, the Clementina, Apocrypha, Decretals, Memoirs of Edessa and Syriac Documents, Remains of the First Ages*, ed. Alexander Roberts, James Donaldson, and A. Cleveland Coxe, trans. B. P. Pratten, vol. 8, The Ante-Nicene Fathers (Buffalo, NY: Christian Literature Company, 1886), 765.

[115] Philip Schaff and Henry Wace, eds., *Eusebius: Church History, Life of Constantine the Great, and Oration in Praise of Constantine*, vol. 1, A Select Library of the Nicene and Post-Nicene Fathers of the Christian Church, Second Series (New York: Christian Literature Company, 1890).

If there were no big concern over the integrity of the New Testament originals, we would not see early church leaders showing such concern. The principle of not adding nor taking away found in Deuteronomy 4:2 and 12:32 can be applied to just one word, or even a single number in the case of Irenaeus in about 180 C.E., who complained about the number 666 found in Revelation 13:18 that had been changed to 616. Irenaeus wrote, "Such, then, being the state of the case, and this number being found in all the most approved and ancient copies [of the Apocalypse], and those men who saw John face to face bearing their testimony [to it]; while reason also leads us to conclude that the number of the name of the beast, [if reckoned] according to the Greek mode of calculation by [the value of] the letters contained in it, will amount to six hundred and sixty and six."[116] The passage ἐν πᾶσι τοῖς σπουδαίοις καὶ ἀρχαίοις ἀντιγράφοις ("in all the most approved and ancient copies") shows that by then the autographs of the New Testament were not available, with various readings creeping into the manuscripts of the canonical books.

Irenaeus went on to let those guilty of willfully adding to or taking away from the Scriptures know that there will be severe punishment. He wrote, "Now, as regards those who have done this in simplicity, and without evil intent, we are at liberty to assume that pardon will be granted them by God. But as for those who, for the sake of vainglory, lay it down for certain that names containing the spurious number are to be accepted, and affirm that this name, hit upon by themselves, is that of him who is to come; such persons shall not come forth without loss, because they have led into error both themselves and those who confided in them. Now, in the first place, it is loss to wander from the truth, and to imagine that as being the case which is not; then again, as there shall be no light punishment [inflicted] upon him who either adds or subtracts anything from the Scripture."[117] Here Irenaeus is referring to John's warning in Revelation 22:18.

Again, the *Letter of Polycarp to the Philippians,* dating to about 110 C.E., reads at 7:1, "For everyone who does not confess that Jesus Christ has come in the flesh is antichrist [cf. 1 John 4:2-3]; and whoever does not acknowledge the testimony of the cross is of the devil [cf. 1 John 3:8]; and whoever twists the sayings of the Lord to suit his own sinful desires and claims that there is neither resurrection nor judgment—well, that person is

---

[116] Irenaeus of Lyons, "Irenæus Against Heresies," in *The Apostolic Fathers with Justin Martyr and Irenaeus,* ed. Alexander Roberts, James Donaldson, and A. Cleveland Coxe, vol. 1, The Ante-Nicene Fathers (Buffalo, NY: Christian Literature Company, 1885), 558.

[117] Irenaeus of Lyons, "Irenæus Against Heresies," in *The Apostolic Fathers with Justin Martyr and Irenaeus,* ed. Alexander Roberts, James Donaldson, and A. Cleveland Coxe, vol. 1, The Ante-Nicene Fathers (Buffalo, NY: Christian Literature Company, 1885), 559.

the first-born of Satan."[118] Of course, "the sayings of the Lord" come from the Gospels. Therefore, Polycarp was declaring a warning to anyone who would alter the Gospels. Some would argue that Polycarp was referring to oral traditions when he used the term "the sayings of the Lord" (τὰ λόγια τοῦ κυρίου), but this simply is not the case, since in the next verse he refers to these "sayings" (κυρίου) again and then quotes Matthew 6:13 and 26:41, where we find Matthew recording Jesus' sayings.

We could cite much more quotations from early church leaders about their concern for the integrity of the New Testament originals being preserved. However, we can see from our limited look at early Christianity's view of the Scriptures that the New Testament books were placed on the same footing as the Hebrew Scriptures from the very beginning. When we look at the first three centuries of Christianity, we find that the manuscripts were prepared for the reading culture of Christians, who placed the highest priority on disseminating a text that was accurate in content and reader-friendly. The Christian texts were prepared in such a way as to place the least demand on the reader, in order to bring the Scriptures to a more diverse audience.

Clearly, both Paul and Peter showed concern for their writings, as well as equating NT books other than their own with the Hebrew Scriptures in authority. Early on, the church leaders were very concerned about preserving the integrity of the original, down to the individual words. The papyri of the first three centuries after Christ **provides evidence** that most scribes (copyists) also cared about preserving the integrity of their exemplars and did not seek to change or alter the wording. On the other hand, we would be misleading others and ourselves if we were to deny that a small minority of the copyists did freely choose to make alterations–as Colwell said for example, that the scribe of P[45] worked "without any intention of exactly reproducing his source. He writes with great freedom, harmonizing, smoothing out, substituting almost whimsically." However, the scribe who worked on P[75] was a "disciplined scribe who writes with the intention of being careful and accurate." Then again, Colwell said that P[66] reflects "a scribe working with the intention of making a good copy, falling into careless errors, ... but also under the control of some other person, or second standard, ... It shows the supervision of a foreman, or a scribe turned proofreader."[119]

---

[118] Michael William Holmes, *The Apostolic Fathers: Greek Texts and English Translations*, Third ed. (Grand Rapids, MI: Baker Books, 2007), 289.

[119] Ernest Colwell, "Method in Evaluating Scribal Habits: A Study of P45, P66, P75," in *Studies in Methodology in Textual Criticism of the New Testament*, New Testament Tools and Studies 9 (Leiden: Brill, 1969), 114–21.

Generally speaking, the early scribes were very concerned about the accuracy of their copying, but while some were more successful than others, every one of them–due to human imperfection–made some transcriptional errors at times which were **unintentional** (Matt. 27:11; Mark 6:51; 10:40; Rom. 5:1; Eph. 1:15; 1 Thess. 2:7; Heb. 12:15). We can also attribute human imperfection to **intentional changes**, *purposeful* scribal alterations, such as *conflation* (Luke 24:53; John 1:34; Rom. 3:32), *interpolation* (Mark 9:29; Lu 23:19, 34; Rom. 8:1; 1 Cor. 15:51), and attempts to clarify the meaning of a text (1 Cor. 3:3) or to enhance a doctrinal position (1 John 5:7).

We can say that **on the whole**, the early church leaders valued the integrity of the original and the scribes valued the integrity of the exemplars which they were copying. In fact, the high value placed on the integrity of the original ironically led to some erroneous changes because scribes were prone at times to correct what they believed to be mistakes within the sacred text. Many modern textual scholars will tell their readers that the early copying period was "'free,' 'wild,' 'in a state of flux,' 'chaotic,' 'a turbid textual morass.'" (Hill and Kruger 2012, 10) The truth was actually the opposite. The church leaders valued the originals above all else, and the scribes saw their exemplars as master copies of those originals and reverentially feared to make any mistakes.

The goal of textual scholarship since the days of Erasmus in the sixteenth century has been to get back to the original, preserving the exact wording of the original twenty-seven New Testament books penned by Matthew, Mark, Luke, John, James, Jude, Peter, and Paul. However, this has not always proved to be the case with recent scholarship. Philip W. Comfort has been one of the leading outspoken proponents of the traditional goal of reconstructing the exact wording of the originals, and I quote the following observation by Comfort at length:

> The time gap between the autographs and the earliest extant copies is quite close—no more than 100 years for most of the books of the New Testament. Thus, we are in a good position to recover most of the original wording of the Greek New Testament. Such optimism was held by the well-known textual critics of the nineteenth century—most notably, Samuel Tregelles, B. F. Westcott, and F. J. A. Hort, who, although acknowledging that we may never recover all of the original text of the New Testament books with absolute certainty, believed that the careful work of textual criticism could bring us extremely close. In the twentieth century, two eminent textual critics, Bruce Metzger and Kurt Aland, affirmed this same purpose, and were instrumental in the production of the two critical editions of the Greek New Testament that are widely used today.

Tregelles, Hort, Metzger, and Aland, as well as Constantine von Tischendorf, the nineteenth-century scholar who famously discovered Codex Sinaiticus, all provided histories of the transmission of the New Testament text and methodologies for recovering the original wording. Their views of textual criticism were derived from their actual experience of working with manuscripts and doing textual criticism in preparing critical editions of the Greek New Testament. Successive generations of scholars, working with ever-increasing quantities of manuscripts (especially earlier ones) and refining their methodologies, have continued with the task of recovering the original wording of the Greek New Testament.

By contrast, a certain number of textual critics in recent years have abandoned the notion that the original wording of the Greek New Testament can ever be recovered. Let us take, for example, Bart Ehrman (author of *The Orthodox Corruption of Scripture*) and David Parker (author of *The Living Text of the Gospels*). Having analyzed their positions, J. K. Elliott writes, "Both [men] emphasize the living and therefore changing text of the New Testament and the needlessness and inappropriateness of trying to establish one immutable original text. The changeable text in all its variety is what we textual critics should be displaying" (1999, 17). Elliott then speaks for himself on the matter: "Despite my own published work in trying to prove the originality of the text in selected areas of textual variation, ... I agree that the task of trying to establish the original words of the original authors with 100% certainty is impossible. More dominant in text critics' thinking now is the need to plot the changes in the history of the text" (1999, 18).

Not one textual critic could or would ever say that any of the critical editions of the Greek New Testament replicates the original wording with 100 percent accuracy. But an accurate reconstruction has to be the goal of those who practice textual criticism as classically defined. To veer from this is to stray from the essential task of textual criticism. It is an illuminating exercise "to plot the changes in the history of the text," but this assumes a known starting point. And what can that starting point be if not the original text? In analyzing Ehrman's book, *The Orthodox Corruption of Scripture*, Silva notes this same paradox: "Although this book is appealed to in support of blurring the notion of an original text, there is hardly a page in that book that does not in fact mention such a text or assume its accessibility .... Ehrman's book is unimaginable unless he can identify an initial form of the text that can be differentiated from a later alteration" (2002, 149). In short, one cannot speak about the text being corrupted if there is not an original text to be corrupted.

I am not against reconstructing the history of the text. In fact, I devoted many years to studying all the early Greek New Testament manuscripts (those dated before A.D. 300) and compiling a fresh edition of them in The Text of the Earliest New Testament Greek Manuscripts (coedited with David Barrett). This work provides a representative sampling of New Testament books that were actually read by Christians in the earliest centuries of the church. But whatever historical insights we may gain by studying the varying manuscript traditions as texts unto themselves, this is no reason to abandon the goal of producing the best critical edition possible, one that most likely replicates the original wording. Thus, I echo Silva's comments entirely, when he says: "I would like to affirm—not only with Hort, but with practically all students of ancient documents—that the recovery of the original text (i.e., the text in its initial form, prior to the alterations produced in the copying process) remains the primary task of textual criticism" (2002, 149).[120]

The author of this work would echo the words of Silva and Comfort, in that the primary task of a textual scholar is the process of attempting to ascertain the original wording of the original text that was published by Matthew, Mark, Luke, John, James, Jude, Peter, and Paul. Even if we acknowledge that we can never say with absolute certainty that we have established the original wording one hundred percent, this should always be the goal. Imagine any other field in life, the certainty of a successful heart transplant by a surgeon, the certainty of astronauts going to the moon and back, or just the certainty that our automobile will get us to our destination, and the like. Do we want a heart surgeon who aims for eighty-percent certainty in a successful operation on us? Most objective textual scholars would agree that between the 1881 Westcott and Hort text and the Nestle-Aland/United Bible Societies Greek text, we are in the very high nineties, if not ninety-nine percent mirror-like reflection of the original wording of the twenty-seven New Testament books. Of course, the ongoing objective is to reach one hundred percent even if it is not achievable.

TEXTUAL CRITICISM is the process of the textual scholar attempting to ascertain the original wording of the original text.

---

[120] Philip Comfort, NEW TESTAMENT TEXT AND TRANSLATUION COMMENTARY: Commentary on the variant readings of the ancient New Testament manuscripts and how they relate to the major English translations (Carol Stream, ILL: Tyndale House Publishers, Inc., 2008), Page xi.

CHAPTER 5 The Early Christian Copyists

Ehrman Wrote: In short, the people copying the early Christian texts were not, for the most part, if at all, professionals who copied texts for a living (cf. Hermas, above); they were simply the literate people in the Christian congregation who could make copies (since they were literate) and wanted to do so. Misquoting Jesus (pp. 50-51).

Ehrman Wrote: Because the early Christian texts were not being copied by professional scribes, at least in the first two or three centuries of the church, but simply by educated members of the Christian congregations who could do the job and were willing to do so, we can expect that in the earliest copies, especially, mistakes were commonly made in transcription. Misquoting Jesus (p. 51).

Ehrman wrote: How could authors guarantee that their texts were not modified once put into circulation? The short answer is that they could not. That explains why authors would sometimes call curses down on any copyists who modified their texts without permission. We find this kind of imprecation already in one early Christian writing that made it into the New Testament, the book of Revelation, whose author, near the end of his text, utters a dire warning: *I testify to everyone who hears the words of the prophecy of this book: If anyone adds to them, God will add to him the plagues described in this book; and if anyone removes any of the words of the book of this prophecy, God will remove his share from the tree of life and from the holy city, as described in this book.* (Rev. 22:18–19) This is not a threat that the reader has to accept or believe everything written in this book of prophecy, as it is sometimes interpreted; rather, it is a typical threat to copyists of the book, that they are not to add to or remove any of its words. Misquoting Jesus (pp. 53-54).

Ehrman wrote: It would be a mistake, however, to assume that the only changes being made were by copyists with a personal stake in the wording of the text. In fact, most of the changes found in our early Christian manuscripts have nothing to do with theology or ideology. Far and away the most changes are the result of mistakes, pure and simple—slips of the pen, accidental omissions, inadvertent additions, misspelled words, blunders of one sort or another. Scribes could be incompetent: it is important to recall that most of the copyists in the early centuries were not trained to do this kind of work but were simply the literate members of their congregations who were (more or less) able and willing. Misquoting Jesus (p. 55).

Today there are about two billion people who call themselves Christians, who own or are aware of the Bible. Most are unaware of just how that book came down to them, yet many if not most would acknowledge that it is inspired by God and free of errors and contradictions. In this chapter, we will take a brief look at how the early Christians went about the work of making copies of what would become known as New Testament books, books that they felt were Scripture, just like the inspired Hebrew Scriptures. Such background cannot only build confidence that we have been carrying the very Word of God, but it also allows us to 'be prepared to make a defense to anyone who asks you for a reason for the hope that is in you.' (1 Pet 3:15) One might say that the 128 New Testament papyrus manuscripts that are known today are hardly a notable amount.[121] When we consider that the ancients wrote on perishable materials, we understand why relatively few manuscripts have been preserved to our day.

Further, early Christianity suffered much persecution. Both emperors Nero (64 C.E.) and Domitian (95 C.E.) persecuted Christians, but this likely did not greatly affect the survival of manuscripts. However, other Roman Emperors throughout the second and third centuries C.E. persecuted Christians on an empire-wide scale, which did significantly affect manuscript survival.

Many scholars tend to speak disapprovingly of the work of the early Christian copyists. First, they maintain that copyists were not concerned with the importance of accurately copying the manuscripts, resulting in many mistakes. Second, they claim that most of the copyists were untrained in the practice of making copies, resulting in more copyist errors. Third, they say that the copyists were freely taking liberties by freely changing words, clauses, even whole sentences, omitting and inserting to improve

---

[121] First, there are close to one million papyrus fragments in various libraries throughout the world that have not yet been published. Since only about one percent of all papyri have been published (about 10,000), there is a very high degree of probability that some of the remainders will be NT fragments. The last NT papyrus to be published was papyrus 127 or P127, a fifth-century fragment of Acts discovered in 2009. Therefore, when we speak of how many have survived, we can understand that the question is not that easy to answer.

NT scholars use the term "extant" to describe MSS that have survived. It means that some have survived and are known to exist. With that definition, you might think that 127 is the number. However, there is a slight problem with that, too. Some fragments, such as P64 and P67, were later determined to belong to the same manuscript. This happens a few times for NT MSS, but mostly for minuscules (of which we now have extant about 2900). However, most scholars do not wrestle with such details. Therefore, 128 is the answer you are looking for.

As for dates, the papyri range in date from early second century C.E. to early seventh century C.E. I have worked up a chart of all NT MSS through the 8th century: as much as 43% of all the verses of the NT are attested by the end of the third century in the extant papyri.-- Dr. Daniel B. Wallace of The Center for the Study of New Testament Manuscripts.

the account, and at times to strengthen orthodoxy. However, as we have seen and will see shortly, this observation is not the case. We do not claim the early copyists were error-free, or that they were inspired. However, professional and semi-professional scribes copied many of the early New Testament manuscripts, with most being done by copyists who at a minimum had experience making documents.[122] Nevertheless, there undoubtedly were copyists with no training at all, who did copy some manuscripts.

Therefore, some of the early Christian copyists, because they were untrained in the task of making copies, did make errors. However, were these errors noteworthy? No. Again, what we can say is that the vast majority of the Greek text is not affected by variants at all. Of the **small amount** of the text that is affected by variants, the vast majority of these are minor slips of the pen, such as misspelling words. Also, they are minor intentional changes, e.g., using a synonym in place of the word in the text, or using a pronoun for a noun, and spelling the same word different ways. With these insignificant mishaps, we are sure what the original reading is in these places. Of our **small amount**, a minor number of variants are difficult in establishing the original reading. Lastly, there are very rare variants where we would say that we are uncertain as to the original reading. However, these latter two categories affect no doctrine; moreover, variant readings can be placed in a footnote, giving the reader access to the original using either the main text or the footnote.

Excursion on How Our Bible Manuscripts Survived the Elements

One may wonder why more Old and New Testament manuscripts have not survived. Really, the better question would be how come so many of our Bible manuscripts survived in comparison to secular ancient manuscripts? The primary materials used to receive writing in ancient times were perishable papyrus and parchment. It must be remembered that the Christians suffered intense persecution during intervals in the first 300 years from Pentecost 33 C.E. With this persecution from the Roman Empire came

---

[122] C. H. Roberts wrote, "In the second century, locally produced texts such as the scrap of *The Shepherd* [of Hermas] on the back of a document from the Fayum or the Baden Exodus-Deuteronomy might be carefully collated and corrected; the numerous duplications and omissions of the first hand of the Chester Beatty Numbers-Deuteronomy codex were put right by the corrector. This scrupulous reproduction of the text may be a legacy from Judaism and reminds us that no more in this period than in any other does quality of book production go hand in hand with quality of text." (C. H. Roberts, Manuscript, Society, and Belief in Early Christian Egypt 1979, 22)

many orders to destroy Christian texts. In addition, these texts were not stored in such a way as to secure their preservation; they were actively used by the Christians in the congregation and were subject to wear and tear. Furthermore, moisture is the enemy of papyrus, and it causes them to disintegrate over time. This is why, as we will discover, the papyrus manuscripts that have survived have come from the dry sands of Egypt. Moreover, it seems not to have entered the minds of the early Christians to preserve their documents, because their solution to the loss of manuscripts was just to make more copies. Fortunately, the process of making copies transitioned to the more durable animal skins, which would last much longer. Those that have survived, especially from the fourth century C.E. and earlier, are the path to restoring the original Greek New Testament.[123]

Both papyrus and parchment jeopardized the survival of the Bible because they were perishable materials. Papyrus, the weakest of the two, can tear and discolor. Because of moist climates, a sheet of papyrus can decay to the point where it is nothing more than a handful of dust. We must remember papyrus is a plant and when the scroll has been stored, it can grow mold and it can rot from dampness. It can even be eaten by starving rodents or also insects, especially white ants (i.e., termites) when it has been buried. When some of the manuscripts were first discovered early on, they were exposed to excessive light and humidity, which hastened their deterioration.

While parchment is far more durable than papyrus, it will also perish in time if mishandled or exposed to the elements (temperature, humidity, and light) over time.[124] Parchment is made from animal skin, so it too is also a victim of insects. Hence, when it comes to ancient records, Everyday Writing in the Graeco-Roman East states, "survival is the exception rather than the rule." (R. S. Bagnall 2009, 140) Think about it for a moment; the Bible and its special revelation could have died from decay in the elements.

The Mosaic Law commanded every future king, "And when he sits on the throne of his kingdom, he shall write for himself in a book a copy of this law, approved by the Levitical priests." (Deuteronomy 17:18) Moreover, the professional copyist of the Hebrew Old Testament made so many manuscripts, by the time of Jesus and the apostles, throughout all of Israel and even into distant Macedonia, there were many copies of the Scriptures in the synagogues (Luke 4:16, 17; Acts 17:11) How did our

---

[123] Cf. J. H. Greenlee, *Introduction to New Testament Textual Criticism* (Peabody: Hendrickson, 1995), 11.

[124] For example, the official signed copy of the U.S. Declaration of Independence was written on parchment. Now, less than 250 years later, it has faded to the point of being barely legible.

Hebrew Old Testament and Greek New Testament survive the elements to the point where there are far more of them than any other ancient document. For example, there are 5,830+ New Testament manuscripts in the original Greek alone.

New Testament scholar Philip W. Comfort writes, "Jews were known to put scrolls containing Scripture in pitchers or jars in order to preserve them. The Dead Sea scrolls found in jars in the Qumran caves are a celebrated example of this. The Beatty Papyri were very likely a part of a Christian library, which was hidden in jars to be preserved from confiscation during the Diocletian persecution."[125] Christianity were initially made up Jewish Christians only for the first seven years (29-36 C.E.), with Cornelius being the first Gentile baptized in 36 C.E. Much of early Christianity (33-350 C.E.) was made up of Jewish Christians, who evidently carried over the tradition of putting "scrolls containing Scripture in pitchers or jars in order to preserve them." It is for this reason that some of our earliest Bible manuscripts have been discovered in unusually dry regions, in clay jars and even dark closets and caves.

Manuscripts Saved from Egyptian Garbage Heaps

Beginning in 1778 and continuing to the end of the 19th century, many papyrus texts were accidentally discovered in Egypt that dated from 300 B.C.E. to 500 C.E., almost 500 thousand documents in all. About 130 years ago, there began a systematic search. At that time, a continuous flow of ancient texts was being found by the native fellahin, and the Egypt Exploration Society, a British non-profit organization, founded in 1882, realized that they needed to send out an expedition team before it was too late. They sent two Oxford scholars, Bernard P. Grenfell and Arthur S. Hunt, who received permission to search the area south of the farming region in the Faiyūm district. Grenfell chose a site called Behnesa because of its ancient Greek name, Oxyrhynchus. A search of the graveyards and the ruined houses produced nothing. The only place left to search was the town's garbage dumps, which were some 30 feet [9 m] high. It seems to Grenfell and Hunt that all was lost but they decided to try.

In January of 1897, a trial trench (excavation or depression in the ground) was dug, and it only took a few hours before ancient papyrus materials were found. These included letters, contracts, and official documents. The sand had blown over them, covering them, and for nearly 2,000 years, the dry climate had served as a protection for them.

---

[125] Philip Wesley Comfort and David P. Barrett, *The Text of the Earliest New Testament Greek Manuscripts* (Wheaton, IL: Tyndale House, 2001), 158.

It took only a mere three months to pull out and recover almost two tons of papyri from Oxyrhynchus. They shipped twenty-five large cases back to England. Over the next ten years, these two courageous scholars returned each and every winter, to grow their collection. They discovered ancient classical writing, along with royal ordinances and contracts mixed in with business accounts private letters, shipping lists, as well as fragments of many New Testament manuscripts.

Of what benefit were all these documents? Foremost, the bulk of these documents were written by ordinary people in Koine (common) Greek of the day. Many of the words that would be used in the marketplace, not by the elites appeared in the Greek New Testament Scriptures, which woke scholars up to the fact that Biblical Greek was not some special Greek, but instead, it was the ordinary language of the common people, the man on the street. Thus, by comparing how the words had been used in these papyri, a clearer understanding of Biblical Greek emerged. As of the time of this writing, less than ten percent of these papyri have been published and studied. Most of the papyri were found in the top 10 feet 93 m] of the garbage heap because the other 20 feet [6 m] had been ruined by water from a nearby canal. If we look at it simply, this would mean that the 500 thousand documents found could have been two million in total. Then, we must ponder just how many documents must have come through Oxyrhynchus that were never discarded in the dumps. We have almost a half million papyrus documents (likely there were millions more that did not survive) in garbage dumps in the dry sands of Oxyrhynchus, Egypt.

The end result is that the New Testament has been preserved in over **5,836** complete or fragmented Greek manuscripts, as well as some **10,000** Latin manuscripts and **9,300 manuscripts** in various other ancient languages, which include Syriac, Slavic, Gothic, Ethiopic, Coptic and Armenian. Some of these are well over 2,000 years old. End of excursion.

Public Reading Indicates the Importance of New Testament Books

Public reading is yet another important inference that the first-century Christian congregation valued the books that were being produced by the New Testament authors Matthew, Mark, Luke, John, Paul, Peter, James, and Jude.

Matthew 24:15 Updated American Standard Version (UASV)

[15] "Therefore when you see the abomination of desolation,[126] which was spoken of through Daniel the prophet, standing in the holy place (let the reader understand),

---

[126] **Abomination of Desolation:** (Gr. *bdelugma eremoseos*) An expression by Jesus recorded in Mathew 24:15 and Mark 13:14 referring to Daniel 11:31 and 12:11. *Bdelugma* refers

This parenthetical "let the reader understand" is a reference to a public reader within the congregations.

1 Timothy 4:13 Updated American Standard Version (UASV)

[13] Until I come, devote yourself to the public reading of Scripture, to exhortation, to teaching.

Only the privileged owned scrolls of the Holy Scriptures. Most Christians in the first century gained access to God's Word, as Paul explains here in his first letter to Timothy, by "the public reading of Scripture." Public reading was a major part of Christian meetings, a traditional practice of the Jews from the time of Moses, and one which was carried over to the Christian congregation. – Acts 13:15; 15:21; 2 Corinthians 3:15.

Revelation 1:3 Updated American Standard Version (UASV)

[3] Blessed is the one who reads and those who hear the words of the prophecy, and who keep what is written in it, for the time is near.

This reference to "he who reads and those who hear" is to the public reader and his audience in each of the seven mentioned congregations. Another factor is how the writers of the Christian Greek Scriptures viewed their own published works.

2 Peter 3:16 Updated American Standard Version (UASV)

[16] as also in all his letters, speaking in them of these things, in which are some things hard to understand, which the untaught and unstable distort, **as they do also the rest of the Scriptures**, to their own destruction. (Bold added.)

Here, about 64 C.E., we have the apostle Peter, who has just canonized Paul's letters, grouping them together as a collection. This is evidence of their being viewed as having authority. At 2 Timothy 3:16 and 2 Peter 1:20, the apostles Paul and Peter respectively appear to be referring to both the Hebrew Old Testament and the Greek Christian writings as [Greek *graphe*] "Scripture." Note that Peter is comparing Paul's letters to "*the rest of the Scriptures.*" What exactly does that mean?

Both Jesus and the writers of the Christian Greek Scriptures often used the Greek word *graphe* in their references to Moses' writings and the prophets, viewing them as having authority from God, being inspired. Many times, Jesus designates these Old Testament books as a whole as *graphe*, i.e., "Scripture." (Matthew 21:42; 22:29; Mark 14:49; John 5:39; Acts 17:11; 18:24, 28) At other times, the singular for "Scripture" was used when quoting a specific text to make a point, referring to it as a part of the whole of writings encompassing our 39 books of the Hebrew Old

---

to something that is an abomination, unclean, which horrifies clean persons, leaving them disgusted. *Eremoseos* has the sense of an extensive desolating act or destruction, which caused total ruin, leaving no place for shelter.

Testament. (Rom. 9:17; Gal. 3:8) Still, at other times *graphe* is used in a single text reference, such as Jesus' reference when dealing with the Jewish religious leaders: "Have you not read this [*graphe*] Scripture: 'The stone that the builders rejected has become the cornerstone.'" (Mark 12:10) Jesus' use of *graphe* in such an authoritative way only strengthens the point that immediately the writings of the New Testament authors were viewed as *graphe*, namely, Scripture.

From an Oral Gospel to the Written Record

Jesus had commanded his disciples to, "Go therefore and make disciples of all nations, baptizing them in the name of the Father and of the Son and of the Holy Spirit, teaching them to observe all that I have commanded you. And behold, I am with you always, to the end of the age." (Matt 28:19-20) How then was this gospel (good news) to be made known?

During the forty-day period between Jesus' resurrection and his ascension, Jesus instructed his disciples in the teaching of the gospel. Accordingly, he prepared them for the tremendous task that awaited them on and after Pentecost.[127]

There were only ten days after Jesus ascension to Pentecost, when "they were all filled with the Holy Spirit." Jesus put it this way, in his words, it being only "a few days." This time would have been filled with the process of replacing Judas Iscariot, prayer, and the established gospel message, which would be the official oral message until it was deemed necessary to have a written gospel some 10 to 15 years later. The gospel message was quite simple: 'Christ died for our sins, was buried, and he was resurrected on the third day according to Scripture.' – 1 Corinthians 15:1-8

1 Corinthians 15:1-2 Updated American Standard Version (UASV)

15 Now I make known to you, brothers, the gospel which I proclaimed to you, which you have also received, in which you also stand, 2 by which you are also being saved, if you hold fast to the message I proclaimed to you, unless you believed in vain.

By the time of the destruction of Jerusalem by General Titus of Rome (70 C.E.), all of the books of the Greek New Testament had been written, except for those penned by the apostle John. The Gospel of Matthew was penned first, published between 45 and 50 C.E. The Gospel of Luke was written about 56-58 C.E. and the Gospel of Mark between 60 to 65 C.E. Matthew, Mark, and Luke are known as the Synoptic Gospels, as they are similar in content, while John chose to convey other information, perhaps

---

[127] Simon J. Kistemaker and William Hendriksen, vol. 17, New Testament Commentary: Exposition of the Acts of the Apostles, New Testament Commentary (Grand Rapids: Baker Book House, 1953-2001), 47-48.

because he wrote his gospel to the second generation of Christians in about 98 C.E. Luke informs us of just how the very first Christians received the gospel message. Very few translations make explicit the exact process.

Luke 1:1-4 Updated American Standard Version (UASV)[128]

[1] Inasmuch as many have undertaken to compile a narrative of the things that have been fulfilled among us, [2] just as they were handed down to us by those who from the beginning were eyewitnesses and servants of the word, [3] It also seemed good to me, since I have carefully investigated everything from the very first, to write an orderly account for you, most excellent Theophilus, [4] so that you may know the certainty concerning the things about which you were **taught** <u>orally</u> [Gr., *katechethes*].

Acts 18:24-25 Updated American Standard Version (UASV)

[24] Now a Jew named Apollos, an Alexandrian by birth, came to Ephesus. He was an eloquent man, competent in the Scriptures. [25] This man had been **orally** [*katechethes*] **instructed** in the way of the Lord, and being fervent in spirit, he spoke and taught accurately the things concerning Jesus, knowing only the baptism of John.

Galatians 6:6 Updated American Standard Version (UASV)

The one who is **orally** [*katechethes*] **taught** the word must share all good things with the one who teaches.

We can see clearly from the above that both Theophilus and Apollos received the initial gospel message, just as all Christians did in the early years, and even after the written gospels were available, the gospel of Jesus was taught by oral instruction (*katechethes*). In time, it was deemed that there was a need for a written record, which is the reason Luke gives for his Gospel. This was not to discount what Theophilus had been orally taught, but rather to give credence to that oral message that he had already received. Of course, the New Testament was not limited to these gospels.

The publishing of these New Testament books in written form would have come about in the following stages:

(1) the inspired author probably would have used a well-trusted, skilled Christian scribe to take down what he was inspired to convey, *some believe* by shorthand;[129]

---

[128] The Updated American Standard Version (UASV) is under production by Christian Publishing House. It is by permission that we use these next few verses before it is published, as their rendering better conveys the original Greek.

[129] "I Tertius, who wrote this letter, greet you in the Lord." (Rom. 16:22) "By Silvanus, a faithful brother as I regard him, I have written briefly to you, exhorting and declaring that this is the true grace of God. Stand firm in it." (1 Pet. 5:12)

(2) The scribe would then make a rough draft *if it had been taken* by shorthand. If shorthand had not been used, this first copy would have been the rough draft;

(3) this draft would then be read by both the scribe and author, making corrections because the copyist, though professional or at least skillful at making documents, was not inspired;

(4) thereafter, the scribe would make what is known as the autograph, original, or initial text, to be signed by the author,

(5) which would then be used as the official exemplar to make other copies.

Both Tertius and Silvanus were very likely skilled Christian scribes, who assisted the writers of the New Testament. (Rom. 16:22; 1 Pet. 5:12) It is unlikely that Paul personally wrote any of his letters that were of great length. It is clear that Peter used the trained Silvanus to pen his first letter, and likely, the second letter was possibly the result of Jude's penman skills, as it is very similar in style to the letter by Jude. This may explain the differences in style between First and Second Peter. We should emphasize that *it is not possible* that the inspired author would give some latitude to his skilled Christian scribe to serve as a coauthor regarding word choices, as some have suggested.

Papyrus or Parchment?

The Hebrew Old Testament that would have been available to the early Christians was written on the processed hide of animals after the hair was removed, and the hide was smoothed out with a pumice stone.[130] Leather scrolls were sent to Alexandria, Egypt in about 280 B.C.E., to make what we now know as the Greek Septuagint.[131] Most of the Dead Sea scrolls that were discovered between 1947 and 1956 are made of leather, and it is almost certain that the scroll of Isaiah that Jesus read from in the synagogue was as well. Luke 4:17 says, "And the scroll of the prophet Isaiah was given to him. He unrolled the scroll and found the place where it was written."

The Dead Sea Scroll of Isaiah (1QIsa) dates to the end of the second century B.C.E., written on 17 sheets of parchment, one of the seven Dead Sea Scrolls that were first recovered by Bedouin shepherds in 1947. The

---

[130] A very light porous rock formed from solidified lava, used in solid form as an abrasive and in powdered form as a polish.

[131] A Greek translation of the Hebrew Bible started in about 280 and completed about 150 B.C.E. to meet the needs of Greek-speaking Jews outside Palestine.

Nash Papyrus is a collection of four papyrus fragments acquired in Egypt in 1898 by W. L. Nash, dating to about 150 B.C.E. It contains parts of the Ten Commandments from Exodus chapter 20, along with some verses from Deuteronomy chapters 5 and 6. It is by far one of the oldest Hebrew manuscript fragments.

Both leather and papyrus were used before the first-century Christians. Vellum is a high-quality parchment made from calfskin, kidskin, or lambskin. After the skin was removed, it would be soaked in limewater, after which the hair would be scraped off, the skin then being scraped and dried, and rubbed afterward with chalk and pumice stone, creating an exceptionally smooth writing material. During the first three hundred years of Christianity, the secular world viewed parchment as being inferior to papyrus, it being relegated to notebooks, rough drafts, and other non-literary purposes.

A couple of myths should be dispelled before continuing. It is often remarked that papyrus is not a durable material. Both papyrus and parchment are durable under normal circumstances. This is not negating the fact that parchment is more durable than papyrus. Another often-repeated thought is that papyrus was fragile and brittle, making it an unlikely candidate to be used for a codex, which would have to be folded in half. Another issue that should be sidelined is whether it was more expensive to produce papyrus or parchment. Presently there is no data to aid in that evaluation. We know that papyrus was used for all of the Christian codex manuscripts up to the fourth century, at which time we find the two great parchment codices, the Sinaiticus and Vaticanus manuscripts. Parchment of good quality has been called "the finest writing material ever devised by man." (Roberts and Skeat, The Birth of the Codex 1987, 8) Why then did parchment take so long to replace papyrus? This may be answered by R. Reed, in *Ancient Skins, Parchments, and Leathers:*

> It is perhaps the extraordinary high durability of the product, produced by so simple a method, which has prevented most people from suspecting that many subtle points are involved.... The essence of the parchment process, which subjects the system of pelt to the simultaneous action of stretching and drying, is to bring about peculiar changes quite different from those applying when making leather. These are (1) reorganization of the dermal fibre network by stretching, and (2) permanently setting this new and highly stretched form of fibre network by drying the pelt fluid to a hard, glue-like consistency. In other words, the pelt fibres are fixed in a stretched condition so that they cannot revert to their original relaxed state. (Reed 1973, 119-20)

Where the medieval parchment makers were greatly superior to their modern counterparts was in the control and modification of the ground substance in the pelt, before the latter was stretched and dried .... The major point, however, which modern parchment manufacturers have not appreciated, is what might be termed the integral or collective nature of the parchment process. The bases of many different effects need to be provided for simultaneously, in one and the same operation. The properties required in the final parchment must be catered for at the wet pelt stage, for due to the peculiar nature of the parchment process, once the system has been dried, and after-treatments to modify the material produced are greatly restricted. (Reed 1973, 124)

This method, which follows those used in medieval times for making parchment of the highest quality, is preferable for it allows the grain surface of the drying pelt to be "slicked" and freed from residual fine hairs while stretching upon the frame. At the same time, any process for cleaning and smoothing the flesh side, or for controlling the thickness of the final parchment may be undertaken by working the flesh side with sharp knives which are semi-lunar in form.... To carry out such manual operations on wet stretched pelt demands great skill, speed of working, and concentrated physical effort. (Reed 1973, 138-9)

Enough has been said to suggest that behind the apparently simple instructions contained in the early medieval recipes there is a wealth of complex process detail which we are still far from understanding. Hence it remains true that parchment-making is perhaps more of an art than a science. (Reed 1973, 172)

The Christian's Use of the Codex

Going back to the first-century once again, let us take a moment to deal with the invention of the codex. Was it the first-century Christians who invented the codex, or at least put it on the stage of the world scene?

The writing tablet of ancient times was made from two flat pieces of wood, held together by a thong hinge, which looks something like our modern book. It had its limits because of the impracticality of fastening more than a few such tablets together. The center of the tablet pages was slightly hollowed, to receive a wax coating. A stylus was the standard instrument used to write on these waxed tablets. The stylus was made of metal, ivory, or bone, and was sharpened to a point on one side while having a rounded knob on the other for erasing, and making corrections.

This was the oldest form of writing for the Greeks, who borrowed it from the Hittites. History and evidence credit the Romans with replacing the wooden tablet with the parchment notebook. The apostle Paul is the only Greek writer of the first-century C.E. to mention the parchment notebook.

2 Timothy 4:13 New American Standard Bible (NASB)

[13] When you come bring the cloak which I left at Troas with Carpus, and the books, especially the parchments. [Gr., *membranai*, parchment notebooks]

However, it should be recognized that the parchment notebook was not used for literature in the first two centuries before the Christian era (B.C.E.); this was done with the roll or scroll. Even though the codex was commonly used for books, the first indication that it was going to displace the roll came toward the end of the first century C.E. (Roberts and Skeat, The Birth of the Codex 1987, 24) Thus, again, the Jews of the late first century C.E. and thereafter used scrolls, while the Christians used codices. However, many of the first Christians were Jewish and likely read their Old Testament from a scroll. Before becoming a Christian, the apostle Paul was a Pharisee and would have used scrolls. However, at least until about the end of the first century C.E. Christians used scrolls primarily.

Only a handful of manuscripts of the New Testament that are still in existence were written on scrolls (P[13], P[18], and P[98]). However, these were written on the backs of other writings, so they were not composed in the scroll form. P[22] was written on a roll, and we await more research there, as it is a peculiarity among the group of papyri. All other New Testament manuscripts were written on codices. As there is evidence that the second-century Christians were trying to set themselves apart from the Jews, so they likely made the transition in part because they wished to be different. We say in part because it is quite evident that the first Christians grouped their writings together, the Gospels and Paul's letters. The codex afforded them the means of doing this, while a scroll of the gospels would have been far too long and bulky, and finding a portion of desired text would have been difficult at best. For example, P[46] dating to about 150 C.E., contained ten of Paul's letters. P[45] dates to about 225 C.E. and originally contained all four Gospels and the book of Acts. In the end, it can be said that the Christians adopted the codex (1) to be different from the Jews, (2) to have the Gospels and the Apostle Paul's letters all in one book, and (3) because of the ease of being able to find a portion of text, and this made the spread of the good news much more convenient.

We do learn a good deal from the New Testament. The apostle Peter writes, "... just as our beloved brother Paul also wrote to you according to the wisdom given him, as he does in all his letters when he speaks in them of these matters ...." (2 Pet 3:15-16, about 64 C.E.) This shows how early Paul's letters were grouped together. The apostle John wrote, "Though I have much to write to you, I would rather not use paper and ink. Instead, I hope to come to you and talk face to face so that our joy may be complete." (2 John 12, about 98 C.E.) We see from this that John used papyrus in writing to a sister congregation. The Greek word *chartou* means "papyrus," "a sheet of paper." The apostle Paul wrote Timothy and asked him, "when you come, bring the cloak that I left with Carpus at Troas, also the books [likely scrolls of OT books], and, above all, the parchments [codices]." (2 Tim 4:13, about 65 C.E) While it is thought by most scholars that Paul was talking about two different items here, it is quite possible that he was referring to only one, which is Skeat's position. Let us look at the verse again:

When you come bring ... the books, especially the parchments.

When you come, bring ... the books, that is my parchment notebooks.

If the second version above is correct, Paul hoped to obtain some of his notebooks, possible rough drafts that he had left behind. The Old Testament books could have been located right where he was, but he would have been highly interested in unpublished works that he wanted to get out before his execution. Of course, this latter thought is the formation of judgments based on incomplete or inconclusive information. However, one thing is sure, that either Paul was asking for codices in complete book form or notebook form. This indicates that Paul was the first to have his books collected into codex form, and we can conclude that the Christians were using the codex at the end of the first century.

The Trustworthiness of Early Copyists

Throughout much of the twentieth century, it was common to form three conclusions about the earliest copyists and their work:

(1) The first three centuries saw copyists who were semiliterate and unskilled in the work of making copies.

(2) Copyists in these early centuries felt as though the end was nigh, so they took liberties with the text in an attempt to strengthen orthodoxy.

(3) In the early centuries, manuscripts could be described as "free," "wild," "in a state of flux," "chaotic," "a turbid textual morass," i.e., a "free text" (so the Alands).

The first in the above would undoubtedly lead to many unintentional changes while the second would escalate intentional changes. J. Harold Greenlee had this to say:

> In the very early period, the NT writings were more nearly "private" writings than the classics . . . the classics were commonly, although not always, copied by professional scribes, the NT books were probably usually copied in the early period by **Christians who were not professionally trained** for the task, and **no corrector** was employed to check the copyist's work against his exemplar (the MS from which the copy was made) .... It appears that a copyist sometimes even took liberty to add or change minor details in the narrative books on the basis of personal knowledge, alternative tradition, or a parallel account in another book of the Bible .... At the same time, the importance of these factors in affecting the purity of the NT text must not be exaggerated. The NT books doubtless came to be considered as "literature" soon after they began to be circulated, with attention to the precise wording required when copies were made.[132]

Greenlee had not changed his position 14 years later when he wrote the following:

> The New Testament, on the other hand, was probably copied during the earliest period mostly by ordinary Christians **who were not professional scribes** but who wanted a copy of the New Testament book or books for themselves or for other Christians.[133]

The Alands in their *Text of the New Testament* saw the New Testament books as not being canonical, i.e., not viewed as Scripture in the first few centuries, so the books were subject to changes. They wrote, "not only every church but each individual Christian felt 'a direct relationship to God.' Well into the second century Christians still regarded themselves as possessing inspiration equal to that of the New Testament writings which they read in their worship service." Earlier they wrote, "That was all the more true of the early period when the text had not attained canonical status, especially in the early period when Christians considered themselves filled with the Spirit." They claimed that "until the beginning of the fourth

---

[132] J. Harold Greenlee, Introduction to New Testament Textual Criticism (Revised Edition, 1995), 51–52.

[133] J. Harold Greenlee, The Text of the New Testament: From Manuscript to Modern Edition (2008), 37.

century the text of the New Testament developed freely." (Aland and Aland, The Text of the New Testament 1995, 295, 69)

Generally, once an established concept is set within the world of textual scholars, it is not easily displaced. During the start of the 20th century (1900–1930), there was a handful of papyri discovered that obviously represented the work of a copyist who had no training. It is during this time that Sir Frederic Kenyon, director and principal librarian of the British Museum for many years, said,

> The early Christians, a poor, scattered, often **illiterate** body, looking for the return of the Lord at no distant date, **were not likely to care** sedulously for minute accuracy of transcription or to preserve their books religiously for the benefit of posterity.[134]

The first papyri discovered (P45, P46, P66) showed this to be the case. However, as more papyri became known, especially after the discovery of P75, it proved to be just the opposite, prompting Sir Frederic Kenyon to write,

> We must be content to know that the general authenticity of the New Testament text has been remarkably supported by the modern discoveries which have so greatly reduced the interval between the original autographs and our earliest extant manuscripts, and that the differences of reading, interesting as they are, do not affect the fundamental doctrines of the Christian faith.[135]

Even though many textual scholars were crediting the Alands' *The Text of the New Testament* with their description of the text as "free," that was not the entire position of the Alands. True, they spoke of the different text styles such as the "normal," "free" "strict" and the "paraphrastic." However, like Kenyon, they saw a need based on the evidence, which suggested a rethinking of how the evidence should be described:

> Our research on the early papyri has yielded unexpected results that require a change in the traditional views of the early text. We have inherited from the past generation the view that the early text was a "free" text, and the discovery of the Chester Beatty papyri seemed to confirm this view. When P45 and P46 were joined by P66 sharing the same characteristics, this position seemed to be definitely established. P75 appeared in contrast to be a loner with its "strict" text anticipating Codex Vaticanus. Meanwhile the other witnesses of the early period had been

---

[134] F. Kenyon, Our Bible and the Ancient Manuscripts (1895), 157.

[135] F. Kenyon, Our Bible and the Ancient Manuscripts (1962), 249.

ignored. It is their collations which have changed the picture so completely.[136]

While we have said this previously, it bears repeating once again that *some* of the earliest manuscripts we now have indicate that a professional scribe copied them.[137] *Many* of the other papyri confirm that a semi-professional hand copied them, while *most* of these early papyri give evidence of being produced by a copyist who was literate and experienced. Therefore, either literate or semi-professional copyist did the vast majority of our early papyri, with some being done by professionals. As it happened, the few poorly copied manuscripts became known first, establishing a precedent that was difficult for some to discard when the enormous amount of evidence came forth that showed just the opposite.

Distribution of Papyri by Century and Type

DATE	ALEX	WEST	CAES	BYZ	Hand
150	P52 P90 P104	0	0	0	0
200	P32 P46 P4/64/67 P66 P77 0189	0	0	0	0
250	P1 P5 P9 P12 P15 P20 P22 P23 P27 P28 P29 P30 P39 P40 P45 P47 P49 P53 P65 P70 P75 P80 P87 0220	0	0	P48 P69	1

---

[136] (Aland and Aland, The Text of the New Testament 1995, 93-5)

[137] Some may argue that we can only be confident that we have good manuscripts of an "early" form of the text but not necessarily of the originally published text. This hypothesis cannot be disproven. However, I think it is highly doubtful for four reasons: (1) The intervening time between the publication date of various New Testament books (from AD 60–90) and the date of several of our extant manuscripts (from AD 100–200) is narrow, thereby giving us manuscripts that are probably only three to five "manuscript generations" removed from the originally published texts. (2) We have no knowledge that any of these manuscripts go back to an early "form" that postdates the original publications. (3) We are certain that there was no major Alexandrian recension in the second century. (4) Text critics have been able to detect any other other second-century textual aberrations, such as the D-text, which was probably created near the end of the second century, not the beginning. Thus, it stands to reason that these "reliable" manuscripts are excellent copies of the authorized published texts." (P. Comfort, Encountering the Manuscripts: An Introduction to New Testament Paleography and Textual Criticism 2005, 269)

300	P13 P16 P18 P37 P72 P78 P115 O162	0	0	P38 0171	1
Acts	14	0	0	0	4

Also, as we noted earlier, textual scholars such as Comfort[138] and others believe that the very early Alexandrian manuscripts that we now possess are a reflection of what would have been found throughout the whole of the Greco-Roman Empire from about 85–275 C.E. So these early papyri can play a major role in our establishing the original readings.

However, Epp asks, "If Westcott-Hort did not utilize papyri in constructing their NT text, and if our own modern critical texts, in fact, are not significantly different from that of Westcott-Hort, then why are the papyri important after all?"[139] From there, Epp goes on to strongly advise that the papyri should play an essential role in three areas: (1) "to isolate the earliest discernable text-types, (2) assisting "to trace out the very early history of the NT text," and, (3) "Finally, the papyri can aid in refining the canons of criticism—the principles by which we judge variant readings—for they open to us a window for viewing the earliest stages of textual transmission, providing instances of how scribes worked in their copying of manuscripts."[140] We should add that the early papyri have changed decisions of textual scholars and committees so that they have not retained the readings of Westcott and Hort at times.

To offer just one example, both Metzger and Comfort inform us that it was the external evidence of the papyri that resulted in the change in the NU text, adopting the reading that was also in the Textus Receptus, as opposed to what was in the Westcott and Hort text.

Matthew 26:20 (WH)	Matthew 26:20 (TRNU)
[20] μετα των δωδεκα μαθητων	[20] μετα των δωδεκα
With the twelve disciples	With the twelve

Metzger writes, "As is the case in 20:17,[141] the reading μαθηταί after οἱ δώδεκα is doubtful. In the present verse [26:20] the weight of the external

---

Philip W. Comfort, The Quest for the Original Text of the New Testament (Eugene, Oregon: Wipf and Stock Publishers, 1992).

[139] The New Testament Papyrus Manuscripts in Historical Perspective, in To Touch the Text: Biblical and Related Studies in Honour of Joseph A. Fitzmyer, S. J. (ed. Maurya P. Horgan and Paul J. Kobelski; New York: Crossroad, 1989), 285 (there italicized) repr. in Epp, Perspectives, 338.

[140] Ibid., 288

[141] 20:17 τοὺς δώδεκα [μαθητάς] {C}

evidence seems to favor the shorter reading." (B. M. Metzger, A Textual Commentary on the Greek New Testament 1994, 53) Comfort in his *New Testament Text and Translation* writes, "Even though both P³⁷ and P⁴⁵ are listed as 'vid,' it is certain that both did not include the word μαθητων because line spacing would not accommodate it. P³⁷ has the typical abbreviation for 'twelve,' as ιβ̄; and P⁴⁵ has it written out as [δω]δεκα. P⁶⁴⁺⁶⁷ is less certain, but line lengths of the manuscript suggest that it reads ιβ̄ (see *Texts of Earliest MSS*, 69)." Comfort more explicitly explains what Metzger hinted at; "The testimony of the papyri (with B and D) created a change in the NU text. Prior to NA26, the NU text included the word μαθητων ("disciples"). But the early evidence shows that this must have been a later addition." Comfort continues, "Such an addition is not necessary in light of the fact that Jesus' closest followers were often designated by the gospel writers as simply "the twelve." (P. W. Comfort 2008, 77)

Again, many textual scholars before 1961 believed that the early copyists of the New Testament papyri were among the untrained in making documents (P⁴⁵, P⁴⁶, P⁴⁷; P⁶⁶ and P⁷² in 2 Peter and Jude), and that the papyri were texts in flux.[142] It was not until the discovery of P⁷⁵ and other papyri that textual scholars began to think differently. Nevertheless, the attitude of the 1930s through the 1950s is explained well by Kurt and Barbara Aland:

> Of special importance are the early papyri, i.e., of the period of the third/fourth century. As we have said, these have an inherent significance for the New Testament textual studies because they witness to a situation before the text was channeled into major text types in the fourth century. Our research on the early papyri has yielded unexpected results that require a change in the traditional views of the early text. We have inherited from the past generation the view that the early text was a "free"

Although copyists often add the word μαθηταίto the more primitive expression οἱ δώδεκα (see Tischendorf's note *in loc.* and 26.20 below), a majority of the Committee judged that the present passage was assimilated to the text of Mark (10:32) or Luke (18:31). In order to represent both possibilities it was decided to employ square brackets. (B. M. Metzger, A Textual Commentary on the Greek New Testament 1994, 42)

On 20:17, Comfort writes, "Either reading could be original because they both have good support and because the gospel writers alternated between the nomenclature 'the twelve disciples' and 'the twelve.'" (P. W. Comfort 2008, 60)

[142] Kurt and Barbara Aland write, "By the 1930s the number of known papyri had grown to more than forty without any of them arousing any special attention, despite the fact that many of them were of a quite early date. (Aland and Aland, The Text of the New Testament 1995, 84)

text,[143] and the discovery of the Chester Beatty papyri seemed to confirm this view. When P[45] and P[46] were joined by P[66] sharing the same characteristics, this position seemed to be definitely established. (Aland and Aland, The Text of the New Testament 1995, 93)

Before P[75], scholars were under the impression that scribes must have used manuscripts of untrained copyists to make a recension (critical revision, i.e., revised text); and this, according to scholars prior to 1961, was how Codex Vaticanus (B) came about. In 1940, Kenyon inferred the following:

> During the second and third centuries, a great variety of readings came into existence throughout the Christian world. In some quarters, considerable license was shown in dealing with the sacred text; in others, more respect was shown to the tradition. In Egypt, this variety of texts existed, as elsewhere; but Egypt (and especially Alexandria) was a country of strong scholarship and with a knowledge of textual criticism. Here, therefore, a relatively faithful tradition was preserved. About the beginning of the fourth century, a scholar may well have set himself to compare the best accessible representatives of this tradition, and so have produced a text of which B is an early descendant.[144]

While Kenyon was correct about the manuscripts coming up out of Egypt being a reasonably pure text, he was certainly mistaken when he suggested that Codex Vaticanus was the result of a critical revision by early scribes. P[75] put this theory to rest. Agreement between P[75] and codex B is 92% in John and 94% in Luke. However, Porter has it at about 85% agreement. Zuntz, on the other hand, went a little further than Kenyon did. Kenyon believed that the critical text had been made in the early part of the fourth century, leading to Codex Vaticanus. Zuntz believed similarly but felt that the recension began back in the mid-second-century and was a process that ran up into the fourth-century. Zuntz wrote:

> The Alexander correctors strove, in ever repeated efforts, to keep the text current in their sphere free from the many faults

---

[143] Early manuscripts (from before the fourth century) are classified by the Alands as "strict," "normal," or "free." The "normal" text "transmitted the original text with the limited amount of variation." Then, there is the "free" text, "characterized by a greater degree of variation than the 'normal' text." Finally, there was the "strict" text, "which reproduced the text of its exemplar with greater fidelity (although still with certain characteristic liberties), exhibiting far less variation than the 'normal' text." (Aland 1987, 93)

[144] F. Kenyon, "Hesychius and the Text of the New Testament," in *Memorial Lagrange* (1940), 250.

that had infected it in the previous period and which tended to crop up again even after they had been obelized [i.e., marked as spurious]. These labours must time and again have been checked by persecutions and the confiscation of Christian books, and counteracted by the continuing currency of manuscripts of the older type. Nonetheless they resulted in the emergence of a type of text (as distinct from a definite edition) which served as a norm for the correctors in provincial Egyptian scriptoria. The final result was the survival of a text far superior to that of the second century, even though the revisers, being fallible human beings, rejected some of its own correct readings and introduced some faults of their own.[145]

P[75], as we can see from the above, influenced the thinking of Kurt Aland. While he said, "We have inherited from the past generation the view that the early text was a 'free' text," he was one of those saying that very thing. However, as he would later say, "Our research on the early papyri has yielded unexpected results that require a change in the traditional views of the early text." P[75] greatly affected the Alands: "P[75] shows such a close affinity with the Codex Vaticanus that the supposition of a recension of the text at Alexandria, in the fourth century, can no longer be held."[146] Gordon Fee clearly states that there was no Alexandrian recension prior to P[75] (175-225 C.E.) and the time of Codex Vaticanus (350 C.E.), as he commented that P[75] and Vaticanus "seem to represent a 'relatively pure' form of preservation of a 'relatively pure' line of descent from the original text."[147] For many decades now, New Testament textual scholarship has been aware that P[75] is an extremely accurate copy. Of the copyist behind P[75], Colwell said, "his impulse to improve style is for the most part defeated by the obligation to make an exact copy."[148] Colwell went on to comment on the work of that scribe:

> In P[75] the text that is produced can be explained in all its variants as the result of a single force, namely the disciplined scribe who writes with the intention of being careful and accurate. There is no evidence of revision of his work by anyone

---

[145] G. Zuntz, *The Text of the Epistles* (1953), 271–272.

[146] Kurt Aland, "The Significance of the Papyri for New Testament Research" in *The Bible in Modern Scholarship* (1965), 336.

[147] Gordon Fee, "P75, P66, and Origen: The Myth of Early Textual Recension in Alexandria" in *New Dimensions in New Testament Study* (1974), 19–43.

[148] Ernest C. Colwell, "Method in Evaluating Scribal Habits: A Study of P45, P66, P75," in *Studies in Methodology in Textual Criticism of the New Testament*, New Testament Tools and Studies 9 (Leiden: Brill, 1969), 121.

else, or in fact of any real revision, or check.... The control had been drilled into the scribe before he started writing.[149]

We do not want to leave the reader with the impression that P[75] is perfect, as it is not. On this Comfort says,

> The scribe had to make several corrections (116 in Luke and John), but there was no attempt 'to revise the text by a second exemplar, and indeed no systematic correction at all.'[150] The scribe of P[75] shows a clear tendency to make grammatical and stylistic improvements in keeping with the Alexandrian scriptorial tradition, and the scribe had a tendency to shorten his text, particularly by dropping pronouns. However, his omissions of text hardly ever extend beyond a word or two, probably because he copied letter by letter and syllable by syllable.[151]

As the early Nestle Greek text moved from edition to edition, the influence of the New Testament papyri increased. It was the son of Eberhard Nestle, Erwin, who added a full critical apparatus in the thirteenth edition of the 1927 Nestle Edition. It was not until 1950 that Kurt Aland began to work on the text that would eventually become known as the Nestle-Aland text. He would begin to add even more evidence from papyri to the critical apparatus of the twenty-first edition. At Erwin Nestle's request, he looked over and lengthened the critical apparatus, adding far more manuscripts. This ultimately led to the 25th edition of 1963. The most significant papyri and recently discovered majuscules, (i.e., 0189), a few minuscules (33, 614, 2814), and rarely also lectionaries were also considered. However, while the critical apparatus was being added to and even altered, the text of the Nestle-Aland was not changed until the 26th edition (1979). Many of these changes to the text were a direct result of the papyri.

Returning to the First Century

The writers of the 27 books comprising the Christian Greek Scriptures were Jews.[152] (Romans 13:1-2) Either these men were apostles, intimate

---

[149] Ibid., 117

[150] James Ronald Royse, "Scribal Habits in Early Greek New Testament Papyri" (Ph.D. diss., Graduate Theological Union, 1981), 538–39.

[151] (Comfort and Barret, The Text of the Earliest New Testament Greek Manuscripts 2001, 506)

[152] Some believe that Luke was a Gentile, basing this primarily on Colossians 4:11, 14. Because Paul first mentioned "the circumcision" (Col 4:11) and thereafter talked about Luke (Col 4:14), the inference is drawn that Luke was not of the circumcision and therefore was not a Jew. However, this is by no means decisive. Romans 3:1-2 says, "Jews were entrusted with

traveling companions of the apostles, or were picked by Christ in a supernatural way, such as the apostle Paul. Being Jewish, they would have viewed the Old Testament as being the inspired, inerrant Word of God. Paul said, "all Scripture is inspired by God" (2 Timothy 3:16). These writers of the 27 New Testament books would have viewed the teachings of Jesus, or their books expounding on his teachings, as Scripture as well as the Old Testament. The teachings of Jesus came to most of these New Testament writers personally from Jesus, being taught orally; thereafter, they would be the ones who published what Jesus had said and taught orally. When it came time to be published in written form, it should be remembered that Jesus had promised them "The Helper, the Holy Spirit, whom the Father will send in my name, he will teach you all things and **bring to your remembrance** all that I have said to you." – John 14:26

The early first-century Christian copyists were very much aware of the traditions that the Jewish scribes followed in meticulously copying their texts. These copyists would have immediately understood that they were copying sacred texts. In fact, the early papyri show evidence of shared features with the Jewish Sopherim, men who copied the Hebrew Scriptures from the time of Ezra in the fifth-century B.C.E. to Jesus' day and beyond. They were extremely careful and were terrified of making mistakes.[153] We will find common features when we compare the Jewish Greek Old Testament with the Christian Greek Scriptures, such things as an enlarged letter at the beginning of each line, and the invention of the nomen sacrum[154] to deal with God's personal name. Marginal notes, accents, breathing marks, punctuation, corrections, double punctuation marks (which indicate the flow of text)—all of these show adoption of scribal practices of the Sopherim by Jewish Christian writers and scribes.

There are, unfortunately, fierce critics who reject any claims of veracity for these early manuscripts. Former evangelical Christian, now agnostic New Testament Bible scholar, Bart Ehrman writes,

> Not only do we not have the originals, we don't have the first copies of the originals. **We don't even have copies of the copies of the originals, or copies of the copies of the copies of the**

---

the whole revelation of God." Luke is one of those to whom such inspired revelations were entrusted.

[153] It is true that they took some liberties with the text, but these few places were the exception to the rule. They intentionally altered some passages that appeared to show irreverence for God or one of his spokespersons.

[154] Nomina sacra (singular: nomen sacrum) means "sacred names" in Latin, and can be used to refer to traditions of abbreviated writing of several frequently occurring divine names or titles in early Greek manuscripts, such as the following:

Lord ($\overline{KC}$), Jesus ($\overline{IH}$, $\overline{IHC}$), Christ ($\overline{XP}$, $\overline{XC}$, $\overline{XPC}$), God ($\overline{\Theta C}$), and Spirit ($\overline{\Pi NA}$).

originals. What we have are copies made later—much later. In most instances, they are copies made many *centuries* later. And these copies all differ from one another, in many thousands of places. As we will see later in this book, these copies differ from one another in so many places that we don't even know how many differences there are. Possibly it is easiest to put it in comparative terms: there are more differences among our manuscripts than there are words in the New Testament. (B. D. Ehrman, Misquoting Jesus: The Story Behind Who Changed the Bible and Why 2005, 10) (Bold mine)

As we read these remarks, it is easy to get a sense of hopelessness because "all feels lost, for there is certainly no way to get back to the originals." Correct? Ehrman has had a long history of creating hopelessness for his readers, as he carries on his alleged truth quest. He asserts that even in the very few numbers of places that we might be sure about the *wording*, we cannot be certain about the *meaning*.

Blinded by Misguided Perceptions

Ehrman clearly has been immensely impacted by the fact that we do not have the originals or immediate copies. Here we have a world-renowned textual and early Christianity scholar who is emphasizing that we do not have the originals, nor the direct copies, and since there are so many copyist errors, it is virtually impossible to get back to the Word of God at all. Even if by some stroke of fortune, we could, we cannot know the meaning with assurance. Ehrman is saying to the lay reader: we can no longer trust the text of the Greek New Testament as the Word of God. If so, we would have to conclude that all translations are untrustworthy as well.

Ehrman has exaggerated the negative to his readers to the detriment of the positive in New Testament textual criticism. Mark Minnick assesses the latter nicely: "Doesn't the existence of these variants undermine our confidence that we have the very words of God inspired? No! The fact is that because we know of them and are careful to preserve the readings of every one of them, *not one word of God's word has been lost to us.*"[155] The wealth of manuscripts that we have for establishing the original Greek New Testament is overwhelming, in comparison to other ancient literature. We can only wonder what Ehrman does with an ancient piece of literature

---

[155] Mark Minnick, "Let's Meet the Manuscripts," in *From the Mind of God to the Mind of Man: A Layman's Guide to How We Got Our Bible*, eds. James B. Williams and Randolph Shaylor (Greenvill, SC: Ambassador-Emerald International, 1999), p. 96.

that has only one copy, and that copy is hundreds or even over a thousand years removed from the time of the original.

Consider a few examples. Before beginning, it should be noted that some of the classical authors are centuries, some many centuries before the first century New Testament era, which is a somewhat unfair comparison. See the chart below.[156]

Author	Work	Writing Completed	Earliest MSS	Years Removed	Number of MSS
Homer	*Iliad*	800 B.C.E.	3rd century B.C.E.[157]	500	1,757
Herodotus	*History*	480–425 B.C.E.	10th cent. C.E.	1,350	109
Sophocles	*Plays*	496–406 B.C.E.	3rd cent. B.C.E.[158]	100-200	193
Thucydides	*History*	460–400 B.C.E.	3rd cent. B.C.E.[159]	200	96
Plato	*Tetralogies*	400 B.C.E.	895 C.E.	1,300	210
Demosthenes	*Speeches*	300 B.C.E.	Fragments from 1st cent. B.C.E.	1,000	340
Caesar	*Gallic Wars*	51-46 B.C.E.	9th cent. C.E.	950	251
Livy	*History of Rome*	59 B.C.E.–17 C.E.	5th cent. C.E.	400	150
Tacitus	*Annals*	100 C.E.	9th-11th cent. C.E.	750–950	33
Pliny, the Elder	*Natural History*	49–79 C.E.	5th cent. C.E. fragment	400	200
Eight Greek NT Authors	27 Books	50 – 98 C.E.	110-125 C.E.	12-27	5,800

The Greek New Testament evidence, as we've mentioned previously, is over 5,830+ Greek manuscripts that have been cataloged, over 9,284 versions, and over 10,000 Latin manuscripts, not to mention an

---

[156] The concept of this chart is taken from *The Bibliographical Test Updated - Christian Research* ... http://www.equip.org/article/the-bibliographical-test-updated/ May 04, 2017. However, some adjustments have been made as well as footnotes added.

[157] There are a number of fragments that date to the second century B.C.E. and one to the third century B.C.E., with the rest dating to the ninth century C.E. or later.

[158] Most of the 193 MSS date to the tenth century C.E., with a few fragments dating to the third century B.C.E.

[159] Some papyri fragments date to the third century B.C.E.

innumerable amount of church fathers' quotations. This places the Greek New Testament in a class by itself, because no other ancient document is close to this. However, there is even more. There are 62 Greek papyri, along with five majuscule manuscripts that date to the second and third centuries C.E.[160] Moreover, these early papyri manuscripts are from a region in Egypt that appreciated books as literature, and were copied by semi-professional and professional scribes, or at least highly skilled copyists. This region produced what are known as the most accurate and trusted manuscripts.

Were the Scribes in the Early Centuries Amateurs?

We could **go on nearly forever** talking about specific places in which the texts of the New Testament came to be changed, either accidentally or intentionally. As I have indicated, the examples are **not just in the hundreds but in the thousands**. The examples given are enough to convey the general point, however: there are lots of differences among our manuscripts, differences created by scribes who were reproducing their sacred texts. **In the early Christian centuries, scribes were amateurs** and as such were more inclined to alter the texts they copied—or more prone to alter them accidentally—than were scribes in the later periods who, starting in the fourth century, began to be

---

[160] **Dr. Daniel B. Wallace**, Executive Director of The Center for the Study of New Testament Manuscripts (CSNTM):

On 1 February 2012, I debated Bart Ehrman at UNC Chapel Hill on whether we have the wording of the original New Testament today. This was our third such debate, and it was before a crowd of more than 1000 people. I mentioned that **seven New Testament papyri had recently been discovered—six of them probably from the second century and one of them probably from the first**. These fragments will be published in about a year.

These manuscripts now increase our holdings as follows: we have as many as eighteen New Testament manuscripts (all fragmentary, more or less) from the second century and one from the first. **Altogether, about 33% of all New Testament verses are found in these manuscripts. But the most interesting thing is the first-century fragment.**

It was dated by one of the world's leading paleographers. He said he was 'certain' that it was from the first century. If this is true, it would be the oldest fragment of the New Testament known to exist. Up until now, no one has discovered any first-century manuscripts of the New Testament. The oldest manuscript of the New Testament has been P52, a small fragment from John's Gospel, dated to the first half of the second century. It was discovered in 1934.

Not only this, but the first-century fragment is from Mark's Gospel. **Before the discovery of this fragment, the oldest manuscript that had Mark in it was P45, from the early third century (c. 200–250 CE). This new fragment would predate that by 100 to 150 years.—http://csntm.org/news**

professionals. (B. D. Ehrman, Misquoting Jesus: The Story Behind Who Changed the Bible and Why 2005, 98) [Bold mine]

Let us take just a moment to discuss Ehrman's statement, "**in the early Christian centuries, scribes were amateurs....**" In this book, we established just the opposite. Literate or semi-professional copyist did the vast majority of our early papyri, with some being done by professionals. As it happened, the few poorly copied manuscripts became known first, establishing a precedent that was difficult for some to discard when the truckload of evidence came forth that showed just the opposite. (P. Comfort 2005, 18-19)

Ehrman is misrepresenting the situation to his readers when he states, "We don't even have copies of the copies of the originals or copies of the copies of the copies of the originals." The way this is worded, he is saying that we do not have copies that are three or four generations removed from the originals. Ehrman cannot know this because we have fifteen copies that are 75 to 100 years removed from the death of the apostle John in 100 C.E. There is the possibility that any of these could be only third or fourth generation removed copies. Furthermore, they could have been copied from a second or third generation. Therefore, Ehrman is misstating the evidence. Moreover, the uncertainty of this rhetoric is exposed by the above fact that we now have "seven New Testament papyri, [which] had recently been discovered, six of them probably from the second century and one of them probably from the first."[161]

Let us do another short review of two very important manuscripts: P75 and Vaticanus 1209 (B). P75 is also known as Bodmer 14, 15. As has already been stated, papyrus is writing material used by the ancient Egyptians, Greeks, and Romans that was made from the pith of the stem of a water plant. These are the earliest witnesses to the Greek New Testament. P75 contains most of Luke and John, dating from 175 C.E. to 225 C.E Vaticanus is designated internationally by the symbol "B" (and 03) and is known as an uncial manuscript written on parchment. It is dated to the mid-fourth-century C.E. [c. 350] and originally contained the entire Bible in Greek. At present, Vaticanus' New Testament is missing parts of Hebrews (Hebrews 9:14 to 13:25), all of First and Second Timothy, Titus, Philemon, and Revelation. Originally, this codex probably had approximately 820 leaves, of which 759 remain.

What kind of weight or evidence do these two manuscripts carry in the eyes of textual scholars? Vaticanus 1209 is a key source for our modern translations. When determining an original reading, this manuscript can

---

161

http://csntm.org/News/Archive/2012/2/10/EarliestManuscriptoftheNewTestamentDiscovered stand against other external evidence that would seem to the non-professional to be much more significant. P75 also is one of the weightiest manuscripts that we have and is virtually identical to Vaticanus 1209, which dates 175 to 125 years later than P75. When textual scholars B. F. Westcott and F. J. A. Hort released their critical text in 1881, Hort said that Vaticanus preserved "not only a very ancient text but a very pure line of a very ancient text." (Westcott and Hort 1882, 251) Later scholars argued that Vaticanus was a scholarly recension: a critical revision or edited text. However, P75 has vindicated Westcott and Hort because of its virtual identity with Vaticanus; it establishes that Vaticanus is essentially a copy of a second-century text, and likely, a copy of the original text, with the exception of a few minor points.

Kurt Aland[162] wrote, "P75 shows such a close affinity with the Codex Vaticanus that the supposition of a recension of the text at Alexandria, in the fourth century, can no longer be held."[163] David C. Parker[164] says of P75 that "it is extremely important for two reasons: "like Vaticanus, it is carefully copied; it is also very early and is generally dated to a period between 175 and 225. Thus, it pre-dates Vaticanus by at least a century. A careful comparison between P75 and Vaticanus in Luke by C.M. Martini demonstrated that P75 was an earlier copy of the same careful Alexandrian text. It is sometimes called proto-Alexandrian. It is our earliest example of a controlled text, one which was not intentionally or extensively changed in successive copying. Its discovery and study have provided proof that the Alexandrian text had already come into existence in the third century." (Parker 1997, 61) Let us look at the remarks of a few more textual scholars: J. Ed Komoszewski, M. James Sawyer, and Daniel Wallace.

> Even some of the early manuscripts show compelling evidence of being copies of a much earlier source. Consider again Codex Vaticanus, whose text is very much like that of P75 (B and P75 are much closer to each other than B is to [Codex Sinaiticus]). Yet the papyrus is at least a century older than Vaticanus. When P75 was discovered in the 1950s, some entertained the possibility that Vaticanus could have been a copy of P75, but this view is no longer acceptable since the wording of Vaticanus is certainly more

---

[162] (1915 – 1994) was Professor of New Testament Research and Church History. He founded the Institute for New Testament Textual Research in Münster and served as its first director for many years (1959–83). He was one of the principal editors of The Greek New Testament for the United Bible Societies.

[163] K. Aland, "The Significance of the Papyri for New Testament Research," 336.

[164] Professor of Theology and the Director of the Institute for Textual Scholarship and Electronic Editing at the Department of Theology and Religion, University of Birmingham. Scholar of New Testament textual criticism and Greek and Latin paleography.

primitive than that of P75 in several places.' They both must go back to a still earlier common ancestor, probably one that is from the early second century. (Komoszewski, M. Sawyer and Wallace 2006, 78)

Comfort comments on how we can know that Vaticanus is not a copy of P[75]: "As was previously noted, Calvin Porter clearly established the fact that P[75] displays the kind of text that was used in making codex Vaticanus. However, it is unlikely that the scribe of B used P[75] as his exemplar because the scribe of B copied from a manuscript whose line length was 12–14 letters per line. We know this because when the scribe of Codex Vaticanus made large omissions, they were typically 12–14 letters long.[165] The average line length for P[75] is about 29–32 letters per line. Therefore, the scribe of B must have used a manuscript like P[75], but not P[75] itself."[166]

Ehrman suggests that the early Christians were not concerned about the integrity of the text, its preservation of accuracy. Let us consult the second-century evidence by way of Tertullian.[167]

> Come now, you who would indulge a better curiosity, if you would apply it to the business of your salvation, run over the apostolic churches, in which the very thrones[168] of the apostles are still pre-eminent in their places,[169] in which their own **authentic writings** are read, uttering the voice and representing the face of each of them severally.[170] (Bold mine)

What did Tertullian mean by "authentic writings"? If he was referring to the Greek originals—and it seems that he was, according to the Latin—it is an indication that some of the original New Testament books were still in existence at the time of his penning this work. However, let us say that it is

---

[165] Brooke F. Westcott and Fenton J. A. Hort, *Introduction to the New Testament in the Original Greek* (New York: Harper & Bros., 1882; reprint, Peabody, Mass.: Hendrickson, 1988), 233–34.

[166] (Comfort and Barret, The Text of the Earliest New Testament Greek Manuscripts 2001)

[167] Tertullian (160 – 220 C.E.), was a prolific early Christian author from Carthage in the Roman province of Africa.

[168] Cathedrae

[169] Suis locis praesident.

[170] Alexander Roberts, James Donaldson and A. Cleveland Coxe, The Ante-Nicene Fathers Vol. III: Translations of the Writings of the Fathers Down to A.D. 325 (Oak Harbor: Logos Research Systems, 1997), 260.

simply referring to copies that were well-preserved. In any case, this shows that the Christians valued the preservation of accuracy.

We need to visit an earlier book by Ehrman for a moment, *Lost Christianities*, in which he writes, "In this process of recopying the document by hand, what happened to the original of 1 Thessalonians? For some unknown reason, it was eventually thrown away, burned, or otherwise destroyed. Possibly, it was read so much that it simply wore out. The early Christians saw no need to preserve it as the `original' text. They had copies of the letter. Why keep the original?" (B. D. Ehrman 2003, 217)

Here Ehrman is arguing from silence. We cannot read the minds of people today, let alone read the minds of persons 2,000 years in the past. It is a known fact that congregations valued Paul's letters, and Paul exhorted them to share the letters with differing congregations. Paul wrote to the Colossians, and in what we know as 4:16, he said, "And when this letter has been read among you, have it **also read in the church of the Laodiceans;** and see that you also read the letter from Laodicea." The best way to facilitate this would be to send someone to a congregation, have them copy the letter and bring it back to their home congregation. On the other hand, someone could make copies of the letter in the congregation that received it and deliver it to interested congregations. In 1 Thessalonians, the congregation that Ehrman is talking about here, at chapter five, verse 27, Paul says, "I put you under oath before the Lord to **have this letter read to all the brothers.**" What did Paul mean by "all the brothers"? It could be that he meant it to be used like a circuit letter, circulated to other congregations, giving everyone a chance to hear the counsel. It may merely be that, with literacy being so low, Paul wanted a guarantee that all were going to get to hear the letter's contents, and he simply meant for every brother and sister locally to have a chance to hear it in the congregation. Regardless, even if we accept the latter, the stress that was put on the reading of this letter shows the weight that these people were placed under concerning Paul's letters.[171] In addition, Comfort comments on how Paul and others would view apostolic letters:

> Paul knew the importance of authorized apostolic letters,
> for he saw the authority behind the letter that came from the first

---

[171] The exhortation ἐνορκίζω ὑμᾶς τὸν κύριον ἀναγνωσθῆναι τὴν ἐπιστολὴν πᾶσιν τοῖς ἀδελφοῖς ("I adjure you by the Lord that this letter be read aloud to all the brothers [and sisters]"), is stated quite strongly. ἐνορκίζω takes a double accusative and has a causal sense denoting that the speaker or writer wishes to extract an oath from the addressee(s). The second accusative, in this case τὸν κύριον ("the Lord"), indicates the thing or person by whom the addressees were to swear. The forcefulness of this statement is highly unusual, and in fact it is the only instance in Paul's letters where such a charge is laid on the recipients of one of his letters.—Charles A. Wanamaker, The Epistles to the Thessalonians: A Commentary on the Greek Text (Grand Rapids, Mich.: W.B. Eerdmans, 1990), 208-09.

Jerusalem church council. The first epistle from the church leaders who had assembled at Jerusalem was the prototype for subsequent epistles (see Acts 15). It was authoritative because it was apostolic, and it was received as God's word. If an epistle came from an apostle (or apostles), it was to be received as having the imprimatur [approval/authority] of the Lord. This is why Paul wanted the churches to receive his word as being the word of the Lord. This is made explicit in 1 Thessalonians (2:13), an epistle he insisted had to be read to all the believers in the church (5:27). In the Second Epistle to the Thessalonians, Paul indicated that his epistles carry the same authority as his preaching (see 2:15). Paul also told his audience that if they would read what he had written, they would be able to understand the mystery of Christ, which had been revealed to him (see Eph. 3:1–6). Because Paul explained the mystery in his writings (in this case, the encyclical epistle known as "Ephesians"), he urged other churches to read this encyclical (see Col. 4:16). In so doing, Paul himself encouraged the circulation of his writings. Peter and John also had publishing plans. Peter's first epistle, written to a wide audience (the Christian diaspora in Pontus, Galatia, Cappadocia, Asia, Bithynia—see 1 Pet. 1:1), was a published work, which must have been produced in several copies from the onset, to reach his larger, intended audience. John's first epistle was also published and circulated—probably to all the churches in the Roman province of Asia Minor. First John is not any kind of occasional epistle; it is more like a treatise akin to Romans and Ephesians in that it contains John's full explanation of the Christian life and doctrine as a model for all orthodox believers to emulate. The book of Revelation, which begins with seven epistles to seven churches in this same province, must have also been inititally published in seven copies, as the book circulated from one locality to the next, by the seven "messengers" (Greek *anggeloi*—not "angels" in this context). By contrast, the personal letters (Philemon, 1 and 2 Timothy, Titus, 2 John, 3 John) were not originally "published"; therefore, their circulation was small. Second Peter also had minimal circulation in the early days of the church. Because of its popularity, the book of Hebrews seemed to have enjoyed wide circulation—this was promoted by the fact that most Christians in the East thought it was the work of Paul and therefore was included in Pauline collections (see discussion below). The book of Acts was originally published by Luke as a sequel to his Gospel (see Acts 1:1–2). Unfortunately, in due course, this book got detached from Luke when the Gospel of

Luke was placed in one-volume codices along with the other Gospels.[172]

Peter, as we have seen, also had this to say about Paul's letters: "there are some things in them [Paul's letters] that are hard to understand, which the ignorant and unstable twist to their own destruction, **as they do the other Scriptures.**" (2 Pet 3:16) Peter viewed Paul's letters as being on the same level as the Old Testament, which was referred to as Scripture. In the second century (about 135 C.E.), Papias, an elder of the early congregation in Hierapolis, made the following comment.

> I will not hesitate to set down for you, along with my interpretations, everything I carefully learned then from the elders and carefully remembered, guaranteeing their truth. For unlike most people I did not enjoy those who have a great deal to say, but those who teach the truth. Nor did I enjoy those who recall someone else's commandments, but those who remember the commandments given by the Lord to the faith and proceeding from the truth itself. In addition, if by chance someone who had been a follower of the elders should come my way, I inquired about the words of the elders--what Andrew or Peter said, or Philip, or Thomas or James, or John or Matthew or any other of the Lord's disciples, and whatever Aristion and the elder John, the Lord's disciples, were saying. For I did not think that information from books would profit me as much as information from a living and abiding voice.[173]

As an elder in the congregation at Hierapolis, in Asia Minor, Papias was an unrelenting researcher, as well as a thorough compiler of information; he exhibited intense indebtedness for the Scriptures. Papias determined properly that any doctrinal statement of Jesus Christ or his apostles would be far more appreciated and respected to explain than the unreliable statements found in the written works of his day. We can compare Jude 1:17, where Jude exhorts his readers to preserve the words of the apostles.

Therefore, the notion that the "early Christians saw no need to preserve it as the 'original' text," is far too difficult to accept when we consider the above. Moreover, imagine a church in middle America being visited by Billy Graham. Now imagine that he wrote them a warm letter, but one also filled with some stern counsel. Would there be little interest in the preservation of those words? Would they not want to share it with

---

[172] (P. Comfort, Encountering the Manuscripts: An Introduction to New Testament Paleography and Textual Criticism 2005, 17)

[173] (Holmes, The Apostolic Fathers: Greek Texts and English Translations 2007, 565)

145

others? Would other churches not be interested in it? The same would have been even truer of early Christianity receiving a letter from an apostle like Peter, John, or Paul. There is no doubt that the "original" wore out eventually. However, they lived in a society that valued the preservation of the apostle's words, and it is far more likely that it was copied with care, to share with others, and to preserve. Moreover, let us acknowledge that their imperfections took over as well. Paul would have become a famous apostle who wrote a few churches, and there were thousands of churches toward the end of the first century. Would they have not exhibited some pride in the fact that they received a letter from the famous apostle Paul, who was martyred for the truth? Ehrman's suggestions are reaching and contrary to human nature. It is simply wishful thinking on his part.

However, Ehrman may not have entirely dismissed the idea of getting back to the original if he agreed with Metzger in their coauthored fourth edition of *The Text of the New Testament*. Metzger's original comments from previous editions are repeated there as follows.

> Besides textual evidence derived from New Testament Greek manuscripts and from early versions, the textual critic compares numerous scriptural quotations used in commentaries, sermons, and other treatises written by early church fathers. Indeed, so extensive are these citations that if all other sources for our knowledge of the text of the New Testament were destroyed, they would be sufficient alone for the reconstruction of practically the entire New Testament. (Metzger and Ehrman 2005, 126)

How are we to view the patristic citations? Let us look at another book for which Ehrman was coeditor and a contributor with other textual scholars: *The Text of the New Testament in Contemporary Research* (1995). The following is from Chapter 12, written by Gordon Fee (*The Use of the Greek Fathers for New Testament Textual Criticism*).

> In NT textual criticism, patristic citations are ordinarily viewed as the third line of evidence, indirect and supplementary to the Greek MSS, and are often therefore treated as of tertiary importance. When properly evaluated, however, patristic evidence is of primary importance, for both of the major tasks of NT textual criticism: in contrast to the early Greek MSS, the Fathers have the potential of offering datable and geographically certain evidence. (B. D. Ehrman 1995, 191)

To conclude, we have established that Ehrman has painted a picture that is not quite the truth of the matter for the average churchgoer while saying something entirely different for textual scholars. Moreover, he does not help the reader to appreciate just how close the New Testament manuscript evidence is to the time of the original writings, in comparison to manuscripts of other ancient works, many of which are few in number and hundreds, if not a thousand years removed.

In addition, Ehrman has exaggerated the variants in the Greek New Testament manuscripts by **not** qualifying the level of variants. In other words, he has not explained how he counts them to obtain such high numbers. Moreover, Ehrman's unqualified statement, "In the early Christian centuries, scribes were amateurs," has been discredited as well. Either literate or semi-professional copyist did **the vast majority** of the early papyri, with some being done by professionals.

CHAPTER 6 What Are Textual Variants [Errors] and How Many Are There?

The first part of this chapter will cover the gist of what is most often discussed in New Testament textual criticism today. After that, we will discuss what should be the primary focus of NTTC (New Testament Textual Criticism). It would seem that Bart D. Ehrman and other Bible critics of his persuasion have sent many textual scholars on a quest. These scholars have become obsessed with discussing how many variants there are, how to count the textual variants, and whether they are significant or insignificant. Below, we will cover what is being said about variants, as well as whether some are more significant than others, and then close the chapter with what actually is the most important mission in NTTC.

Some Bible critics seem, to begin with, the belief that if the originals were inspired of God and fully inerrant, the subsequent copies must continue to be inerrant in order for the inerrancy of the originals to have value. They seem to be asking, "If only the originals were inspired, and the copies were not inspired, and we do not have the originals, how are we to be certain of any passage in Scripture?" In other words, God would never allow the inspired, inerrant Word to suffer copying errors. Why would he perform the miracle of inspiring the message to be fully inerrant and not continue with the miracle of inspiring the copyists throughout the centuries to keep it inerrant? First, we must acknowledge that God has not given us the specifics of every decision he has made in reference to humans. If we begin asking, "Why did God not do this or do that," where would it end? For example, why didn't God just produce the books himself, and miraculously deliver them to people as he gave the commandments to Moses? Instead of using humans, why did he not use angelic messengers to pen the message, or produce the message miraculously? God has chosen not to tell us why he did not move the copyists along with the Holy Spirit, so as to have perfect copies, and it remains an unknown. However, it should be noted that if we can restore the text to its original wording through the science of textual criticism, i.e. to an exact representation thereof, we have, in essence, the originals.

We do know that the Jewish copyists and later Christian copyists were not infallible as were the original writers. The Holy Spirit inspired the original writers, while the most that can be said about the copyists is that they were **guided** by the Holy Spirit. However, do we not have a treasure-load of evidence from centuries of copies, unlike ancient secular literature? Regardless of the recopying, do we not have the Bible in a reliable critical text and trustworthy translations, with both improving all the time? It was only inevitable that imperfect copyists, who were not under inspiration, would cause errors to creep into the text. However, the thousands of copies that we have enable textual scholars to identify and reject these errors. How? For one thing, different copyists made different errors. Therefore, the textual scholar compares the work of different copyists. He is then able to identify their mistakes.

A Simple Example

Suppose 100 people were invited or hired to make a handwritten copy of Matthew's Gospel, with 18,345 words. Further suppose that these people fit in one of four categories as writers: (1) struggle to write and have no experience as a document maker; (2) skilled document makers (recorders of events, wills, business, certificates, etc.); (3) trained copyists of literature; and (4) the professional copyists. There is little doubt that these copyists would make some copying errors, even the professionals. However, it would be impossible that they would all make the same errors. If a trained textual scholar with many years of religious education, including textual studies, and decades of experience, were to compare the 100 documents carefully, he could identify the errors and restore the text to its original form, even if he had never seen that original.

The textual scholars of the last 250 years, especially the last 70 years have had over 5,800 Greek manuscripts at their disposal. A number of the manuscripts are portions dating to the second and third centuries C.E. Moreover, more manuscripts are always becoming known; technology is ever advancing, and improvements are always being made.

Hundreds of scholars throughout the last three centuries have produced what we might call a master text, by way of lifetimes of hard work and careful study. Are there places where we are not certain of the reading? Yes, of course. However, we are considering very infrequent places in the text of the Greek NT that contains about 138,020 words, which would be considered difficult in arriving at what the original reading was. In all these places the alternative readings are provided in the apparatus. Bible critics who exaggerate the extent of errors are misleading the public on several fronts. First, some copies are almost error-free and negate the critics, who claim, "We have only error-ridden copies."[174] Second, the vast majority of the Greek New Testament has no scribal errors. Third, textual scholarship can easily identify and correct the majority of the scribal errors. In addition, of the remaining errors, we can still say most are

---

[174] (Bart D. Ehrman, Misquoting Jesus: The Story Behind Who Changed the Bible and Why 2005, 7)

solved with satisfaction. Of the small number of scribal errors remaining, we can say that most are solved with some difficulty, and there remain very few errors of which textual scholarship continues to be uncertain about the original reading at this time.

400,000 to 500,000 Supposed Variants in the Manuscripts

With this abundance of evidence, what can we say about the total number of variants known today? Scholars differ significantly in their estimates—some say there are 200,000 variants known, some say 300,000, some say **400,000 or more!** We do not know for sure because, despite impressive developments in computer technology, no one has yet been able to count them all. Perhaps, as I indicated earlier, it is best simply to leave the matter in comparative terms. There are more variations among our manuscripts than there are words in the New Testament.[175]

Bart D. Ehrman has some favorite, unprofessional ways of describing the problems, which he stresses without qualification, in every interview he has for a lay audience or seminary students. Below are several, the first two from the quotation above:

- Scholars differ significantly in their estimates—some say there are 200,000 variants known, some say 300,000, some say **400,000 or more!**

- There are **more variations** among our manuscripts **than there are words** in the New Testament.

- We have only **error-ridden copies,** and the vast majority of these are centuries removed from the originals and different from them, evidently, in thousands of ways. (*Whose Word is It,* 7)

- We don't even have copies of the copies of the originals, or **copies of the copies of the copies of the originals.** (*Misquoting Jesus,* 10)

- **In the early Christian centuries, scribes were amateurs** and as such were more inclined to alter the texts they copied. (*Misquoting Jesus,* 98)

- **We could go on nearly forever** talking about specific places in which the texts of the New Testament came to be changed, either accidentally or intentionally. (*Misquoting Jesus,* 98)

- The Bible began to appear to me as a very **human book.** (*Misquoting Jesus,* 11)

---

[175] Ibid., 89-90

Each of the bullet points above claimed by Ehrman can be categorized as an exaggeration, misinformation, misleading, or just a failure to be truthful. Many laypersons-churchgoers have been spiritually shipwrecked in their faith by such unexplained hype. What the uninformed person hears is that we can never get back to the originals or even close, that there are hundreds of thousands of significant variants that have so scarred the text, we no longer have the Word of God, and it is merely the word of man. How such a knowledgeable man cannot know the impact his words are having is beyond this author.

Miscounting Textual Variants

In 1963, Neil R. Lightfoot penned a book that has served to help over a million readers, *How We Got the Bible*. It has been revised two times since 1963, once in 1988, and again in 2003. There is a "miscalculation" in the book which has contributed to a misunderstanding in how textual variants are counted. In fact, there are several other books repeating it. A leading textual scholar, Daniel B. Wallace, has brought this to our attention in an article entitled, *The Number of Textual Variants an Evangelical Miscalculation.*[176] World-renowned Bible apologist Norman L. Geisler has commented on it as well.

Lightfoot wrote,

From one point of view, it may be said that there are 200,000 scribal errors in the manuscripts. Indeed, the number may well considerably exceed this and obviously will grow, as more and more manuscripts become known. However, it is wholly misleading and untrue to say that there are 200,000 errors in the text of the New Testament. (Actually, textual critics consciously avoid the word "error;" they prefer to speak of "textual variants.") This large number is gained by counting all the variations in all of the manuscripts (over 5,800). This means that if, for example, one word is misspelled in 4,000 different manuscripts, and it amounts to 4,000 "errors." Actually, in a case of this kind, only one slight error has been made, and it has been copied 4,000 times. But this is the procedure which is followed in arriving at the large number of 200,000 "errors."[177]

Wallace makes this observation in his article:

[176] http://bible.org/article/number-textual-variants-evangelical-miscalculation

[177] *How We Got the Bible* (Grand Rapids: Baker, 2003; p). Lightfoot says (53-54)

In other words, Lightfoot was claiming that textual variants are counted by the number of manuscripts that support such variants, rather than by the wording of the variants. This book has been widely influential in evangelical circles. I believe over a million copies of it have been sold. And this particular definition of textual variants has found its way into countless apologetic works." He goes on to clarify just what a textual variant is, "The problem is, the definition is wrong. Terribly wrong. A textual variant is simply any difference from a standard text (e.g., a printed text, a particular manuscript, etc.) that involves spelling, word order, omission, addition, substitution, or a total rewrite of the text. No textual critic defines a textual variant the way that Lightfoot and those who have followed him have done.

Geisler writes,

> Some have estimated there are about 200,000 of them. First of all, these are not "errors" but variant readings, the vast majority of which are strictly grammatical. Second, these readings are spread throughout more than 5300 manuscripts, so that a variant spelling of one letter of one word in one verse in 2000 manuscripts is counted as 2000 "errors."[178]

Lightfoot evidently was thought to have erred by counting manuscripts, rather than the variants in the text. In fairness to Lightfoot, it should be pointed out that he deplored the system of counting "errors" by the number of manuscripts, as the quotation above reveals. He was simply saying that critics were doing this, not that it was proper. It is difficult to see why Wallace would attribute responsibility for the system to Lightfoot. Also, Wallace cited Lightfoot's 1963 edition that did not include the distinction between "error" and "textual variant."

Let me offer the reader an example for our purposes. First, we should underscore a few important points raised: 1) we have so many variants because we have so many manuscripts. 2) We do *not* count the manuscripts; we count the variants. 3) A variant is any portion of the text that exhibits variations in its reading between two or more different manuscripts. This is more precisely called a **variation unit**. It is important to distinguish variation units from variant readings. Variation units are the places in the text where manuscripts disagree, and each variation unit has at least two variant readings. Setting the limits and range of a variation unit is sometimes difficult or even controversial because some variant readings

---

[178] *Baker Encyclopedia of Christian Apologetics*, by Norm Geisler (Grand Rapids: Baker, 1998; p. 532)

affect others nearby. Such variations may be considered individually, or as elements of a longer single reading.

We should also note that the terms "manuscript" and "witness" may appear to be used interchangeably in this context. Strictly speaking, "witness" (see below) only refers to the content of a given manuscript or fragment, so the witness predates the physical manuscript on which it is written to a greater or lesser extent. However, the only way to reference the "witness" is by referring to the manuscript or fragment that contains it. In this book, we have sometimes used the terminology "witness *of* x or y manuscript" to distinguish the content in this way.

We begin by choosing our "base" or "standard text." We are using the *standard text* (critical or master text), Nestle-Aland (NA) Greek Text (28th edition) and the United Bible Society (UBS) Greek Text (5th edition). These two critical texts are actually the same. Therefore,

Note: When the acronym **NU** is used, **N** stands for Nestle-Aland, the **U** for United Bible Societies, since the texts are the same. The apparatuses are different, the UBS version designed primarily for translators (more on this below).

In this writer's opinion, the critical NU text is as close as we can get to what the original would have been like.[179] Therefore, we can use the reading in the critical text as the original reading, and anything outside of that in the manuscript history is a variant: spelling, word order, omission, addition, substitution, or a total rewrite of the text. Any difference in two different manuscripts is a variant, technically speaking.

Before going to our example, I want to emphasize that Bible critics, who grumble and repeat over and over again how there are 400,000 variants in the text of the New Testament, have only one agenda: they want to discredit the Word of God. They use the issue of variants as a misrepresented excuse for their having lost their faith, having shipwrecked their faith, or having had no faith from the start. These Bible critics are no different from the religious leaders Jesus dealt with in the first century. Jesus said of them, "Blind guides! You strain out a gnat, yet gulp down a camel!" (Matt. 23:24). They thrust aside 99.95 percent because 0.05 of one per

---

[179] It is true that some scholars, such as Philip Comfort, argue that the NU could be improved upon because in many cases it is too dependent on internal evidence, when the documentary evidence should be more of a consideration in choosing readings. It should be pointed out, however, that this is in only a relative handful of places, when one considers 138,020 words in the Greek New Testament, and it is hardly consequential. I would also mention that this writer would agree with Comfort in the matter of giving more weight to documentary evidence.

cent is in not absolutely certain! Now let's turn to our example, which comes from the Apostle Paul's letter to the Colossians.

Example of a Textual Variant

Colossians 2:2 Updated American standard Version (UASV)

2 that their hearts may be comforted, having been knit together in love, and into all riches of the full assurance of understanding, and that they may have a complete knowledge[180] of the mystery **of God**, namely **Christ**, [τοῦ θεοῦ Χριστοῦ; tou theou Christou]

See the chart below.

Variants	Variant	MSS or Versions
NU[181]	of the God of Christ	Standard Text
1	of the God	10 MSS[182]
2	of the Christ	1 MS
3	of the God who is Christ	4 MSS
4	of the God who is concerning Christ	2 MSS
5	Of the God in the Christ	2 MSS
6	of the God in the Christ Jesus	1 MS
7	of the God and Christ	1 MS
8	Of God the father Christ	4 MSS
9	Of God the father of Christ	5 MSS
10	Of God and Father of Christ	2 MSS
11	Of God father and of Christ	4 MSS
12	Of God father and of Christ Jesus	3 MSS
13	Of God father and of Lord of us Christ Jesus	2 MSS
14	Of God and father and of Christ	38 MSS
Total 14	14 Variants in 79 MSS	79 MSS

---

[180] *Epignosis* is a strengthened or intensified form of *gnosis* (*epi*, meaning "additional"), meaning, "true," "real," "full," "complete" or "accurate," depending upon the context. Paul and Peter alone use *epignosis*.

[181] Recall that NU is an acronym for two critical manuscripts: (1) Nestle-Aland Greek Text (28th ed.) and (2) United Bible Societies Greek Text (5th ed.)

[182] This is only a partial list of the manuscripts, as we are just offering an example, to see how we count the variants.

These variants are found in 79 MSS, Thus, we have 14 variants in 79 manuscripts, not 79 variants. We do not count manuscripts, as most textual scholars know. In trying to paint a picture about the trustworthiness of the text, this author does not think talking about variants is really helpful, and it can confuse the layperson. It is important for the churchgoer to know what a variant is and the general extent of the variants, but in the long run, it is the places in the text that are affected by variants that most matter, and what we have as our text in the end.

The United Bible Society's "A" "B" "C" and "D" ratings are fine, and the definitions by UBS, i.e., [A] **certain**, [B] **almost certain**, [C] **difficulty in deciding**, and [D] **great difficulty in arriving at**, are helpful but should be better qualified, with some numbers of what percentage of the text fall under each area.

All Variant Units (Places)

What we need to talk about is how many **places** there are where we find variants. What percentage is this of the entire New Testament text?

We can then discuss:

- What percentage of the text is untouched by variants?
- Of the percentage affected, how much can we say or surmise to be given an "A" rating, a "B" Rating, a "C," or "D" rating?

Variant Reading and Variation Unit

This section is based in large part on the work by Eldon Jay Epp and Gordon D. Fee, *Studies in the Theory and Method of New Testament Textual Criticism* (Grand Rapids, MI: Eerdmans, 1993), wherein Eldon J. Epp expands on the brief 1964 article of Ernest C. Colwell (1901–74) and Ernest W. Tune on "Variant Readings: Classification and Use."

Again, what we need to discuss is how many variation units (places) there are where we find variations. Before doing so, let us define some terms.

SIGNIFICANT AND INSIGNIFICANT READINGS AND OR VARIANTS: Below we have what are commonly described as significant and insignificant variants. *Significant* would mean any reading that has an impact on the transmission history of a variant unit. For example, it would apply to how we determine the relationship of the manuscripts to one another, such as where a particular manuscript would fall in the history and transmission of the manuscripts. It would also be impactful if the reading could help the textual scholar establish the original. Therefore, *insignificant* would mean just the opposite, referring to a reading that has very little to no impact at all in *many* aspects of a transmission history. The reason we stop at "many" aspects here is that all readings in a manuscript play a role in some aspects of the transmission history, such as the characteristics of the manuscript it is in and the scribal activity within that individual manuscript.

Insignificant—Nonsense Reading: As Epp points out, a nonsense reading is "a reading that fails to make sense because it cannot be construed grammatically, either in terms of grammatical/lexical form or in terms of grammatical structure, or because in some other way it lacks a recognizable meaning. Since authors and scribes do not produce nonsense intentionally, it is to be assumed (1) that nonsense readings resulted from errors in transmission, (2) that they, therefore, cannot represent either the original text or the intended text of any MS or alert scribe, and (3) that they do not aid in the process of discerning the relationships among MSS."[183] It should also be stated that the original did not contain any nonsense readings, as the writers were led by the Holy Spirit. The inspired author before publication would have corrected any error by a scribe such as Tertius or Silvanus.

Insignificant—Certainty of Scribal Errors: while these errors "can be construed grammatically and make sense," there is a certainty on the part of textual scholars that these are scribal errors. These are not nonsense readings but rather readings that make sense, which are scribal errors beyond all reasonable doubt. These would "be certain instances of haplography and dittography, cases of harmonization with similar contexts, hearing errors producing a similar-sounding word, and the transposition of letters or words with a resultant change in meaning."[184] The problem that we sometimes encounter here is that what may be *certainty* of scribal error to one scholar may instead be an *almost certainty* to another, and even less so to another. The key element here in determining a reading that is understandable as insignificant is that it can be "demonstrated" so by the scholar making such a claim.

Insignificant—Incorrect Orthography (Greek for "correct writing"): this term is used loosely to refer to the spelling of words, which (for Greek) can include breathing and accent marks. Thus, one can refer to variations in the orthography of a word, or even to incorrect orthography. When a variation in orthography is due merely to dialectical or historical changes in spelling for variant readings, the variations are often ignored in the decision process because the reading in question is identical to another

---

[183] Eldon Jay Epp and Gordon D. Fee, *Studies in the Theory and Method of New Testament Textual Criticism* (Grand Rapids, MI: Eerdmans, 1993), 58.

[184] Ibid. 58.

reading, once the orthographical differences are factored in (*mutatis mutandis*). Epp writes, "Mere orthographic differences, particularly itacisms and nu-movables (as well as abbreviations) are 'insignificant' as here defined; they cannot be utilized in any decisive way for establishing manuscript relationships, and they are not substantive in the search for the original text. Again, the exception might be the work of a slavish scribe, whose scrupulousness might be considered useful in tracing manuscript descent, but the pervasive character of itacism, for example, over wide areas and time-spans precludes the 'significance' of orthographic differences for this important text-critical task."[185]

Insignificant—Singular Readings: a singular reading is technically a variant reading that occurs only once in only one Greek manuscript and is therefore immediately suspect. There is some quibbling over this because critics who reject the Westcott and Hort position on the combination of 01 (Sinaiticus) and 03 (Vaticanus) might call a reading "nearly singular" if it has only the support of these two manuscripts. Moreover, it is understood that not all manuscripts are comparable. Thus, for example, one would comfortably reject a reading found only in a single late manuscript, while many critics would not find it so easy to reject a reading supported uniquely by 03. Some also give more credit to singular readings that have additional support from versions. Singular readings that are insignificant would be nonsense readings, transcriptional errors, meaningless transpositions, and itacisms.

Significant Variants: a *significant* reading/variant is any reading that has an impact on any major facet of transmission history of a variant unit. One approach to identifying these is to remove the insignificant variants first: nonsense readings, determined (without doubt) scribal errors, incorrect orthography, and singular readings. Those readings that cannot be ruled out in this process are probably significant.

Number of Variants, Significant and Insignificant Variants vs. Level of Certainty

It would seem that some scholars have lost sight of the most important goal of textual criticism, namely, reconstructing the original. There is little doubt that agnostic Bible scholar Dr. Bart D. Ehrman has led the conversation on how many textual variants exist. The author of this publication are focusing their attention on the initial goal of textual criticism, returning to the original. We believe that even now the Greek New Testament completely reliable. However, there are some 2,000

---

[185] Ibid. 58.

textual places within the New Testament that need to be dealt with because the witnesses and internal evidence require consideration and deliberation.

Level of Certainty

The level of certainty charts below is generated from A TEXTUAL COMMENTARY ON THE GREEK NEW TESTAMENT (Second Edition), A Companion Volume to the UNITED BIBLE SOCIETIES' GREEK NEW TESTAMENT (Fourth Revised Edition) by Bruce M. Metzger.

The letter {A} signifies that the text is certain.

The letter {B} indicates that the text is almost certain.

The letter {C} indicates that the Committee had difficulty in deciding which variant to place in the text.

The letter {D}, which occurs only rarely, indicates that the Committee had great difficulty in arriving at a decision. In fact, among the {D} decisions sometimes none of the variant readings commended itself as original, and therefore the only recourse was to print the least unsatisfactory reading.

The word count below is taken from the Nestle-Aland Novum Testamentum Graece using Logos Bible Software.[186] While this author has compiled the numbers regarding the level of certainty of readings from Metzger's Textual Commentary, he has not gone to the point of counting the letters or words at each variant place. We will just offer the reader the general statement that almost all textual variants in the commentary were based on a letter or a few letters in a Greek word, to two-three words. Seldom was it an entire sentence or verse, very rarely several verses like the long ending of Mark. Therefore, we have chosen three words as the average to multiply the total number of variants, so that the reader can see the truly small number of variants that are even worthy of consideration, as opposed to the total number of words in the New Testament. For example, Matthew has 18,346 words with a mere 153 places where we find variants selected for the GNT, affecting about 459 words.

We need to add and emphasize, that all of the variants counted were selected by the GNT editors as relevant for translation, and the total does not include other variant units that were not considered relevant for that purpose. A good number of these additional variants can be found in the NA apparatus, but only with considerable difficulty in many cases because the same variants are frequently handled differently in the GNT and NA apparatuses. The author of this book do consider all variant units relevant

---

[186] Word Counts for Every Book of the Bible ..., http://overviewbible.com/word-counts-books-of-bible/ (accessed April 20, 2017).

even if a good number of them are difficult or virtually impossible to represent in translation (depending on the target language), and we recommend that the reader adjust the figures offered below by multiplying the numbers of variants by a factor of two, which should compensate for any variants that are not reported in the GNT text. We see no reason to assume a significantly different outcome in the ratings that might have been assigned to these variants if they had been included in the GNT, except possibly where no decisions might be possible in the cases of competing readings that were fully acceptable (rather than difficult).

For readers who have a working knowledge of NT Greek, it may be informative simply to select a few random pages of corresponding text from the GNT and NA and compare the apparatuses to see what is missing from the GNT relative to the NA apparatus. We believe that our suggestion of multiplying the variant figures below by a factor of two will appear more than reasonable; however, even using a factor of three or four will still leave a relatively minute percentage of "C" and "D" readings, as revealed below.

So then, if we look at Matthew and first multiply the GNT variant units by three for an average three words a variant, we have 459 words. Of the 153 variant units found in Matthew, we are certain of about 32 of them, almost certain about 70, have a little difficulty deciding on 50, and great difficulty deciding on only one variant unit. When we say that we have difficulty deciding, this does not mean that we cannot decide, as we can. Moreover, a good translation will list the alternative reading in a footnote. So, in the entirety of the Gospel of Matthew, there is only one variant place (Matt 23:26) which we would count as about three out of 18,346 words, where there was great difficulty in deciding the original. As it turns out, in this case, the GNT apparatus handles it as a variant of eight words, while NA breaks it into two variants, thus illustrating our point about the difficulty of comparing the two apparatuses. Some translations have incorporated the variant (ESV, NASB, NIV, TNIV, NJB, and the NLT), viewing it as the original, while other translations (NRSV, NEB, REB, NAB, CSB, and the UASV) see the variant as an addition taken from the previous verse.

Matthew 23:26 Blind Pharisee, cleanse first the inside of the cup,[187] so that the outside of it may also become clean. (UASV)

NU has καθάρισον πρῶτον τὸ ἐντὸς τοῦ ποτηρίου, ἵνα γένηται καὶ τὸ ἐκτὸς αὐτοῦ καθαρόν "first cleanse the **inside of the cup, that the outside**

---

[187] The NU (D Θ f¹ itᵃ,ᵉ syrˢ) has the above reading. A variant, WH and Byz (ℵ (B²) C L W 0102 0281 Maj) add "and of the dish." The variant is an addition taken from the previous verse.

of it may also become clean," which is supported by D Θ f¹ itᵃ·ᵉ syrˢ (bold mine).

Variant/Byz WH καθαρισον πρωτον το εντος του ποτηριου και της παροψιδος ινα γενηται και το εκτος αυτων καθαρον have "first cleanse the inside of the cup [and the dish], that the outside of them may also become clean," which is supported by ℵ (B²) C L W 0102 0281 Maj.

Looking at the above support alone, it would seem that the witnesses for the longer reading ("and the dish") are weightier, making the longer reading the likely original. Then, when we consider the presence of a few manuscripts (B* f¹³ 28 *al*) that are not listed for the shorter reading because they have the longer reading ("and the dish"), the weight shifts over to the shorter reading's being the original. Why? Because these few manuscripts have the singular αυτου instead of αὐτῶν, even though they have the longer reading. This tells us that the archetype text was the shorter reading. Clearly, the copyist added ("and the dish") from the previous verse, Matthew 23:25, which reads, "Woe to you, scribes and Pharisees, hypocrites! because you cleanse **the outside of the cup and of the dish,** but inside they are full of greediness and self-indulgence."

Below, we will look at all of the numbers, the total words in the Greek New Testament, the number of A, B, C, and D variants in each book as they were selected by the GNT committee, followed by the total number of variants listed in Metzger's textual commentary.

The Entire New Testament (138,020 Words)

{A-D}	New Testament
{A}	505
{B}	523
{C}	354
{D}	10
Total Var.	1,392
Words	138,020

The Gospels (64,767 Words)

{A-D}	Matt	Mark	Luke	John
{A}	32	45	44	44
{B}	70	49	73	62
{C}	50	45	44	41

{D}	1	1	0	2
Total Var.	153	140	161	149
Words	18,346	11,304	19,482	15,635

The Acts of the Apostles (18,450 Words)

{A-D}	Acts
{A}	74
{B}	82
{C}	40
{D}	1
Total Var.	197
Words	18,450

Paul's Fourteen Epistles (37,361 Words)

{A-D}	Rom	1 Cor	2 Cor	Gal.	Eph.	Php	Col.
{A}	39	21	12	16	16	10	8
{B}	19	22	17	3	11	7	12
{C}	20	15	10	8	7	3	8
{D}	1	1	0	0	0	0	0
Total Var.	79	59	39	27	34	20	28
WORDS	7,111	6,830	4,477	2,230	2,422	1,629	1,582

{A-D}	1 Th	2 Th	1 Tim	2 Tim	Tit	Phm.	Heb.
{A}	9	3	15	2	2	2	20
{B}	2	3	2	6	1	3	11
{C}	3	2	2	1	1	0	12
{D}	0	0	0	0	0	0	0
Total Var.	14	8	19	9	4	5	43
WORDS	1,481	823	1,591	1,238	659	335	4,953

The General Epistles (7,591 Words)

{A-D}	Jam	1 Pet	2 Pet	1 Jn	2 Jn	3 Jn	Jude
{A}	7	21	8	18	4	1	9
{B}	12	9	7	7	1	1	0
{C}	4	7	6	4	0	0	3
{D}	0	0	1	0	0	0	1
Total Var.	23	37	22	29	5	2	13
WORDS	1,742	1,684	1,099	2,141	245	219	461

The Book of Revelation (9,851 Words)

{A-D}	Revelation
{A}	23
{B}	31
{C}	18
{D}	1
Total Var.	73
Words	9,851

As noted above, the author of this publication maintain that all variation units or places where variations occur are significant because we are dealing with the Word of God, and reconstructing the original wording is of the utmost importance. Recall Lightfoot once more. "What about the significance of these variations? Are these variations immaterial or are they important? What bearing do they have on the New Testament message and on faith? To respond to these questions, it will be helpful to introduce three types of textual variations, classified in relation to their significance for our present New Testament text. 1. Trivial variations which are of no consequence to the text. 2. Substantial variations which are of no consequence to the text. 3. Substantial variations that have bearing on the text."[188]

Whether we are talking about the addition or omission of such words as "for," "and," and "the," or different forms of similar Greek words, differences in spelling, or the addition of a whole verse or even several verses, the importance lies **not with the significance of impact** on the meaning of the text but rather **the certainty** of the wording in the original. What we want to focus on is the certainty level of reconstructing every single word that Matthew, Mark, Luke, John, Paul, Peter, James, and Jude penned.

We will use Lightfoot's example of Matthew 11:10-23, that is, fourteen verses of 231 words; we have eleven variants in verses 10, 15, 16, 17, 18, 19(2), 20, 21, and 23(2). This may seem worrisome to the churchgoer or someone new to textual criticism. However, while all of the variants are found in the NA28 critical apparatus (2012), pp. 31-32,[189] the following sources below only covered seven of them because four are not even an

---

[188] *How We Got the Bibles*, by Neil R. Lightfoot (Grand Rapids: Baker, 1998; p. 95-103)

[189] Eberhard Nestle and Erwin Nestle, *Nestle-Aland: NTG Apparatus Criticus*, ed. Barbara Aland et al., 28. revidierte Auflage. (Stuttgart: Deutsche Bibelgesellschaft, 2012), 31–32.

issue. Why are they not an issue? We know what the original reading is with absolute certainty. The seven that have some uncertainty are mentioned in the textual commentaries below.

- Comfort *New Testament Text and Translation* covers verses 15 and 19

- Comfort *Commentary on the Manuscripts* and Text *of the New Testament* covers verses 12 and 19

- Metzger's *Textual Commentary on the Greek New Testament* covers 15, 17, 19, and 23.

Immediately we need to note that verse 12 is absolutely certain as to the original words as well. Verse 19a is mentioned in Comfort's textual commentary because he is drawing attention to the "Son of Man" being written as a nomen sacrum ("sacred name" that is abbreviated) in two early manuscripts (א W), as well as in L. Therefore, verse 19a is absolutely certain as well. We are now down to five variants. The original readings of verses 15, 17, 19a and the two in verse 23 where variants occur are almost certain. The textual scholars on the committees for four leading semi-literal and literal translations (ESV, LEB, CSB, and the NASB) agree on ten of the eleven variants. There is disagreement on **Matthew 11:15**. Even so, the reader has access to the original and alternatives in the footnote.

"He who has ears to hear, let him hear." (ESV, NASB, UASV)

The variant is ο εχων ωτα ακουειν ακουετω "the one having ears to hear let him hear," which is supported by א C L W Z Θ f¹,¹³ 33 Maj syr^c,h,p cop

"The one who has ears to hear, let him hear!" (LEB, cf. CSB)

WH and NU have ὁ ἔχων ὦτα ἀκουέτω "the one having ears let him hear," which is supported by B D 700 it^k syr^s

As is usually the case in more difficult decisions, the variant readings are divided in their support between the leading Alexandrian manuscripts. One reading has 01 (Sinaiticus) on its side, the other has 03 (Vaticanus). This tends to cancel out the weight of documentary evidence.

Now, we return to the charts above. There are 138,020 words in the New Testament. Just 1,392 textual variants deemed relevant for translation have enough of an issue to even be considered in the textual commentary. Again, if we average three words per variant, this amounts only to about 3.026 percent of the 138,020 words, or about 6 percent when we compensate for variant units ignored by the GNT editors. We can also remove the 505 {A} ratings because they are certain. Then, we really have no concerns about the {B} ratings because they are almost certain as well.

This means that out of 138,020 words in the Greek New Testament, we only have 364 variants (1,092 words by our average) with which we have difficulty, a mere 10 of which involve great difficulty in deciding which reading to put in the text. Our average would make these variants 0.791 percent of the text without accounting for any difficult variants not included because they were considered irrelevant for translation.

We need not be disturbed or distracted by worries of how many variants there are, or whether they are significant or insignificant. We need only to deal with the certainty of each variation unit, endeavoring to determine the original reading. We should also be concerned with the role textual criticism plays in apologetics. There is no possibility of apologetics if we do not have an authoritative and true Word of God. J. Harold Greenlee was correct when he wrote, "Textual criticism is the basic study for the accurate knowledge of any text. New Testament textual criticism, therefore, is the basic biblical study, a prerequisite to all other biblical and theological work. Interpretation, systemization, and application of the teachings of the NT cannot be done until textual criticism has done at least some of its work."[190] We would add apologetics to that list for which textual criticism is a prerequisite. How are we to defend the Word of God as inspired, inerrant, true, and authoritative, if we do not know whether we even have the Word of God? Therefore, when Bible critics try to muddy the waters of truth with misinformation, it is up to the textual scholar to correct the Bible critic's misinformation.

Again, it is true that Lightfoot erred if he was counting the manuscripts instead of the variants. However, we need not count variants either but rather variation units, namely, the places where there are variations. The above Colossians 2:2 example of variations that are found in 79 manuscripts was seen to have 14 variants in 79 manuscripts, not 79 variants. While this is true, it is also true that this is simply one variation unit, i.e. one place, where a variation occurs. This may sound as though we are trying to rationalize a major problem of hundreds of thousands of variants. However, it is actually the other way around. The Bible critic is misrepresenting the facts, trying to talk about an issue without giving the reader or listener all of the facts. We need to consider Benjamin Disraeli's words on statistics: "There are three types of lies: lies, damn lies, and statistics."

---

[190] *Introduction to New Testament Textual Criticism*, by J. Harold Greenlee (Peabody: Hendrickson Publishers, 1995; p. 7)

Certainty of the Original Words of the Original Authors

Virgil (70-19 B.C.E.) wrote the *Aeneid* between 29 and 19 B.C.E. for which there are only five manuscripts dating to the fourth and fifth centuries C.E.[191] Jewish historian Josephus (37-100 C.E.) wrote *The Jewish Wars* about 75 C.E., for which we have nine complete manuscripts, seven of major importance dating from the tenth to the twelfth centuries C.E.[192] Tacitus (59-129 C.E.) wrote *Annals of Imperial Rome* sometime before 116 C.E., a work considered vital to understanding the history of the Roman Empire during the first century, and we have only thirty-three manuscripts, two of the earliest that date 850 and 1050 C.E. Julius Caesar (100-44 B.C.E.) wrote his Gallic Wars between 51-46 B.C.E.,[193] which is a firsthand account in a third-person narrative of the war, of which we have 251 manuscripts dating between the ninth and fifteenth centuries.[194]

On the other hand, New Testament textual scholars have over 5,800 Greek manuscripts, not to mention ancient versions such as Latin, Coptic, Syriac, Armenian, Georgian, and Gothic, which number into the tens of thousands. We have many early and reliable manuscripts in Greek and the versions, a good number that cover almost the entire New Testament dating within 100 years of the originals. Therefore, reconstructing the original Greek New Testament is a realistic goal for Bible scholars. This belief and goal that we could anticipate a time when we would recover the original wording of the Greek New Testament had its greatest advocates in the nineteenth century, in Samuel Tregelles (1813-75), B. F. Westcott (1825-1901), and F. J. A. Hort (1828-92). While they acknowledged that we would never recover every word with absolute certainty, they knew that it was always the primary goal to come extremely close to the original. When we entered the twentieth century, there were two textual scholars

---

[191] Preface | Dickinson College Commentaries. (April 25, 2017) http://dcc.dickinson.edu/vergil-aeneid/manuscripts

[192] Honora Howell Chapman (Editor), Zuleika Rodgers (Editor), 2016, A *Companion to Josephus* (Blackwell Companions to the Ancient World), Wiley-Blackwell: p. 307.

[193] Carolyn Hammond, 1996, Introduction to *The Gallic War*, Oxford University Press: p. xxxii.

Max Radin, 1918, The date of composition of Caesar's Gallic War, *Classical Philology* XIII: 283–300.

[194] O. Seel, 1961, *Bellum Gallicum*. (Bibl. Teubneriana.) Teubner, Leipzig.

W. Hering, 1987, *C. Iulii Caesaris commentarii rerum gestarum, Vol. I: Bellum Gallicum.*(Bibl. Teubneriana.) Teubner, Leipzig.

Virginia Brown, 1972, *The Textual Transmission of Caesar's Civil War*, Brill.

Caesar's Gallic war - Tim Mitchell. (April 25, 2017) http://www.timmitchell.fr/blog/2012/04/12/gallic-war/

who have since stood above all others, Kurt Aland and Bruce Metzger. These two men carried the same purpose with them, as they were instrumental in bringing us the Nestle-Aland and the United Bible Societies critical editions, which are at the foundation of almost all modern translations.

From the days of Johann Jacob Griesbach (1745-1812), to Constantin Von Tischendorf (1815-1874), to Samuel Prideaux Tregelles (1813-1875), to Fenton John Anthony Hort (1828-1892), to Kurt Aland (1915-1994), to Bruce M. Metzger (1914-2007),[195] we have been blessed with extraordinary textual scholars. These scholars have devoted their entire lives to providing us the transmission of the New Testament text and the methodologies by which we can recover the original words of the New Testament authors. They did not construct these histories and methodologies from textbooks or in university classrooms. No, they spent decades upon decades in working with manuscripts and putting their methods of textual criticism into practice, as they provided us with one improved critical edition after another. As their knowledge grew, the number of manuscripts which they had to work with fortunately grew as well.

Samuel Tregelles stated that it was his purpose to restore the Greek New Testament text "as nearly as can be done on existing evidence."[196] B. F. Westcott and F. J. A. Hort declared that their goal was "to present exactly the original words of the New Testament, so far as they can now be determined from surviving documents."[197] Metzger said that the goal of textual criticism is "to ascertain from the divergent copies which form of the text should be regarded as most nearly conforming to the original."[198] Sadly, after centuries, textual criticism is losing its way, as new textual scholars have begun to set aside the goal of recovering and establishing the original wording of the Greek New Testament. They have little concern for the certainty of a reading as to whether it is the original.

---

[195] These textual scholars provided us with histories of the transmission of the New Testament text and methodologies. However, we have had dozens of textual scholars who have given their lives to the text of the New Testament. To mention just a few, we have Brian Walton (1600-1661), John Fell (1625-1686), John Mill (1645-1707), Edward Wells (1667-1727), Richard Bentley (1662-1742), Johann Albert Bengel (1687-1752), Johann Jacob Wettstein (1693-1754), Johann Salomo Semler (1725-1791), Johann Leonard Hug (1765-1846), Johann Martin Augustinus Scholz (1794-1852), Karl Lachmann (1793-1851), Erwin Nestle (1883-1972), Allen Wikgren (1906-1998), Matthew Black, (1908-1994), Barbara Aland (1937-present), and Carlo Maria Martini (1927-2012).

[196] Tregelles, *An Account of the Printed Text of the Greek New Testament*, 174.

[197] Westcott and Hort, *Introduction to the New Testament in the Original Greek*, 1.

[198] Metzger, *The Text of the New Testament*, v.

In speaking of the positions of agnostic Bart D. Ehrman (author of *The Orthodox Corruption of Scripture*) and David Parker (author of *The Living Text of the Gospels*), Elliott overserved, "Both emphasize the living and therefore changing text of the New Testament and the needlessness and inappropriateness of trying to establish one immutable original text. The changeable text in all its variety is what we textual critics should be displaying."[199] Elliott then reflects further on his goals within textual criticism: "Despite my own published work in trying to prove the originality of the text in selected areas of textual variation ... I agree that the task of trying to establish the original words of the original authors with 100% certainty is impossible. More dominant in text critics' thinking now is the need to plot the changes in the history of the text. That certainly seemed to be the consensus at one of the sessions of the 1998 SBL conference in Orlando, where the question of whether the original text was an achievable goal received generally negative responses."[200]

We strongly disagree. The goal of textual criticism had been and still should be **to restore** the New Testament Greek text **in every word that was originally penned** by the New Testament authors, in a critical edition. If we are aiming only "to plot the changes in the history of the text," as Elliott put it, we are unable to do so precisely at the time when we have the greatest need to see what happened, i.e. soon after the NT books were first published, if we actually deny and rob ourselves of any chance to recover the original. Then we must admit either that we can never have the complete word of God (the new position), or that any and potentially every quality Greek witness must be considered the word of God. The latter might even be said of a quality version, or at least of readings clearly inferred from such a version. In reality, however, any manuscript that departs from the original in its witness is more or less damaged goods.

We obviously do not think such pessimism is the necessary or inevitable response. In looking at the numbers above as to the certainty level of the restoration of the original Greek New Testament, we have come a long way since John Fell (1625-1686). A spot comparison of changes in ratings between GNT5 and previous GNT editions indicates that the level of certainty is increasing in most cases, and when it does not, the preference tends toward the earliest and most reliable manuscripts.[201] To set aside the

---

[199] J. K. Elliott, *New Testament Textual Criticism: The Application of Thoroughgoing Principles: Essays on Manuscripts and Textual Variation*, 592.

[200] Ibid. 592.

[201] Sample comparisons of the General Epistles in GNT5 with previous GNT editions led to this conclusion. When the level of certainty decreased—which was infrequent compared to the reverse—the trend seemed to be that more weight was being given to 03 and/or 01 in

primary goal of textual criticism now would be an insult to the lives of many textual scholars who preceded us, not to mention to the authors who penned the New Testament books and the Almighty God who inspired them.

---

opposition to internal factors. It is also expected that certainty levels will increase with the use of the CBGM (discussed in detail below).

CHAPTER 7 Bible Difficulties Explained

Ehrman wrote: "Hmm…maybe Mark did make a mistake." Once I made that admission, the floodgates opened. For if there could be one little, picayune [petty, worthless] mistake in Mark 2, maybe there could be mistakes in other places as well. **Misquoting Jesus (p. 9).**

IT SEEMS THAT the charge that the Bible contradicts itself has been made more and more in the last 20 years. Generally, those making such claims are merely repeating what they have heard, because most have not even read the Bible, let alone done an in-depth study of it. I do not wish, however, to set aside all concerns as though they have no merit. There are many who raise legitimate questions that seem, on the surface anyway, to be about well-founded contradiction. Sadly, these issues have caused many to lose their faith in God's Word, the Bible. The purpose of this books is, to help its readers to be able to defend the Bible against Bible critics (1 Pet. 3:15), to contend for the faith (Jude 1:3), and help those, who have begun to doubt. – Jude 1:22-23.

Before we begin explaining things, let us jump right in, getting our feet wet, and deal with two major Bible difficulties, so we can see that there are reasonable, logical answers. After that, we will delve deeper into explaining Bible difficulties.

Is God permitting Human Sacrifice at Judges 11:30-31?

Judges 11:29-34, 37-41 English Standard Version (ESV)

[29] Then the Spirit of the Lord was upon Jephthah, and he passed through Gilead and Manasseh and passed on to Mizpah of Gilead, and from Mizpah of Gilead he passed on to the Ammonites. [30] And Jephthah **made a vow** to the Lord and said, "If you will give the Ammonites into my hand, [31] then **whatever**[202] comes out from the doors of my house to meet me when I return in peace from the Ammonites shall be the Lord's, and I will offer it up for a burnt offering." [32] So Jephthah crossed over to the Ammonites to fight against them, and the Lord gave them into his hand. [33] And he struck them from Aroer to the neighborhood of Minnith, twenty cities, and as far as Abel-keramim, with a great blow. So the Ammonites were subdued before the people of Israel.

---

[202] Whoever

³⁴ Then Jephthah came to his home at Mizpah. And behold, **his daughter came out** to meet him with tambourines and with dances. She was his only child; besides her he had neither son nor daughter.

³⁷ So she said to her father, "Let this thing be done for me: leave me alone two months, that I may go up and down on the mountains and weep for my virginity, I and my companions." ³⁸ So he said, "Go." Then he sent her away for two months, and she departed, **she and her companions, and wept for her virginity** on the mountains. ³⁹ And at the end of two months, she returned to her father, who **did with her according to his vow that he had made.** She had never known a man [been intimate with a man], and it became a custom in Israel ⁴⁰ that the daughters of Israel went year by year to **lament [or commemorate] the daughter** of Jephthah the Gileadite four days in the year.

It is true; to infer that having the idea of an animal sacrifice would really have not been an impressive vow, which the context requires. Human sacrifice would be repugnant, if we are talking about taking a life. Jephthah had no sons, so he likely knew it was the daughter, who would come to greet him.

First, the text does not say he killed his daughter. The idea of some that he did kill her is concluded only by an inference. While it is not good policy to interpret backward, using Paul on Judges, he does say humans are to be **"as a living sacrifice."** Therefore, Jephthah could have offered his daughter at the temple, "as a living sacrifice" in service, like Samuel.

This is not to be taken dismissively, because under Jewish backgrounds, it is no small thing to offer a **perpetual virginity** as a sacrifice. This would mean Jephthah's lineage would not be carried on, the family name, was no more.

Second, the context says she went out to weep for two months, not mourn her death. It says, "she left with her friends and **mourned her virginity**."

If she was facing impending death, she could have married, and spent that last two months as a married woman. There would be absolutely no reason for her to mourn her virginity, if she were not facing perpetual virginity. – Exodus 38:8; 1 Samuel 2:22

Third, it was completely forbidden to offer a human sacrifice. – Leviticus 18:21; 20:2-5; Deuteronomy 12:31; 18:10

Imagine an Israelite believing that he could please God with a human sacrifice that was intended to offer up a human life. To do so would have been a rejection of Jehovah's Sovereignty (the very person you are asking for help), and a rejection of the Law that made them a special people.

Worse still, this interpretation would have us believe that Jehovah, this was coming, allowed the vow, and then aided this type of man succeed over his enemies.

The last point is simple enough. If such a man as one who would make such a vow, in gross violation of the law, and then carry it out; there is no way he would be mentioned by Paul in Hebrews chapter 11.

There is no way God would have granted and helped in Jephthah's initial success knowing the vow that was coming, because both Jehovah and Jephthah would be as bad as the Canaanites. There is no way that God would accept such a vow and then go on to help Jephthah with his enemies yet again. Then, to allow such a vow to be carried out, to then put Jephthah on the wall of star witnesses for God in Hebrews chapter 11.

Does Isaiah 45:7 mean that God Is the Author of Evil?

Isaiah 45:7 King James Version (KJV)

7 I form the light, and create darkness: I make peace, and **create evil**: I the Lord do all these things.

Isaiah 45:7 English Standard Version (ESV)

7 I form light and create darkness,

I make well-being and **create calamity**,

I am the Lord, who does all these things.[203]

Encarta Dictionary: (Evil) (1) morally bad: profoundly immoral or wrong (2) deliberately causing great harm, pain, or upset

QUESTION: Is this view of evil always the case? No, as you will see below.

Some apologetic authors try to say, 'we are not understanding Isaiah 45:7 correctly, because there are other verses that say God is not evil (1 John 1:5), cannot look approvingly on evil (Hab. 1:13), and cannot be tempted by evil. (Jam. 1:13)' Well, while all of these things are Scripturally true, the question at hand is not: Is God evil, can God approvingly look on evil, or can God be tempted with evil? Those questions are not relevant to the one at hand, as God cannot be those things, and at the same time, he can be the yes to our question. The question is, is God the author, the creator of evil?

---

[203] See Jeremiah 18:11, Lamentations 3:18, and Amos 3:6

dly argue that God was **not just** in his bringing
down on Adam and Eve. Thus, we have Isaiah 45:7
ne creator of "calamity" or "evil."

simple, without trying to be philosophical. When God
ind Eve from the Garden of Eden, he sentenced them and
ness, old age, and death. (Rom. 5:8; i.e., enforce penalty
for . 1 was to bring "calamity" or "evil" upon humankind.
Therefore, .. we can "evil" does not always mean wrongdoing. Other
examples of God bringing "calamity" or "evil" are Noah and the flood, the
Ten Plagues of Egypt, and the destruction of the Canaanites. These acts of
evil were not acts of wrongdoing. Rather, they were righteous and just,
because God, the Creator of all things, was administering justice to
wrongdoers, to sinners. He warned the perfect first couple what the penalty
was for sin. He warned the people for a hundred years by Noah's
preaching. He warned the Canaanites centuries before.

Nevertheless, there are times, when God extends mercy, refraining
from the execution of his righteous judgment to one worthy of calamity.
For example, he warned Nineveh, the city of blood, and they repented, so
he pardoned them. (Jon 3:10) God has made it a practice to warn persons
of the results of sin, giving them undeservedly many opportunities to
change their ways. – Ezekiel 33:11.

God cannot sin; it is impossible for him to do so. So, when did he
create evil? Without getting into the eternity of his knowing what he was
going to do, and when, let us just say, evil did not exist when he was the
only person in existence. We might say the idea of evil existed because he
knew what he was going to do. However, the moment he created creatures
(spirit and human), the potential for evil came into existence because both
have a free will to sin. Evil became a reality the moment Satan entertained
the idea of causing Adam to sin, to get humanity for himself, and then acted
on it.

God has the right and is just to bring calamity of or evil down on
anyone that is an unrepentant sinner. God did not even have to give us the
underserved kindness of offering us his Son. God is the author or agent of
evil regardless of the source books that claim otherwise. If he had never
created free will beings, evil would have never gone from the idea of evil
to the potential of evil, to the existence of evil. However, God felt that it
was better to get the sinful state out of angel and human existence, recover,
and then any who would sin thereafter, he would be justified in handing
out evil or calamity to just that person or angel alone.

Who among us would argue that he should have created humans and
angels like robots, automatons with no free will? The moment he chose the

free will, he moved evil from an idea to a potential, and Satan moved it to a reality. God has a moral nature that does not bring about evil and sin when he is the only person in existence. However, the moment he created beings in his image, who had the potential to sin, he brought about evil. The moment we have a moral code of good and evil that is placed upon one's with free will; then, we have evil.

In English, the very comprehensive Hebrew word ra' is variously translated as "bad," "downcast (sad, NASB)," "ugly," "evil," "grievous (distressing, NASB)," "sore," "selfish (stingy, HCSB)," and "envious," depending upon the context. (Gen 2:9; 40:7; 41:3; Ex 33:4; Deut. 6:22; 28:35; Pro 23:6; 28:22)

Evil as an adjective **describes** the **quality of** a class of people, places, or things, or of a specific person, place, or thing

Evil as a noun, **defines** the **nature** of a class of people, places, or things, or of a specific person, place, or thing (e.g., the evil one, evil eye).

We can agree that "evil" is a thing. Create means to bring something into existence, be it people, places, or things, as well something abstract, for lack of a better word at the moment. We would agree that when God was alone evil was not a reality, it did not exist? We would agree that the moment that God created free will creatures (angels and humans), creating humans in his image, with his moral nature, he also brought the potential for evil into existence, and it was realized by Satan?

Inerrancy: Can the Bible Be trusted?

If the Bible is the Word of God, it should be in complete agreement throughout; there should be no contradictions. Yet, the rational mind must ask, why is it that some passages appear to be contradictions when compared with others? For example, Numbers 25:9 tells us that 24,000 died from the scourge, whereas at 1 Corinthians 10:8, the apostle Paul says it was 23,000. This would seem to be a clear error. Before addressing such matters, let us first look at some background information.

Full inerrancy in this book means that the original writings are fully without error in all that they state, as are the words. The words were not dictated (automaton), but the intended meaning is inspired, as are the words that convey that meaning. The Author allowed the writer to use his style of writing, yet controlled the meaning to the extent of not allowing the writer to choose a wrong word, which would not convey the intended meaning. Other more liberal-minded persons hold with *partial inerrancy*, which claims that as far as faith is concerned, this portion of God's Word is without error, but that there are historical, geographical, and scientific errors.

There are several different levels of inerrancy. *Absolute Inerrancy* is the belief that the Bible is fully true and exact in every way; including not only relationships and doctrine, but also science and history. In other words, all information is completely exact. *Full Inerrancy* is the belief that the Bible was not written as a science or historical textbook, but is phenomenological, in that it is written from the human perspective. In other words, speaking of such things as the sun rising, the four corners of the earth, or the rounding-off of number approximations are all from a human perspective. *Limited Inerrancy* is the belief that the Bible is meant only as a reflection of God's purposes and will, so the science and history is the understanding of the author's day, and is limited. Thus, the Bible is susceptible to errors in these areas. *Inerrancy of Purpose* is the belief that it is only inerrant in the purpose of bringing its readers to a saving faith. The Bible is not about facts, but about persons and relationships, thus, it is subject to error. *Inspired: Not Inerrant* is the belief that its authors are human and thus subject to human error. It should be noted that this author holds the position of full inerrancy.

For many today, the Bible is nothing more than a book written by men. The Bible critic believes the Bible to be full of myths and legends, contradictions, and geographical, historical, and scientific errors. University professor Gerald A. Larue had this to say, "The views of the writers as expressed in the Bible reflect the ideas, beliefs, and concepts current in their own times and are limited by the extent of knowledge in those times."[204] On the other hand, the Bible's authors claim that their writings were inspired of God, as Holy Spirit moved them along. We will discover shortly that the Bible critics have much to say, but it is inflated or empty.

2 Timothy 3:16-17 Updated American Standard Version (UASV)

[16] All Scripture is inspired by God and profitable for teaching, for reproof, for correction, for training in righteousness; [17] so that the man of God may be fully competent, equipped for every good work.

2 Peter 1:21 Updated American Standard Version (UASV)

[21] for no prophecy was ever produced by the will of man, but men carried along by the Holy Spirit spoke from God.

The question remains as to whether the Bible is a book written by imperfect men and full of errors, or is written by imperfect men, but inspired of God. If the Bible is just another book by imperfect man, there is

---

[204] Gerald Larue, "The Bible as a Political Weapon," *Free Inquiry* (Summer 1983): 39.

no hope for humankind. If it is inspired of God and without error, although penned by imperfect men, we have the hope of everything that it offers: a rich happy life now by applying counsel that lies within and the real life that is to come, everlasting life. This author contends that the Bible is inspired of God and free of human error, although written by imperfect humans.

Before we take on the critics who seem to sift the Scriptures looking for problematic verses, let us take a moment to reflect on how we should approach these alleged problem texts. The critic's argument goes something like this: 'If God does not err and the Bible is the Word of God, then the Bible should not have one single error or contradiction, yet it is full of errors and contradictions.' If the Bible is riddled with nothing but contradictions and errors as the critics would have us believe, why, out of 31,173 verses in the Bible, should there be only 2-3 thousand Bible difficulties that are called into question, this being less than ten percent of the whole?

First, let it be said that it is every Christian's obligation to get a deeper understanding of God's Word, just as the apostle Paul told Timothy:

1 Timothy 4:15-16 Updated American Standard Version (UASV)

15 Practice these things, be absorbed in them, so that your progress will be evident to all. 16 Pay close attention to yourself and to your teaching; persevere in these things, for as you do this you will ensure salvation both for yourself and for those who hear you.

Paul also told the Corinthians:

2 Corinthians 10:4-5 Updated American Standard Version (UASV)

4 For the weapons of our warfare are not of the flesh[205] but powerful to God for destroying strongholds.[206] 5 We are destroying speculations and every lofty thing raised up against the knowledge of God, and we are taking every thought captive to the obedience of Christ,

Paul also told the Philippians:

Philippians 1:7 Updated American Standard Version (UASV)

7 It is right for me to feel thus about you all, because I hold you in my heart, for you are all partakers with me of grace, both in my imprisonment and in the defense and confirmation of the gospel.

In being able to defend against the modern-day critic, one has to be able to reason from the Scriptures and overturn the critic's argument(s) with

---

[205] That is *merely human*

[206] That is *tearing down false arguments*

mildness. If someone were to approach us about an alleged error or contradiction, what should we do? We should be frank and honest. If we do not have an answer, we should admit such. If the text in question gives the appearance of difficulty, we should admit this as well. If we are unsure as to how we should answer, we can simply say that we will look into it and get back with them, returning with a reasonable answer.

However, do not express disbelief and doubt to your critics, because they will be emboldened in their disbelief. It will put them on the offense and you on the defense. With great confidence, you can express that there is an answer. The Bible has withstood the test of 2,000 years of persecution and is the most printed book of all time, currently being translated into 2,287 languages. If these critical questions were so threatening, the Bible would not be the book that it is.

When you are pursuing the text in question, be unwavering in purpose, or resolved to find an answer. In some cases, it may take hours of digging to find the solution. Consider this: as you resolve these difficulties, you are also building your faith that God's Word is inerrant. Moreover, you will want to do preventative maintenance in your personal study. As you are doing your Bible reading, take note of these surface discrepancies and resolve them as you work your way through the Bible. Make this a part of your prayers as well. I recommend the following program. At the end of this chapter I list several books that deal with difficult passages. As you read your Bible from Genesis to Revelation, do not attempt it in one year; make it a four-year program. Use a good exegetical commentary like *The New International Commentary of the Old and New Testament* (NICOT/NICNT) or *The New American Commentary* set, and *The Big Book of Bible Difficulties* by Norman L. Geisler, as well as *The Encyclopedia of Bible Difficulties* by Gleason Archer.

You should be aware that the originally written books were penned by men under inspiration. In fact, we do not have those originals, what textual scholars call autographs, but we do have thousands of copies. The copyists, however, were not inspired; therefore, as one might expect, throughout the first 1,400 years of copying, thousands of errors were transmitted into the texts that were being copied by imperfect hands that were not under inspiration when copying. Yet, the next 450 years saw a restoration of the text by textual scholars from around the world. Therefore, while many of our best literal translations today may not be inspired, they are a mirror-like reflection of the autographs by way of textual criticism.[207] Therefore, the fallacy could be with the copyist error

---

[207] Textual criticism is the study of copies of any written work of which the autograph (original) is unknown, with the purpose of ascertaining the original text. Harold J. Green, Introduction to New Testament Textual Criticism (Peabody, MA: Hendrickson, 1995), 1.

that has simply not been weeded out. In addition, you must keep in mind that God's Word is without error, but our interpretation and understanding of that Word is not.

In this chapter, we are not going to take the space that we will in later chapters that are dedicated to one difficulty. Here, in short, we will address a number of them. Before looking at a few examples, it should be noted that the Bible is made up of 66 smaller books that were hand-written over a period of 1,600 years, having some 40 writers of various trades such as shepherd, king, priest, tax collector, governor, physician, copyist, fisherman, and tentmaker. Therefore, it should not surprise us that some difficulties are encountered as we casually read through the Bible. Yet, if one were to take a deeper look, one would find that these difficulties are easily explained. Let us take a few pages to examine some passages that have been under attack.

Again, our objective here is not to be exhaustive, not even close. What we are looking to do is cover a few alleged contradictions and a couple of alleged mistakes. This is to give you, the reader, a small sampling of the reasonable answers that you will find in the recommended books at the end of the chapter. Remember, your Bible is a sword that you must use both offensively and defensively. One must wonder how long a warrior of ancient times would last who was not expertly trained in the use of his weapon. Let us look at a few scriptures that support our need to learn our Bible well so will be able to defend what we believe to be true.

When "false apostles, deceitful workmen, disguising themselves as apostles of Christ" were causing trouble in the congregation in Corinth, the apostle Paul wrote that under such circumstances, we are to *tear down their arguments* and *take every thought captive*. (2 Corinthians 10:4, 5; 11:13–15) All who present critical arguments against God's Word, or contrary to it, can have their arguments overturned by the Christian who is able and ready to defend that Word in mildness. – 2 Timothy 2:24–26.

1 Peter 3:15 Updated American Standard Version (UASV)

[15] but sanctify Christ as Lord in your hearts, always being prepared to make a defense[208] to anyone who asks you for a reason for the hope that is in you; yet do it with gentleness and respect;

Peter says that we need to be prepared to make a *defense*. The Greek word behind the English 'defense' is *apologia*, which is actually a legal term that refers to the defense of a defendant in court. Our English apologetics is just what Peter spoke of, having the ability to give a reason to any who

---

[208] Or *argument*, or *explanation*

may challenge us, or to answer those who are not challenging us but who have honest questions that deserve to be answered.

2 Timothy 2:24-25 Updated American Standard Version (UASV)

24 For a slave of the Lord does not need to fight, but needs to be kind to all, qualified to teach, showing restraint when wronged 25 with gentleness correcting those who are in opposition, if perhaps God may grant them repentance leading to accurate knowledge[209] of the truth,

Look at the Greek word (*epignosis*) behind the English "knowledge" in the above. "It is more intensive than *gnosis* (1108), knowledge, because it expresses a more thorough participation in the acquiring of knowledge on the part of the learner."[210] The requirement of all of the Lord's servants is that they be able to teach, but not in a quarrelsome way, and in a way to correct his opponents with mildness. Why? Because the purpose of it all is that by God, and through the Christian teacher, one may come to repentance and begin taking in an accurate knowledge of the truth.

Inerrancy: Practical Principles to Overcoming Bible Difficulties

Below are several ways of looking at the Bible that enable the reader to see he is not dealing with an error or a contradiction, but rather a Bible difficulty.

Different Points of View

At times, you may have two different writers who are writing from two different points of view.

Numbers 35:14 New International Version (NIV)

14 Give three on this side of the Jordan and three in Canaan as cities of refuge.

Joshua 22:4 New International Version (NIV)

4 Now that the Lord your God has given them rest as he promised, return to your homes in the land that Moses the servant of the Lord gave you on the other side of the Jordan.

---

209 *Epignosis* is a strengthened or intensified form of *gnosis* (*epi*, meaning "additional"), meaning, "true," "real," "full," "complete" or "accurate," depending upon the context. Paul and Peter alone use *epignosis*.

210 Spiros Zodhiates, *The Complete Word Study Dictionary: New Testament*, Electronic ed. (Chattanooga, TN: AMG Publishers, 2000, c1992, c1993), S. G1922.

Here we see that Moses is speaking about the east side of the Jordan when he says "on this side of the Jordan." Joshua, on the other hand, is also speaking about the east side of the Jordan when he says "on the other side of the Jordan." So, who is correct? Both are. When Moses was penning Numbers the Israelites had not yet crossed the Jordan River, so the east side was "this side," the side he was on. On the other hand, when Joshua penned his book, the Israelites had crossed the Jordan, so the east side was just as he had said, "on the other side of the Jordan." Thus, we should not assume that two different writers are writing from the same perspective.

A Careful Reading

At times, it may simply be a case of needing to slow down and carefully read the account, considering exactly what is being said.

Joshua 18:28 New American Standard Bible (NASB)

[28] and Zelah, Haeleph and the Jebusite (that is, Jerusalem), Gibeah, Kiriath; fourteen cities with their villages. This is the inheritance of the sons of Benjamin according to their families.

Judges 1:21 New International Version (NIV)

[21] The Benjamites, however, did not drive out the Jebusites, who were living in Jerusalem; to this day the Jebusites live there with the Benjamites.

Joshua 15:63 New International Version (NIV)

[63] Judah could not dislodge the Jebusites, who were living in Jerusalem; to this day the Jebusites live there with the people of Judah.

Judges 1:8-9 New American Standard Bible (NASB)

[8] Then the sons of Judah fought against Jerusalem and captured it and struck it with the edge of the sword and set the city on fire. [9] Afterward the sons of Judah went down to fight against the Canaanites living in the hill country and in the Negev and in the lowland.

2 Samuel 5:5-9 New American Standard Bible (NASB)

[5] At Hebron he reigned over Judah seven years and six months, and in Jerusalem he reigned thirty-three years over all Israel and Judah.

[6] Now the king and his men went toJerusalem against the Jebusites, the inhabitants of the land, and they said to David, "You shall not come in here, but the blind and lame will turn you away"; thinking, "David cannot enter here." [7] Nevertheless, David captured the stronghold of Zion, that is the city of David. [8] David said on that day, "Whoever would strike the

Jebusites, let him reach the lame and the blind, who are hated by David's soul, through the water tunnel." Therefore they say, "The blind or the lame shall not come into the house." [9] So David lived in the stronghold and called it the city of David. And David built all around from the Millo and inward.

There is no doubt that even the advanced Bible reader of many years can come away confused because the above accounts seem to be contradictory. In Joshua 18:28 and Judges 1:21, we see that Jerusalem was an inheritance of the tribe of Benjamin, yet the Benjamites were unable to conquer Jerusalem. But in Joshua 15:63 we see that the tribe of Judah could not conquer them either, with the reading giving the impression that it was a part of their inheritance. In Judges 1:8, however, Judah was eventually able to conquer Jerusalem and burn it with fire. Yet, to add even more to the confusion, we find at 2 Samuel 5:5–8 that David is said to have conquered Jerusalem hundreds of years later.

Now that we have the particulars, let us look at it more clearly. The boundary between Benjamin's inheritances ran right through the middle of Jerusalem. Joshua 8:28 is correct, in that what would later be called the "city of David" was in the territory of Benjamin, but it also in part crossed over the line into the territory of Judah, causing both tribes to go to war against this Jebusite city. It is also true that the tribe of Benjamin was unable to conquer the city and that the tribe of Judah eventually did. However, if you look at Judges 1:9 again, you will see that Judah did not finish the job entirely and moved on to conquer other areas. This allowed the remaining ones to regroup and form a resistance that neither Benjamin nor Judah could overcome, so these Jebusites remained until the time of David, hundreds of years later.

Intended Meaning of Writer

First, the Bible student needs to understand the level that the Bible intends to be exact in what is written. If Jim told a friend that 650 graduated with him from high school in 1984, it is not challenged, because it is all too clear that he is using rounded numbers and is not meaning to be exactly precise. This is how God's Word operates as well. Sometimes it means to be exact, at other times, it is simply rounding numbers, in other cases, the intention of the writer is a general reference, to give readers of that time and succeeding generations some perspective. Did Samuel, the author of judges, intend to pen a book on the chronology of Judges, or was his focus on the falling away, oppression, and the rescue by a judge, repeatedly. Now, it would seem that Jeremiah, the author of 1 Kings was more interested in giving his readers an exact number of years.

Acts 2:41 English Standard Version (ESV)

⁴¹ So those who received his word were baptized, and there were added that day about three thousand souls.

As you can see here, numbers within the Bible are often used with approximations. This is a frequent practice even today, in both written works and verbal conversation.

Acts 7:2-3 English Standard Version (ESV)

² And Stephen said:

"Brothers and fathers, hear me. The God of glory appeared to our father Abraham when he was in Mesopotamia, before he lived in Haran, ³ and said to him, 'Go out from your land and from your kindred and go into the land that I will show you.'

If you were to check the Hebrew Scriptures at Genesis 12:1, you would find that what is claimed to have been said by God to Abraham is not quoted word-for-word; it is simply a paraphrase. This is a normal practice within Scripture and in writing in general.

Numbers 34:15 English Standard Version (ESV)

¹⁵ The two tribes and the half-tribe have received their inheritance beyond the Jordan east of Jericho, toward the sunrise."

Just as you would read in today's local newspaper, the Bible writer has written from the human standpoint, how it appeared to him. The Bible also speaks of "to the end of the earth" (Psalm 46:9), "from the four corners of the earth" (Isa 11:12), and "the four winds of the earth" (Revelation 7:1). These phrases are still used today.

Unexplained Does Not Mean Unexplainable

Considering that there are 31,173 verses in the Bible, encompassing 66 books written by about 40 writers, ranging from shepherds, to kings, an army general, fishermen, tax collector, a physician and on and on, and being penned over a 1,600 year period, one does find a few hundred Bible difficulties (about one percent). However, 99 percent of those are explainable. Yet no one wants to be so arrogant to say that he can explain them all. It has nothing to do with the inadequacy of God's Word, but is based on human understanding. In many cases, science or archaeology and the field of custom and culture of ancient peoples has helped explain difficulties in hundreds of passages. Therefore, there may be less than one percent left to be answered, yet our knowledge of God's Word continues to grow.

Guilty Until Proven Innocent

This is exactly the perception that the critic has of God's Word. The legal principle of being "innocent until proven guilty" afforded mankind in courts of justice is withheld from the very Word of God. What is ironic here is that this policy has contributed to these Bible critics looking foolish over and over again when something comes to light that vindicates the portion of Scripture they are challenging.

Daniel 5:1 English Standard Version (ESV)

[1] King Belshazzar made a great feast for a thousand of his lords and drank wine in front of the thousand.

Bible critics had long claimed that Belshazzar was not known outside of the book Daniel; therefore, they argue that Daniel was mistaken. Yet it hardly seems prudent to argue error from absence of outside evidence. Just because archaeology had not discovered such a person did not mean that Daniel was wrong, or that such a person did not exist. In 1854, some small clay cylinders were discovered in modern-day southern Iraq, which would have been the city of Ur in ancient Babylonia. The cuneiform documents were a prayer of King Nabonidus for "Bel-sar-ussur, my eldest son." These tablets also showed that this "Bel-sar-ussur" had secretaries as well as a household staff. Other tablets were discovered a short time later that showed that the kingship was entrusted to this eldest son as a coregent while his father was away.

He entrusted the 'Camp' to his oldest (son), the firstborn [Belshazzar], the troops everywhere in the country he ordered under his (command). He let (everything) go, entrusted the kingship to him and, himself, he [Nabonidus] started out for a long journey, the (military) forces of Akkad marching with him; he turned towards Tema (deep) in the west."[211]

Ignoring Literary Styles

The Bible is a diverse book when it comes to literary styles: narrative, poetic, prophetic, and apocalyptic; also containing parables, metaphors, similes, hyperbole, and other figures of speech. Too often, these alleged errors are the result of a reader taking a figure of speech as literal, or reading a parable as though it is a narrative.

Matthew 24:35 English Standard Version (ESV)

[35] Heaven and earth will pass away, but my words will not pass away.

If some do not recognize that they are dealing with a figure of speech, they are bound to come away with the wrong meaning. Some have

---

[211] J. Pritchard, ed., *Ancient Near Eastern Texts* (1974), 313.

concluded from Matthew 24:35 that Jesus was speaking of an eventual destruction of the earth. This is hardly the case, as his listeners would not have understood it that way based on their understanding of the Old Testament. They would have understood that he was simply being emphatic about the words he spoke, using hyperbole. What he was conveying is that his words are more enduring than heaven and earth, and with heaven and earth being understood as eternal, this merely conveyed even more so that Jesus' words could be trusted.

Two Accounts of the Same Incident

If you were to speak to officers that take accident reports for their police department, you would find that there is cohesion in the accounts, but each person has merely witnessed aspects that have stood out to them. We will see that this is the case as well with the examples below, which is the same account in two different gospels:

Matthew 8:5 English Standard Version (ESV)

⁵ When he had entered Capernaum, a centurion came forward to him, appealing to him,

Luke 7:3 English Standard Version (ESV)

³ When the centurion heard about Jesus, he sent to him elders of the Jews, asking him to come and heal his servant.

Immediately we see the problem of whether the centurion or the elders of the Jews spoke with Jesus. The solution is not really hidden from us. Which of the two accounts is the more detailed account? You are correct if you said Luke. The centurion sent the elders of the Jews to represent him to Jesus, so; that whatever response Jesus might give, it would be as though he were addressing the centurion; therefore, Matthew gave his readers the basic thought, not seeing the need of mentioning the elders of the Jews aspect. This is how a representative was viewed in the first century, just as some countries see ambassadors today as being the very person they represent. Therefore, both Matthew and Luke are correct.

Man's Fallible Interpretations

Inspiration by God is infallible, without error. Imperfect man and his interpretations over the centuries, as bad as many of them have been, should not cast a shadow over God's inspired Word. The entire Word of God has one meaning and one meaning only for every penned word, which is what God willed to be conveyed by the human writer he chose to use.

The Autograph Alone Is Inspired and Inerrant

It has been argued by conservative scholars that only the autograph manuscripts were inspired and inerrant, not the copying of those manuscripts over the next 3,000 years for the Old Testament and 1,500 years for the New Testament. While I would agree with this position as well, it should be noted that we do not possess the autographs, so to argue that they are inerrant is to speak of nonexistent documents. However, it should be further understood that through the science of textual criticism, we can establish a mirror reflection of the autograph manuscripts. B. F. Westcott, F. J. A. Hort, F. F. Bruce, and many other textual scholars would agree with Norman L Geisler's assessment: "The New Testament, then, has not only survived in more manuscripts than any other book from antiquity, but it has survived in a purer form than any other great book—*a form that is 99.5 percent pure.*"[212]

An example of a copyist error can be found in Luke's genealogy of Jesus at Luke 3:35–37. In verse 37 you will find a Cainan, and in verse 36 you will find a second Cainan between Arphaxad (Arpachshad) and Shelah. As one can see from most footnotes in different study Bibles, the Cainan in verse 36 is seen as a scribal error, and is not found in the Hebrew Old Testament, the Samaritan Pentateuch, or the Aramaic Targums, but is found in the Greek Septuagint. (Genesis 10:24; 11:12, 13; 1 Chronicles 1:18, but not 1 Chronicles 1:24) It seems quite unlikely that it was in the earlier copies of the Septuagint, because the first-century Jewish historian Josephus lists Shelah next as the son of Arphaxad, and Josephus normally followed the Septuagint.[213] So one might ask why this second Cainan is found in the translations at all if this is the case? The manuscripts that do contain this second Cainan are some of the best manuscripts that are used in establishing the original text: 01 B L A^1 33 (Kainam); A 038 044 0102 A^{13} (Kainan).

Look at the Context

Many alleged inconsistencies disappear by simply looking at the context. Taking words out of context can distort their meaning. *Merriam-Webster's Collegiate Dictionary* defines context as "the parts of a discourse that surround a word or passage and can throw light on its meaning."[214] Context can also be "the circumstances or events that form the environment within which something exists or takes place." If we were to look in a thesaurus for a synonym, we would find "background" for this second

---

[212] Norman L. Geisler and William E. Nix: *A General Introduction to the Bible* (Chicago, Moody Press, 1980), 367. (Emphasis is mine.)

[213] *Jewish Antiquities*, I, 146 [vi, 4].

[214] Merriam-Webster, Inc: *Merriam-Webster's Collegiate Dictionary*. Eleventh ed. (Springfield, Mass.: Merriam-Webster, Inc. 2003).

meaning. At 2 Timothy 2:15, the apostle Paul brings home the point of why context is so important: "Do your best to present yourself to God as one approved, a worker who has no need to be ashamed, rightly handling the word of truth."

Ephesians 2:8-9 English Standard Version (ESV)

8 For by grace you have been saved through faith. And this is not your own doing; it is the gift of God, 9 not a result of works, so that no one may boast.

James 2:26 English Standard Version (ESV)

26 For as the body apart from the spirit is dead, so also faith apart from works is dead.

So, which is it? Is salvation possible by faith alone as Paul wrote to the Ephesians, or is faith dead without works as James wrote to his readers? As our subtitle brings out, let us look at the context. In the letter to the Ephesians, the apostle Paul is speaking to the Jewish Christians who were looking to the works of the Mosaic Law as a means to salvation, a righteous standing before God. Paul was telling these legalistic Jewish Christians that this is not so. In fact, this would invalidate Christ's ransom, because there would have been no need for it if one could achieve salvation by meticulously keeping the Mosaic Law. (Rom. 5:18) But James was writing to those in a congregation who were concerned with their status before other men, who were looking for prominent positions within the congregation, and not taking care of those that were in need. (Jam. 2:14–17) So, James is merely addressing those who call themselves Christian, but in name only. No person could truly be a Christian and not possess some good works, such as feeding the poor, helping the elderly. This type of work was an evident demonstration of one's Christian personality. Paul was in perfect harmony with James on this. – Romans 10:10; 1 Corinthians 15:58; Ephesians 5:15, 21–33; 6:15; 1 Timothy 4:16; 2 Timothy 4:5; Hebrews 10:23-25.

Inerrancy: Are There Contradictions?

Below I will follow this pattern. I will list the critic's argument first, followed by the text of difficulty, and conclude with an answer to the critic. What should be kept at the forefront of our mind is this: one is simply looking for the best answer, not absoluteness. If there is a reasonable answer to a Bible difficulty, why are the critics able to set them aside with ease? Because they start with the premise that this is not the Word of God, but only a book by imperfect men and full of contradictions; thus, the bias toward errors has blinded their judgment.

Critic: The critic would argue that there was an Adam and Eve, and an Abel who was now dead, so, where did Cain get his wife? This is one of the most common questions by Bible critics.

Genesis 4:17 New English Translation (NET Bible)

[17] Cain had marital relations with his wife, and she became pregnant and gave birth to Enoch. Cain was building a city, and he named the city after his son Enoch.

Answer: If one were to read a little further along, they would come to the realization that Adam had a son named Seth; it further adds that Adam "became father to sons *and daughters.*" (Genesis 5:4) Adam lived for a total of 800 years after fathering Seth, giving him ample opportunity to father many more sons and daughters. So it could be that Cain married one of his sisters. If he waited until one of his brothers and sisters had a daughter, he could have married one of his nieces once she was old enough. In the beginning, humans were closer to perfection; this explains why they lived longer and why at that time there was little health risk of genetic defects in the case of children born to closely related parents, in contrast to how it is today. As time passed, genetic defects increased and life spans decreased. Adam lived to see 930 years. Yet Shem, who lived after the Flood, died at 600 years, while Shem's son Arpachshad only lived 438 years, dying before his father died. Abraham saw an even greater decrease in that he only lived 175 years, while his grandson Jacob was 147 years when he died. Thus, due to increasing imperfection, God prohibited the marriage of closely related people under the Mosaic Law because of the likelihood of genetic defects.— Leviticus 18:9.

Critic: If God is here hardening Pharaoh's heart, what exactly makes Pharaoh responsible for the decisions he makes?

Exodus 4:21 Revised Standard Version (RSV)

[21] And the Lord said to Moses, "When you go back to Egypt, see that you do before Pharaoh all the miracles which I have put in your power; but I will harden his heart, so that he will not let the people go.

Answer: This is actually a prophecy. God knew that what he was about to do would contribute to a stubborn and obstinate Pharaoh, who was going to be unwilling to change or give up the Israelites so they could go off to worship their God. Therefore, this is not stating what God is going to do; it is prophesying that Pharaoh's heart will harden because of the actions of God. The fact is, Pharaoh allowed his own heart to harden because he was determined not to agree with Moses' wishes or accept Jehovah's request to let the people go. Moses tells us at Exodus 7:13 (ESV) that "Pharaoh's heart was hardened, and he would not listen to them, as the Lord had said." Again, at 8:15 we read, "When Pharaoh saw that there was a respite, he hardened his heart and would not listen to them, as the Lord had said."

Critic: The Israelites had just received the Ten Commandments, with one commandment being: "You shall not make for yourself a carved image, or any likeness of anything that is in heaven above, or that is in the earth beneath, or that is in the water under the earth." Therefore, how is the bronze serpent not a violation of this commandment?

Numbers 21:9 English Standard Version (ESV)

[9] So Moses made a bronze serpent and set it on a pole. And if a serpent bit anyone, he would look at the bronze serpent and live.

Answer: First, an idol is "a representation or symbol of an object of worship; *broadly:* a false god."[215] Second, it should be noted that not all images are idols. The bronze serpent was not made for the purpose of worship, or for some passionate devotion or veneration. There were times, however, when images were created with absolutely no intention of it receiving devotion, veneration, or worship, yet were later made into objects of veneration. That is exactly what happened with the copper serpent that Moses had formed in the wilderness. Many centuries later, "in the third year of Hoshea son of Elah, king of Israel, Hezekiah the son of Ahaz, king of Judah, began to reign. He removed the high places and broke the pillars and cut down the Asherah. And he broke in pieces the bronze serpent that Moses had made; for until those days the people of Israel had made offerings to it (it was called Nehushtan)."–2 Kings 18:1, 4.

Critic: Deuteronomy 15:11 (NET) says: "*There will never cease to be some poor people in the land;* therefore, I am commanding you to make sure you open your hand to your fellow Israelites who are needy and poor in your land." Is this not a contradiction of Deuteronomy 15:4? Will there be no poor among the Israelites, or will there be poor among them? Which is it?

Deuteronomy 15:4 New English Translation (NET Bible)

---

[215] Merriam-Webster, Inc: *Merriam-Webster's Collegiate Dictionary.* Eleventh ed. (Springfield, Mass.: Merriam-Webster, Inc., 2003).

⁴ However, there should not be any poor among you, for the Lord will surely bless you in the land that he is giving you as an inheritance,

Answer: If you look at the context, Deuteronomy 15:4 is stating that if the Israelites obey Jehovah's command to take care of the poor, "there should not be any poor among" them. Thus, for every poor person, there will be one to take care of that need. If an Israelite fell on hard times, there was to be a fellow Israelite ready to step in to help him through those hard times. Verse 11 stresses the truth of the imperfect world since the rebellion of Adam and inherited sin: there will always be poor among mankind, the Israelites being no different. However, the difference with God's people is that those who were well off were to offset conditions for those who fell on difficult times. This is not to be confused with the socialistic welfare systems in the world today. Those Jews were hard-working men, who labored from sunup to sundown to take care of their families. But if disease overtook their herd or unseasonal weather brought about failed crops, an Israelite could sell himself into the service of a fellow Israelite for a period of time; thereafter, he would be back on his feet. And many years down the road, he may very well do the same for another Israelite who fell on difficult times.

Critic: Joshua 11:23 says that Joshua took the land according to what God had spoken to Moses and handed it on to the nation of Israel as planned. However, in Joshua 13:1, God is telling Joshua that he has grown old and much of the Promised Land has yet to be taken possession of. How can both be true? Is this not a contradiction?

Joshua 11:23 English Standard Version (ESV)

²³ So Joshua took the whole land, according to all that the Lord had spoken to Moses. And Joshua gave it for an inheritance to Israel according to their tribal allotments. And the land had rest from war.

Joshua 13:1 English Standard Version (ESV)

13 Now Joshua was old and advanced in years, and the Lord said to him, "You are old and advanced in years, and there remains yet very much land to possess.

Answer: No, it is not a contradiction. When the Israelites were to take the land, it was to take place in two different stages: the nation as a whole was to go to war and defeat the 31 kings of this land; thereafter, each Israelite tribe was to take their part of the land based on their individual actions. (Joshua 17:14–18; 18:3) Joshua fulfilled his role, which is expressed in 11:23, while the individual tribes did not complete their campaigns, which is expressed in 13:1. Even though the individual tribes failed to live up to taking their portion, the remaining Canaanites posed no real threat. Joshua 21:44, *ASV*, reads: "Jehovah gave them rest round about."

Critic: The critic would point out that John 1:18 clearly says that "*no one has ever seen God*," while Exodus 24:10 explicitly states that Moses and Aaron, Nadab and Abihu, and seventy of the elders of Israel "*saw the God of Israel*." Worse still, God informs them in Exodus 33:20: "You cannot see my face, for man shall not see me and live." The critic with his knowing smile says, 'This is a blatant contradiction.'

John 1:18 New American Standard Bible (NASB)

[18] No one has seen God at any time; the only begotten God who is in the bosom of the Father, He has explained *Him.*

Exodus 24:10 New American Standard Bible (NASB)

[10] and they saw the God of Israel; and under His feet there appeared to be a pavement of sapphire, as clear as the sky itself.

Exodus 33:20 English Standard Version (ESV)

[20] But," he [God] said, "you cannot see my face, for man shall not see me and live."

Answer: Exodus 33:20 is one-hundred percent correct: No human could see Jehovah God and live. The apostle Paul at Colossians 1:15 tell us that Christ is the image of the invisible God, and the writer informs us at Hebrews 1:3 that Jesus is the "exact representation of His nature." Yet if you were to read the account of Saul of Tarsus (the apostle Paul), you would see that a mere partial manifestation of Christ's glory blinded Saul – Acts 9:1–18.

When the Bible says that Moses and others have seen God, it is not speaking of *literally* seeing him, because first of all He is an invisible spirit person. It is a *manifestation* of his glory, which is an act of showing or demonstrating his presence, making himself perceptible to the human mind. In fact, it is generally an angelic representative that stands in his place and not him personally. Exodus 24:16 informs us that "the glory of the Lord dwelt on Mount Sinai," not the Lord himself personally. When texts such as Exodus 24:10 explicitly state that Moses and Aaron, Nadab and Abihu, and seventy of the elders of Israel "*saw the God of Israel*," it is this "glory of the Lord," an angelic representative. This is shown to be the case at Luke 2:9, which reads: "And *an angel of the Lord* appeared to them, and *the glory of the Lord shone around them* [the shepherds], and they were filled with fear."

Many Bible difficulties are cleared up elsewhere in Scripture; for example, in the New Testament you will find a text clarifying a difficulty from the Old Testament, such as Acts 7:53, which refers to those "who received the law *as delivered by angels* and did not keep it." Support comes from Paul at Galatians 3:19: "Why then the law? It was added because of transgressions, until the offspring should come to whom the promise had been made, and it was put in place through angels by an intermediary." The writer of Hebrews chimes in at 2:2 with "For since the message *declared by angels* proved to be reliable, and every transgression or disobedience received a just retribution. . . ." As we travel back to Exodus again, to 19:19 specifically, we find support that it was not God's own voice, which Moses heard; no, it was an angelic representative, for it reads: "Moses was speaking and God was answering him with a voice." Exodus 33:22–23 also helps us to appreciate that it was the back of these angelic representatives of Jehovah that Moses saw: "While my glory passes by . . . Then I will take away my hand, and you shall see my back, but my face shall not be seen."

Exodus 3:4 states: "God called to him out of the bush, 'Moses, Moses!' And he said, 'Here I am.'" Verse 6 informs us: "I am the God of your father, the God of Abraham, the God of Isaac, and the God of Jacob." Yet, in verse 2 we read: "And the angel of the Lord appeared to him in a flame of fire out of the midst of a bush." Here is another example of using God's Word to clear up what seems to be unclear or difficult to understand at first glance. Thus, while it speaks of the Lord making a direct appearance, it is really an angelic representative. Even today, we hear such comments, as 'the president of the United States is to visit the Middle East later this week.' However, later in the article it is made clear that he is not going personally, but it is one of his high-ranking representatives. Let us close with two examples, starting with,

Genesis 32:24-30 English Standard Version (ESV)

24 And Jacob was left alone. And a man wrestled with him until the breaking of the day. 25 When the man saw that he did not prevail against Jacob, he touched his hip socket, and Jacob's hip was put out of joint as he wrestled with him.26 Then he said, "Let me go, for the day has broken." But Jacob said, "I will not let you go unless you bless me." 27 And he said to him, "What is your name?" And he said, "Jacob."28 Then he said," Your name shall no longer be called Jacob, but Israel, for you have striven with God and with men, and have prevailed."29 Then Jacob asked him, "Please tell me your name." But he said, "Why is it that you ask my name?" And there he blessed him. 30 So Jacob called the name of the place Peniel, saying, "For I have seen God face to face, and yet my life has been delivered."

It is all too obvious here that this man is simply a materialized angel in the form of a man, another angelic representative of Jehovah God. Moreover, the reader of this book should have taken in that the Israelites as a whole saw these angelic representatives, and spoke of them as though they were dealing directly with Jehovah God himself.

This proved to be the case in the second example found in the book of Judges where an angelic representative visited Manoah and his wife. Like the above mentioned account, Manoah and his wife treated this angelic representative as if he were Jehovah God himself: "And Manoah said to the angel of the Lord, 'What is your name, so that, when your words come true, we may honor you?' And the angel of the Lord said to him, 'Why do you ask my name, seeing it is wonderful?' Then Manoah knew that he was the angel of the Lord. And Manoah said to his wife, "We shall surely die, *for we have seen God.*" – Judges 13:3–22.

Inerrancy: Are There Mistakes?

I have addressed the alleged contradictions, so it would seem that our job is done here, right? Not hardly. Yes, there are just as many who claim that the Bible is full of mistakes.

Critic: Matthew 27:5 states that Judas hanged himself, whereas Acts 1:18 says that "falling headlong he burst open in the middle and all his bowels gushed out."

Matthew 27:5 English Standard Version (ESV)

5 And throwing down the pieces of silver into the temple, he departed, and he went and hanged himself.

Acts 1:18 English Standard Version (ESV)

18 (Now this man acquired a field with the reward of his wickedness, and falling headlong he burst open in the middle and all his bowels gushed out.

Answer: Neither Matthew, nor Luke made a mistake. What you have is Matthew giving the reader the manner in which Judas committed suicide. On the other hand, Luke is giving the reader of Acts, the result of that suicide. Therefore, instead of a mistake, we have two texts that complement each other, really giving the reader the full picture. Judas came to a tree alongside a cliff that had rocks below. He tied the rope to a branch and the other end around his neck, and jumped over the edge of the cliff in an attempt at hanging himself. One of two things could have happened: (1) the limb broke plunging him to the rocks below, or (2) the rope broke with the same result, and he burst open onto the rocks below.

Critic: The apostle Paul made a mistake when he quotes how many people died.

Numbers 25:9 English Standard Version (ESV)

⁹ Nevertheless, those who died by the plague were twenty-four thousand.

1 Corinthians 10:8 English Standard Version (ESV)

⁸ We must not indulge in sexual immorality as some of them did, and twenty-three thousand fell in a single day.

Answer: We must keep in mind the above principle that we spoke of, the *Intended Meaning of the Writer*. We live in a far more precise age today, where specificity is highly important. However, we round large numbers off (even estimate) all the time: "there were 237,000 people in Time Square last night." The simplest answer is that the number of people slain was in between 23,000 and 24,000, and both writers rounded the number off. However, there is even another possibility, because the book of Numbers specifically speaks of "all the chiefs of the people" (25:4-5), which could account for the extra 1,000, which is mentioned in Numbers 24,000. Thus, you have the people killing the chiefs of the people and the plague killing the people. Therefore, both books are correct.

Critic: After 215 years in Egypt, the descendants of Jacob arrived at the Promised Land. As you recall they sinned against God and were sentenced to forty years in the wilderness. But once they entered the Promised Land, they buried Joseph's bones "at Shechem, in the piece of land that *Jacob bought* from the sons of Hamor the father of Shechem," as stated at Joshua 24:32. Yet, when Stephen had to defend himself before the Jewish religious leaders, he said that Joseph was buried "in the tomb that *Abraham had bought* for a sum of silver from the sons of Hamor." Therefore, at once it appears that we have a mistake on the part of Stephen.

Acts 7:15-16 English Standard Version (ESV)

¹⁵ And Jacob went down into Egypt, and he died, he and our fathers,¹⁶ and they were carried back to Shechem and laid in the tomb that Abraham had bought for a sum of silver from the sons of Hamor in Shechem.

Genesis 23:17-18 English Standard Version (ESV)

¹⁷ So the field of Ephron in Machpelah, which was to the east of Mamre, the field with the cave that was in it and all the trees that were in the field, throughout its whole area, was made over ¹⁸ to Abraham as a possession in the presence of the Hittites, before all who went in at the gate of his city.

Genesis 33:19 English Standard Version (ESV)

¹⁹ And from the sons of Hamor, Shechem's father, he [Jacob] bought for a hundred pieces of money the piece of land on which he had pitched his tent.

Joshua 24:32 English Standard Version (ESV)

[32] As for the bones of Joseph, which the people of Israel brought up from Egypt, they buried them at Shechem, in the piece of land that Jacob bought from the sons of Hamor the father of Shechem for a hundred pieces of money. It became an inheritance of the descendants of Joseph.

Answer: If we look back to Genesis 12:6-7, we will find that Abraham's first stop after entering Canaan from Haran was Shechem. It is here that Jehovah told Abraham: "To your offspring I will give this land." At this point Abraham built an altar to Jehovah. It seems reasonable that Abraham would need to purchase this land that had not yet been given to his offspring. While it is true that the Old Testament does not mention this purchase, it is likely that Stephen would be aware of such by way of oral tradition. As Acts chapter seven demonstrates, Stephen had a wide-ranging knowledge of Old Testament history.

Later, Jacob would have had difficulty laying claim to the tract of land that his grandfather Abraham had purchased, because there would have been a new generation of inhabitants of Shechem. This would have been many years after Abraham moved further south and Isaac moved to Beersheba, and including Jacob's twenty years in Paddan-aram (Gen 28:6, 7). The simplest answer is that this land was not in use for about 120 years because of Abraham's extensive travels and Isaac's having moved away, leaving it unused; likely it was put to use by others. So, Jacob simply repurchased what Abraham had bought over a hundred years earlier. This is very similar to the time Isaac had to repurchase the well at Beersheba that Abraham had already purchased earlier. – Genesis 21:27–30; 26:26–32.

Genesis 33:18–20 tells us that 'Jacob bought this land for a hundred pieces of money, from the sons of Hamor.' This same transaction is also mentioned at Joshua 24:32, in reference to transporting Joseph's bones from Egypt, to be buried in Shechem.

We should also address the cave of Machpelah that Abraham had purchased in Hebron from Ephron the Hittite. The word "tomb" is not mentioned until Joshua 24:32, and is in reference to the tract of land in Shechem. Nowhere in the Old Testament does it say that Abraham bought a "tomb." The cave of Machpelah obtained by Abraham would eventually become a family tomb, receiving Sarah's body and, eventually, his own, and those of Isaac, Rebekah, Jacob, and Leah. (Genesis 23:14–19; 25:9; 49:30, 31; 50:13) Gleason L. Archer, Jr., concludes this Bible difficulty, saying,

> The reference to a *mnema* ("tomb") in connection with Shechem must either have been proleptic [to anticipate] for the later use of that shechemite tract for Joseph's tomb (i.e., 'the

tomb that Abraham bought' was intended to imply 'the tomb location that Abraham bought"); or else conceivably the dative relative pronoun *ho* was intended elliptically [omission] for *en to topo ho onesato Abraam* ("in the place that Abraham bought") as describing the location of the *mnema* near the Oak of Moreh right outside Shechem. Normally Greek would have used the relative-locative adverb *hou* to express 'in which' or 'where'; but this would have left o*nesato* ("bought") without an object in its own clause, and so *ho* was much more suitable in this context. (Archer 1982, 379–81)

Another solution could be that Jacob is being viewed as a representative of Abraham, for he is the grandson of Abraham. This was quite appropriate in Biblical times, to attribute the purchase to Abraham as the Patriarchal family head.

Critic: 2 Samuel 24:1 says that God moved David to count the Israelites, while 1 Chronicles 21:1 Satan, or a resister did. This would seem to be a clear mistake on the part of one of these authors.

2 Samuel 24:1 English Standard Version (ESV)

[1] Again the anger of the Lord was kindled against Israel, and he incited David against them, saying, "Go, number Israel and Judah."

1 Chronicles 21:1 English Standard Version (ESV)

[1] Then Satan stood against Israel and incited David to number Israel.

Answer: In this period of David's reign, Jehovah was very displeased with Israel, and therefore he did not prevent Satan from bringing this sin on them. Often in Scripture, it is spoken of as though God did something when he allowed an event to take place. For example, it is said that God 'hardened Pharaoh's heart' (Exodus 4:21), when he actually allowed the Pharaoh's heart to harden.

Inerrancy: Are There Scientific Errors?

Many truths about God are beyond the scope of science. Science and the Bible are not at odds. In fact, we can thank modern day science, as it has helped us to better under the creation of God, from our solar system, to the universes, to the human body and mind. What we find is a level of order, precision, design and sophistication, which points to a Designer, the eyes of many Christians, to an Almighty God, with infinite intelligence and power. The apostle Paul makes this all too clear, when he writes, "For his invisible attributes, namely, his eternal power and divine nature, have been clearly perceived, ever since the creation of the world, in the things that have been made. So they are without excuse." – Romans 1:20.

Back in the seventeenth century, the world-renowned scientist Galileo proved beyond any doubt that the earth was not the center of the universe, nor did the sun orbit the earth. In fact, he proved it to be the other way around (no pun intended), with the earth revolving around the sun. However, he was brought up on charges of heresy by the Catholic Church and ordered to recant his position. Why? From the viewpoint of the Catholic Church, Galileo was contradicting God's Word, the Bible. As it turned out, Galileo and science were correct and the Church was wrong, for which it issued a formal apology in 1992. However, the point we wish to make here is that in all the controversy, the Bible was never in the wrong. It was a misinterpretation on the part of the Catholic Church, and not a fault with the Bible. One will find no place in the Bible that claims the sun orbits the earth. So where would the Church get such an idea? The Church got such an idea from Ptolemy (b. about 85 C.E.), an ancient astronomer, who argued for such an idea.

As it usually turns out, the so-called contradiction between science and God's Word lies at the feet of those who are interpreting Scripture incorrectly. To repeat the sentiments of Galileo when writing to a pupil– Galileo expressed the same sentiments: "Even though Scripture cannot err, its interpreters and expositors can, in various ways. One of these, very serious and very frequent, would be when they always want to stop at the purely literal sense."[216] I believe that today's scholars, in hindsight, would have no problem agreeing.

While the Bible is not a science textbook, it is scientifically accurate when it touches on matters of science.

The Circle of the Earth Hangs on Nothing

Isaiah 40:22 English Standard Version (ESV)

22 It is he who sits above **the circle of the earth,**
    and its inhabitants are like grasshoppers;
who stretches out the heavens like a curtain,
    and spreads them like a tent to dwell in;

More than 2,500 years ago, the prophet Isaiah wrote that the earth is a circle or sphere. First, how would it be possible for Isaiah to know the earth is a circle or sphere, if not from inspiration? Scientific America writes, "As countless photos from space can attest, Earth is round—the "Blue Marble," as astronauts have affectionately dubbed it. Appearances,

---

[216] Letter from Galileo to Benedetto Castelli, December 21, 1613.

however, can be deceiving. Planet Earth is not, in fact, perfectly round."[217] Scientifically speaking, the sun is not perfectly, absolutely 100 percent round but in everyday speech, this verse is both acceptable and accurate, when we keep in mind it is written from a human perspective, not from a scientific perspective. Moreover, Isaiah was not discussing astronomy; he was simply making an inspired observation that man came to realize once he was in space, looking back at the earth, it is round. See the section about title, "Intended Meaning of Writer."

Job 26:7 English Standard Version (ESV)

[7] He stretches out the north over the void
and hangs the earth on nothing.

Here the author describes the earth as hanging upon nothing. Many have never heard of the Greek mathematician and astronomer Eratosthenes. He was born in about 276 B.C.E. and received some of his education in Athens, Greece. In 240 B.C., the "Greek astronomer, geographer, mathematician and librarian Eratosthenes calculates the Earth's circumference. His data was rough, but he wasn't far off."[218] While man very early on used their God given intelligence to arrive at some outstanding conclusion that were actually very accurate, we learn two points here. Eratosthenes was a very astute scientist, while Isaiah, who wrote some 500 years earlier, was no scientist at all. Moreover, Moses, who wrote the book of Job over 1,230 years before Eratosthenes, knew that the earth hung upon nothing.

How Is the Sun Standing Still Possible?

Joshua 10:13 English Standard Version (ESV)

[13]And the sun stood still, and the moon stopped, until the nation took vengeance on their enemies.

The Canaanites had besieged the Gibeonites, a group of people that gained Jehovah God's backing because they had faith in Him. In this battle, Jehovah helped the Israelites continue their attack by causing "the sun [to stand] still, and the moon stopped, until the nation took vengeance on their enemies." (Jos 10:1-14) Those who accept God as the creator of the universe and life can accept that he would know a way of stopping the earth from rotating. However, there are other ways of understanding this account. We

---

[217] Charles Q. Choi (April 12, 2007). Scientific America. Strange but True: Earth Is Not Round. Retrieved Monday, August 03, 2015.

http://www.scientificamerican.com/article/earth-is-not-round/

[218] Alfred, Randy (June 19, 2008). "June 19, 240 B.C.E: The Earth Is Round, and It's This Big". Wired. Retrieved Monday, August 03, 2015.

must keep in mind that the Bible speaks from an earthly observer point of view, so it need not be that he stopped the rotation. It could have been a refraction of solar and lunar light rays, which would have produced the same effect.

Psalm 136:6 English Standard Version (ESV)

[6]to him who spread out the earth above the waters, for his steadfast love endures forever;

Hebrews 3:4 English Standard Version (ESV)

[4](For every house is built by someone, but the builder of all things is God.)

2 Kings 20:8-11 English Standard Version (ESV)

[8]And Hezekiah said to Isaiah, "What shall be the sign that the LORD will heal me, and that I shall go up to the house of the LORD on the third day?" [9]And Isaiah said, "This shall be the sign to you from the LORD, that the LORD will do the thing that he has promised: shall the shadow go forward ten steps, or go back ten steps?" [10]And Hezekiah answered, "It is an easy thing for the shadow to lengthen ten steps. Rather let the shadow go back ten steps." [11]And Isaiah the prophet called to the LORD, and he brought the shadow back ten steps, by which it had gone down on the steps of Ahaz.

How is it that the stars fought on behalf of Barak?

Judges 5:20 English Standard Version (ESV)

[20] From heaven the stars fought, from their courses they fought against Sisera.

Judges 4:15 English Standard Version (ESV)

[15] And the LORD routed Sisera and all his chariots and all his army before Barak by the edge of the sword. And Sisera got down from his chariot and fled away on foot.

In the Bible, you have Biblical prose, and Biblical poetry.

Prose: language that is not poetry: (1) writing or speech in its normal continuous form, without the rhythmic or visual line structure of poetry **(2)** ordinary style of expression: writing or speech that is ordinary or matter-of-fact, without embellishment.

Poetry: literature in verse: (1) literary works written in verse, in particular verse writing of high quality, great beauty, emotional sincerity or intensity, or profound insight **(2) beauty or grace:** something that resembles poetry in its beauty, rhythmic grace, or imaginative, elevated, or decorative style.

We have a beautiful example of both of these forms of writing-communication in chapters four and five of the book of Judges. Judges Chapter 4 is a prose account of Deborah and Barak, while Judges Chapter 5 is a poetic account. As we have learned from the above, poetry is less concerned with accuracy than evoking emotions. Poetry has a license to say things like what we find in of 5:20, which is in the poetry chapter: "from heaven the stars fought." This can be said and the reader is expected to not take the language literally. What we can surmise from it though, is that God was acting against Sisera in some way, there was divine intervention.

Procedures for Handling Biblical Difficulties

1. You need to be completely convinced a reason or understanding exists.

2. You need to have total trust and conviction in the inerrancy of the Scripture as originally written down.

3. You need to study the context and framework of the verse carefully, to establish what the author meant by the words he used. In other words, find the beginning and the end of the context that your passage falls within.

4. You need to understand exegesis: find the historical setting, determine author intent, study key words, and note parallel passages. You need to slow down and carefully read the account, considering exactly what is being said

5. You need to find a reasonable harmonization of parallel passages.

6. You need to consider a variety of trusted Bible commentaries, dictionaries, lexical sources, encyclopedias, as well as books on Bible difficulties.

7. You should investigate as to whether the difficulty is a transmissional error in the original text.

8. You must always keep in mind that the historical accuracy of the biblical text is unmatched; that thousands of extant manuscripts some of which date back to the second century B.C. support the transmitted text of Scripture.

9. We must keep in mind that the Bible is a diverse book when it comes to literary styles: narrative, poetic, prophetic, and apocalyptic; also containing parables, metaphors, similes, hyperbole, and other figures of

speech. Too often, these alleged errors are the result of a reader taking a figure of speech as literal, or reading a parable as though it is a narrative.

10. The Bible student needs to understand what level that the Bible intends to be exact in what is written. If Jim told a friend that 650 graduated with him from high school in 1984, it is not challenged, because it is all too clear that he is using rounded numbers and is not meaning to be precise.

CHAPTER 8 'What We Have Here Are the Error-Ridden Copies of the Autographs'

Ehrman wrote: The Moody experience was intense. I decided to major in Bible theology, which meant taking a lot of biblical study and systematic theology courses. Only one perspective was taught in these courses, subscribed to by all the professors (they had to sign a statement) and by all the students (we did as well): the Bible is the **inerrant word of God**. It contains no mistakes. It is inspired completely and in its very words— "verbal, plenary inspiration." All the courses I took presupposed and taught this perspective; any other was taken to be misguided or even heretical. Some, I suppose, would call this brainwashing. *Misquoting Jesus* (p. 4) So rather than actually having the inspired words of the autographs (i.e., the **originals**) of the Bible, what we have are the **error-ridden copies** of the autographs. *Misquoting Jesus* (p. 5). What good is it to say that the autographs (i.e., the originals) were inspired? We don't have the originals! We have only **error-ridden copies**, and the vast majority of these are centuries removed from the originals and different from them, evidently, in thousands of ways. *Misquoting Jesus* (p. 7) I've indicated, already at Wheaton I had begun to question some of the foundational aspects of my commitment to the Bible as the inerrant word of God. That commitment came under serious assault in my detailed studies at Princeton. **Misquoting Jesus (p. 8).**

Ehrman seems to start with the belief that if the originals were inspired by God and fully inerrant, it must remain that way, in order to remain inerrant. He seems to be asking, 'if only the originals were inspired, and the copies were not inspired, and we do not have the originals, how are we to be certain of any passage of Scripture?' In other words, God would never allow the inspired, inerrant Word to suffer copying errors. Why would he perform the miracle of inspiring the message to be fully inerrant, and not follow up with the miracle of inspiring the copyist, to keep it inerrant? First, we must note that God has not given us the specifics of every decision he has made in reference to man. If we start the, 'why did God not do this or do that,' where would it end? For example, why did God just not produce the books himself, and miraculously deliver them to persons such as Moses? Why did he not use angelic messengers to pen the message, or produce the message miraculously? God has chosen not to tell us why he did not inspire the copyists, so it remains an unknown. However, I would contend that if one can restore the text to its original wording through the work of textual criticism, to an exact representation thereof, you have, in essence, the originals.

In the end, what we do know is that the Jewish copyists and later Christian copyists were not infallible like the original writers. The original writers were **inspired** by "Holy Spirit," while the copyists were **guided** by "Holy Spirit." However, do we not have a treasure-load of evidence from centuries of copies? Regardless of the recopying, do we not have the Bible in a reliable critical text and trustworthy translations, with both improving all the time? It was only inevitable that imperfect copyists, who were not under inspiration, would have errors creep into the text. However, the thousands of copies that we do have, these enable the textual scholars to trace these errors. How? Different copyists made different errors. Therefore, the textual scholar compares the work of different copyists. He is able to identify their mistakes.

A Simple Example

What if 100 persons were asked or hired to make a handwritten copy of Matthew's Gospel, with 18,345 words. These persons fit in one of four categories as writers: (1) struggles to write, and has no experience as a document maker, (2) a skilled document maker [recorder of events, wills, business, certificates, etc.], (3) a trained copyist of literature, and (4) the professional copyist. There is little doubt that these copyists would make some copying errors. However, it would be impossible that they would all make the same errors. If a trained textual scholar with many years of religious education, including textual studies, and decades of experience, were to compare these 100 documents carefully, he could determine which are erroneous, and restore the text to its original form, even if he had never seen that original.

The textual scholars of the last 250 years, especially the last 50 years have had over 5,750 Greek manuscripts to work with, several of them dating back to the second century C.E. Some of these textual scholars were very skilled in their craft, and to study the life of any of the hundreds that have lived throughout this era, would impress on us that we have nothing short of a mirror reflection of the original in our critical text (Greek New Testament, 5th Revised Edition[219] and Nestle-Aland Greek New Testament 28th edition),[220] namely, an exact representation.

Hundreds of scholars throughout the last three centuries have produced what we might call a master text, by way of lifetimes of hard work and careful study. Are there a few places where we are not 100 percent certain? Yes, of course. However, we are considering merely a handful of places in a text that contains 138,020 words. In addition, in these places, the alternative reading is in the footnote. Ehrman's expression

---

[219] The UBS5 is designed for translators and students.

[220] NA28 is designed for scholarly research.

'error-ridden copies' is a bit misplaced, and certainly misleading indeed, because we have many manuscripts that were copied by professional copyists that are just the opposite, almost error-free. So, when he says 'we only have error-ridden' copies, he is misleading us by the emphatic expression on two fronts. First, there are many copies that are almost error-free and negates his "only." Second, textual scholarship can easily identify 99 percent of those errors that only make up 25 percent of the text, as 75 percent of the text is error-free.

400,000 to 500,000 Variants in the Manuscripts

> With this abundance of evidence, what can we say about the total number of variants known today? Scholars differ significantly in their estimates—some say there are 200,000 variants known, some say 300,000, some say 400,000 or more! We do not know for sure because, despite impressive developments in computer technology, no one has yet been able to count them all. Perhaps, as I indicated earlier, it is best simply to leave the matter in comparative terms. There are more variations among our manuscripts than there are words in the New Testament. *Misquoting Jesus* (pp. 89-90)

Ehrman has some favorite layman ways of expressing the problems that he uses without qualification, in every interview I have seen of him before a lay audience (which includes seminary students), he presents one or more of his favorites, without qualifying them:

- Scholars differ significantly in their estimates—some say there are 200,000 variants known, some say 300,000, some say **400,000 or more!**
- There are **more variations** among our manuscripts **than there are words** in the New Testament.
- We have only **error-ridden copies,** and the vast majority of these are centuries removed from the originals and different from them, evidently, in thousands of ways.
- We don't even have copies of the copies of the originals, or **copies of the copies of the copies of the originals.**
- In the early Christian centuries, **scribes were amateurs** and as such were more inclined to alter the texts they copied.
- **We could go on nearly forever** talking about specific places in which the texts of the New Testament came to be changed, either accidentally or intentionally.
- The Bible began to appear to me as a very **human book.**

202

It is true that Ehrman has said that, the majority of the manuscript variants are not substantial. However, from my observation, this comes when he is in front of scholars that would know otherwise. I would argue that in a larger number of cases he is focusing the laypersons on a large number of variants and there being substantial. Each of the above favorite snippets by Ehrman left unexplained are an exaggeration, misinformation, misleading, and just a failure to be truthful. Many layperson-churchgoers have been spiritually shipwrecked in their faith by such unexplained hype. What the uninformed person hears is that we can never get back to the originals or even close, that there are hundreds of thousands of significant variants that have so scarred the text, we no longer have the Word of God, and it is merely the word of man. How such a knowledgeable man cannot know the impact, his words are having is beyond this writer.

How to Count Textual Variants

Now, let us return to the mindset of Bart Ehrman. Let us look at what he says to a person, who asked him a sincere Bible question in a recent debate with Daniel Wallace. Since the debate, Wallace has called him on his words, and Ehrman offers a reason that is really no reason at all, for which Wallace correctly informs him that his words have an impact.[221]

Daniel Wallace Calling Ehrman out on His Words

During the Q&A time in our debate, someone from the audience asked a question of you about what it would take for you to regard our copies of Mark to be "trustworthy." You responded:

Well, if we had early copies—if we had copies of Mark—suppose next week there's an archaeological find... say it's in Rome, and we have reason to think that these ten manuscripts that were discovered were all copied within a week of the original copy [sic] of Mark and they disagree in, uh, .001 percent of their textual variation, then I would say 'that's good evidence!' And that's precisely what we don't have.

Ehrman's Weak Reply

I'm sorry you took an off-the-cuff comment of mine with intentional exaggeration to be a literal statement of my standards of evidence. (Why do you do that??) Of course, I didn't calculate

---

[221] textualcriticism@yahoogroups.com

in my mind that I would require one-millionth deviation for it to be good evidence. Good grief!

Wallace Informs Ehrman How Words Impact

Regarding your post on the TC-list, you're saying that before more than 1400 people who were deciding whether the manuscript evidence was at all reliable—people who sincerely and earnestly wanted to get straightforward answers by both of us—you intentionally exaggerated your standard when folks were hanging on your every word? To call this off-the-cuff is unwarranted. The individual was asking a serious question, and you gave no hint in your mannerism or tone that you were giving anything but a straightforward answer. Why do you do that?

You have a responsibility when making public statements to be more accurate than sensationalist in your assessment. I've talked to several folks about your comment; no one thought you were intentionally exaggerating. As a master teacher, you know how important clear communication is.

Wallace has offered the truth of the matter here, words have an impact, if you do not qualify them, they can cause serious damage. Ehrman has a tendency to offer what I perceive to be as sarcastic jokes during debates. I believe he does this at times, to get the audience laughing so he can sidestep his inability to offer a response to something that has been asked of him. He has debated many scholars at present, and this writer feels that he has not done well with any of them because his information in such popular books for laypersons does not hold up under the scrutiny of textual scholars that possess the same equal level of knowledge.

Concession or Concealment?

In fact, most of the changes found in our early Christian manuscripts have nothing to do with theology or ideology. Far and away the most changes are the result of mistakes, pure and simple—slips of the pen, accidental omissions, inadvertent additions, misspelled words, blunders of one sort or another. Scribes could be incompetent: it is important to recall that most of the copyists in the early centuries were not trained to do this kind of work but were simply the literate members of their congregations who were (more or less) able and willing. *Misquoting Jesus* (p. 55)

One might think that the above is Ehrman's concession, where he is going to help the reader finally, when he says, "most changes are the result of mistakes, pure and simple—slips of the pen, accidental omissions, inadvertent additions, misspelled words, blunders." You might have thought that Ehrman was going to say thereafter that 'these types of blunders are easy to recognize and correct, giving us confidence that most of the changes are easily fixed.' If you thought that, you were sadly mistaken because this concession is only a means to propagate the 'incompetence of the scribes.' As you saw earlier in this book and will see later, this is not the case.

Ehrman's Missing Information on the Textual Variants

As he has already conceded, most variants are accidental. He also was kind enough to help us appreciate just what kind of accidents we are considering. However, this is as far as Ehrman takes us, for we are not told that they are *trivial* and *easily* resolved. Let us list some of the most common variants.

Division of Words: As we learned early on, the manuscripts were written without any division between words (GODISNOWHERE is either 'God is no where,' or God is now here.) Therefore, it was quite easy to come up with the wrong division.

Similar Endings: The scribe looks away from the exemplar[222] to pen the word or phrase, and when he looks back, to see what is next, his eyes skip down the page to a similar ending, picking up there, leaving out what lie in between.

(Homoioteleuton) Similar Endings: Some of the Greek letters were quite similar (whether capital or lower case), making them easy to confuse.

(Haplography) Single Writing: The scribe writes a letter or word once when it should have been written twice.

(Dittography) Double Writing: The scribe writes a letter or word twice when it should have been written once.

(Metathesis) Change of Place: The scribe accidentally changes the order of the letters or words.

Sight Issues: A scribe or lector has poor eyesight, and so he would have found it difficult to distinguish between the Greek letters. This would be especially true if the exemplar he was working from had not been written with care.

---

[222] A master copy of a text, from which further copies were made from

Memory Issues: The scribe looks at his exemplar and takes a clause into his mind, and in the process of looking away to perform the task of copying it, he struggles with his recall, and writes any of the following: a synonym for one of the words, or alters a couple of the words, transposed letters in one of the words, inserts words from a parallel passage.

Hearing Issues: The scribe possesses faulty hearing, and when the lector[223] is reading the words from the exemplar, which is to be taken down in the scribe's copy, the pronunciation is unclear, causing the scribe to choose the wrong word at times. (An English example being 'there' and 'their.') In addition, early on, Greek vowels and diphthongs were pronounced alike, which could cause confusion.

Writing Issues: The scribe here would make mistakes that are similar to the ones under the hearing issues. The error is not derived from what he saw in his exemplar, but in what he penned in his copy.

In the beginning, I had asked you to keep the phrase **"accuracy of statement"** in mind, because there are many ways that one can express the information, leading the person to believe or think one thing, which is completely not the case. We have seen that thus far and there is more ahead.

---

[223] A lector is a reader of an exemplar text to a room full of scribes, who are taking down and producing manuscript copies.

CHAPTER 8 'We Don't Have Copies of the Copies of the Copies of the Originals'

Ehrman wrote: Not only do we not have the originals, we don't have the first copies of the originals. **We don't even have copies of the copies of the originals, or copies of the copies of the copies of the originals.** What we have are copies made later—much later. In most instances, they are copies made many *centuries* later. And these **copies all differ from one another, in many thousands of places.** As we will see later in this book, these copies differ from one another in so many places that we don't even know how many differences there are. Possibly it is easiest to put it in comparative terms: **there are more differences among our manuscripts than there are words in the New Testament. Misquoting Jesus (p. 10)**

As one reads this little section of intensity, he gets a sense of hopelessness, because 'all feel lost, for there is certainly no way to get back to the originals.' As you will see before we finish this book, Ehrman hangs, even more, hopelessness on the back of the Christian, for he asserts that even in the few minute places that we might be certain about the wording, we cannot be certain about the meaning.

Blinded by Misguided Perceptions

It seems that Ehrman has been very blinded by the fact that we do not have the originals or immediate copies. Here we have a world-renowned textual and early Christianity scholar, who is suggesting all throughout his book that we do not have the originals, nor the immediate copies, and there are so many copyist errors, it is nigh impossible to get back to the Word of God at all. Even if by some mere fortune that we do, we cannot know the meaning for sure. Ehrman is saying to the lay reader; we can no longer trust the text of the Greek New Testament as the Word of God.

Ehrman has been so busy over exaggerating the negative to his readers; he has failed to mention what we do have. Dr. Mark Minnick assesses what we do have quite nicely, "Doesn't the existence of these variants undermine our confidence that we have the very words of God inspired? No! The fact is that because we know of them and are careful to preserve the readings of every one of them, *not one word of God's word has been lost to us.*"[224]

---

[224] Mark Minnick, "Let's Meet the Manuscripts," in from the Mind of God to the Mind of Man: A Layman's Guide to How We Got Our Bible, eds. James B. Williams and Randolph Shaylor (Greenvill, SC: Ambassador-Emerald International, 1999), p. 96.

The wealth of manuscripts that we have for establishing the original Greek New Testament is shameless, in comparison to other ancient literature. We can only wonder what Ehrman does with an ancient piece of literature that has only one copy, and that copy is 1,000 years removed from the time of the original.

Virgil (70-19 B.C.E.) wrote the *Aeneid* between 29 and 19 B.C.E. for which there are only five manuscripts dating to the fourth and fifth centuries C.E.[225] Jewish historian Josephus (37-100 C.E.) wrote *The Jewish Wars* about 75 C.E., for which we have nine complete manuscripts, seven of major importance dating from the tenth to the twelfth centuries C.E.[226] Tacitus (59-129 C.E.) wrote *Annals of Imperial Rome* sometime before 116 C.E., a work considered vital to understanding the history of the Roman Empire during the first century, and we have only thirty-three manuscripts, two of the earliest that date 850 and 1050 C.E. Julius Caesar (100-44 B.C.E.) wrote his Gallic Wars between 51-46 B.C.E.,[227] which is a firsthand account in a third-person narrative of the war, of which we have 251 manuscripts dating between the ninth and fifteenth centuries.[228]

The Greek New Testament evidence is over 5,836 Greek manuscripts, over 9,284 versions, and over 10,000 Latin manuscripts, not to mention an innumerable amount of church father quotations. This places the Greek New Testament in a world of its own, because no other ancient document is close to this, except the Hebrew Old Testament. However, there is even more. There are about 66+ papyri manuscripts that date to the 2nd and 3rd centuries C.E. Moreover, these early papyri manuscripts are from a region in Egypt that appreciated books as literature, and was copied by semi-professional and professional scribes, or at least a highly skilled copyist. This region produced what is known as the most accurate and trusted manuscripts.

---

[225] Preface | Dickinson College Commentaries. (April 25, 2017) http://dcc.dickinson.edu/vergil-aeneid/manuscripts

[226] Honora Howell Chapman (Editor), Zuleika Rodgers (Editor), 2016, A *Companion to Josephus* (Blackwell Companions to the Ancient World), Wiley-Blackwell: p. 307.

[227] Carolyn Hammond, 1996, Introduction to *The Gallic War*, Oxford University Press: p. xxxii.

Max Radin, 1918, The date of composition of Caesar's Gallic War, *Classical Philology* XIII: 283–300.

[228] O. Seel, 1961, *Bellum Gallicum*. (Bibl. Teubneriana.) Teubner, Leipzig.

W. Hering, 1987, *C. Iulii Caesaris commentarii rerum gestarum, Vol. I: Bellum Gallicum.*(Bibl. Teubneriana.) Teubner, Leipzig.

Virginia Brown, 1972, *The Textual Transmission of Caesar's Civil War*, Brill.

Caesar's Gallic war - Tim Mitchell. (April 25, 2017) http://www.timmitchell.fr/blog/2012/04/12/gallic-war/

Were the Scribes in the Early Centuries Amateurs

> We could **go on nearly forever** talking about specific places in which the texts of the New Testament came to be changed, either accidentally or intentionally. As I have indicated, the examples are **not just in the hundreds but in the thousands.** The examples given are enough to convey the general point, however: there are lots of differences among our manuscripts, differences created by scribes who were reproducing their sacred texts. **In the early Christian centuries, scribes were amateurs** and as such were more inclined to alter the texts they copied—or more prone to alter them accidentally—than were scribes in the later periods who, starting in the fourth century, began to be professionals. *Misquoting Jesus* (p. 98)

Let us take just a moment, to discuss Ehrman's statement, "**in the early Christian centuries, scribes were amateurs.**" In chapter four of this book, we established just the opposite. Here is a summary paragraph of that evidence. Some of the earliest manuscripts that we now have established that a professional scribe copied them. Many of the other papyri give evidence that a semi-professional hand copied them, while most of these early papyri give evidence of being done by a copyist that was literate and experienced. Therefore, either literate or semi-professional copyist did the vast majority of our early papyri, with some being done by professionals. As it happened, the few poorly copied manuscripts came to light first, establishing a precedent that was difficult for some to shake when the truckload of evidence came forth that showed just the opposite. (Aland and Aland 1987, 18-19)

Ehrman is distorting the facts to his readers when he goes off the rails, to say, "We don't even have copies of the copies of the originals or copies of the copies of the copies of the originals." The way this is worded, he is saying that we do not have copies that are third or fourth generations removed from the original. Ehrman cannot know this because we have fifteen copies that are 75-100 years removed from the death of the apostle John in 100 C.E. There is the possibility that any of these could be only third or fourth generation removed copies. Moreover, they could have been copied from a second or third generation. Therefore, Ehrman is misstating the evidence.

Let us do a short review of two very important manuscripts: P[75] and Vaticanus 1209. The "P" in P[75] (also known as Bodmer 14, 15) stands for papyrus document, an ancient manuscript written on papyrus. Papyrus is writing material used by the ancient Egyptians, Greeks, and Romans that was made from the pith of the stem of a water plant. These are the earliest witnesses to the Greek New Testament. P[75] contains most of Luke and John, dating from 175 C.E. to 225 C.E The Vaticanus is designated internationally by the symbol "B," and is known as an uncial manuscript, written on parchment, a creamy or yellowish material made from dried and treated sheepskin, goatskin, or other animal hides. The Vaticanus is of the mid-fourth-century C.E., originally contained the entire Bible in Greek. At present, Vaticanus' New Testament is missing parts of Hebrews (Hebrews 9:14 to 13:25), all of First and Second Timothy, Titus, Philemon, and Revelation. Originally, this codex probably had approximately 820 leaves, of which 759 remain.

What kind of weight or evidence do these two manuscripts carry in the eyes of textual scholars? Vaticanus 1209 is a key source for our modern translations. When determining an original reading, this manuscript could stand against other external evidence that would seem to the nonprofessional as being so much more. P[75] also is one of the weightiest manuscripts that we have, and is virtually identical to Vaticanus 1209, which dates 175 to 125 years later, about 350 C.E. When textual scholars B. F. Westcott and F. J. A. Hort released their critical text in 1881, Hort said that Vaticanus preserved a "not only a very ancient text but a very pure line of a very ancient text." (Westcott and A., The New Testament in the Original Greek, Vol. 2: Introduction, Appendix 1882, 251) However, later scholars have argued that Vaticanus was a scholarly recension; a critical revision carried out on Vaticanus, an edited text. However, P[75] has vindicated Westcott and Hort, because of its virtual likeness with Vaticanus, establishes that Vaticanus is essentially a copy of a second-century text, and likely, a copy of the original text, with the exception of a few minor points.

Kurt Aland,[229] wrote, "P[75] shows such a close affinity with the Codex Vaticanus that the supposition of a recension of the text at Alexandria, in the fourth century, can no longer be held."[230] David C. Parker,[231] says of P[75] that "it is extremely important for two reasons: "like Vaticanus it is carefully copied; it is also very early, and is generally dated to a period between 175 and 225. Thus, it pre-dates Vaticanus by at least a century. A careful comparison between P75 and Vaticanus in Luke by C.M. Martini demonstrated that P75 was an earlier copy of the same careful Alexandrian

---

[229] (1915 –1994) was Professor of New Testament Research and Church History. He founded the Institute for New Testament Textual Research in Münster and served as its first director for many years (1959–83). He was one of the principal editors The Greek New Testament for the United Bible Societies.

[230] K. Aland, "The Significance of the Papyri for New Testament Research," 336.

[231] Professor of Theology and the Director of the Institute for Textual Scholarship and Electronic Editing at the Department of Theology and Religion, University of Birmingham. Scholar of New Testament textual criticism and Greek and Latin paleography.

text. It is sometimes called a proto-Alexandrian. It is our earliest example of a controlled text, one which was not intentionally or extensively changed in successive copying. Its discovery and study have provided proof that the Alexandrian text had already come into existence in the third century." (D. C. Parker 1997, 61) Let us look at a few more textual scholars, just to nail the coffin shut, J. Ed Komoszewski; M. James Sawyer; Daniel Wallace.

> Even some of the early manuscripts show compelling evidence of being copies of a much earlier source. Consider again Codex Vaticanus, whose text is very much like that of P75 (B and P75 are much closer to each other than B is to [Codex Sinaiticus]). Yet the papyrus is at least a century older than Vaticanus. When P75 was discovered in the 1950s, some entertained the possibility that Vaticanus could have been a copy of P75, but this view is no longer acceptable since the wording of Vaticanus is certainly more primitive than that of P75 in several places.' They both must go back to a still earlier common ancestor, probably one that is from the early second century. (Komoszewski, M. Sawyer and Wallace 2006, 78)

Ehrman suggests that the early Christians were not concerned about the integrity of the text, its preservation of accuracy. Let us visit the second-century evidence by way of Tertullian.[232]

> Come now, you who would indulge a better curiosity, if you would apply it to the business of your salvation, run over the apostolic churches, in which the very thrones[233] of the apostles are still pre-eminent in their places,[234] in which their own **authentic writings** are read, uttering the voice and representing the face of each of them severally.[235] (Bold mine)

What did Tertullian mean by "authentic writings"? If he is referring to the Greek originals, which it likely seems that he is, according to the Latin, it is a reference that some of the original New Testament books are still in existence at the time of his penning this work. However, let us say that it is

---

[232] (160 – 220 C.E.), was a prolific early Christian author from Carthage in the Roman province of Africa.

[233] Cathedrae

[234] Suis locis praesident.

[235] Alexander Roberts, James Donaldson and A. Cleveland Coxe, The Ante-Nicene Fathers Vol. III: Translations of the Writings of the Fathers Down to A.D. 325 (Oak Harbor: Logos Research Systems, 1997), 260.

simply referring to copies that were well preserved. In any case, this still shows that the Christians valued the preservation of accuracy.

We need to visit an earlier book by Ehrman for a moment, *Lost Christianities*, in which he writes, "In this process of recopying the document by hand, what happened to the original of 1 Thessalonians? For some unknown reason, it was eventually thrown away, burned, or otherwise destroyed. Possibly, it was read so much that it simply wore out. The early Christians saw no need to preserve it as the `original' text. They had copies of the letter. Why keep the original?" (B. D. Ehrman 2003, 217)

Here Ehrman is arguing from silence. We cannot read the minds of people today; let alone read the minds of persons 2,000 years before we were born. It is a known fact that congregations valued Paul's letters, and Paul exhorted them to share the letters amongst differing congregations. Paul wrote to the Colossians, and in what we know as 4:16 he said, "And when this letter has been read among you, have it **also read in the church of the Laodiceans**; and see that you also read the letter from Laodicea." The best way would be to send someone to a congregation, have them copy the letter and bring it back to their home congregation. On the other hand, someone could make copies of the letter in the congregation that received it and delivered it to interested congregations. In 1 Thessalonians, the congregation that Ehrman is talking about here, chapter five, verse 27, Paul says, "I put you under oath before the Lord to **have this letter read to all the brothers.**" What did Paul mean by "all the brothers"? It could be that he meant it to be used like a circuit letter, circulated to other congregations, giving everyone a chance to hear the counsel. It may merely be that, with the ability to read being so low, Paul wanted a guarantee that all were going to get to hear its contents, and it simply meant that every brother and sister locally would have had a chance to hear it in the congregation. Regardless, even if we live with the latter, the stress that was put on the reading of this letter, shows the weight that these people were placed under concerning Paul's letters.[236]

Peter also had this to say about Paul's letters, "there are some things in them [Paul's letters] that are hard to understand, which the ignorant and unstable twist to their own destruction, **as they do the other Scriptures.**" (2

---

[236] The exhortation ἐνορκίζω ὑμᾶς τὸν κύριον ἀναγνωσθῆναι τὴν ἐπιστολὴν πᾶσιν τοῖς ἀδελφοῖς ("I adjure you by the Lord that this letter be read aloud to all the brothers [and sisters]") is stated quite strongly. ἐνορκίζω takes a double accusative and has a causal sense denoting that the speaker or writer wishes to extract an oath from the addressee(s). The second accusative, in this case τὸν κύριον ("the Lord"), indicates the thing or person by whom the addressees were to swear. The forcefulness of this statement is highly unusual, and in fact it is the only instance in Paul's letters where such a charge is laid on the recipients of one of his letters. —Charles A. Wanamaker, The Epistles to the Thessalonians: A Commentary on the Greek Text (Grand Rapids, Mich.: W.B. Eerdmans, 1990), 208-09.

Pet 3:16) Peter just compared Paul's letters to being on the same level as the Old Testament that was referred to as Scripture. Jumping ahead, about 135 C.E., Papias, an elder of the early congregation in Hierapolis, put what he had to tell into a book.

Papias explains: "I will not hesitate to set down for you, along with my interpretations, everything I carefully learned then from the elders and carefully remembered, guaranteeing their truth. For unlike most people I did not enjoy those who have a great deal to say, but those who teach the truth. Nor did I enjoy those who recall someone else's commandments, but those who remember the commandments given by the Lord to the faith and proceeding from the truth itself. In addition, if by chance someone who had been a follower of the elders should come my way, I inquired about the words of the elders--what Andrew or Peter said, or Philip, or Thomas or James, or John or Matthew or any other of the Lord's disciples, and whatever Aristion and the elder John, the Lord's disciples, were saying. For I did not think that information from books would profit me as much as information from a living and abiding voice." (Holmes, The Apostolic Fathers: Greek Texts and English Translations 2007, 565)

As an elder in the congregation at Hierapolis in Asia Minor, Papias was an unrelenting researcher. Moreover, he was also a thorough compiler of information, he exhibited intense indebtedness for the Scriptures. Papias determined properly that any doctrinal statement of Jesus Christ or his apostles would be far more appreciated and respected to explain than the unreliable statements found in the written works of his day.—Jude 17.

Therefore, the idea of that the "early Christians saw no need to preserve it as the `original' text," is far too difficult to swallow when we consider the above. Moreover, imagine a Church in Middle America getting a visit from Billy Graham. Now imagine that he wrote them a warm letter, but filled with some stern counsel. Would there be little interest in the preservation of those words? Would they not want to share it with others? Would other churches not be interested in it? The same would have been true of early Christianity receiving a letter from an apostle like Peter, John, or Paul. There is no doubt that the 'original' wore out eventually. However, they lived in a society that valued the preservation of the apostle's words, and it is far more likely that it was copied, to share with others, and to preserve. Moreover, let us assume that their imperfections took over as well. Paul would have become a famous apostle that wrote a few churches, and there were thousands of churches toward the end of the first-century. Would they have not exhibited some pride in that they received a letter from the famous apostle Paul, who was martyred for the truth? Ehrman's suggestions are reaching and contrary to human nature. It is simply wishful thinking on his part.

The idea of getting back to the original seems not really to be so far removed from the mind of Ehrman, who pens the fourth edition of *The Text of the New Testament*, with Bruce Metzger: "Besides textual evidence derived from New Testament Greek manuscripts and from early versions, the textual critic compares numerous scriptural quotations used in commentaries, sermons, and other treatises written by early church fathers. Indeed, so extensive are these citations that if all other sources for our knowledge of the text of the New Testament were destroyed, they would be sufficient alone for the reconstruction of practically the entire New Testament." (Metzger and Ehrman 2005, 126)

How are we to view the patristic citations? Well, let us look at another book that Bart Ehrman coauthored with other textual scholars. The following is from chapter 12, written by Gordon Fee (The Use of the Greek Fathers for New Testament Textual Criticism), "In NT textual criticism, patristic citations are ordinarily viewed as the third line of evidence, indirect and supplementary to the Greek MSS, and are often therefore treated as of tertiary importance. When properly evaluated, however, patristic evidence is of primary importance, for both of the major tasks of NT textual criticism: in contrast to the early Greek MSS, the Fathers have the potential of offering datable and geographically certain evidence." (B. D. Ehrman 1995, 191)

In closing out this chapter, we have certainly established that Ehrman is once again, painting a picture that is not quite the truth of the matter. We have also established that the manuscript evidence is not as far removed as he suggests with his sarcasm. Moreover, he does not help the reader to appreciate just how close the New Testament manuscript evidence is to the time of the original writings, in comparison to other ancient literature, many of which are few in number and a thousand years removed.

In addition, he has exaggerated the variants in the Greek New Testament manuscripts by not qualifying the level of variants and just how he is counting to get such high numbers. In addition, Ehrman's unqualified statement, "In the early Christian centuries, scribes were amateurs," has been debunked as well, because it is a statement without explanation. True, there were amateur scribes in the first few centuries, but the manuscript evidence suggests the opposite is true when it comes to copying the New Testament manuscripts. Again, **some** of the earliest manuscripts that we now have established that a professional scribe copied them. **Many** of the other papyri give evidence that a semi-professional hand copied them, while **most** of these early papyri give evidence of being done by a copyist that was literate and experienced. Therefore, either literate or semi-professional copyist did **the vast majority** of our early papyri, with some being done by professionals.

CHAPTER 9 'This was a Human Book from Beginning to End'

Ehrman wrote: For me, though, this was a compelling problem. It was the words of Scripture themselves that God had inspired. Surely we have to know what those words were if we want to know how he had communicated to us, since the very words were his words, and having some other words (those inadvertently or intentionally created by scribes) didn't help us much if we wanted to know His words. **Misquoting Jesus (p. 5)**

Ehrman wrote: The Bible began to appear to me as **a very human book.** Just as human scribes had copied, and changed, the texts of scripture, so too had human authors originally written the texts of Scripture. This was **a human book from beginning to end.** It was written by different human authors at different times and in different places to address different needs. *Misquoting Jesus* **(p. 11)** Lindsey, like those of us at Moody, believed that the Bible was absolutely inerrant in its very words, to the extent that you could read the New Testament and know not only how God wanted you to live and what he wanted you to believe, but also what God himself was planning to do in the future and how he was going to do it. The world was heading for an apocalyptic crisis of catastrophic proportions, and the inerrant words of scripture could be read to show what, how, and when it would all happen. **Misquoting Jesus (p. 12)**

Sadly, Ehrman is not alone here in his thinking. It is quite common today, to be skeptical about everything: ideas, customs, values, the existence of God, and whether the Bible is the Word of God. In the last 20-30-years, there has been an all-out attack on the Bible, viewing it as nothing more than the word of man. Many seem to view it as out of date, or unconnected to our modern-day world. Few, who we might consider intellectuals, see the Bible as the Word of God. Bart Ehrman and other scholars would agree with James Barr, who wrote, "My account of the formation of the biblical tradition is an account of a human work. It is man's statement of his beliefs."[237]

Do you think the Bible is the Word of God or the word of man? Herein so far, we have debunked many of the arguments made by one of the leading agnostic Bible scholars, Dr. Bart D. Ehrman. We have disclosed his mindset, and his desire to mislead by withholding certain evidence from lay audiences or manipulating the evidence, to make it seem more egregious

---

[237] *The Bible in the Modern World*, by James Barr, 1973, p. 120.

than it is while being very honest when in front of scholars that would know better. Below, you will find more of the same, and at the end of this book, you will find some recommended books by leading authorities in textual studies that will help you defend against those that would seek to mislead you.

Ehrman views the authors of the Bible, as the final line, there is no Creator or heavenly Father that moved them to pen their books. After losing confidence in the Bible, especially the Gospels, Ehrman shipwrecked his faith and became an agnostic, and has now plummeted to the depths of turning on the Word of God. You have to wonder how Ehrman got through Moody Bible College and Wheaton College and failed to discover textual inconsistencies. One must also wonder why some seminary students are infected with doubt, while the far majority seems to see the same evidence and maintain their faith.

While I certainly cannot read Ehrman's heart or mind, it is as though some doubts plagued him, because once he discovered them, he closed his eyes to the evidence and failed to reason from the evidence. Moreover, the moment he had one professor open the gate for him, by saying, 'maybe Mark was just wrong,' this opened the floodgates for Ehrman. He has continued to maintain his downward plummet because he has a mindset that the evidence is heavily in the extreme against inspiration, and thus he is looking through binoculars the opposite way, so the eyes are always focused narrowly.

For example, many of the Scriptures that Ehrman uses as his examples are solved quite easily and are not known in the textual community as even being significant, but more as insignificant. As Lightfoot put it in his enormously popular book, *How We Got the Bible*, there are "textual variations, classified in relation to their significance for our present New Testament text. He goes on to speak of "trivial variants which are of no consequence to the text. The great majority of variant readings in the manuscripts have to do with trivial matters, many of them so minute that they cannot be represented in translation." (N. R. Lightfoot 1963, 1988, 2003, 96)

What Lightfoot meant by the latter part is that these "trivial variants" are so insignificant that they are not listed in the footnotes in your Bible translations. Of the hundreds of thousands of textual variants, the vast majority are differences in spelling that have no effect on the meaning of the text. With other examples that make up the more significant variety, you are looking at a handful of verse out of the 7,956 verses in the Greek New Testament. Even with this handful of verses that Ehrman continues to cite, the evidence is quite clear. Examples of this would be the woman caught in adultery, John 7:53-8:11. Another would be when Jesus is in prayer on the Mount of Olives, Luke 22:41-45. Another being the ending that was added to close off the Gospel of Mark, Mark 16:9-20. Ehrman has an obsessive-compulsive issue of over exaggerating the evidence.

Ehrman's Misleading Views on Literacy Versus Illiteracy

. . . but for the most part, Christians came from the ranks of the illiterate. This is certainly true of the very earliest Christians, who would have been the apostles of Jesus. In the Gospel accounts, we find that most of Jesus's disciples are simple peasants from Galilee—uneducated fishermen, for example. Two of them, Peter and John, are explicitly said to be "illiterate" in the book of Acts (4:13). The apostle Paul indicates to his Corinthian congregation that "not many of you were wise by human standards" (1 Cor. 1:27)—which might mean that some few were well educated, but not most. As we move into the second Christian century, things do not seem to change much. As I have indicated, some intellectuals converted to the faith, but most Christians were from the lower classes and uneducated. **Misquoting Jesus (pp. 39-40)**.

We can start by clarifying that the level of literacy in the first century is quite subjective (based on opinions or feelings rather than on real facts or evidence), because of the limited evidence that is available. Let us take a moment to look at the historian today, as compared to the historian during the first few centuries of Christianity. Today, we are capable of covering almost anything that goes on in life, from the most insignificant, to the most noteworthy. We in the United States may watch live on CNN as some firefighters in New Zealand rescue a puppy that had been trapped in a storm drain. Then again, we can watch a 9.0 earthquake as it hits Japan, causing the deaths of over 15,000 people.

What about the first few centuries of our Common Era? The coverage of people, places, and events are not even remotely comparable. The coverage at that time was of the most prominent people, like the emperor of Rome, with very little press being given to the lower officials, let alone the lower class. We do not have much on Pontius Pilate at all, but what we do have is an exception to the rule.

History from antiquity, then, is recoverable but incomplete due to the limited extent and frequently tendentious nature of the sources. Ancient historiography, more than its modern counterpart, is to a greater degree approximate or provisional. A new discovery may alter previous perceptions. Until the discovery of Claudius's Letter to the Alexandrians, written on his

217

accession in 41 but lost until modern times, that emperor's steely resolve could not have been guessed. In short, evidence from Greco-Roman antiquity is fragmentary, generally devoted to "important" people and events and its texts overtly "interpreted." (Barnett 2005, 13)

Now let us offer some basic comments about the literacy level in the first century. Literacy in the first century was determined by being able to read, not write. The need for writing today is far greater than antiquity. Richards offers a great analogy in that 'I am right-handed, so to pen a long paper with my left hand would be quite difficult, and not very legible. The man of antiquity would write with the same difficulty because the need to write was so seldom.' (Richards, Paul And First-Century Letter Writing: Secretaries, Composition and Collection 2004, 28) Like Ehrman, many argue that the lower class was almost all illiterate. However, this is not really the case, as literacy was more every day than they are suggesting.[238] However, let us give Ehrman the benefit of the doubt, and say that illiteracy was very high among the lower class, and even relatively high among the upper class, which might pay for that service.

What does that say about individual Christians throughout the Roman Empire? It is believed that more than 30–40 million people lived in the combined eastern and western Roman Empire (50–200 C.E.). Now, let us say that statistically, the literacy rate is low in a certain region, or in a certain city, like Rome. Does that mean that everyone is illiterate in that region or city? Do we equate the two? If we accept Ehrman's belief that the lower class were likely to be illiterate, meaning they cannot write, or struggle to write; what does this really mean for Christianity? Nothing. Because if 40 million people are living throughout the Roman Empire, and only 400 thousand of them are Christian, we are only talking one percent of the population. There is no way to judge the level of literacy for this tiny selection, because of a statistic, in a time period when history focused on the prominent. If a person says anything about the lower class, this is only based on the sphere of who he knows or what he has seen in his life, which would be minuscule when compared to the whole. Even still, let us look at the texts that Ehrman cited.

---

[238] Exler, Form. P. 126, warns "The papyri discovered in Egypt have shown that the art of writing was more widely, and more popularly, known in the past, than some scholars have been inclined to think." For example, see PZen. 6, 66, POxy. 113,294, 394, 528, 530, 531 and especially 3057.

Were Peter and John Uneducated?

Acts 4:13 Updated American Standard Version (UASV)

[13] Now when they saw the boldness of Peter and John, and perceived that **they were uneducated**[239] and untrained men, they were astonished, and they recognized that they had been with Jesus.

How are we to understand the statement that Peter and John **were uneducated**? This did not necessarily mean that they could not read and write, as the letters that were penned by these apostles (or their secretary) testify that they could. What this means is that they were not educated in higher learning of the Hebrew schools, like studying under someone like Gamaliel. It was the same reason that the Jewish religious leaders were surprised by the extensive knowledge that Jesus had. They said of him, "How is it that this man has learning when he has never studied?" (John 7:15) This is a reference to not studying at the Hebrew schools.

Ehrman also points to secular historians like "Celsus, the first writer against Christianity, makes it a matter of mockery, that labourers, shoemakers, farmers, the most uninformed and clownish of men, should be zealous preachers of the Gospel." (The History of the Christian Religion and Church, During the Three First Centuries, by Augustus Neander; translated from the German by Henry John Rose, 1848, p. 41) Paul explained it in this way: "For consider your calling, brothers: not many of you were wise according to worldly standards, not many were powerful, not many were of noble birth. But God chose what is foolish in the world to shame the wise; God chose what is weak in the world to shame the strong"–1 Corinthians 1:26-27.

First, Celsus was an enemy of Christianity. In addition, like was stated above, what Celsus observed is only within the sphere of his personal experiences. What did he know, a few dozen Christians out of almost a million at the time of his writing? Moreover, although not highly educated in schools, it need not be assumed that the most or all of the early Christians were illiterate, in that they could read and write (with difficulty).

Let us return to Peter and John. We will give Ehrman the benefit of the doubt one more time. We will accept that Peter and John were illiterate in the sense that he wishes it to be true. At the time of this statement in Acts about being **"uneducated,"** it was about 33 C.E. Peter would not pen his first letter for 30 more years. Throughout that 30 years, Peter progressed spiritually maturing into the position of being one of the leaders of the

---

[239] Or *unlettered* (YLT) that is, not educated in the rabbinic schools; not meaning illiterate.

entire first-century Christian congregation. A few years later, Peter and John are viewed as maturing and growing into their new position, as leaders in the Jerusalem congregation, as Paul said of them, "when James and Cephas and John, who seemed to be pillars" of the community. John, on the other hand, did not pen his books until 60 years after Acts 4:13. Can we assume that he too had not grown in 60 years?

Would Ehrman want historians in 2150, to look back, and evaluate his literacy level, based on when he was 18-years-old? What about a person that never graduated from high school, such as the owner of Wendy's restaurant franchise, Dave Thomas? As of March 2010, Wendy's was the world's third largest hamburger fast food chain with approximately 6,650 locations. Are we to look back on Dave Thomas (1932 – 2002), and evaluate his level of education at the age of 18 in 1940? Are we to assume that Dave Thomas was uneducated at the age of 68 in the year 2000? Hardly!

CHAPTER 10 "And So It Goes for Centuries"

Ehrman wrote: That is to say, once a scribe changes a text—whether accidentally or intentionally—then those changes are permanent in his manuscript (unless, of course, another scribe comes along to correct the mistake). The next scribe who copies that manuscript copies those mistakes (thinking they are what the text said), and he adds mistakes of his own. The next scribe who then copies that manuscript copies the mistakes of both his predecessors and adds mistakes of his own, and so on. The only way mistakes get corrected is when a scribe recognizes that a predecessor has made an error and tries to resolve it. There is no guarantee, however, that a scribe who tries to correct a mistake corrects it correctly. That is, by changing what he thinks is an error, he may in fact change it incorrectly, so now there are three forms of the text: the original, the error, and the incorrect attempt to resolve the error. Mistakes multiply and get repeated; sometimes they get corrected and sometimes they get compounded. **And so it goes. For centuries. Misquoting Jesus (p. 57)**

Ehrman is correct in his assessment of human error, and that a scribe copying 138,020 words is bound to make many scribal errors. In addition, the next scribe to use this copy as an exemplar, will make his own copying errors, and incorporate the ones from his exemplar. Moreover, a scribe may attempt to correct what he perceives to be an error, which is not, and actually add an error himself. Generally speaking, then, the further removed the manuscript is from the original, the more errors it will contain. However, you may have a manuscript that was copied in the twelfth-century, but the scribe was using a fourth-century manuscript, meaning that this twelfth-century manuscript will have fewer errors than another twelfth-century that was copied from an exemplar that was created from a line of manuscripts through all those intervening centuries.

This is a textually oriented religion whose texts have been changed, surviving only in copies that vary from one another, **sometimes** in highly **significant** ways. The task of the textual critic is to **try to recover the oldest form** of these texts. This is obviously a **crucial task**, since we **can't interpret the words of the New Testament if we don't know what the words were**. Moreover, as I hope should be clear by now, knowing the words is important not just for those who consider the words divinely inspired. **Misquoting Jesus (p. 70).**

Again, Ehrman is correct, and it is well appreciated that he uses the adverb "sometimes," as opposed to "many times." There are variations within the manuscripts that are "significant" and have a bearing on the text. While the above is correct, it all depends on what a person's perceived goals are before he considers such concepts. A number of textual scholars are not trying to "recover the oldest form," but are trying to recover the original. Yes, the task is "crucial." Why? Because of the reason offered by Ehrman, we **"can't interpret the words of the New Testament if we don't know what the words were."** However, only on a handful of texts out of 7,956 verses, are we talking about a level of 'significance' being enough that they affect the text. I feel that Ehrman is trying to act as though the entire text is in doubt when the only "significant" variants that affect the text are but a handful. Moreover, those few that are "significant" (e.g., Mark 16:9-20; 1 John 5:7; Acts 8:37; John 7:53-8:11; 1 Timothy 3:16)[240], should not be viewed as affecting the Christian message or faith in the least, because the textual evidence is quite **certain**. Let us just consider our five examples listed above. Our resource tools are respected by textual scholarship. We will be using, *A Textual Commentary on the Greek New Testament* (**TCGNT**) by Bruce M. Metzger *United Bible Societies*, 1994 This work is a companion volume to the fourth edition of the United Bible Societies' Greek New Testament (UBS4), published by the German Bible Society on behalf of the United Bible Societies early in 1993. Here are a few words from Metzger on how they indicate the degree of certainty.

> In order to indicate the relative degree of certainty in the mind of the Committee for the reading adopted as the text,[241] an identifying letter is included within braces at the beginning of each set of textual variants. The letter {A} signifies that the text is certain, while {B} indicates that the text is almost certain. The letter {C}, however, indicates that the Committee had difficulty in deciding which variant to place in the text. The letter {D}, which occurs only rarely, indicates that the Committee had great difficulty in arriving at a decision. In fact, among the {D} decisions sometimes none of the variant readings commended itself as

---

[240] Only a few are listed, this is not to suggest that these five texts are the only significant variants.

[241] It will be noted that this system is similar in principle but different in application from that followed by Johann Albrecht Bengel in his edition of the Greek New Testament (Tübingen, 1734).

original, and therefore the only recourse was to print the least unsatisfactory reading.[242]

We will also be using the *New Testament Text and Translation Commentary* (**NTTTC**) by Philip W. Comfort, 2008. We will not go into the textual arguments, but we will consider Metzger's **TCGNT**, of how a committee viewed the degree of certainty, as well as the new work by Comfort, **NTTTC**.

Mark 16:9-20:[243] TCGNT and NTTTC say it is **certain** that this ending is not original, and neither are the other three endings and that Mark ended abruptly in verse 8.

1 John 5:7: TCGNT and NTTTC say it is **certain** that John never penned the addition "for there are three that bear record in heaven, the Father, the Word, and the Holy Ghost: and these three are one."

Acts 8:37: TCGNT and NTTTC say it is **certain** that this verse should be omitted, "Philip said to him: 'If you believe with all your heart, it is permissible.' In reply, he said: 'I believe that Jesus Christ is the Son of God.'"

John 7:53-8:11: TCGNT and NTTTC say it is **certain** that the woman caught in adultery should be omitted.

1 Timothy 3:16: TCGNT and NTTTC say it is **certain** that this verse should read, "who was manifested."

If you were to delve into these resources, you would discover that while these are "significant" to the text, they create no real problem, because, in every case, we are **certain** about the original reading. The doctrinal positions that can be established from the New Testament are not affected by these being omitted. No doctrine stands on one verse.

'The Meaning of the Text is at Stake'?

It would be wrong, however, to say—as people sometimes do—that the changes in our text have no real bearing on what the texts mean or on the theological conclusions that one draws from them. We have seen, in fact, that just the opposite is the case. **In some instances, the very meaning of the text is at stake,**

---

[242] Bruce Manning Metzger and United Bible Societies, A Textual Commentary on the Greek New Testament, Second Edition a Companion Volume to the United Bible Societies' Greek New Testament (4th Rev. Ed.) (London; New York: United Bible Societies, 1994), xxviii.

[243] There are actually four endings of the Gospel according to Mark, which are current in the manuscripts. The above verses 9-20 are the traditional ending.

depending on how one resolves a textual problem: *Misquoting Jesus* (pp. 207-208)

In short, determining the original text is neither simple nor straightforward! It requires a lot of thought and careful sifting of the evidence, and different scholars invariably come to different conclusions—not only about minor matters that have no bearing on the meaning of a passage (such as the spelling of a word or a change of word order in Greek that can't even be replicated in English translation), but also about matters of major importance, matters that **affect the interpretation of an entire book of the New Testament.** *Misquoting Jesus* (p. 132)

If Ehrman would have stayed with "**in some instances, the very meaning of the text is at stake,**" he would have remained in the realm of realistic, but he had to exaggerate to the "matters that **affect the interpretation of an entire book of the New Testament.**" Certainly, if one removes an interpolation of twelve verses, as was done with the long ending of Mark, the interpretation of the text is affected, because it is no longer there. However, to say that the removal of an interpolation affects a whole Bible book is a bit incredulous, to say the least. We will take one of Ehrman's illustrations and see if this is truly the case.

The textual problem of **Mark 1:41** occur in the story of Jesus healing a man with a skin disease. The surviving manuscripts preserve verse 41 in two different forms; *Misquoting Jesus* (p. 133)

Mark 1:41 (TR[244] WH[245] NU KJV NKJV ASV RSV NRSV ESV NASB NIV NJB NAB NLT GCSB NET); (א A B C L W f[1,13] 33 565 700 syr cop Diatessaron)

[41]**Moved with** pity [splanchnon], he stretched out his hand and touched him and said to him, "I will; be clean."

Mark 1:41 (TNIV NEB REB); (D a, d, ff[2])

[41]**Moved with** anger [orgistheis], he stretched out his hand and touched him and said to him, "I will; be clean."

The reason that this text is considered difficult is because of one having to go against the grain of textual principles: *Which reading is it that the other reading(s) most likely came from?* Well, it is certainly easy to see how

---

[244] TR stands for the Textus Receptus ("received text"). This is the name given to the succession of printed Greek texts of the New Testament, which was the foundation for all English translations up until the 19th century.

[245] WH stands for the Westcott and Hort text of the New Testament published in 1881.

"moved with anger" would have been changed to "move with pity." In that case, the scribe would have been softening the reading. It is very difficult to see why a scribe would be tempted to go from "moved with pity" to "moved with anger." On the other hand, the textual evidence for "moved with pity" is very weighty, while the textual evidence "moved with anger" has no real weight at all. However, the irony is that most persons who define textual criticism say, 'it is an art and a science.' What they mean is that it is a science in that there are rules and principles, like the one above, and it is an art, because one needs to be balanced in the application of those rules and principles. The irony comes in when we come to the actual act of being balanced, as this text is no real struggle. The textual rule above is not to be rigidly applied; there are times that it does not apply, this being one of them.

First, the Western text **D**, which gives us the reading of "moved with anger," is notorious for making "significant" changes to the text. Comfort and Metzger, as well as others, offer a very real reason as to why the scribe may have chosen to do so. "He may have decided to make Jesus angry with the leper for wanting a miracle--in keeping with the tone of voice Jesus used in 1:43 when he sternly warned the leper." (P. W. Comfort 2008, 98) However, as Comfort goes on to point out, this would have been a misunderstanding on the part of the scribe, because Jesus was not warning him about seeking a miracle, it was rather "a warning about keeping the miracle a secret." Another motive for the scribe to alter the text to the harder reading is because he felt the man was slow to believe that Jesus was serious about healing him (v. 40) In addition, why would the scribes soften the text here from "move with anger" to "moved with pity," but not do the same at Mark 3:12 and 10:14?

Now, we are about to see Ehrman agree with the above textual information but go into his misleading the reader mode. He writes,

> As we have already seen, **we are never completely safe in saying that when the vast majority of manuscripts have one reading and only a couple have another, the majority are right.** Sometimes a few manuscripts appear to be right even when all the others disagree. In part, this is because the vast majority of our manuscripts were produced hundreds and hundreds of years after the originals, and they themselves were copied not from the originals but from other, much later copies. Once a change made its way into the manuscript tradition, it could be perpetuated until it became more commonly transmitted than the original wording. In this case, both readings we are considering appear to be very ancient. Which one is original? *Misquoting Jesus* (p. 134)

Ehrman has stated the textual principle correctly, well almost anyway. The principle is, 'count evidence, not manuscripts.' In other words, the majority of manuscripts mean nothing; it is the weight of the manuscript evidence that counts. What Ehrman is leaving out of his declaration is why that rule is a valuable principle to the textual scholar. The corrupt Byzantine text became the standard text from the sixth century forward and is the largest cache of manuscripts that we have, numbering in the thousands. The Alexandrian text is few in number but is "considered to be the best text and the most faithful in preserving the original."[246] You see 2-3 of the right Alexandrian texts (say P[75], B and ℵ) could be the weightier evidence against hundreds of Byzantine texts. The minute textual evidence for "moved by anger" comes from the Western text, which is known for its "fondness for paraphrase." As "words, clauses, and even whole sentences are freely changed, omitted, or inserted."[247]

Thus, he is choosing a principle that is generally used in reference to the Alexandrian text ["moved with pity"] (which is few in number but rated best), over against the Western ["moved with anger"] and Byzantine texts (which are far more numerous and corrupt). The rule of 'count the manuscript evidence, not the number of manuscripts' is used, because the manuscripts that are few are more weightier than the many, and are more trustworthy. Well, that just is not the case here as Ehrman is using the textual principle; the Western manuscripts are far less trustworthy than the Alexandrian manuscripts. Therefore, he is invoking a rule in a misleading way. If it were the case that these few Western texts that support "moved with anger" were rated as the best text and the most faithful in preserving the original, and the more numerous Alexandrian that supports "moved with pity" were rated untrustworthy; then, he would have a point. However, it is just the opposite. (Wegner, A Student's Guide to Textual Criticism of the Bible: Its History Methods & Results 2006, 240-1)

Another Argument that is no Real Argument at All

There is even better evidence than this speculative question of which reading the scribes were more likely to invent. As it turns out, we don't have any Greek manuscripts of Mark that contain this passage until the end of the fourth century, nearly three hundred years after the book was produced. But we do have two

---

[246] Bruce Manning Metzger and United Bible Societies, A Textual Commentary on the Greek New Testament, Second Edition a Companion Volume to the United Bible Societies' Greek New Testament (4th Rev. Ed.) (London; New York: United Bible Societies, 1994), xix.

[247] IBID., xx.

authors who copied this story within twenty years of its first production. **Misquoting Jesus (p. 135)**

We have asked this question already, but I am certain that Ehrman cannot read any other classical literature that is based on one or a handful of manuscripts at best, which are upwards of a thousand years removed from the time of writing. Anyway, we do have a manuscript, P75 (dating to 175 C.E.), that is, in essence, the same as the Vaticanus 1209 codex of 350 C.E., the latter here containing the Gospel of Mark. We have already discussed what it means that these two are virtually identical, but we will take a moment to touch on that once more. What this shows is the Vaticanus text is a text that existed in the second century C.E. While Vaticanus may have been copied in the middle of the fourth-century, it has a text from the second-century.

In fact, Hort's view of Vaticanus is that it preserves a "very pure line of very ancient text" (Westcott and A., The New Testament in the Original Greek, Vol. 2: Introduction, Appendix 1882, 251), as well as the belief that Vaticanus, with the exception of a few minor points, is essentially the original text. How do other textual scholars feel about the Vaticanus 1209 Codex? Bruce M. Metzger "is one of the great scholars of modern times," according to Ehrman, wrote the following about Vaticanus, "one of the most valuable of all manuscripts of the Greek Bible." (B. M. Metzger 1964, 1968, 1992, 47) Kurt Aland, a scholar on the same par as Metzger, wrote, "is by far the most significant of the uncials."[248] (K. a. Aland 1987, 109), Harold Greenlee, another scholar on par with Metzger, has written this about Vaticanus, "it is probably the best single MS of the NT." (Greenlee, Introduction to New Testament Textual Criticism 1995, 30)

Now, when Ehrman gives you, the reader, the dreadful news that **"we don't have any Greek manuscripts of Mark that contain this passage until the end of the fourth century, nearly three hundred years after** the book was produced." What sense is he trying to instill in you? How do you feel when he does not inform you that, one of those manuscripts that he refers to as 'not being until the late fourth century' is actually containing a second-century text, and is rated the best manuscript out of the 5,750 we have? Is it not just as deceptive to withhold pertinent information that you need to make a balanced judgment?

---

[248] An uncial is a letter of the kind used in Greek manuscripts written between the 2nd and 11th centuries that resembles a modern capital letter but is more rounded, numbering at 274.

Mark was the First Gospel?

Scholars have long recognized that **Mark was the first Gospel to be written, and that both Matthew and Luke used Mark's account as a source for their own stories about Jesus**. It is possible, then, to examine Matthew and Luke to see how they changed Mark, wherever they tell the same story but in a (more or less) different way. When we do this, we find that Matthew and Luke have both taken over this story from Mark, their common source. It is striking that Matthew and Luke are almost word for word the same as Mark in the leper's request and in Jesus's response in verses 40–41. Which word, then, do they use to describe Jesus's reaction? Does he become compassionate or angry? Oddly enough, Matthew and Luke both omit the word altogether. *Misquoting Jesus* (p. 135)

This is just not the case. His whole argument is based on more higher criticism, liberal scholarship, and historical criticism. I penned chapter five of this book to give you a taste of the subject matter. Thus, if you have not read that chapter, please go back and do so. It takes a whole book to deal with the subject matter of what is known as the Synoptic Problem. However, while I have merely introduced you to the subject in chapter five, I have also offered you some the best books that deal with that subject matter at the end of chapter 5, in the Recommended Reading.

Literary Dependency Revisited

It is striking that Matthew and Luke are almost word for word the same as Mark in the leper's request and in Jesus's response in verses 40–41. Which word, then, do they use to describe Jesus's reaction? Does he become compassionate or angry? **Oddly enough, Matthew and Luke both omit the word altogether.**

If the text of Mark available to Matthew and Luke had described Jesus as feeling compassion, why would each of them have omitted the word? Both Matthew and Luke describe Jesus as compassionate elsewhere, and whenever Mark has a story in which Jesus's compassion is explicitly mentioned, **one or the other of them retains this** description in his own account.

What about the other option? What if both Matthew and Luke read in Mark's Gospel that Jesus became angry? Would they have been inclined to eliminate that emotion? There are, in fact, other occasions on which Jesus becomes angry in Mark. In each instance, Matthew and Luke have modified the accounts. **In Mark 3:5 Jesus looks around "with anger" at those in the synagogue who are watching to see if he will heal the man with the withered hand.** Luke has the verse almost the same as Mark, but he removes the reference to Jesus's anger. Matthew completely rewrites this section of the story and says nothing of **Jesus's wrath.** Similarly, in **Mark 10:14 Jesus is aggravated at his disciples** (a different Greek word is used) for not allowing people to bring their children to be blessed. **Both Matthew and Luke have the story, often verbally the same, but both delete the reference to Jesus's anger** (Matt. 19:14; Luke 18:16). Ehrman, Bart D. (2009-01-23). *Misquoting Jesus* **(pp. 135-136).** Harper Collins, Inc.. Kindle Edition.

Is There Literary Dependence Found Within the Synoptic Gospels?

The oral gospel had been proclaimed throughout the Roman Empire between 33 CE and about 50 CE and the Gospels were written thereafter because it was time to establish the certainty of that message and for its posterity after the apostles died. The process was the scribe would initially take down the author's letter or gospel in shorthand as he dictated it. After creating a rough draft, which was edited by the scribe and author. Then the scribe would create an official copy, which would be signed by the author, validating it as his work, this being known as the *original* or initial exemplar. We are aware of at least two scribes who worked with Paul and Peter, and possibly James as well: Tertius (Rom. 16:22) and Silvanus (1 Pet 5:12). The *Tyndale Bible Dictionary* states what we have already considered in the above from Comfort: "At one point Papias states, 'The Elder used to say this also: Mark became Peter's interpreter and wrote down accurately, though not in order, all that [Peter] remembered concerning the things both said and done by the Lord.'"[249] So, here we have the possibility that Mark may have served as a secretary for Peter. If Mark spent time with Paul, as he did with Peter, Mark would have had the necessary material to write his Gospel based on the inspired memories of Peter.—John 14:26.

The Hypothetical Q Document (30 – 65 CE)

The story of Q (German Quelle "source") dates to over 120 years ago. It originates as part of what is known as the "two-source" theory of gospel

---

[249] Walter A. Elwell and Philip Wesley Comfort, *Tyndale Bible Dictionary*, Tyndale reference library (Wheaton, Ill.: Tyndale House Publishers, 2001), 857.

origins. As history reports, the 1800s could be known as the period of ignorance, not the period of enlightenment. Nevertheless, during this time it was decided that the gospels were *not* historically dependable. According to the **Q** Document theory, early on there were oral sayings and deeds of Jesus that were not written (*agrapha*, "not written). Several examples of these supposed *agrapha* were found in the writings of second century Church Fathers. It is the hypothetical **Q** Document, which is allegedly a collection of these oral sayings and deeds that were written. These writings served as the source for Mark's Gospel and by extension Matthew and Luke. It is also argued that Matthew and Luke did *not* pen their gospels from memory, or the memories of others, but instead by using the dual sources of Mark and this hypothetical document called **Q**.

Some establish the **Q** document by looking to the verses in Matthew and Luke that are similar to each other, yet do not appear in the Gospel of Mark. There is just one small problem with this theory: the so-called **Q** document is not in existence, and as far as evidence goes, there is none to show that it ever existed. For example, it has never been quoted by any of the Church Fathers. One would not know this by listening to the factual way the higher critics present their hypothetical document. The expressions below bring to life a nonexistent document:

- "Q originally played a critical role";

- "Q demonstrates";

- "Q forces the issue";

- "Q calls into question";

- "Q is the most important text we have"; and

- "Q tells us."[250]

Scholars as B. F. Westcott (1825-1901), Theodor Zahn (1883-1933) and Adolf Schlatter (1852-1938) rejected this "two-source" theory, with the latter two being German. As with most other damage done to the Bible's validity, it started with German scholarship and was soaked up by other academic scholars. Eta Linnemann, who studied under Bultmann and Fuchs, supported the two-source hypothesis. Eventually, she did her own extensive re-evaluation, which contributed to her break with historical-critical scholarship, as well as her taking up the Independence View. She

---

[250] Eta Linnemann, *Biblical Criticism on Trial: How Scientific is "Scientific Theology"?* (Grand Rapids, MI: Kregel Publications, 1990), 20-21.

expresses her strong disapproval of the position today's seminary students find themselves in if they adopt the Independent View:

> What student in seminar discussion is going to risk being labeled as uncritical and hopelessly behind the times by raising the possibility that the three Gospels are equally original, in keeping with their own claims and early church tradition?[251] . . . I am shocked when I look at the books of my former colleagues, which I used to hold in highest esteem, and examine the justification for their position. Instead of proof, I find only assertions. Instead of arguments there is merely circular reasoning.[252]

What are the Facts About Q?

No Church Father or early source makes a reference to such a source. If the Q Document was distributed so widely that Mark, Matthew, and Luke had copies, why do we not even have a fragment? Paul in all likelihood did not know of the Gospel of Matthew and definitely not Mark and Luke. There is no reason why he would not have been aware of such a document that is claimed to have affected and played a very influential role on the start of Christianity and existed before he became a Christian. But Paul is dead silent on the Q Document. The Independent View stood as the dominant understanding until the era of enlightenment when the philosophical giants, such as Grotius (1593-1645), Kant (1724-1804), Reimarus 1694-1768), Spinoza (1632-1677), and Tindal (1656-1733) brought us errancy of Scripture, Biblical criticism, and their views on the origins of the Synoptic Gospels, Two-Source Hypothesis.[253]

Papias (c. 110 CE) states:

> (3) I will not hesitate to set down for you . . . everything I carefully learned then from the elders and carefully remembered, guaranteeing their truth. For unlike most people I did not enjoy those who have a great deal to say, but those who teach the truth. Nor did I enjoy those who recall someone else's commandments, but those who remember the commandments given by the Lord to the faith and proceeding from the truth itself.

---

[251] Linnemann. *Is There A Synoptic Problem? Rethinking the Literary Dependance of the First Three Gospels.* Grand Rapids, MI: Baker Book House, 1992, 45.

[252] Ibid., 10

[253] Thomas, Robert L. *Three Views of the Origins of the Synoptic Gospels.* Grand Rapids, MI: Kregel, 2002, 235-41.

(4) And if by chance someone who had been a follower of the elders should come my way, I inquired about the words of the elders—what Andrew or Peter said, or Philip, or Thomas or James, or John or Matthew or any other of the Lord's disciples.[254]

(15) And the Elder used to say this: "Mark, having become Peter's interpreter, wrote down accurately everything he remembered, though not in order, of the things either said or done by Christ. For he neither heard the Lord nor followed him, but afterward, as I said, followed Peter, who adapted his teachings as needed but had no intention of giving an ordered account of the Lord's sayings. Consequently, Mark did nothing wrong in writing down some things as he remembered them, for he made it his one concern not to omit anything which he heard or to make any false statement in them." Such, then, is the account given by Papias with respect to Mark. (16) But with respect to Matthew, the following was said: So Matthew composed the oracles in the Hebrew language and each person interpreted them as best he could.[255]

Ehrman states the following about Papias:

There's an even bigger problem with taking Papias at his word when he indicates that Mark's Gospel is based on an eyewitness report of Peter: virtually everything else that Papias says is widely, and rightly, discounted by scholars as pious imagination rather than historical fact.[256]

It is true Papias exaggerated and expanded the death of Judas Iscariot based on Matthew 27:5 and Acts 1:18. However, much of what we read on Papias is found in the New Testament, whether one likes it or not. Other aspects of Papias concerning Gospel writers receive validation by other writers, such as Irenaeus who lived shortly thereafter and would have had firsthand information. Many of these renowned Church Fathers had access to Papias and other sources that validate the truthfulness of Papias' message. In short, if we discounted all things Papias said because he exaggerated or tried to explain Judas Iscariot's death, we would discount every statement Ehrman has ever made based on the same principles. Ehrman has been

---

[254] Michael William Holmes, *The Apostolic Fathers: Greek Texts and English Translations*, Third ed. (Grand Rapids, Mich.: Baker Books, 2007), 735.

[255] Ibid., 739-41

[256] Ehrman, Bart D. *Peter, Paul and Mary Magdalene: The Followers of Jesus in History and Legend.* New York, NY: Oxford University Press, 2006.

found guilty of misrepresenting numbers on many occasions for the sole purpose of manipulating the information in an attempt to deceive.[257]

The Gospel of Matthew proved the most influential up until the time of Irenaeus (c. 180 CE). If there was a Q document and Mark was written first, with Matthew and Luke merely copying from Mark and Q, why has Matthew become the most popular among the congregations? Moreover, why were the early congregations united in Matthew's Gospel being written first, giving him first place in the canon? We will look at just one example in Clement of Alexandria. It is Eusebius, the fourth century Church historian, who tells the tradition that Mark is one of the founders of the Alexandrian congregation: a congregation that Clement would later lead. Eusebius also informs us that Clement wrote of "a tradition of primitive elders," who gave him the order of the Gospels as Matthew, Luke, Mark, and John, being written in that order. Being that Mark was one of the founders, and Clement placed him as the third Gospel writer, gives, even more, credence to Clement's words, as it would be tempting to place your founding leader in the first place.

Again, going back to the evidence of the Church Fathers, none of them addressed literary dependence, even when opportunity presented itself. The in-depth answer is found in a publication by Eta Linnemann, *Is There a Synoptic Problem?* In short, she found absolutely no evidence that either "Matthew or Luke were literary dependent on Mark." At the end of this investigation, nothing negates the fact they were composed independently of one another.[258] She is joined by *many* prominent scholars, who have viewed the evidence, and find independence to be the preferred option: Louis Berkhof, Henry C. Thiessen, Robert G. Gromacki, Merrill C. Tenney, Jacob Von Bruggen, John M. Rist, John Wenham, and Bo Reicke. While listing world-renowned scholars does not in and of itself prove anything, it lends credence to the Independent View.

While listing the world renowned scholars do not in and of itself prove anything, it does lend some credence to the Independent View. Moreover, the evidence that Matthew was penned first, followed by Luke, and then Mark is almost certain. Therefore, it is almost certain that Matthew and Luke did not have Mark to "copy" from. In addition, the evidence does not demonstrate literary dependence regardless. Even still, let us concede

---

[257] "Scholars differ significantly in their estimates — some say there are 200000 variants known, some say 300000, some say *400000* or more! . . . There are more variations among our manuscripts than there are words in the New Testament." (Ehrman 2005, 89-90) While the statement is true on the surface, it is very misleading to the lay churchgoer, as well as Ehrman's audience. as we saw in chapter 10 of this book.

[258] Linnemann. *Is There A Synoptic Problem? Rethinking the Literary Dependance of the First Three Gospels.* Grand Rapids, MI: Baker Book House, 1992, 155-91

that Mark was available at the time Matthew and Luke penned their gospels.

In the English New Testament, the Greek word *orge* is generally translated "wrath," while *thymos* is usually rendered "anger." Anger may be justified or unjustified. Jesus divine anger does not come from a quick impulse, to be later regretted. He sees all the issues involved in a matter and has complete, entire knowledge of a situation. He reads the inner person; he notes the amount of ignorance, negligence, or willfulness; and he acts with impartiality. Anger for Jesus is righteous indignation, displeasure with someone or something.

Luke 5:12-16 (ESV)	Mark 1:40-45 (ESV)	Matt 8:2-4 (ESV)
12 While he was in one of the cities, there came a man full of leprosy. And when he saw Jesus, he fell on his face and begged him, "Lord, if you will, you can make me clean." 13 And Jesus stretched out his hand and touched him, saying, "I will; be clean." And immediately the leprosy left him. 14 And he charged him to tell no one, but "go and show yourself to the priest, and make an offering for your cleansing, as Moses commanded, for a proof to them." 15 But now even more the report about him went abroad, and great	40 And a leper came to him, imploring him, and kneeling said to him, "If you will, you can make me clean." 41 Moved with pity, he stretched out his hand and touched him and said to him, "I will; be clean." 42 And immediately the leprosy left him, and he was made clean. 43 And Jesus sternly charged him and sent him away at once, 44 and said to him, "See that you say nothing to anyone, but go, show yourself to the priest and offer for your cleansing what Moses commanded, for a proof to them." 45 But he went out and began to talk freely about it, and to spread the news, so that Jesus could no longer openly enter a town, but was out in desolate places, and people were	2 And behold, a leper came to him and knelt before him, saying, "Lord, if you will, you can make me clean." 3 And Jesus stretched out his hand and touched him, saying, "I will; be clean." And immediately his leprosy was cleansed. 4 And Jesus said to him, "See that you say nothing to anyone, but go, show yourself to the priest and offer the gift that Moses commanded, for a proof to them."

crowds gathered to hear him and to be healed of their infirmities. [16] But he would withdraw to desolate places and pray.	coming to him from every quarter.	

Is there really literary dependence in the above texts about the account of Jesus healing a leper. (Luke 5:12-16; Mark 1:40-45; Matthew 8:2-4) No, there is no literary dependence. Luke used 98 Greek words to inform his readers of the account, while, Mark used 99 words, with Matthew using only 52 words. Here we might lean toward the close amount of words between Luke and Mark, but as we move on, we will see that this is where the similarity ends. Therefore, we will focus our initial interest in Luke and Mark. However, first, of all the accounts of Jesus' life, Mark's is the most graphic, the most vivid, fast-moving as well as the richest in interesting details.

For example, in telling about Jesus' curing the man with the withered hand, Mark records not only that Jesus looked around at the Pharisees watching what Jesus would do, but that he did so "with anger, grieved at their hardness of heart." (Mark 3:5, ESV) And in reporting Jesus' cleansing of the literal temple in Jerusalem, Mark alone informs us that Jesus "would not allow anyone to carry anything through the temple." (Mark 11:16, ESV) When the people began bringing him young children for him to touch these, the disciples were holding the children back from getting to Jesus; Mark alone writes, "Jesus saw it; he was indignant." What Ehrman is discounting is the style of the writer. Mark's own style is also obvious in a stronger wording of the rebukes Jesus directed to his own disciples. Compare Matthew 8:26 and 16:8 with Mark 4:40 and 8:17.

Luke starts the account with: "While he was in one of the cities, there came a man full of leprosy. And when he saw Jesus, he fell on his face and begged him, 'Lord, if you will, you can make me clean.'"

Mark begins the account with: "And a leper came to him, imploring him, and kneeling said to him, "If you will, you can make me clean."

[Luke 5:12; Mark 1:40] Notice that (1) Luke mentions being in one of the cities, while Mark does not. (2) Notice that Luke, a physician says a man came to Jesus, who was "full of leprosy." Luke felt the need to inform his readers that the man's disease was in an advanced stage. For Mark, it was enough to mention leprosy. (3) In the Greek, Luke says the man "fell on his face," while Mark uses a different Greek expression, informing us the man was "falling on his knees." (4) Luke in the Greek says the man "begged,"

235

while Mark uses a differed Greek word, saying the man "entreated" him. In just the first verse, we find points of difference in content and style.

[Luke 5:13; Mark 1:41-42] (5) Notice that Mark says that Jesus was "moved with pity," while Luke did not. (6) Notice too that Mark reiterates the cleanness with the parting comment, "he was made clean," while Like does not. In the first part of the account, we kept noticing differences where Luke stood out as different from Mark, and here we see Mark is different from Luke. In essence, they are really just different from one another, because it is two people retelling what they saw and heard, so personality and style will creep into each person's account.

[Luke 5:14; Mark 1:43-44] (7) Notice that Mark informs his readers that "Jesus" addressed the man, but Luke uses a pronoun. (8) Notice too that Mark says that Jesus "sternly" charged the man to tell no one, but look does not comment on Jesus' demeanor. (9) In addition, note that Mark informs the reader of the added detail that Jesus "sent him away at once," which Luke did not include this observation.

[Luke 5:15-16; Mark 1:45] (10) Notice that Luke says the "report about him went abroad;" not mentioning how this came about, but Mark says "he went out and began to talk freely about it, and to spread the news." (11) Not too that Mark informs his readers of the result of the leper's actions, "so that Jesus could no longer openly enter a town," but Luke address a different aspect of the result, "and great crowds gathered to hear him and to be healed of their infirmities." Both Mark and Luke would inform their readers that Jesus had to withdraw to a desolate place, (12) but Luke adds to pray. (13) Mark goes on to conclude with "and people were coming to him from every quarter."

We can see that there is no literary dependency between Mark and Luke at all. There are thirteen major differences in just a five verse account of Jesus healing of a leper. What we have here are two different observations of the same account. The differences come by way of the author's different styles, as well as what they wished to convey to their prospective audiences. Like any eyewitness testimony, there will be differences, but the gist of the story will be the same. Some differences arise when we have two or more accounts of the same incident.

This chapter does not extensively investigate the evidence for or against the dependence of either Matthew, Luke, or Mark and the so-called Q document. The best we can offer is a summary of Linnemann's conclusions. The final analysis in determining the amount of dependence, the findings are there is no dependency. Mark contains 116 passages, of which 40 (3635 words, 32.28 percent), are not found in Matthew or Luke. Of the 76 passages that remain, 7,625 words, or 67.72 percent, occur in

Matthew and Luke. Taking these 7,625 words, we find there are only 1,539 words (20.19 percent) completely identical in Matthew, Mark, and Luke. In Matthew and Mark alone, we find only 1,640 words (21.51 percent) are completely identical. In Mark and Luke alone, it is a mere 877 words (11.5 percent). In Matthew and Luke, it is 381 words (5 percent).

There are words that are basic, and not relevant to literary dependency. In Biblical Greek, the definite article "the" is the only article, and it plays a large role, far different and more extensive than English. The definite article "the" is found in the Greek New Testament as the most often occurring, 19,870 times, with the Greek word και "and" coming in second at 9,153 times. If we remove the basic words of the article, και, and pronouns the percentage falls drastically. Looking at our 1,539 identical words, we find the basic words of Matthew and Mark to be 530 (32.32 percent), with Mark and Luke having 286 words that are basic (32.61 percent), and Matthew and Luke at 91 words (23.88 percent).

Thus, we only find 970 words of importance in Matthew, Mark, and Luke. In other words, a mere 12.72 percent of the 7,695 words have any bearing in the synoptic passages. These commonalities do not consider there are another 3,635 words, or 32.28 percent, of Mark that are not found in Matthew or Luke.[259]

For a very in-depth article on the fact that there is no literary dependency in the synoptic Gospels, please see Dr. F. David Farnell' artiicle on the CPH Blog.

The Synoptic Gospels in the Ancient Church: The Testimony to the Priority of the Gospel of Matthew—F. David Farnell

http://tiny.cc/l8z1ky

---

[259] Eta Linnemann, *Biblical Criticism on Trial: How Scientific is "Scientific Theology"?* (Grand Rapids, MI: Kregel Publications, 1990), 42-72.

CHAPTER 11 "Sometimes In Highly Significant Ways"

Ehrman wrote: Christianity from the outset was a bookish religion that stressed certain texts as authoritative scripture. As we have seen in this chapter, however, **we don't actually have** these authoritative texts. This is a textually oriented religion whose texts have been changed, surviving only in copies that vary from one another, **sometimes in highly significant ways.** The task of the textual critic is to try to recover the oldest form of these texts. *Misquoting Jesus* (p. 70)

Since we are digging into the mind of Bart D. Ehrman, you might find it interesting that he informs the reader 19 times in his book that we do not have the originals, 13 times in first 16 pages. It is a given that when you have 5,750 Greek New Testament manuscripts, they are going to differ, and in "highly significant" ways. As stated in an earlier section, the idea that the earliest copies were mostly copied by untrained scribes is a misconception that was created because the first papyri to show up on the scene were such. However, as others were discovered, a new picture appeared. Most of the early copies were worked on by a trained or skilled copyist, with some being copied by professional scribes. However, we have no problem conceding that the early copyists sometimes took liberties to add or change the text. Having other manuscripts makes us very much more aware of what those changes were, helping us to undo them.

As we have already acknowledged, the copyists were imperfect humans, who were not moved by inspiration. Like us, they had limits of concentration, some having bad eyesight or hearing. Some were even moved to make changes to the text, hoping to strengthen orthodoxy, or correct what they perceived to be an error. We have established, and Ehrman agrees that there are many reasons that an imperfect copyist would introduce unintentional and at times intentional errors into the text. However, the real issue is, can we get back to the original reading through textual criticism?

Ehrman's Mixed Messages

As we have seen throughout the whole of this book so far, Ehrman has stressed the fact we do not have the originals, there are 400,000 errors or more in the texts, more than the words that exist in the New Testament; we have only error-ridden copies, with the vast majority of them being centuries removed from the originals, the Bible is nothing but a human book, and the early scribes were amateurs. This bleak picture is presented for 260 pages by an expert wordsmith. However, we also find a mixed message in *Misquoting Jesus*.

Ehrman has dedicated *Misquoting Jesus* to his former professor at Princeton, Bruce M. Metzger, who he refers to as "one of the greatest scholars of modern times." He also had this to say, "I have nothing but respect and admiration for him. In addition, even though we may disagree on important religious questions--he is a firmly committed Christian and I am not--we are in complete agreement on a number of very important and historical and textual questions. If he and I were put in a room and asked to hammer out a consensus statement on what we think the original text of the New Testament probably looked like, there would be very few points of disagreement—maybe one or two dozen places out of many thousands." (*Misquoting Jesus*, 252)

This is certainly a telling statement, and it certainly flies in the face of his entire book. It is like a car that has been driven a 140 MPH, and then, all of a sudden hits reverse. I have argued all along that there are 7,956 verses in the Greek New Testament, but only a handful of these textual issues create any kind of serious difficulty. Here, Ehrman has just said that he and Bruce Metzger could sit down and get back to the original in many thousands of places, with the exception of two dozen. Just who is Bruce M. Metzger again? I have introduced him already, but it is worth doing it again.

"Bruce Manning Metzger (February 9, 1914, to February 13, 2007) was a professor at Princeton Theological Seminary and Bible editor who served on the board of the American Bible Society and United Bible Societies. He was a scholar of Greek New Testament, New Testament Textual Criticism, and wrote prolifically on these subjects." (Wikipedia) Metzger penned many books that had to do with the Greek text, as well as chaired or worked on many Bible translation committees. Moreover, he penned the *Textual Commentary on the Greek New Testament* (1994), which is the companion to the *United Bible Societies' Greek New Testament*. Members of the Editorial Committee of the United Bible Societies' Greek New Testament comprise Barbara Aland, Kurt Aland, Johannes Karavidopoulos, Carlo Maria Martini, and Bruce Metzger.

Considering that Bruce Metzger is one of the chief people responsible for the United Bible Societies' Greek New Testament, which is the foundation for almost all modern translations, and Ehrman has said, he could agree on all but two dozen places, this whole 266 page book that has gone to great lengths to stress what we do not have (the originals), and what we do have (intervening copying period), being corrupted has just informed us that we can get back to the original 7,956, minus two dozen places. Moreover, he is the co-author with Bruce Metzger of the fourth edition, *The Text of the New Testament: It Transmission, Corruption, **and Restoration*** (2005). Have you taken note of the last period of the Greek New Testament history? Yes, the **restoration period.** What does the word restoration mean, and when did that period actually start? Restoration means the restoring of something to its former condition. If we are starting with the very beginning, it will go back to Robert Estienne, known as Stephanus (1503-1559), who made a few corrections to the Greek text. What Greek text did Stephanus make corrections to? The Textus Receptus is the text that he corrected, known as the Received Text. The question naturally follow: What is the origin of the Received Text? Let us take a moment and **briefly** walk through the three time periods that Ehrman's book *The Text of the New Testament* refers to and keep in mind that if this were thoroughly covered, it would require many enormous volumes, for each of the three periods.

The Transmission Period

It must be understood that the synoptic Gospels were published orally for many years before the written text came to market. With many of the writers of the Christian Greek Scriptures, you have the author himself penning the book (rough draft), making needed corrections, and then producing the 'authorized' text. From this authorized text, other copies were made. For those authors who dictated their writings, the scribe would take it down initially, in shorthand, and then create a rough draft to be corrected by the author and himself. From this, the scribe would produce the authorized text for the author to sign in his own hand. After the individual books had been in circulation for a few decades, the community of Christians throughout the Roman Empire started to form collections, such as combined books of the Gospels, and compilations of the Apostle Paul's letters. These groupings were accomplished by 125 C.E., with the total collection of the 27 books of the Christian Greek Scriptures coming together by 325 C.E. There is no doubt that throughout this process of publishing, copying, collecting, and canonizing of the Christian Greek Scriptures, those involved recognized these writings as being authoritative, no less than the *graphe* [Scriptures] of the Hebrew Old Testament books.

Were the Early Copyist Trained?

The perception expressed in the above heading is a long-held belief that is mistaken. The early Christian congregations were not isolated from one another. The Roman roads and maritime travel connected all the regions from Rome to Greece, to Asia, to Syria and Palestine and Egypt.[260] From the days of Pentecost onward, Jewish or Jewish proselyte Christians returned to Egypt with the good news of Christ. (Acts 2:10) Three years thereafter, the Ethiopian eunuch traveled home with the good news as well. (Acts 8:26–39). Apollos of Alexandria, Egypt, a renowned speaker, came out of Egypt with the knowledge of John the Baptizer and arrived in Ephesus in about 52 C.E. (Acts 18:24, 25) The apostle Paul traveled over 20,000 miles throughout the Roman Empire establishing congregations. The apostles were a restraint to the apostasy and division within the whole of the 1st-century Christian congregation. (2 Thessalonians 2:6, 7; 1 John 2:18) It was not until the 2nd century that the next generation of religious leaders gradually moved left of center. Conservative Christianity was strong and centered against Gnosticism, Roman persecution, and Jewish hatred.

It is conceivable that by 55 C.E. there would have been a thriving congregation in Alexandrian Egypt, with its huge Jewish population.[261] (Acts 11:19) "Now those who were scattered because of the persecution that arose over Stephen traveled as far as Phoenicia and Cyprus and Antioch, speaking the word to no one except Jews." While this indicates a traveling north to Antioch, it does not negate a traveling south to Egypt. Antioch is obviously mentioned because it played the major role as a commencement for 1st century Christianity, especially for the apostle Paul.

The Coptic Church claims the Gospel writer Mark as its founder and first patriarch. Tradition has it that he preached in Egypt just before the middle of the 1st century. At any rate, Christianity spread to Egypt and North Africa at an early date. In fact, it became a prominent religious center, with a noted scholar named Pantaenus, who founded a catechetical school in Alexandria, Egypt, about 160 C.E. In about 180 C.E. another prominent scholar, Clement of Alexandria, took over his position. It was Clement who really put this religious, educational institution on the map as the possible center for the whole of the Christian congregation throughout the Roman Empire. The persecution that came about the year 202 C.E. forced Clement to flee Alexandria, but one of the most noted scholars of early Christian history, Origen, replaced him. In addition, Origen took this scholarly environment to Caesarea in 231 C.E. and started yet another prominent school and scriptorium.

---

[260] People of the first three centuries sent and received letters and books from all over the Roman Empire. To give just two examples: the Shepherd of Hermas was written in Rome and found its way to Egypt within a few decades; Irenaeus' Against Heresies was written in Gaul and made it to Egypt (Oxyrhynchus) within short order.

[261] Macquarie University, *Ancient History Documentary Research Center* (AHDRC), Papyri from the Rise of Christianity in Egypt (PCE), http://www.anchist.mq.edu.au/doccentre/PCEhomepage.html.

What does all of this mean? Of course, we cannot know absolutely, but textual scholars Philip W. Comfort,[262] Larry W. Hurtado,[263] and Eldon Jay Epp believe that the very early Alexandrian manuscripts that we now possess are a reflection of what would have been found throughout the whole of the Greco-Roman Empire from about 85–275 C.E. In other words, if we were to discover early manuscripts from other regions, such as Rome, Greece, Asia, and Palestine, they would be very similar to the early Alexandrian manuscripts. This means that these early papyri are the means of establishing the original text, and we are in a far better position today than were Westcott and Hort of 1881.

Those who have abandoned all hope of such a venture would argue differently, saying that 'oldest is not necessarily best.' For these scholars, the original reading could be found in any manuscript. They continue with the approach that the reading that produced the other readings is likely the original. While on the surface this sounds great, it is not as solid a principle as one might think. On this issue, Comfort writes:

> For example, two scholars, using this principle to examine the same variant, may not agree. One might argue that a copyist attempting to emulate the author's style produced the variant; the other could claim the same variant has to be original because it accords with the author's style. Or, one might argue that a variant was produced by an orthodox scribe attempting to rid the text of a reading that could be used to promote heterodoxy or heresy; another might claim that the same variant has to be original because it is orthodox and accords with Christian doctrine (thus a heterodoxical or heretical scribe must have changed it). Furthermore, this principle allows for the possibility that the reading selected for the text can be taken from any manuscript of any date. This can lead to subjective eclecticism.[264]

Either reasoned eclecticism or the local-genealogical method[265] will lean more heavily on internal evidence, setting off external evidence as being of less importance. However, as Ernest Colwell suggested in 1968, we need to get back to the principles of Westcott and Hort. Hort wrote in

---

[262] Philip W. Comfort, *The Quest for the Original Text of the New Testament* (Eugene, Oregon: Wipf and Stock Publishers, 1992).

[263] Larry W. Hurtado, *The Earliest Christian Artifacts: Manuscripts and Christian Origins* (Grand Rapids, Michigan: Eerdmans, 2006).

[264] P. W. Comfort (1992), 38–39.

[265] *This method holds that any variant can be established as original and can be from any given manuscript(s).

his 1882 Introduction: "Documentary attestation has been in most cases allowed to confer the place of honour as against internal evidence."[266]

Trustworthiness of Early Copyists

It has become common to suggest that the earliest copyists were of two types: (1) semiliterate and unskilled in the work of making copies; (2) feeling the end was nigh and chose to take liberties with the text in an attempt to strengthen orthodoxy. The former would undoubtedly lead to many unintentional changes, while the latter would certainly escalate intentional changes. J. Harold Greenlee had this to say,

> In the very early period, the NT writings were more nearly "private" writings than the classics . . . the classics were commonly—although not always—copied by professional scribes, the NT books were probably usually copied in the early period by Christians who were not professionally trained for the task, and no corrector was employed to check the copyist's work against his exemplar (the MS from which the copy was made). . . . It appears that copyist sometimes even took liberty to add or change minor details in the narrative books on the basis of personal knowledge, alternative tradition, or a parallel account in another book of the Bible. . . . At the same time, the importance of these factors in affecting the purity of the NT text must not be exaggerated. The NT books doubtless came to be considered as "literature" soon after they began to be circulated, with attention to the precise wording required when copies were made.[267]

Greenlee had not changed his position 14 years later, when he wrote the following:

> The New Testament, on the other hand, was probably copied during the earliest period mostly by ordinary Christians who were not professional scribes but who wanted a copy of the New Testament book or books for themselves or for other Christians.[268]

---

[266]Westcott and Hort, *The New Testament in the Original Greek*, Vol. 2: Introduction, Appendix, (1882), 17.

[267] J. Harold Greenlee, *Introduction to New Testament Textual Criticism* (Revised Edition, 1995), 51–52.

[268] J. Harold Greenlee, *The Text of the New Testament: From Manuscript to Modern Edition* (2008), 37.

Generally, once an established concept is set within the world of textual scholars, it is not so easily displaced. During the start of the 20th century (1900–1930), there were a handful of papyri discovered that obviously were the work of a copyist who had no training in making copies. It is during this time that Sir Frederic Kenyon, director and principal librarian of the British Museum for many years, said:

> The early Christians, a poor, scattered, often illiterate body, looking for the return of the Lord at no distant date, were not likely to care sedulously for minute accuracy of transcription or to preserve their books religiously for the benefit of posterity.[269]

The first papyri discovered showed this to be the case. However, as more papyri became known, it proved to be just the opposite, prompting Sir Frederic Kenyon to write:

> We must be content to know that the general authenticity of the New Testament text has been remarkably supported by the modern discoveries which have so greatly reduced the interval between the original autographs and our earliest extant manuscripts, and that the differences of reading, interesting as they are, do not affect the fundamental doctrines of the Christian faith.[270]

Some of the earliest manuscripts that we now have provide evidence that a professional scribe copied them. Many of the other papyri give evidence that a semiprofessional hand copied them, while most of these early papyri reveal that they were the work of a copyist who was literate and experienced. Therefore, either literate or semiprofessional copyists did the vast majority of our early papyri, with some being done by professionals. As it happened, the few poorly copied manuscripts came to light first, establishing a precedent that was difficult for some to shake when the truckload of evidence came forth that showed just the opposite.

The writers of the 27 books comprising the Christian Greek Scriptures were Jews. (Romans 3:1-2) Either these men were apostles, intimate traveling companions of the apostles, or picked by Christ in a supernatural way, such as the apostle Paul. Being Jewish, they would have viewed the Old Testament as being the inspired, inerrant Word of God. When Paul said, "all Scripture is inspired of God," he was likely referring to the Septuagint as well as the Hebrew Old Testament. These writers of the 27 New Testament books would have viewed the teachings of Jesus, or their books expounding on his teachings, as Scripture as well as the Old

---

[269] F. Kenyon, *Our Bible and the Ancient Manuscripts* (1895), 157.

[270] F. Kenyon, *Our Bible and the Ancient Manuscripts* (1962), 249.

Testament. The teachings of Jesus came to most of these New Testament writers personally from Jesus, being taught orally; thereafter, they would be the ones who published what Jesus had said and taught orally. When it came time to be published in written form, it should be remembered that Jesus had promised them: "The Helper, the Holy Spirit, whom the Father will send in my name, he will teach you all things and bring to your remembrance all that I have said to you.--John 14:26, *ESV*.

The early first-century Hebrew Christian [or Gentile] copyists were very much aware of the traditions that the Jewish scribes followed in meticulously copying their texts. These copyists would have immediately understood that they were copying sacred texts. In fact, our early papyri show evidence of shared features with the Jewish Sopherim, those men who copied the Hebrew Scriptures in Jesus' day. You will find common features when you compare the Jewish Greek Old Testament and the Christian Old Testament with the Christian Greek Scriptures—such things as an enlarged letter at the beginning of each line, and the invention of the nomen sacrum to deal with God's personal name. Instead of penning the Tetragrammaton from the Greek Septuagint in front of them, the copyists invented the nomen sacrum *KC*. Marginal notes, accents, breathing marks, punctuation, corrections, double punctuation marks (which indicate the flow of text); all of this indicates an adoption of scribal practices of the Sopherim by Jewish Christian writers and scribes.

With the exception of Matthew, all writers of the New Testament published their books in koinē, the common Greek of the day. Matthew initially published his Gospel in Hebrew, and shortly thereafter in koinē Greek. In his work, *Concerning Illustrious Men*, chapter III, Jerome says, "Matthew, who is also Levi, and who from a publican came to be an apostle, first of all composed a Gospel of Christ in Judaea in the Hebrew language and characters for the benefit of those of the circumcision who had believed."[271] Early in the 3rd century, Origen, in discussing the Gospels, is quoted by Eusebius as saying that the "first was written . . . according to Matthew, . . . who published it for those who from Judaism came to believe, composed as it was in the Hebrew language."[272] Initially, the primary focus of the first seven years of Christianity was to bring in fellow Jews; thereafter, the Gentile population became more the target audience. Therefore, we see that Matthew's publishing of his Gospel in two languages was simply responding to two audience needs.

We might ask if these writers of the Christian Greek Scriptures were bringing their material to their audience in any way different from the other

---

[271] Translation from the Latin text edited by E. C. Richardson and published in the series "Texte und Untersuchungen zur Geschichte der altchristlichen Literatur," Leipzig, 1896, Vol. 14: 8–9.
[272] *The Ecclesiastical History*, VI, XXV, 3–6.

writers of their time. The Apostle Paul's formal letters were styled after such Greek notables as Isocrates and Plato. Matthew, Mark, Luke, and John followed the form of the Greek historian Herodotus. Many of these New Testament writers used professional scribes to bring their works to market: Tertius with Paul, Silas with Peter, Silas composing the letter from the governing body of elders in Jerusalem to Antioch, Theophilus funding Luke's two productions. Philip Comfort helps us to appreciate the following:

> As recorded by Eusebius (Ecclesiastical History 3:24:5–7), Irenaeus tells us that Mark and Luke "published their Gospels" using the Greek word *ekdosis*, the standard term for the public dissemination of any writing. Irenaeus (Against Heresies 3:1:1) also said, "John, the disciple of the Lord, he who had leaned on his breast, also published [ekdoke] the Gospel, while living at Ephesus in Asia." For John to publish his Gospel means that he (with the help of the Johannine community) made a distribution of multiple copies of his Gospel.[273]

Public Reading

Public reading is yet another serious inference that the first century Christian congregation valued the books that were being produced by Matthew, Mark, Luke, John, Paul, Peter, James, and Jude, and copied for future generations.

Matthew 24:15 (ESV): So when you see the abomination of desolation spoken of by the prophet Daniel, standing in the holy place (let the reader understand), . . .

This parenthetical "let the reader understand" is reference to a public reader within the congregations.

1 Timothy 4:13 (ESV): Until I come, devote yourself to the public reading of Scripture, to exhortation, to teaching.

Again, this is Paul exhorting Timothy in public reading, which would have been before the Christian congregation.

Revelation 1:3 (ESV): Blessed is the one who reads aloud the words of this prophecy, and blessed are those who hear, and who keep what is written in it, for the time is near.

This reference to the "one who reads aloud" is to the public reader of those in each of the seven mentioned congregations. Another factor is how

---

[273] P. W. Comfort (1992), 45.

the writers of the Christian Greek Scriptures view their own published works.

2 Peter 3:16: . . . as he does in *all his* [*Paul's*] *letters* when he speaks in them of these matters. There are some things in them that are hard to understand, which the ignorant and unstable twist to their own destruction, as *they do the other Scriptures.* – (Italics added.)

Here, about 64 C.E., we have the apostle Peter, who has just canonized Paul's letters, grouping them together as a collection. This is evidence of their being viewed as having authority. At 2 Timothy 3:16 and 2 Peter 1:20 (*ESV*), both the apostles Paul and Peter appear to be referring to both the Hebrew Old Testament and the Christian Greek writings as [*graphe*] "Scripture." Please take note that Peter is comparing Paul's letters to "*the other Scriptures.*" What exactly does that mean?

Both Jesus and the other writers of the Christian Greek Scriptures often used *graphe* in their references to Moses' writings and the prophets, viewing them as having authority from Jehovah God, being inspired. Many times Jesus designates these Old Testament books as a whole as graphe, "Scripture." (Matthew 21:42; 22:29; Mark 14:49; John 5:39; Acts 17:11; 18:24, 28, *ESV*) At other times, the singular for "Scripture" was used when quoting a specific text to make a point, referring to it as a whole of writings encompassing our 39 books of the Hebrew Old Testament. (Romans 9:17; Galatians 3:8) Still, at other times "graphe" is used in a single text reference, such as Jesus' reference when dealing with the Jewish religious leaders: "Have you not read this [graphe] Scripture: 'The stone that the builders rejected has become the cornerstone.'" (Mark 12:10) Jesus' use of "graphe" in such an authoritative way only strengthens my point that immediately the writings of the Christian Greek Scriptures were viewed as "graphe."

With what we have already discussed as to the level of skilled copying of the early papyri, obviously, the scribal practices of Alexandria, Egypt, have played a large role in this. As historical records have shown, Alexandria had a huge Jewish population. We can imagine a large, predominately Jewish, Christian congregation early on as the Gospel made its way throughout that land. This congregation maintained serious ties with their brothers in Jerusalem and Antioch. Then, there was the Didaskelion catechetical school of Alexandria that had some of the most influential Church Fathers as head instructors, as has already been stated, but is worth repeating. Pantaenus took over and was in charge from about 160–180 C.E., Clement being his greatest student, and Origen, who took this school to Caesarea in 231, establishing a second school and scriptorium.

As the Greek Septuagint originated from Alexandria, and the vast majority of the earliest New Testament papyri also originate in Egypt

[Fayum and Oxyrhynchus], it is quite clear that the above-mentioned Church Fathers would have accessed the Septuagint and the Christian Greek Scriptures in their writings and evangelistic work. Origen, who learned from both Clement and Pantaenus, has written more than most early leaders of Christianity, and his writings are a reflection of the early New Testament papyri, as is true with Clement and his writings. Considering that Clement studied under Pantaenus, it is not difficult to surmise that his would as well. Therefore, it truly is not a stretch to suggest going in reverse chronologically. Thus, we have Origen, Clement, Pantaenus, and those who studied with Pantaenus and who brought him into Christianity from Stoic philosophy were using texts that were mirror-like reflections of the original texts of the Christian Greek Scriptures. Church historian Eusebius helps us to appreciate just how early this school was; note how he expresses it:

About the same time, a man most distinguished for his learning, whose name was Pantaenus, governed the school of the faithful. There had been a school of sacred learning *established there from ancient times*, which has continued down to our own times, and which we have understood was held by men able in eloquence and the study of divine things. The tradition is that this philosopher was then in great eminence, as he had been first disciplined in the philosophical principles of those called stoics.[274]

What does all of this mean? It means that in the second and third centuries C.E., the scholarship and scribal practices of Alexandria had a tremendous impact on all of Egypt and as far south as the Fayum and Oxyrhynchus. It means that a standard text of the Christian Greek Scriptures reflecting the originals came up out of Egypt during the second century. The Alexandrian Library had been a force for influencing stringent scholarship and setting high standards from the third century B.C.E. onward. Is it mere coincidence that the four greatest libraries and learning centers were located in the very places that Christianity had its original growth: Alexandria, Pergamum near Ephesus, Rome, and Antioch? The congregations within these cities and nearby ones would be greatly influenced by their book production. We saw in our section on textual criticism, how the text was transmitted under inspiration, how a period of corruption took place, but also a centuries long period of restoration.

---

[274] Eusebius, *Ecclesiastical History* 5:10:1.

CHAPTER 12 Ehrman Equates the Apocryphal Gospels as Being Equal to the Canonical Gospels

Ehrman wrote: To be sure, of all the hundreds of thousands of textual changes found among our manuscripts, **most of them are completely insignificant, immaterial, of no real importance** for anything other than showing that scribes could not spell or keep focused any better than the rest of us. Misquoting Jesus (p. 207)

From this section of Ehrman's book, we get the impression that he too agrees that 'most of the hundreds of thousands of textual changes are completely insignificant,' and are able to be restored. In other words, textual scholarship has no problem discerning what the correct reading is, and what is not the correct reading. In another place in *Misquoting Jesus*, Ehrman uses another strong adjective to describe the level of agreement among textual scholars being able to restore the text where scribes had made intentional changes.

In a **remarkable** <u>number of instances—most of them, actually</u>—scholars by and large agree. It is perhaps useful for us here to consider an array of the kinds of intentional changes one finds among our manuscripts, as these can show us the reasons scribes had for making alterations. *Misquoting Jesus* (p. 94)

Here again, we offer an example, where we would agree with Ehrman's assessment. Most textual scholars agree on the vast majority of intentional and unintentional changes. If we search throughout his book and find these isolated comments, it seems that one picture of Ehrman emerges. One that places him in the same camp with modern-day textual scholarship that believes the restoration of the original New Testament is quite possible. Let us investigate another quoted portion.

Moreover, in the **early centuries** of the church, some locales had better scribes than others. Modern scholars have come to recognize that **the scribes in Alexandria**—which was a major intellectual center in the ancient world—**were particularly scrupulous**, even in these early centuries, and that there, in Alexandria, **a very pure form of the text of the early Christian writings was preserved**, decade after decade, by dedicated and relatively skilled Christian scribes. Misquoting Jesus (p. 72)

Here again, Ehrman is right on the mark with modern textual scholarship, in that the Alexandrian scribes produces a very pure form of text, because they viewed literature in a whole other way, as opposed to the rest of the Roman Empire. However, this does not negate that early Christianity as a whole respected the books they possessed and viewed them as Scripture on par with the Old Testament. Moreover, the modern scholarship also believes that if other early manuscripts from throughout the Roman Empire would have survived, they would have differed very little from the Alexandrian papyri. Textual scholar Philip W. Comfort writes, "The early papyrus manuscripts represent not only the Egyptian New Testament text but also the text of the entire early church." (P. W. Comfort 1992, 34) Kurt Aland of the Nestle-Aland critical text also affirms this position.

When did the church begin to use professional scribes to copy its texts? There are good reasons for thinking that this happened sometime near the beginning of the fourth century. **Misquoting Jesus (p. 72)**

However, we find a conflicting statement on the very same page. We had just established the pure quality of the Alexandrian manuscripts "in the **early centuries** of the church," and now Ehrman is saying that the church did not begin to use professional scribes until the fourth-century. I am certain that he would agree that the following were done by a professional scribe: $P^{4,64,67}$, P^{30}, P^{39}, P^{46}, P^{66}, P^{75}, P^{77} + P^{103}, P^{95}, P^{104}.

The scribes—whether non-professional scribes in the early centuries or professional scribes of the Middle Ages—were intent on "conserving" the textual tradition they were passing on. Their ultimate concern was **not** to modify the tradition, **but to preserve** it for themselves and for those who would follow them. **Most scribes**, no doubt, tried to do a faithful job in making sure that the text they reproduced was the same text they inherited. **Misquoting Jesus (p. 177)**

Here again, we agree. One could almost get whiplash in trying to get a clear picture of Ehrman's trustworthy or not trustworthy. As soon as you feel he is suggesting that we can get back to something, or that something is trustworthy, or that the most of something is easily resolved, or that most textual scholars agree, you get just the opposite view in other places in *Misquoting Jesus*. At times, this takes place on the same page. With no disrespect intended, it is as though he has two personalities that are at odds with each other: his textual scholarship personality versus his liberal scholarship personality. Of the 7,956 verses and 138,020 words in the critical Greek text, only one percent is significant to the point that they affect the text as to meaning. However, the evidence to make a textual decision leans in one direction, and once again, we have no problem restoring the original.

Canonical Gospels and Apocryphal Gospels

Four such Gospels became most widely used—those of Matthew, Mark, Luke, and John in the New Testament—but many others were written. We still have some of the others: for example, Gospels allegedly by Jesus's disciple Philip, his brother Judas Thomas, and his female companion Mary Magdalene. Other Gospels, including some of the very earliest, have been lost. We know this, for example, from the Gospel of Luke, whose author indicates that in writing his account he consulted "many" predecessors (Luke 1:1), which obviously no longer survive. One of these earlier accounts may have been the source that scholars have designated Q, which was probably a written account, principally of Jesus's sayings, used by both Luke and Matthew for many of their distinctive teachings of Jesus (e.g., the Lord's Prayer and the Beatitudes). **Misquoting Jesus (p. 24)**

I dealt with the Q document in chapter five, so there is no reason to take it up again here. However, I am going to examine the worth of Apocryphal writings in comparison to the Canonical[275] writings because Ehrman appears to equate them equally. What should trouble the reader is the scholarship of a person that equates the Apocryphal Gospels on the same level as our four canonical Gospels. Commenting on such post-apostolic Apocryphal writings, Bible scholar, Norman L. Geisler states:

During the first few centuries, numerous books of a fanciful and heretical nature arose that are neither genuine nor valuable as a whole. Eusebius of Caesarea called these "totally absurd and impious." Virtually no orthodox Father, canon, or council considered these books canonical and, so far as the church is concerned, they are primarily of historical value, indicating the heretical teaching of gnostic, docetic, and ascetic groups, as well as the exaggerated fancy of religious lore in the early church. At best, these books were revered by some of the cults and referred

---

[275] The word "canon" refers to the collection of Bible books that give convincing proof of being inspired of God. There are 66 books that are generally recognized as canonical and are an integral and indispensable part of God's Word.

to by some of the orthodox Fathers, but they were never considered canonical by the mainstream of Christianity.[276]

When Were the Canonical Gospels Written and by Whom?

Many factors support that the Gospel of Matthew was written sometime between 50-55 C.E. It was written before the destruction of Jerusalem in 70 C.E. (Matt 24:1-2, 15; 27:53) The early church supports that Matthew was the first Gospel to have been penned in Hebrew and shortly thereafter translated into Greek. There being closer to the date certainly gives them the better position to know. Since most date Luke to about 60 C.E., and he speaks of other Gospels, this would put Matthew and Mark prior to this date. Since Matthew is considered earliest, this would mean Mark, who had the help of Peter, was second, likely between 55-60 C.E. John wrote his Gospel after his arrival back from banishment on the island of Patmos. (Rev. 1:9) The Roman emperor Nerva, 96-98 C.E., returned many who had been banished at the close of the reign of his predecessor, Domitian. After penning his Gospel in about 98 C.E., John is believed to have died at Ephesus in the third year of Emperor Trajan, 100 C.E.

Those who had spent time with Jesus while he was alive were around for his death and resurrection were still living then; they could confirm the Gospel accounts. They could also definitely make known any inaccuracies as well. Professor F. F. Bruce observes,

> One of the strong points in the original apostolic preaching is the confident appeal to the knowledge of the hearers; they not only said, 'We are witnesses of these things,' but also, 'As you yourselves also know' (Acts 2:22). (Bruce, The New Testament Documents: Are they Reliable? 1981, 43)

What do we know about the writers of the canonical New Testament? Some of the apostles were moved to pen books, and it was they who had traveled with Jesus in his three and a half year ministry. **Matthew**, who penned what is considered to be the first Gospel, was an apostle. **James** and **Jude** penned a letter each and were Jesus' half-brothers, both being doubters during Jesus' ministry and death. These two and **Mark**, who penned one of the Gospels, were likely present on the day of Pentecost in 33 C.E., at the birth of the Christian congregation. **Luke**, who penned a Gospel and the book of Acts of Apostles was a traveling companion of Paul

---

[276] Norman L. Geisler and William E. Nix, A General Introduction to the Bible, Rev. and expanded. (Chicago: Moody Press, 1996), 301.

and was closely involved with the older men in Jerusalem. **Peter** was an apostle and penned two letters. Jesus selected **Paul** personally, after he was visited by him on the road to Damascus, and penned 14 books. **John** was an apostle, the beloved of Jesus, who penned one Gospel, three letters, and the book of Revelation.—1 Corinthians 15:1-7; Acts 15:2, 6, 12-14, 22; Galatians 2:7-10.

Mathew. There is both internal and external evidence that the Gospel bearing the name Matthew was, in fact, written by Matthew even though the title "According to Matthew" was added in the second century. There are many references to money throughout this Gospel, which one would expect from a tax collector. Moreover, the humility of multiple references to his being a tax collector. His ability as a record keeper is borne out in his recording the long discourses of Jesus. That Matthew is the author of this Gospel is also established by the church Fathers as far back as Papias of Hierapolis (written works published about 130-140 C.E.), also by Justin Martyr, by Hegesippus, Irenæus, Tatian, Athenagoras, Theophilus, Clement, Tertullian, and Origen.

Mark. Mark had a history with many of the major people in the birth of Christianity. He was a cousin of Barnabas and traveled with the missionaries. His mother, Mary's home, was used as a place of worship. He was the young man that fled the night of Jesus' betrayal, meaning he was a follower of Christ before Jesus' execution. He was a friend of the Apostle Peter. The person who penned the Gospel entitled Mark was familiar with the geography of the land and Jerusalem, knew Aramaic, and understood Jewish traditions and customs, familiarity with James, Peter and John. Most agree that Mark penned the letter, but it was mainly through the recounting of Peter. Some of Peter's characteristics are to be seen in Mark's style, which is impetuous, living, energetic, dynamic, and expressive. It seems Mark (Peter) can scarcely relate events fast enough. For example, the word "immediately" or "at once" occurs 23 times in this short Gospel, transporting the story along in intense style. It was Peter who referred to Mark as "my son." (1 Pet. 5:13) Again, Papias attributed the Gospel to him along with many other early church Fathers (Irenaeus, Clement of Alexander, Justin Martyr, Tatian, Tertullian, Origen, Jerome, and Eusebius).

Luke. Luke was a traveling companion of the Apostle Paul, as he uses the first person in parts of Acts. (16:10, 17; 20:6; 27:1) Both Timothy and Mark are referred to in the third person. (20:5) The use of medical terms fits Luke, as he is a physician. Luke uses more than 300 medical terms or words to which he gives a medical meaning.[277] The earliest Gospel manuscripts bear the name Luke. Again, the early church Fathers supported

---

[277] The Medical Language of Luke, 1954, W. K. Hobart, pages xi-xxviii.

him as the author, such as Irenaeus, Tertullian, Clement, Origen, Gregory of Nasianzus, Jerome, and Eusebius. The Muratorian Fragment (c. 170 C.E.) attributes the Gospel to Luke.

John. In this final Gospel, the writer is referred to as the "disciple whom Jesus loved," (20:17) this and comparable expressions being used numerous times in the record, though the name of the apostle John is not ever mentioned. Jesus is here quoted as saying about him: "If it is my will that he remain until I come, what is that to you?" (John 21:20, 22) This certainly fit the historical facts, because John lived a life that is decades beyond the others. He was a follower of John the Baptist (1:35-40), and one of the first to follow Jesus (1:40). He was one of the three disciples (James, Peter, and John) that were pulled aside by Jesus at times, into an inner circle (Matt 17:1). The author was a Jew, who had a good knowledge of the customs, traditions, and the Old Testament. He knew the geography and topography of the land. He was an eyewitness to persons, time, numbers, places, and other details. (21:24) What is known as P^{52}, the John Ryland's papyrus fragment, dating to between 110-125 C.E., evidence that John was written in the first-century. Also, Irenaeus of Lyons (b. 120-140 – d. 202 C.E.), knew Polycarp (69-155 C.E.), who had studied under John the Apostle. The Muratorian Fragment (c. 170 C.E.), Clement of Alexandria, Tertullian, and Eusebius attribute the Gospel to John.

Who Selected the Books to go into the Canon?

Some liberal scholars have claimed that the canon of the Gospels was chosen centuries after the fact by the church that was an established power in the direction of Emperor Constantine. Nevertheless, the facts show otherwise.

For example, note what Professor of Church History Oskar Skarsaune states: "Which writings that were to be included in the New Testament, and which were not, was never decided upon by any church council or by any single person . . . The criteria were quite open and very sensible: Writings from the first century C.E. that were regarded as written by apostles or by their fellow workers were regarded as reliable. Other writings, letters, or 'gospels' that were written later were not included . . . This process was essentially completed a long time before Constantine and a long time before his church of power had been established. It was the church of martyrs, not the church of power; that gave us the New Testament."

Carl F. H. Henry writes,

Jesus altered the prevailing Jewish view of Scripture in several ways: (1) he subjected the authority of tradition to the superior and normative authority of the Old Testament; (2) he emphasized that he himself fulfills the messianic promise of the inspired writings; (3) he claimed for himself an authority not below that of the Old Testament and definitively expounded the inner significance of the Law; (4) he inaugurated the new covenant escalating the Holy Spirit's moral power as an internal reality; (5) he committed his apostles to the enlargement and completion of the Old Testament canon through their proclamation of the Spirit-given interpretation of his life and work. At the same time he identified himself wholly with the revelational authority of Moses and the prophets—that is, with the Old Testament as an inspired literary canon insisting that Scripture has sacred, authoritative and permanent validity, and that the revealed truth of God is conveyed in its teachings.[278]

Norman L. Geisler writes,

First, a book is not the Word of God because it is accepted by the people of God. Rather, it was accepted by the people of God because it is the Word of God. That is, God gives the book its divine authority, not the people of God. They merely recognize the divine authority which God gives to it. Further, this view shifts the "locus of authority" from God to man, from the divine to the human. Thus, the divine authority of Scripture is determined by man. Finally, the final acceptance of a book by the church of God often did not come for many generations, even centuries.[279]

J. I. Packer writes,

The Church no more gave us the New Testament canon than Sir Isaac Newton gave us the force of gravity. God gave us gravity, by His work of creation, and similarly He gave us the New Testament canon, by inspiring the individual books that make it up.[280]

Edward J. Young writes,

---

[278] arl F. H. Henry, God, Revelation and Authority, vol. 3: God Who Speaks and Shows: Fifteen Theses, Part Two, p. 47.

[279] Norman L. Geisler and William E. Nix, A General Introduction to the Bible, Rev. and expanded. (Chicago: Moody Press, 1996), 210-11.

[280] J. I. Packer, God Speaks to Man, p. 81.

When the Word of God was written it became Scripture and, inasmuch as it had been spoken by God, possessed absolute authority. Since it was the Word of God, it was canonical. That which determines the canonicity of a book, therefore, is the fact that the book is inspired by God. Hence a distinction is properly made between the authority which the Old Testament possesses as divinely inspired, and the recognition of that authority on the part of Israel.[281]

1 Corinthians 12:4, 10 Updated American Standard Version (UASV)

[4] Now there are different gifts, but there is the same Spirit; [10] to yet another operations of miraculous powers, to another prophesying, to another the **distinguishing of spirits**, to another different tongues, and to another interpretation of tongues.

According to Paul, one of the gifts of the "Spirit" was the ability "to distinguish between spirits." Therefore, just like those that were given the superhuman ability to speak in tongues, or inspired to pen Scripture, these were given the ability to discern inspired writings from uninspired writings. Therefore, we can be most confident that the 66 books that are found in our Bibles were recognized as inspired.

It is true that the canon was mentioned in the writings of second and third-century writers. However, as the above Bible scholars testify, these church Fathers did not determine canonicity, they merely acknowledge what God has already established through representatives there were gifted by the "Spirit."

What Are the Differences Between Apocryphal and the Canonical?

Internal evidence sanctions the clear separation that was made between the canonical writings and writings that were false or uninspired. The Apocryphal writings are substandard and often imaginary and juvenile. They are often erroneous. Note what the following scholars have to say about the noncanonical books:

M. R. James writes,

---

[281] Edward J. Young, The Canon of the Old Testament," in Carl F. H. Henry, ed., Revelation and the Bible, p. 156.

It will be very quickly seen that there is no question of any one's having excluded them from the New Testament: they have done that for themselves.[282]

G. Milligan writes,

We have only to compare our New Testament books as a whole with other literature of the kind to realize how wide is the gulf which separates them from it. The uncanonical gospels, it is often said, are in reality the best evidence for the canonical.[283]

N. R. Lightfoot writes,

Anyone who doubts about the New Testament Canon should take the time to read some of the New Testament Apocrypha. Here are a few examples of what one may find: (1) Infancy Story of Thomas. When a child bumps his [Jesus'] shoulder, Jesus strikes him dead. (2) Gospel of Peter. Three men come out of Jesus' tomb, with a cross following them; the head of two of them reaches to heaven, the head of the other overpasses the heavens. (3) Protevangelium of James. Mary is brought up in the temple, dedicated as a virgin from the age of three. (4) Acts of John. John, on finding bedbugs in his bed at an inn, commands the bugs to leave and behave themselves. (5) Acts of Paul. Paul baptizes a lion, who later spares him from death in an amphitheater at Ephesus.[284]

As we can see from the few examples given to us from Lightfoot, the apocryphal writings are very different from the canonical writings. The apocryphal books are not written by any of the people they claim as authors, and were penned about 150 C.E. and later. The picture portrayed in these Pseudepigraphal gospels of Jesus and Christianity is nothing like the canonical Gospels.

The Gospel of Thomas has Jesus saying that he will transform Mary into a man so that she would be eligible to enter the Kindom of heaven. The apocryphal Acts of Paul and Acts of Peter stress complete self-denial of sexual intercourse and even portray the apostles as advising women to separate from their husbands. The Gospel of Judas portrays Jesus as laughing at his disciples for praying to God in reference to a meal. Of course, these are in contrary to what we find in the canonical books.— Mark 14:22; 1 Corinthians 7:3-5; Galatians 3:28; Hebrews 7:26.

---

[282] M. R. James, *The Apocryphal New Testament*, pages xi, xii.

[283] G. Milligan, *The New Testament Documents*, page 228.

[284] N. R. Lightfoot, *How We Got the Bible*, page 171

Numerous apocryphal writings reflect the beliefs of the Gnostics.[285] They believe that the Creator, Jehovah God was evil. In addition, they believed that the resurrection is not literal because to them physical matter is also evil. Also, they believed that it was Satan, who was behind marriage and procreation.

Apocryphal and Apostasy Prophecy

Acts 20:30 Updated American Standard Version (UASV)

[30] and from among your own selves men will arise, speaking twisted things, to draw away the disciples after them.

2 Thessalonians 2:3, 6-7 Updated American Standard Version (UASV)

[3] Let no one deceive[286] you in any way, for it will not come unless the apostasy[287] comes first, and the man of lawlessness is revealed, the son of destruction, [6] And now you know the thing restraining him, so that in his time he will be revealed. [7] For the mystery[288] of lawlessness is already at work; but only until the one who is right now acting as a restraint is out of the way.

1 Timothy 4:1-3 Updated American Standard Version (UASV)

[4] But the Spirit explicitly says that in later times some will fall away from the faith, paying attention to deceitful spirits and doctrines of demons, [2] by means of the hypocrisy of men who speak lies, whose conscience is seared as with a branding iron, [3] men who forbid marriage and command to abstain from foods that God created to be partaken of with thanksgiving by those who have faith and accurately know the truth.

2 Peter 2:1 Updated American Standard Version (UASV)

[2] But false prophets also arose among the people, just as there will also be false teachers among you, who will secretly introduce destructive

---

[285] A pre-Christian and early Christian religious movement teaching that salvation comes by learning esoteric spiritual truths that free humanity from the material world, believed in this movement to be evil.

[286] Or *seduce*

[287] **Apostasy:** (Gr. *apostasia*) The term literally means "to stand away from" and is used to refer to ones who 'stand away from the truth.' It is abandonment, a rebellion, an apostasy, a refusal to accept or acknowledge true worship. In Scripture, this is used primarily concerning the one who rises up in defiance of the only true God and his people, working in opposition to the truth. – Ac 21:21; 2 Thess. 2:3.

[288] **Mystery; Secret:** (Gr. *mystērion*) A sacred divine mystery or secret doctrine that lies with God alone, which is withheld from both the angelic body and humans, until the time he determines that it is to be revealed, and to those to whom he chooses to make it known. – Mark 4:11; Rom. 11:25; 16:25; 1 Cor. 2:1; 4:1; 13:2; 14:2; 15:51; Eph. 1:9; 6:19; Col. 1:26; 2:2; 2 Thess. 2:7; 1 Tim. 3:9; Rev. 17:5.

heresies, even denying the Master who bought them, bringing swift destruction upon themselves.

John 2:18-19 Updated American Standard Version (UASV)

¹⁸ So the Jews answered and said to him, "What sign do you show us for doing these things?" ¹⁹ Jesus answered and said to them, "Destroy this temple, and in three days I will raise it up."

1 John 4:1-3 Updated American Standard Version (UASV)

4 Beloved ones, do not believe every spirit, but test the spirits to see whether they are from God, for many false prophets have gone out into the world. ² By this you know the Spirit of God: every spirit that confesses that Jesus Christ has come in the flesh is from God; ³ and every spirit that does not confess Jesus is not from God; this is the spirit of the antichrist,[289] of which you have heard that it is coming, and now it is in the world already.

More could have been listed, but in the above, you will find numerous warnings about a coming apostasy. The apostles were to be a restraint to this great apostasy that was coming. As long as they were alive, it would not fully infiltrate and cause divisions. However, as we see, John tells us that at the time of his writing, it was "the last hour," meaning that he was about 98 years old, serving as the last restraint, and his death was imminent. Therefore, in essence, he was in the last hour of his life. Is it mere coincidence that all of the more than fifty Pseudepigraphal gospels started to be penned within decades of John's death?

Some liberal scholars get overly absorbed in them, because they go back to 150 C.E. forward, meaning that they are very early. However, what if scholars almost 2,000 years from now were to look back to 2012, and gather up a bunch of tabloid magazines. Just because they date back almost 2,000 years to the time in American history that they are interested in, would the gossip and lies within them be accepted as historical facts, simply because the dated early to the beginning of the 21st century?

---

[289] **Antichrist**: (Gr. *antichristos*) The term "Antichrist," occurs in the NT five times. From those five times, we gather this entity is "against" (i.e. denies Christ) or "instead of" (i.e., false Christs) Jesus Christ. There are *many antichrists* that began back in the apostle John's day and will continue up unto Jesus' second coming. (1 John 2:18) The antichrist is referred to as a number of individuals taken together, i.e., collectively. (2 John 1;7) Persons who deny Jesus Christ are the antichrist. (1 John 2:22) All who deny the divinity of Jesus Christ as the One and Only Son of God is the antichrist. (1 John 2:22; John 10:36; Lu 9:35) Some antichrists are apostates, one who left the faith and are now in opposition to the truth. (1 John 2:18-19) Those who oppose the true followers of Jesus are the antichrist. (John 15:20-21) Individuals or nations that oppose Jesus or try to supplant his kingly authority are antichrists. – Ps. 2:2; Matt. 24:24; Rev. 17:3, 12-14; 19:11-21.

That would hardly be the case. Therefore, we should see the more than fifty Pseudepigraphal gospels as nothing but tabloid gossip trying to be passed off as official Gospels, such as the claim Jesus married Mary Magdalene.

A Scrap of Historical Criticism

Would any Christian living in 1700 C.E. have ever doubted the Bible was the Word of God? Hardly! So how did historical criticism[290] (a principal aspect of higher criticism) become the predominant view among Bible scholars? All it took was for some leading professors at major universities to plant seeds of doubt within their students. Being at the entrance of the era of skepticism of the mid-19th century to the early 20th century, this historical criticism had a well-cultivated field in which to grow. You had liberal scholars mixing rationalism and Christianity. It created a domino effect as a few scholars produced a generation of students, who would then be the next generation of scholars, and so on.

As we moved into the twentieth century, these questions had become "facts" in the eyes of many; in fact, it became in vogue to challenge the Bible. Leading schools and leading scholars of historical criticism were the norm, and soon the conservative Christian was isolated. The twentieth-century student received a lean diet from those few scholars who still accepted God's Word as just that, the Word of God, fully inerrant, with 40 writers of 66 books over a period of about 1,600 years. No, these students would now be fed mostly liberal theology, and any who disagreed were portrayed as ignorant and naïve. This planting of uncertainty or mistrust, with question after question bringing canonical books into doubt, with most literature focusing on this type of propaganda, would create the latest generation of scholars, and today they dominate the world of scholarship.

How did this progressive takeover come off without a hitch? The conservative scholarship of the mid-19th century to the early 20th century saw these liberal naysayers as nothing more than a fly at a picnic.[291] Most did not even deem it necessary to address their questions, so by 1950–1970, the historical criticism machine was in full throttle. It was about this same time that the sleeping giant finally woke to find that conservative scholarship had taken a backseat to this new creature, liberal scholarship. It

---

[290] Historical criticism comprises several disciplines, which include: (1) Source criticism, (2) Form criticism, (3) Redaction criticism, (4) Traditional criticism, (5) Radical criticism, to mention just a few.

[291] This is not to say that the 19th and early 20th century did not have any apologist defending against biblical criticism. There were some giants in this field, like R. A. Torrey, and many others.

is only within the last 30–40 years that some very influential conservative scholars have started to publish books in a move to dislodge this liberal movement. Was it too little, too late?

It is possible to displace historical criticism, but many factors stand in the way. For one, any opposition is painted as uninformed and inexperienced regarding the subject matter. Moreover, the books that tear down the Bible with all their alleged critical analysis sell far better than those do that encourage putting faith in God's Word. In addition, many conservative scholars tend to sit on the sideline and watch as a few leading scholars attempt to do the work of the many. In addition, there are liberal scholars continually putting out numerous articles and books, dominating the market. Unlike the conservative scholars in the first part of the twentieth century, these liberal scholars in the first part of the twenty-first century are not slowing down. Moreover, they have become more aggressive. I will not make the *possible* correlation, but will only mention that early textual scholarship of the 19th century believed that it was possible to restore the original text. As liberal scholarship has overrun our universities throughout the last one hundred and fifty years, is it a mere coincidence that now many textual scholars do not talk about getting back to the original, but to the earliest form, and other middle of the road scholars are just more careful in their commitments? Since this is the crucial point that *Misquoting Jesus* is really all about, we will address this briefly one more time in our concluding section.

Getting Back to the Original

When we discuss getting back to the original, it is really the originals, because each of the books was penned outside of each other, and had their own history of being copied and recopied. We do not find the New Testament as a whole until the fourth century. As we discussed earlier, the Sinaiticus manuscript (325 C.E.) contains the whole New Testament, and the Vaticanus manuscript (350 C.E.) did at one time as well. As you may recall, up until the fourth-century, there were many groupings that circulated together, such as P[72] (Peter's letters and Jude), or P[45] (Gospels with Acts), or P[46] (Paul's letters). In fact, individual books have been copied by themselves as well: P[1] (Matthew), P[88] (Mark), P[69] (Luke), P[5] (John), or P[18] (Revelation). Therefore, each of the books needs to be recovered based on itself, and the manuscripts that would be most beneficial to its recovery.

It is the papyrus manuscripts of the second and third-centuries C.E. that is going to get back to the original(s). These manuscripts are 50 to 240 years older than our famed Sinaiticus and Vaticanus manuscripts. Westcott and Hort were the pioneers to the idea of creating a critical text that, to them was the original(s). Of course, they did not have the papyri that we have today. Kurt Aland of the Nestle-Aland text is of the same mind as well, as he writes in his *The Text of the New Testament*, where he writes that the NA text "comes closer to the original text of the New Testament than did Tischendorf or Westcott and Hort, not to mention Von Sodon." (K. a. Aland 1987, 24) Some textual scholars today will look down on any scholar suggesting such and idea.

If you think about the families of manuscripts that we have discussed thus far in this book (Western, Byzantine, Caesarean, and Alexandrian), it is the Alexandrian family that makes up the earliest manuscripts, the Egyptian text if you will. Therefore, many textual scholars shrink back from the idea that the early church manuscripts were reflective of the Egyptian New Testament text. Kurt Aland has successfully dealt with this criticism by stating that "(1) we are not sure if all of the papyri discovered in Egypt actually originated in Egypt and (2) that the text typically called the Egyptian text (as opposed to the 'Western' or Byzantine text) was the text displayed in the writings of the early church fathers who lived outside of Egypt—Such as Irenaeus, Marcion, and Hippolytus. (Bruce, Packer, et al. 1992, 2003, 203)

The modern man tends to believe that the ancient world was isolated from one another because travel was nothing like today. In the first three centuries, Christians benefited from the Pax Romana, or Roman Peace, with its law and order, good roads, and relatively safe maritime travel. The stable rule of law and order, the good roads, and the relatively safe maritime travel created an environment that favored the expansion of Christianity throughout the whole of the Roman Empire.[292]

Historically, we know that there as a church in Alexandria, Egypt as early as 100 C.E. Pantaenus (was a Christian theologian who became the head of the Catechetical School of Alexandria about 160-180 C.E. The fourth-century church historian Eusebius informs us that the school was already there and that Pantaenus simply took over. When Pantaenus left, it was Clement (c.150-c. 215), who then replaced him as head of the school. Around 200 C.E. Clement had built the Alexandrian school into a well-educated Christian center, which brought with it a thriving community as well.

Historically, we also know that there were Christian communities far south of Alexandria as well, in such rural places as Fayum and Oxyrhynchus, as early as 110-125 C.E. This is the area where almost all of our papyri come from. The dry air preserved the manuscripts, which would not have

---

[292] Areas touched by the Gospel in the first-century alone: SPAIN, ITALY, MALTA, Mediterranean Sea, ILLYRICUM, MESOPOTAMIA, MEDIA, PARTHIA, Caspian Sea, ELAM, ARABIA, Cyrene, LIBYA, EGYPT, ETHIOPIA, Red Sea.

survived the moisture of Alexandria. Moreover, the library in Alexandria had been destroyed twice. As we have argued twice now, agreeing with Kurt Aland, Philip Comfort, and other textual scholars, if we were to find second-century manuscripts in other parts of the Roman Empire, they would resemble the Egyptian text.

CHAPTER 13 Why Has God Permitted Wickedness and Suffering?

Ehrman includes a Question and Answer section at the end of his book, in which he is asked about "*What big question(s) would have to be answered to your satisfaction for you to return to the Christian faith or some form of religious observance?*"

Ehrman wrote: The big issue that drove me to Agnosticism has to do not with the Bible, but with the pain and suffering in the world. I eventually found it impossible to explain the evil so rampant among us—whether in terms of genocides (which continue), unspeakable human cruelty, war disease, hurricanes, tsunamis, mudslides, the starvation of millions of innocent children, you name it—if there was a good and loving God who was actively involved in this world. **Misquoting Jesus (p. 248)**

"God has morally sufficient reasons for permitting the evil and suffering in the world." – William Lane Craig

That *morally sufficient reason* lies below.

As you will see below, Ehrman's issue is simply a matter of starting with the wrong assumption. **Point One:** He starts with 'if God is a God of love, who has the power to fix anything, how can there have been such horrific pain and suffering in imperfection over the last 6,000 years?' **Point Two:** He also likely begins with the premise that 'God is responsible for everything that happens.' If one starts with the wrong assumption, there is no doubt that he will reach the wrong conclusion(s). **Point One** is dealt with below, but let it be said that Ehrman is looking through the binoculars from the opposite end, the big side through the small. When we do that, we get a narrow, focused outlook. God looks through the binoculars the correct way and can see the big picture. Ehrman can only see but a fraction and a moment of time, 70 – 80 years, while God has seen everything that has happened over these past 6,000 plus years in the greatest of detail, and can see what the outcome would be if he had handled things in a variety of ways.

Point Two is certainly one reason suffering and evil is often misunderstood. God is responsible for everything, but not always directly. If he started the human race, and we end up with what we now have, in essence, he is responsible. Just as parents, who have a child are similarly responsible for the child committing murder 21 years into his life, because they procreated and gave birth to the child. The mother and father are indirectly responsible. King David commits adultery with Bathsheba and has her husband Uriah killed to cover things up, and impregnates Bathsheba, but the adulterine child, who remains nameless, died. Is God responsible for the death of that child? We can answer yes and no to that question. He is responsible in two ways: (1) He created humankind, so there would have been no affair, murder, adulterine child if he had not. (2) He did not step in and save the child when he had the power to do so. However, he is not directly responsible, because he did not make King David and Bathsheba commit the acts that led to the child being born, nor did he bring an illness on the adulterine child, he just did not move in to protect the child, in a time that had a high rate of infant deaths.

The reason people think that God does not care about us is the words of some religious leaders, which have made them, feel this way. When tragedy strikes, what do some pastors and Bible scholars often say? When 9/11 took place, with thousands dying in the twin towers of New York, many ministers said: "It was God's will. God must have had some good reason for doing this." When religious leaders make such comments or similar ones, they are actually blaming God for the bad things that happened. Yet, the disciple James wrote, "Let no one say when he is tempted, 'I am being tempted by God,' for God cannot be tempted with evil, and he himself tempts no one." (James 1:13) God never directly causes what is bad. Indeed, "far be it from God that he should do wickedness, and from the Almighty that he should do wrong." Job 34:10.

The history of humans has been inundated with pain and suffering on an unprecedented scale, much of which they have brought on themselves. The problem/question that has plagued many persons is, 'why if there is a loving God, would he allow it to start with, and worse still, why allow it to go on for over 6,000 years?' Some apologist scholars have struggled to answer this question, because they are over analyzing, as opposed to just looking for the answer in God's Word. Therefore, if we are to answer this question, we must go back to Adam and Eve at the time of the first sin. Many have read this account, but I will list the texts as a refresher.

Genesis 2:17 Updated American Standard Version (UASV)

[17] but from the tree of the knowledge of good and evil you shall not eat,[293] for in the day that you eat from it you shall surely die."[294]

---

[293] Lit *eat from it*

[294] Lit *dying you* [singular] *shall die.* Heb *moth tamuth*; the first reference to death in the Scriptures

Genesis 3:1-5 Updated American Standard Version (UASV)

3 Now the serpent was more crafty than any beast of the field which Jehovah God had made. And he said to the woman, "Did God actually say, 'You[295] shall not eat of any tree in the garden'?" 2 And the woman said to the serpent, "From the fruit of the trees of the garden we may eat, 3 but from the tree that is in the midst of the garden, God said, 'You shall not eat from it, nor shall you touch it, lest you die.'" 4 And the serpent said to the woman, "You shall not surely die. 5 For God knows that when you eat of it your eyes will be opened, and you will be like God, knowing good and evil." knowing good and evil.

Later Bible texts establish Satan the Devil as the one using a serpent as his mouthpiece like a ventriloquist would a dummy. Anyway, take note that Satan contradicts the clear statement that God made to Adam at Genesis 2:17, "you will not surely die." Backing up a little, we see Satan asking an inferential question, "Did God actually say, 'You shall not eat of any tree in the garden'?" First, he is overstating what he knows to be true, not "any tree," just one tree. Second, Satan is inferring, 'I can't believe that God would say . . . how dare he say such.' Notice too that Eve has been told so thoroughly about the tree that she even goes beyond what Adam told her, not just that you 'do not eat from it,' no, 'you do not even touch it!' Then, Satan out and out lied and slandered God as a liar, saying that 'they would not die.' To make matters much worse, he infers that God is withholding good from them, and by rebelling they would be better off, being like God, 'knowing good and bad.' This latter point is not knowledge of; it is the self-sovereignty of choosing good and bad for oneself and act of rebellion for created creatures. What was symbolized by the tree is well expressed in a footnote on Genesis 2:17, in The Jerusalem Bible (1966):

This knowledge is a privilege, which God reserves to himself and which man, by sinning, is to lay hands on, 3:5, 22. Hence it does not mean omniscience, which fallen man does not possess; nor is it moral discrimination, for unfallen man already had it and God could not refuse it to a rational being. It is the power of deciding for himself what is good and what is evil and of acting accordingly, a claim to complete moral independence by which man refuses to recognize his status as a created being. The first sin was an attack on God's sovereignty, a sin of pride.

The Issues at Hand

(1) Satan called God a liar and said he was not to be trusted, as to the life or death issue.

---

[295] In Hebrew *you* is plural in verses 1–5

(2) Satan's challenge, therefore, took into question the right and legitimacy of God's rightful place as the Universal Sovereign.

(3) Satan also suggested that people would remain obedient to God only as long as their submitting to God was to their benefit.

(4) Satan all but said that humankind was able to walk on his own, there being no need for dependence on God.

(5) Satan argued that man could be like God, choosing for himself what is right and wrong.

(6) Satan claimed that God's way of ruling was not in the best interests of humans, and they could do better without God.

Job 1:6-11 Updated American Standard Version (UASV)

6 Now there was a day when the sons of God came to present themselves before Jehovah, and Satan also came among them. 7 Jehovah said to Satan, "From where do you come?" Then Satan answered Jehovah and said, "From roaming about on the earth and walking around on it." 8 Jehovah said to Satan, "Have you considered my servant Job? For there is no one like him on the earth, a blameless and upright man, fearing God and turning away from evil." 9 Then Satan answered Jehovah, "Does Job fear God for nothing? 10 Have you not made a hedge about him and his house and all that he has, on every side? You have blessed the work of his hands, and his possessions have increased in the land. 11 But put forth your hand now and touch all that he has; he will surely curse you to your face."

Job 2:4-5 Updated American Standard Version (UASV)

4 Satan answered Jehovah and said, "Skin for skin! Yes, all that a man has he will give for his life. 5 However, put forth your hand now, and touch his bone and his flesh; he will curse you to your face."

This general reference to "a man," as opposed to explicitly naming Job, is suggesting that all men [and women] will only obey God when things are good, but when the slightest difficulty arises, he will not obey. If you were put to the test, would you prove your love for your heavenly Father and show that you preferred His rule to that of any other?

God Settles the Issues

There is one thing that Satan did not challenge, namely, the power of God. Satan did not suggest that God was unable to destroy him as an opposer. However, he did challenge God's way of ruling, not His right to rule. Therefore, a moral issue must be settled.

An illustration of how God chose to deal with the issue can be demonstrated in human terms. A neighbor down the street slandered a man, who had a son and daughter. The slanderer said that he was not a good father, i.e., he withheld good from his children and was so overbearing, to the point of being abusive. The slanderer stated that the children would be better off without their father. He further argued that the children had no real love for their father and only obeyed him because of the food and shelter. How should the father deal with these false, i.e., slanderous accusations? If he were to go down the road and pummel the slanderer, it would only validate the lies, making the neighbors believe the accuser is telling the truth.

The answer lies within his family as they can serve as his witnesses. (Pro 27:11; Isa 43:10) If the children stay obedient and grow to be successful adults, turning out to be loving, caring, honest people with spotless character, it proves the accusations false. If the children accept the lies and rebel and grow up to be despicable people, it just further validates that they would have been better off by staying with the father. This is how God chose to deal with the issues. The issues that were raised must be settled beyond all reasonable doubt.

If God had destroyed the rebellious three: Satan, Adam, and Eve; he would not have resolved the issues of

(1) Whether man could walk on his own,

(2) if he would be better off without his Creator,

(3) if God's rulership were not best, and

(4) if God were hiding good from man.

(5) In addition, there was an audience of untold billions of angelic spirit creatures looking on.

If God destroyed without settling things, these spirit persons would be following God out of dreadful fear, not love, fear of displeasing God. Moreover, say He did kill them and start over, and ten thousand years down the road (with billions of humans now on earth), the issues were raised again, He would have to destroy billions of people again, and again, and again all throughout time, until these issues were laid to rest.

What God has done is, allow time to pass, and the issues to be resolved. Man thought he was better off without God, and could walk on his own. In addition, man has attempted every kind of rulership imaginable, and one must ask, 'have they proven themselves better than rulership under the sovereignty of their Creator?' (Proverbs 1:30-33; Isaiah 59:4, 8) Sadly, the issues must be taken up to the brink of destroying man. (Rev 11:18)

Otherwise, the argument would be that if given enough time, they could have turned things around. If man goes up to the point of destroying himself and Armageddon comes at the last minute, it will have set a case law, solved the issue, and the Bible can serve as the example forever. If the issues of God's sovereignty or the loyalty of His created creatures, angelic or human, is ever questioned again, we would have the Holy Bible that will serve as a law established based on previous verdicts of not guilty, please see below.

What Have the Results Been?

(1) God does not cause evil and suffering. Romans 9:14.

(2) The fact that God has allowed evil, pain and suffering have shown that independence from God has not brought about a better world. Jeremiah 8:5, 6, 9.

(3) God's permission of evil, pain, and suffering has also proved that Satan has not been able to turn all humans away from God. Exodus 9:16; 1 Samuel 12:22; Hebrews 12:1.

(4) The fact that God has permitted evil, pain, and suffering to continue has provided proof that only God, the Creator, has the capability and the right to rule over humankind for their eternal blessing and happiness. Ecclesiastes 8:9.

(5) Satan has been the god of this world since the sin in Eden (over 6,000 years), and how has that worked out for man, and what has been the result of man's course of independence from God and his rule? Matthew 4:8-9; John 16:11; 2 Corinthians 4:3-4; 1 John 5:19; Psalm 127:1.

Satan's impact on the earth's activities has carried with it conflict, evil and death, and his rulership has been by means of deception, power and his own self-interest. He has demonstrated himself an unfit ruler of everything. Therefore, God is now completely vindicated in putting an end to this corrupted rebel along with all who have shared in his evil deeds. – Romans 16:20.

God has tolerated evil, sickness, pain, suffering and death until our day in order to resolve all the issues raised by Satan. We are self-centered in thinking that this has only pained us. Imagine that you are holding a rope on a sinking ship that 20 other men, women, and children are clinging to, when your child loses her grip and falls into the ocean. You can hold the rope, saving 20 people, or you can let go and attempt to rescue your daughter. God has been watching the suffering of billions from the day of Adam and Eve's sin. Moreover, it has been His great love for us, which causes Him to cling to the rope of issues, saving us from a future of repeated

269

issues. Nevertheless, he will not allow this evil to remain forever. He has set a fixed time when He will end this wicked system of Satan's rule.

Daniel 11:27 Updated American Standard Version (UASV)

²⁷ As for both kings, their heart will be inclined to do what is evil, and they will speak lies to each other at the same table; but it will not succeed, for the end is still to come <u>at the appointed time</u>.

Unlike what many people of the world may think (the world that lies in the hands of Satan), being obedient to God is not difficult. We simply must set our pride aside and accept that the wisdom of God is so far greater than our own and accept that He has worked for the good of obedient humankind, as He loves each one of us.

Matthew 7:21 Updated American Standard Version (UASV)

²¹ "Not everyone who says to me, 'Lord, Lord,' will enter the kingdom of heaven, but <u>the one who does the will of my Father</u> who is in heaven.

1 John 2:15-17 Updated American Standard Version (UASV)

¹⁵ Do not love the world or the things in the world. If anyone loves the world, the love of the Father is not in him. ¹⁶ For all that is in the world, the lust of the flesh and the lust of the eyes and the boastful pride of life, is not from the Father, but is from the world. ¹⁷ The world is passing away, and its lusts; but the one who does the will of God remains forever.

As Christians, there is a love we must not have. We must 'not love the world or anything in it.' Instead, we need to keep from becoming infected by the corruption of unrighteous human society that is alienated from God and must not breathe in its mental disposition or be moved by its sinful dominant attitude. (Ephesians 2:1-2; James 1:27) If we were to have the views of those in the world that are in opposition to God, "the love of the Father" would not be in us. (James 4:4)

Was Satan Punished?

Yes.

COMMON QUESTION: Why did God not destroy the Satan, Adam, and Eve right away?

I would follow up with what would have happened if God had chosen that path. Hundreds of billions of angels with free will were watching, and they knew of the issues raised. What would their love of God have been like if God did not address the issues raised? Was Satan right? Was God lying? Would free will creatures, spirit and humans, be better off? Will God just destroy us over anything? First, the spirit creatures would have followed God out of dreadful fear, rather than fear of displeasing the one they loved so much up to that point, like a child to a parent. Second, what happens if the issue is raised a hundred thousand years after a restart and there are 30 billion perfect humans on the planet? Would God simply destroy everyone again and start over. Do we think it wise that he does this reboot every time or was it not better that he settled the issue once and for all?

POINT: Satan raised Issues of sovereignty in the Garden of Eden.

POINT: Can humans walk on their own; do they really need their Creator? Are they better off without God?

POINT: Was God lying and withholding?

When a teenager becomes a rebel in our house, we have a choice: (1) severe punishment or (2) teach them an object lesson.

HUMANS AND ANGELS are a created product no different than a car coming off of an assembly line, i.e., (1) they owe their existence to their creator and (2) they were created to function based on the design of the creator. If we take a ford escort and treat it like a heavy duty four-wheel drive truck and go off roading (not what the car was designed to do), what will happen?

God wisely chose to teach both angels and humans an object lesson. Neither was designed to walk on their own. Both angel and human were given relative freedom (under the sovereignty of God), not absolute freedom. They were not designed to choose what is right and what is wrong on their own. They were given God's moral standards by way of an internal conscience. How can we tell a rebel that we do not have absolute freedom, we are better off under the umbrella of our creator's sovereignty, we cannot walk on our own? They will just reject it as a rebel teenager would.

OBJECT LESSON: We let them learn from their choice, no matter how painful it is, and hard love means that we do not step in until the lesson is fully learned. Humankind was essentially told, "Oh, you think you can walk on your own, well go ahead, we will see how that works out." After six-thousand-years, God could actually use a common saying among young people today: "How is that absolute freedom working out for you?"

When will the lesson fully be learned? Humankind will walk right up to the very edge of the cliff of killing themselves, actually falling over, when God will step in and stop the object lesson. To stop it anytime before, will cause doubts. If it had been stopped a century ago, the argument would have been; God simply stepped in before we got to the scientific age because he knew we were going to find true peace and security, along with something to give us eternal life. However, if humanity has actually fallen over the edge of the cliff and the destruction of us is definite, and God steps in, no argument can be raised, the object lesson is learned.

Why Was Satan Not Kicked Out of Heaven Right Away?

Satan stayed in his realm, just as humans stayed in theirs. God changed nothing right away because he would have been accused of adjusting the pieces on the chessboard to get the desired outcome, i.e., cheating. When will Satan be kicked out of heaven? Satan and the Demons lost access to the person of God long age, and they lost some of their powers, such as being able to materialize in human form, like they did when they took human women for themselves at the flood, producing the Nephilim.

Satan would be thrown to the earth very shortly before the end of his age of rulership, when "he knows that his time is short." (Rev 12:9-12) This, then, means that Satan will be thrown from heaven likely sometime before the Great Tribulation and Christ's return. Revelation 12:12 says, "'Therefore, rejoice, O heavens and you who dwell in them! But woe to you, O earth and sea, for the devil has come down to you in great wrath because he knows that his time is short!'"

Notice that it is at a time, when "Satan knows that his time is short!" What comes next for Satan? He will be abyssed, thrown into a super-maximum-security prison for a thousand years (for lack of a better way to explain it) while Jesus fixes all that Satan done. After the thousand years, he will be let loose for a little while, and he will tempt perfect humans, and sadly some will fall away. In the end, Satan and those humans will be destroyed, and Jesus will hand the kingdom back over to the father.

CHAPTER 14 The Bible was Penned by Men But Still God's Word

Ehrman responds in a Question and Answer section at the end of his book, in which he is asked about his view of "*the Bible encapsulating the very words of God.*"

Ehrman wrote: . . . . When I started out as a believer in high school, though, I thought (and was taught) that the Bible was unsullied by human hands, that it was completely divine, down to its very words. This was the view taught at Moody Bible Institute, where I went to college; we called it the 'verbal plenary inspiration' of Scripture. Inspiration was verbal (down to the very words) and plenary (complete from beginning to end). **Misquoting Jesus (p. 250-1)**

Here again, Ehrman is starting with the wrong premise, 'that the Word of God was dictated to the writers, and every word was specifically chosen by God, with the writer simply penning it.' Let us take a long look at how we can say that the Bible was penned by men but was still the Word of God.

The sixty-six books of the Bible (39 old Testament, 27 New Testament), were written by some forty men over a period of about sixteen-hundred years. These writers were no different from you and me, simply imperfect humans, specifically chosen for the task of the author. They too suffered from weaknesses and errors. Some were viewing Barnabas and Paul as gods, to which Paul responded, "Men, why are you doing these things? We also are men, of like nature with you." (Acts 14:15) Moreover, many of the writers of the Bible did not have any sort of exceptional learning or abilities. These were ordinary men, from different walks of life, like a herdsman or fisherman.

Certainly, the first obvious question should be, 'how then can imperfect, ordinary men pen a record that we can rightly call the Word of God?' These ones were not writing by their own spirit, behaving in a way that has a particular feeling, mood, or character, what we today in the Western world would call 'being in a zone.' No, these ones were inspired by the "Spirit" of God."

Traditional

2 Timothy 3:16 New American Standard Bible (NASB)

[16] All Scripture is **inspired by God** and profitable for teaching, for reproof, for correction, for training in righteousness

Literal

2 Timothy 3:16 English Standard Version (ESV)

[16] All Scripture is **breathed out by God** and profitable for teaching, for reproof, for correction, and for training in righteousness

> The word God-breathed, occurring only here[296] indicates that "all scripture" owes its origin and contents to the divine breath, the Spirit of God. The human authors were powerfully guided and directed by the Holy Spirit. As a result, what they wrote is not only without error but of supreme value for man. It is all that God wanted it to be. It constitutes the infallible rule of faith and practice for mankind.[297]

Without taking away from the concerns of Ehrman, as being trivial, it must be asked how one can so quickly abandon their faith, while others, stay the course under far greater tests. We can think of William Tyndale, John Wycliffe, or John Hus. However, let us look at Jeremiah the prophet.

Jeremiah 20:8 American Standard Version (ASV)

[8] For as often as I speak, I cry out; I cry, Violence and destruction! because the word of Jehovah is made a reproach unto me, and a derision, all the day.

We must ask ourselves, have we invested enough of ourselves into an understanding of inspiration, inerrancy that we know it to be the Word of God, and would suffer verbal abuse, physical mistreatment and even death for it? If we have never suffered a tragedy (i.e., losing a child) that could rob us of our faith, we may not know if we would come up short in such horrific circumstances. When we are under the pressure of suffering, there may begin a slow drip, drip, drip of doubts that creep in about the inspiration and inerrancy of God's Word, which can give way to greater

---

[296] theopneustos does not mean "God-breathing," "breathing the divine spirit," but is passive: "God-breathed." Cf. II Peter 1:21. See the detailed argument in B. B. Warfield, The Inspiration and Authority of the Bible, Philadelphia, Pa., 1948, pp. 245–296.

[297] William Hendriksen and Simon J. Kistemaker, vol. 4, New Testament Commentary: Exposition of the Pastoral Epistles, New Testament Commentary (Grand Rapids: Baker Book House, 1953-2001), 302.

doubts, undermining our faith, causing us to have a spiritual shipwreck. (1 Tim 1:19) However, if we have gathered a correct understanding of inspiration and inerrancy, avoiding the wrong premises, we can be in a far better position to withstand pressure and to resist following a course of expediency.

Once a person slips a step below the inspired Word of God, fully inerrant to a Bible, in part at least, that is the product of human thinking; he will not stand strong in temptation or difficult times, but will look for an easy way out. Therefore, it is vitally important that we show more than a passing interest of how the book on one hand can be penned by men, and on the other, is truly the Word of God.

How was it that the Bible Writers received what they were to Pen?

There is no doubt that dictation was one of the ways that the Word of God was transmitted to man on earth. (Heb. 1:1- 2) One example of dictation would have been the Ten Commandments, which was also provided in written form on two tablets of stone. This would also include all of the other laws in the covenant between God and the Israelites. We are informed of this at Acts 7:53, which reads, "You who received the law as delivered by angels and did not keep it." Moses was then instructed to "Write these words, for in accordance with these words I have made a covenant with you and with Israel." (See 2 Samuel 7:5-16; Isaiah 7:3-9 and Jeremiah 7:1-34.) The specific passages mentioned here were spoken by the angel of God. – Genesis 31:11-13.

The Bible writers also received their messages from God through visions and dreams. (Num. 12:6; 1 Sam. 3:4-14; 2 Sam. 7:17; Dan. 9:20-27) If we consider the dreams, we find that the person would have had a message from God superimposed on his mind. Likely, this was far more than we have ever experienced in our dreams that seem to fade as we awaken. Others were actually awake when they had their visions, but still had information pictorially impressed upon the conscious mind. (Matt. 17:2-9; Luke 9:32) While likely not too similar, this may be a deeper or different version of our daydreaming, a deep trance, yet still aware of their surroundings. Have you have spaced out while driving, and then shook yourself more fully awake, to wonder how far you had been driving like that? (Acts 10:10-16; 11:5-10) Here is where the human author comes into the picture, as he would have to select words and expressions then to describe in meaningful terms what they had seen. – Habakkuk 2:2; Revelation 1:1, 11.

A vast portion of the Bible is simply historical narrative, the lives of persons, families, tribes and nations. In what way did the writers receive this information? In some cases, they were eyewitnesses to the events. However, regularly they had to draw on sources outside of themselves. These sources would include historical records, genealogical records, family records, state records, and interviewing those who were there for the events. Ezra for example was an extensive and careful researcher, who penned a book bearing his name, and the book of Chronicles, which covered 410 years of Israelite history. The physician Luke, writing about his Gospel, commented that he had "followed all things closely for some time past, to write an orderly account for you, most excellent Theophilus." Many scholars have recognized Luke's work in the book of Acts as something that would have been done by a first-rate historian. (Luke 1:3) The events in the book of Genesis could have been passed on to Moses through just five human links, that is, Methuselah, Shem, Isaac, Levi, and Amram. Another possibility is by written records. – Genesis 2:4; 5:1; 6:9; 10:1; 11:10, 27; 25:12, 19; 36:1, 9; 37:2.

Another portion of Scripture, aside from historical narrative and law, would be wise proverbs and counsel. The writers were moved to draw on their own life experiences, in conjunction with their study of Scripture. Psalm 37:25 informs the reader, "I have been young, and now am old, yet I have not seen the righteous forsaken or his children begging for bread." King Solomon stated, "There is nothing better for a person than that he should eat and drink and find enjoyment in his toil. This also, I saw, is from the hand of God. Even though the "Holy Spirit" moved the writer of wise sayings to pen his message he still had to put forth the diligent effort. This is evident from Ecclesiastes 12:9, 10, which reads, "Besides being wise, the Preacher also taught the people knowledge, weighing and studying and arranging many proverbs with great care. The Preacher sought to find words of delight, and uprightly he wrote words of truth."

The Role of the Holy Spirit

Because there was so much human effort in the penning of the Bible books, the Bible critic will likely surmise that there is no alternative, but to have errors creep in due to human imperfection. Should we only accept those portions that we know to be dictation from God or one of his representative angelic messengers? The answer would be a resounding, no! These writers, in their effort to pen a book were moved by the "Holy Spirit."

David wrote,

2 Samuel 23:2 American Standard Version (ASV)

[2] The Spirit of Jehovah spoke by me, And his word was upon my tongue.

How did the "Spirit of Jehovah" put such powerful messages into the minds of the Bible writers and safeguard that they continued to be His "word"?

2 Peter 1:20-21 Updated American Standard Version (UASV)

[20] But know this first, that no prophecy of Scripture comes from one's own interpretation, [21] for no prophecy was ever produced by the will of man, but men carried along by the Holy Spirit spoke from God.

Peter informs us that Bible prophecy was not the result of the writer's own examination and interpretation of the present-day events of the writer, nor the future results of these events. Instead, the writer had his mental faculties stimulated by "Holy Spirit," which moved him to express the intended message, usually in his own words. Therefore, the word selection, the syntax, and grammar were the writer, but the message belonged to Jehovah God, who would not allow a wrong word or expression to be chosen if it did not convey his message.

There is often a complaint about the amount of time that would go by before events were penned, like the Gospel accounts of Jesus' life and ministry. Matthew waited for at least 15-years, Luke and Mark about 30-years, and John more than 60-years before penning their Gospels. Jesus guaranteed them that they would have a great recall, "But the Helper, the Holy Spirit, whom the Father will send in my name, he will teach you all things and bring to your remembrance all that I have said to you." —John 14:26.

Because the "Holy Spirit," moved the writers, to select and pen, what God wanted to be conveyed, does this mean they had no personal involvement in the selection of their subject matter? No, not really. Certainly, they would write about matters that affected them and their circumstances because this would have been according to the will and purpose of God as well. Many times, they would answer questions, clarify certain points, or correct misunderstandings. Let us use Paul's second letter to the Thessalonian congregation. Some had wrongly concluded that the presence of Christ was already at hand. Then, in addition, there were those who had not taken to heart his previous counsel about 'working hard and walking decently as regards people outside the congregation.' Paul uses this second occasion to clarify the proper Christian view of these points. (1 Thess. 4:10-12; 2 Thess. 2:1-3; 3:10-15) Writers like the Apostle Paul were simply responsive to the leading of the "Holy Spirit," and what they chose to cover was merely their working in harmony with the "Holy Spirit."

What About When a Writer Seems to be Expressing a Personal View?

What are we to make of those moments when the Bible writers appear to be offering his personal view? We can use the Apostle Paul as an example of this,

1 Corinthians 7:12, 25, 40 Updated American Standard Version (UASV)

[12] But to the rest I say, not the Lord, that if any brother has a wife who is an unbeliever, and she consents to live with him, he must not divorce her. [25] Now concerning virgins I do not have a command from the Lord, but I am giving an opinion as one shown mercy by the Lord to be trustworthy. [40] Yet in my judgment she is happier if she remains as she is. And I think that I too have the Spirit of God.

Concerning the circumstances, there was no direct quote that he could refer to, as a direct teaching of the Lord Jesus Christ, and therefore, he offered his personal view. However, this changes nothing, as he was still writing under the influence of the "Holy Spirit," and according to his vast knowledge of Scripture, all of which is reflected in God's view. Another inspired writer, the Apostle Peter places Paul's writings in the same category as the Old Testament, *Scripture.*

2 Peter 3:15-16 Updated American Standard Version (UASV)

[15] and regard the patience of our Lord as salvation; just as also our beloved brother Paul, according to the wisdom given him, wrote to you, [16] as also in all his [Paul's] letters, speaking in them of these things, in which are some things hard to understand, which the untaught and unstable distort, as they do also the rest of the **Scriptures**, to their own destruction.

In conclusion, the evidence indicates that the forty plus writers of Scripture were not automatons, just taking down dictated material. The Apostle John informs his readers of the book of Revelation that, "the revelation of Jesus Christ, which God gave him to show to his servants the things that must soon take place. He made it known by sending his angel to his servant John, who bore witness to the word of God and to the testimony of Jesus Christ, even to all that he saw." (Rev. 1:1, 2) He goes on,

Revelation 1:10-11 Updated American Standard Version (UASV)

[10] I was **in the Spirit** on the Lord's day, and I heard behind me a loud voice like a trumpet, [11] saying, "Write what you see in a book and send it

to the seven churches, to Ephesus and to Smyrna and to Pergamum and to Thyatira and to Sardis and to Philadelphia and to Laodicea."

Therefore, Just as God gave man free will and intelligence, he has saw fit, to allow the writers of His Word to use their own mental faculties, as they selected the words and expression that would convey His message. (Hab. 2:2) However, God exercised sufficient control, in that he would never allow them to choose a word or expression that would fail to communicate His message. – Proverbs 30:5-6

Bibliography

Abbot, Nabia. 1938. *STUDIES IN ANCIENT ORIENTAL CIVILIZATIONS.* Chocago: The University of Chicago Press.

Aland, Kurt and Barbara. 1987. *The Text of the New Testament.* Grand Rapids: Eerdmans.

Aland, Kurt, and Barbara Aland. 1995. *The Text of the New Testament.* Grand Rapids: Eerdmans.

—. 1987. *The Text of the New Testament.* Grand Rapids: Eerdmans.

—. 1987. *The Text of the New Testament.* Grand Rapids: Eerdmans.

Aland, Kurt, Matthew Black, and Carlo M. Martini. 1993; 2006. *The Greek New Testament, Fourth Revised Edition (Interlinear With Morphology).* Deutsche Bibelgesellschaft: United Bible Society.

Arndt, William, Frederick W. Danker, and Walter Bauer. 2000. *A Greek-English Lexicon of the New Testament and Other Early Christian Literature. 3rd ed.* . Chicago: University of Chicago Press.

Baer, Daniel. 2007. *The Unquenchable Fire.* Maitland, FL: Xulon Press.

Bagnall, Roger S. 2009. *The Oxford Handbook of Papyrology (Oxford Handbooks).* Oxford: Oxford University Press.

Bagnall, Roger S. 2012. *Everyday Writing in the Græco-Roman East.* Berkeley and Los Angeles, CA: University of California Press.

Balz, Horst, and Gerhard Schneider. 1978. *Exegetical Dictionary of the New Testament.* Edinburgh: T & T Clark Ltd.

Barnett, Paul. 2005. *The Birth of Christianity: The First Twenty Years (After Jesus, Vol. 1)* . Grand Rapids, MI: Wm. B. Eerdmans .

Bercot, David W. 1998. *A Dictionary of Early Christian Beliefs.* Peabody: Hendrickson.

Black, David Alan. 1994. *New Testament Textual Criticism: A Concise Guide.* Grand Rapids, MI: Baker Books.

—. 2002. *Rethinking New Testament Textual Criticism.* Grand Rapids: Baker Books.

Bock, Darrell L, and Daniel B Wallace. 2007. *Dethroning Jesus: Exposing Popular Culture's Quest to Unseat the Biblical Christ.* Nashville: Thomas Nelson.

Borgen, Peder. 1997. *Philo of Alexandria: An Exegete for His Time.* Leiden, Boston: Brill.

Bowman, Alan K. 1998. *Life and Letters on the Roman Frontier: Vindolanda and its People.* London and New York: Routledge.

Brand, Chad, Charles Draper, and England Archie. 2003. *Holman Illustrated Bible Dictionary: Revised, Updated and Expanded.* Nashville, TN: Holman.

Brown, Virginia. 1972. *The Textual Transmission of Caesar's Civil War.* Leiden: Brill.

Bruce, F. F. 1981. *The New Testament Documents: Are they Reliable?* Downer Groves: Inter Varsity. Accessed April 03, 2009. http://www.libertyparkusafd.org/lp/Burgon/cd-roms/121bible.html.

Bruce, F. F., J. I. Packer, Philip Cmfort, and Carl F. H. Henry. 1992, 2003. *The Origin of the Bible.* Carol Steam, IL: Tyndale House.

Capes, David B, Rodney Reeves, and E. Randolph Richards. 2007. *Rediscovering Paul: An Introduction to His World, Letters and Theology .* Downers Grove: IVP Academic.

Carson, D. A, and Douglas J Moo. 2005. *An Introduction to the New Testament.* Grand Rapids, MI: Zondervan.

Carson, D. A. 1994. *New Bible Commentary: 21st Century Edition. 4th ed.* Downers Grove: Inter-Varisity Press.

Clayton, Joseph. 2006. *Luther and His Work.* Whitefish: Kessinger Publishing.

Cmfort, Philip Wesley. 2015. *A Commentary On the Manuscripts and Text of the New Testament.* Grand Rapids: Kregel Publications.

Colwell, E. C. 1969. *Methods in Evaluating Scribal Habits: A Study of P45, P66, P75, in Studies in Methodology in Textual Criticism of the New Testament.* Leiden and Boston: Brill.

Colwell, Ernest C. 1965. *Scribal Habits in Early Papyri: A Study in the Corruption of the Text.* Grand Rapids: Eerdmans.

Comfort, Philip. 2005. *Encountering the Manuscripts: An Introduction to New Testament Paleography and Textual Criticism.* Nashville: Broadman & Holman.

Comfort, Philip W. 2008. *New Testament Text and Translation Commentary.* Carol Stream: Tyndale House Publishers.

Comfort, Philip Wesley. 1992. *The Quest for the Original Text of the New Testament.* Eugene: Wipf and Stock.

Comfort, Philip, and David Barret. 2001. *The Text of the Earliest New Testament Greek Manuscripts.* Wheaton: Tyndale House Publishers.

Cruse, C. F. 1998. *Eusebius' Eccliatical History.* Peabody, MA: Hendrickson.

Deissmann, Adolf. 1910. *LIGHT FROM THE ANCIENT EAST: The New Testament Illustrated by Recently Discovered Texts of the Graeco-Roman World.* New York and London: Hodder and Stoughton.

Dell'Orto, Luisa Franchi. 1990. *Riscoprire Pompei (Rediscovering Pompeii).* Italy: L'Erma di Bretschneider.

Durant, Will & Ariel. 1950. *The Story of Civilization: Part IV—The Age of Faith.* New York, NY: Simon & Schuster.

Ehrman, Bart D. 2005. *Misquoting Jesus: The Story Behind Who Changed the Bible and Why.* New York: Harper One.

—. 2006. *Peter, Paul and Mary Magdalene: The Followers of Jesus in History and Legend.* Oxford: Oxford University Press.

Ehrman, Bart D, and Michael W. Holmes. 2012. *The Text of the New Testament in Contemporary Research: Essays on the Status Quaestionis. Second Edition.* Leiden and Boston: Brill.

Ehrman, Bart D. Holmes, Michael W. 1995. *The Text of the New Testament in Contemporary Research: Essays on the Status Quaestionis .* Grand Rapids, MI: Eerdmans.

Ehrman, Bart D. 2003. *Lost Christianities: The Battles for Scripture and the Faiths We Never Knew .* New York: Oxford University Press.

Elliott, J. K. 2010. *New Testament Textual Criticism: The Application of Thoroughgoing Principles: Essays on Manuscripts and Textual Variation (Novum Testamentum, Supplements).* Leiden: Brill.

Epp, Eldon J. 1993. *Studies in the Theory and Method of New Testament Textual Criticism.* Grand Rapids: Wm. B. Eerdmans Publishing Co.

—. 1989. *Textual Criticism.* Atlanta: Scholars Press.

Evans, Craig A. 2002. *Fabricating Jesus: How Modern Scholars Distort the Gospels.* Downers Grove, IL: InterVaristy Press.

—. 2012. *Jesus and His World: The Archaeological Evidence.* Louisville: Westminster John Knox Press.

Fahlbusch, Erwin (Editor), Jan Milic (Editor) Lochman, John (Editor) Mbiti, Jaroslav (Editor) Pelikan, and Lukas (Editor) Vischer. German 1986, 1989, 1992, 1996, 1997; English 1999, 2001, 2003, 2005. *The Encyclopedia of Christianity (Vol. 1-3)*. Grand Rapids: Eerdmans Publishing Company and Koninklijke Brill NV.

Fee, Gordon D. 1993. *P75, P66, and Origen: The Myth of Early Textual Recension in Alexandria, in: E. J. Epp & G. D. Fee, Studies in the Theory & Method of NT Textual Criticism*. Grand Rapids: Wm. Eerdmans.

Fee, Gordon D. 1974. *P75, P66, and Origen: The Myth of the Early Textual Recension in Alexandria*. Grand Rapids: Zondervan.

—. 1979. *The Textual Criticism of the New Testament*. Grand Rapids: Zondervan.

Ferguson, Everett. 2003. *Backgrounds of Early Christianity*. Grand Rapids, MI: Wm. B. Eerdmans.

Freeman, James M. 1998. *THE NEW MANNERS & CUSTOMS OF THE BIBLE*. Gainesville: Bridge-Logos.

Gamble, Henry Y. 1995. *Books and Readers in the Early Church: A History of Early Christian Texts*. New Haven: New Haven University Press.

Geisler, Norman L, and William E Nix. 1996. *A General Introduction to the Bible*. Chicago: Moody Press.

Geisler, Norman, and David Geisler. 2009. *CONVERSATION EVANGELISM: How to Listen and Speak So You Can Be Heard*. Eugene: Harvest House Publishers.

Goldberg, Sander M. 2005. *Constructing Literature in the Roman Republic (1st Ed.)*. Cambridge: Cambridge University Press.

Greenlee, J Harold. 1995. *Introduction to New Testament Textual Criticism*. Peabody: Hendrickson.

—. 2008. *The Text of the New Testament*. Peabody: Henrickson.

Guthrie, Donald. 1990. *Introduction to the New Testament (Revised and Expanded)*. Downers Grove, IL: InterVarsity Press.

Haines-Eitzen, Kim. 2000. *Guardians of Letters: Literacy, Power, and the Transmitters of Early Christian Literature*. New York, NY: Oxford University Press.

Hammond, Carolyn. 1996. *Introduction to The Gallic War*. Oxford: Oxford University Press.

Harris, William V. 1989. *Ancient Literacy.* Cambridge, MA: Harvard University Press.

Hatch, William Henry Paine. 45. "A Recently Discovered Fragmrnt of the Epistle to the Romans." *Harvard Theological Review* 81-85.

Head, Peter M. 2004. "The Habits of New Testament Copyists Singular Readings in the Early Fragmentary Papyri of John." *Biblica, Vol. 85, No. 3* 399-408.

Hezser, Catherine. 2001. *Jewish Literacy in Roman Palestine (Texts and Studies in Ancient Judaism)* . Tübingen, Germany: Mohr Siebeck.

Hill, Charles E., and Michael J. Kruger. 2012. *The Early Text of the New Testament.* Oxford: Oxford University Press.

Holmes, Michael W. 1989. *New Testament Textual Criticism.* Grand Rapids: Baker.

—. 2007. *The Apostolic Fathers: Greek Texts and English Translations.* Grand Rapids: Baker Academics.

Hurtado, Larry. 1989. *New International Bible Commentary: Mark.* .: . Peabody, Mass: Hendrickson.

Hurtado, Larry. 1998. "The Origin of the Nominal Sacra." *Journal of Biblical Literature* 655-673.

Jeffers, James S. 1989. *The Greco-Roman World of the New Testament Era: Exploring the Background of Early Christianity.* Downers Grove, IL: InterVarsity Press.

Johnson, William A. 2012 (Reprint). *Readers and Reading Culture in the High Roman Empire: A Study of Elite Communities (Classical Culture and Society).* Oxford, New York: Oxford University Press.

Johnson, William A, and Holt N Parker. 2011. *Ancient Literacies: The Culture of Reading in Greece and Rome.* Oxford: Oxford University Press.

Jones, Timothy Paul. 2007. *Misquoting Truth: A Guide to the Fallacies of Bart Ehrman's Misquoting Jesus.* Downer Groves: InterVarsity Press.

Komoszewski, J. Ed, James M. Sawyer, and Daniel Wallace. 2006. *Reinventing Jesus* . Grand Rapids, MI: Kregel Publications.

Kyrtatas, Dimitris J. 1987. *The Social Structure of the Early Christian Communities.* Brooklyn, NY: Verso.

Lane Fox, Robin. 2006. *Pagans and Christians: In the Mediterranean World from the Second Century AD to the Conversion of Constantine.* City of Westminster, London: Penguin.

Lea, Thomas D., and Hayne P. Griffin. 1992. *The New American Commentary, vol. 34, 1, 2 Timothy, Titus.* Nashville: Broadman & Holman Publishers.

Lightfoot, Joseph Barber, and J. R Harmer. 1891. *The Apostolic Fathers.* London: Macmillan and Co.

Lightfoot, Neil R. 1963, 1988, 2003. *How We Got the Bible.* Grand Rapids, MI: Baker Books.

Malherbe, Abraham J. 1986. *Social Aspects of Early Christianity (2nd ed).* Eugene, OR: Wipf & Stock Pub.

McCarthy, Dan, and Charles Clayton. 1994. *Let the Reader Understand: A guide to Interpreting and Applying the Bible.* Wheaton, Illinois: BridgePoint.

McKenzie, John L. 1975. *Light on the Epistles: A Reader's Guide.* Chicago, IL: Thomas More Press.

McRay, John. 2003. *Paul: His Life and Teaching.* Grand Rapids: Baker Academics.

Meeks, Wayne A. 2003. *The First Urban Christians: The Social World of the Apostle Paul (2nd ed.).* New Haven, CT: Yale University Press.

Metzger, Bruce M. 1964, 1968, 1992. *The Text of the New Testament: Its Transmission, Corruption, and Transmission.* New York: Oxford University Press.

Metzger, Bruce M. 1994. *A Textual Commentary on the Greek New Testament.* New York: United Bible Society.

Metzger, Bruce M., and Bart D. Ehrman. 2005. *The Text of the New Testament: Its Transmission, Corruption, and Restoration (4th Edition).* New York: Oxford University Press.

Metzger, Bruce. 1981. *Manuscripts of the Greek Bible: An Introduction to Palaeography .* New York, NY: Oxford University Press.

Millard, Alan. 2000. *READING AND WRITING IN THE TIME IF JESUS.* New York, NY: NYU Press.

Milnor, Kristina. 2014. *Graffiti and the Literary Landscape in Roman Pompeii.* Eugene, OR: Oxford University Press.

Mounce, Robert H. 2001. *The New American Commentary.* Nashville, TN: Broadman & Holman Publishers.

Mounce, William D. 2006. *Mounce's Complete Expository Dictionary of Old & New Testament Words.* Grand Rapids, MI: Zondervan.

Myers, Allen C. 1987. *The Eerdmans Bible Dictionary .* Grand Rapids, Mich: Eerdmans.

Nestle, Eberhard, and Erwin Nestle. 2012. *Nestle-Aland: NTG Apparatus Criticus, ed. Barbara Aland et al., 28. revidierte Auflage (Revised Edition).* Stuttgart: Deutsche Bibelgesellschaft.

Ohlson, Kristin. 2010. *Smithsonian.com.* July 26. Accessed March 27, 2019. https://www.smithsonianmag.com/history/reading-the-writing-on-pompeiis-walls-1969367/.

Orchard, Bernard (Editor), Longstaff, Thomas R. W. (Editor). 2005. "J. J. Griesbach: Synoptic and Text - Critical Studies 1776-1976." *Society for New Testament Studies Monograph Series (Book 34)* xi.

Orchard, Bernard. 1776-1976, 2005. *J. J. Griesbach: Synoptic and Text - Critical Studies .* Cambridge: Cambridge University Press.

Pagels, Elaine. 1989. *The Gnostic Gospels.* New York: Vintage.

Parker, David C. 1992. *Codex Bezae: An Early Christian Manuscript and its Text.* Cambridge: Cambridge University Press.

Parker, David C. 1997. *The living Text of the Gospels.* Cambridge: Cambridge University Press.

Porter, Stanley E. 2013. *How We Got the New Testament (Acadia Studies in Bible and Theology).* Grand Rapids, MI: Baker Publishing Group.

Price, Randall. 2007. *Searching for the Original Bible.* Eugene: Harvest House.

Richards, E. Randolph. 2004. *Paul And First-Century Letter Writing: Secretaries, Composition and Collection.* Downers Grove: InterVarsity Press.

—. 1990. *The Secretary in the Letters of Paul.* Tübingen: J.C.B. Mohr.

Roberts, C. H. 1970. *Books in the Graeco-Roman World and in the New Testament in the Cambridge History of the Bible, Vol. 1, From the Beginnings to Jerome .* Cambridge: Cambridge University Press.

Roberts, Colin H. 1979. *Manuscript, Society, and Belief in Early Christian Egypt.* London: Oxford University Press.

Roberts, Colin H., and Theodore C. Skeat. 1987. *The Birth of the Codex.* London: Oxford University Press.

Robertson, A. T. 1925. *An Introduction to the Textual Criticism of the New Testament.* London: Hodder & Stoughton.

Royse, James R. 2008. *Scribal Habits in Early Greek New Testament Papyri (New Testament Tools and Studies) (New Testament Tools, Studies and Documents).* Leiden & Boston: Brill Academic Pub.

Schaff, Philip, and David Schley Schaff. 1910. *History of the Christian Church, vol. 2.* New York: Charles Scribner's Sons.

Schurer, Emil. 1890. *A HISTORY OF THE JEWISH PEOPLE IN THE TIME OF JESUS CHRIST (Volume II).* Edinburgh: T. & T. Clark.

Scott, Julius J. Jr. 1995. *Jewish Backgrounds of the New Testament.* Grand Rapids, MI: Baker Academic.

Souter, Alexander. 1913. *The Text and Canon of the New Testament.* New York: Charles Scribner's Sons.

Starr, Raymond J. 1987. "The Circulation of Literary Texts in the Roman World." *The Classical Quarterly* 213-223.

Theissen, Gerd. 2004. *The Social Setting of Pauline Christianity.* Eugene, OR: Wipf & Stock Pub.

Towns, Elmer L. 2006. *Concise Bible Dictrines: Clear, Simple, and Easy-to-Understand Explanations of Bible Doctrines.* Chattanooga: AMG Publishers.

Tregelles, Samuel Prideaux. 1854. *An Account of the Printed Text of the Greek New Testament: With Remarks on Its Revision Upon Critical Principles.* London: S. Bagster and Sons.

Tuckett, Christopher M. 2001. "P52 and Nomina Sacra." *New Testament Study* 544-48.

Wachtel, Klaus, and Michael W Holmes. 2011. *The Textual History of the Greek New Testament: Changing Views in Contemporary Research, Text-Critical Studies.* Atlanta: Society of Biblical Literature.

Wallace, Daniel B. 2011. *Revisiting the Corruption of the New Testament: Manuscript, Patristic, and Apocryphal Evidence.* Grand Rapids, MI: Kregel Publications.

Wallace, Daniel. 2011. *The Reliability of the New Testament: Bart Ehrman and Daniel Wallace in Dialogue.* Minneapolis, MN: Fortress Press.

Wegner, Paul D. 2006. *A Student's Guide to Textual Criticism of the Bible: Its History Methods & Results.* Downers Grove: InterVarsity Press.

—. 1999. *The Journey from Text to Translation.* Grand Rapids: Baker Academic.

Westcott, B. F., and F. J. A. Hort. 1882. *Introduction to the New Testament in the Original Greek.* New York: Harper & Brothers.

—. 1882. *The New Testament in the Original Greek, Vol. 2: Introduction, Appendix.* London: Macmillan and Co.

Westcott, B. F., and Hort F. J. A. 1882. *The New Testament in the Original Greek, Vol. 2: Introduction, Appendix.* London: Macmillan and Co.

Whiston, William. 1987. *The Works of Josephus.* Peabody, MA: Hendrickson.

Wright, Brian J. 2016. "Ancient Rome's Daily News Publication With Some Likely Implications For Early Christian Studies," *TynBull 67.1 (2016): 145-160.* Accessed March 22, 2017. https://www.academia.edu/18281056/_Ancient_Romes_Daily_Ne ws_Publication_With_Some_Likely_Implications_For_Early_Christi an_Studies_TynBull_67.1_2016_145-160.

Yonge, Charles Duke. 1995. *With Philo of Alexandria, The Works of Philo: Complete and Unabridged.* Peabody, MA: Hendrickson.

Zuntz, Gunther. 1953. *The Text of the Epistles: A Disquisition upon the Corpus Paulinum.* London: Oxford University Press.

Made in the USA
Middletown, DE
13 August 2020

15212150R00161